| Gymnasium Bayern |

access 5

LEHRERFASSUNG

Vokabel Trainer

Cornelsen

Vokabeltrainer-App

Verfügbar für: iOS, Android und Windows Phone

Cornelsen

Access Bayern 5
Lehrerfassung

Im Auftrag des Verlages herausgegeben von
Prof. Dr. Engelbert Thaler, Augsburg
Prof. Jörg Rademacher, Mannheim

Erarbeitet von
Jennifer Seidl, München; Laurence Harger, Nürnberg; Cecile Niemitz-Rossant, Berlin

unter Mitarbeit von
Dr. Annette Leithner-Brauns, Dresden; Birgit Ohmsieder, Berlin; Mervyn Whittaker, Bad Dürkheim; Dominik Eberhard (Vocabulary, Dictionaries), Bonn

in Zusammenarbeit mit der Englischredaktion
Filiz Bahşi (Projektkoordination), Bonnie Glänzer (Lehrerfassung), Dr. Philip Devlin, Stefan Höhne, Dr. Christiane Kallenbach (Redaktionsleitung), Uwe Tröger *sowie* Mailin Neubauer

Beratende Mitwirkung
Thomas Bohlen, Traunstein; Gerhard Finster, Dillingen; Carmen Mendez, Bad Tölz; Ingola Seger, Augsburg; Jörg Wunderlich, München

Illustrationen
Tobias Dahmen, Utrecht/NL; Elke Hanisch, Köln; Burkhard Schulz, Düsseldorf *sowie* Roland Beier, Berlin; Judy Brown, Hove *und* Jane Smith, London

Fotos
Trevor Burrows Photography, Plymouth

Umschlaggestaltung
hawemannundmosch, Berlin

Layout und technische Umsetzung
zweiband.media, Berlin

Für die freundliche Unterstützung danken wir der Plymstock School in Plymouth.

Soweit in diesem Lehrwerk Personen fotografisch abgebildet sind und ihnen von der Redaktion fiktive Namen, Berufe, Dialoge und Ähnliches zugeordnet oder diese Personen in bestimmte Kontexte gesetzt werden, dienen diese Zuordnungen und Darstellungen ausschließlich der Veranschaulichung und dem besseren Verständnis des Inhalts.

Dieses Werk berücksichtigt die Regeln der reformierten Rechtschreibung und Zeichensetzung.

Legende zur Lehrerfassung

1 12	CD- und Tracknummern
school	Lernwortschatz (produktiv)
°spy	Situativer Wortschatz (nicht produktiv)
Box "when", Voc, S. 237	Verweis auf Wortschatzbox im *Vocabulary*
+(to) groan	Hinweis auf zusätzl. Wortschatz im *Vocabulary*
rooms of the house	Grammatische Strukturen
KV 1 • Folie 1 • …	Verweise auf Begleitmedien
www	Verweise auf interaktive Übungen
['priːjaː, 'priːjə]	Aussprachehinweis
Die S können …	Didaktische Hinweise, Alternativen
learned • sat	Lösungen (geschlossene Aufgaben)

www.cornelsen.de

In diesem Werk wird in Form von Symbolen auf Audio-Material verwiesen; dieses enthält – bis auf die Hörverstehensübungen – ausschließlich optionale Unterrichtsmaterialien. Die Audio-Materialien unterliegen nicht dem staatlichen Zulassungsverfahren.

Die Mediencodes enthalten zusätzliche Unterrichtsmaterialien, die der Verlag in eigener Verantwortung zur Verfügung stellt.

1. Auflage, 1. Druck 2017

Alle Drucke dieser Auflage sind inhaltlich unverändert und können im Unterricht nebeneinander verwendet werden.

Druck: Firmengruppe APPL, aprinta Druck, Wemding

ISBN 978-3-06-034287-7

ISBN 978-3-06-034321-8 (E-Book)

PEFC
PEFC/04-32-0928

PEFC zertifiziert
Dieses Produkt stammt aus nachhaltig bewirtschafteten Wäldern und kontrollierten Quellen.

www.pefc.de

Access Bayern 5 enthält folgende Teile:

Here we go!	Los geht's: der Einstieg ins Buch
Book rally	eine „Rundfahrt" durch dein Englischbuch
Units	die fünf Kapitel des Buches
Access to cultures	landeskundliche Informationen
Access story	*Reading for fun* – eine spannende Geschichte
Wordbank	Mini-Bildwörterbuch zu verschiedenen Themen
Skills File	eine Beschreibung wichtiger Lern- und Arbeitstechniken
Grammar File	eine Zusammenfassung der Grammatik jeder Unit
Vocabulary	das Wörterverzeichnis zum Lernen der neuen Wörter jeder Unit
Dictionary	alphabetisches Wörterverzeichnis zum Nachschlagen (Englisch-Deutsch / Deutsch-Englisch)

In den Units findest du diese Überschriften:

Background file	Informationen über Land und Leute
Everyday English	Englisch in Alltagssituationen
Looking at language	Beispiele sammeln und sprachliche Regeln entdecken
Language help	Hilfe in Form von sprachlichen Regeln
Practice	Aufgaben und Übungen
Pronunciation course	englische Aussprache trainieren
The world behind the picture	vom Bild in den Film – Videoclips mit Aufgaben
Text	eine spannende oder lustige Geschichte
Your task	In der Lernaufgabe kannst du in jeder Unit zeigen, was du gelernt hast und dich selbst einschätzen.
Let's prepare for a test	Auf diesen Seiten kannst du den Wortschatz und die Grammatik einer Unit wiederholen und dich auf Schulaufgaben vorbereiten.

Du findest auch diese Symbole:

(Symbol: Hören online)	Texte, die du dir anhören kannst: *www.cornelsen.de/webcodes* (Webcode ACC332076-1)
(Symbol: Übungssequenz)	Übungssequenz: neue Grammatik intensiv üben und dann anwenden
Early finisher	zusätzliche Aktivitäten und Übungen für Schüler/innen, die früher fertig sind
More help	zusätzliche Hilfen für eine Aufgabe
You choose	eine Aufgabe auswählen
EXTRA	zusätzliche Aktivitäten und Übungen für alle
My Book	schöne und wichtige Arbeiten sammeln
Study skills	Einführung in Lern- und Arbeitstechniken
(Symbole)	Hören Sprechen Lesen Schreiben
(Symbole)	Mediation (zwischen zwei Sprachen vermitteln), Thinking about language (Sprachreflexion)
(Symbole)	Partnerarbeit Partnercheck Gruppenarbeit Kooperative Lernform

Justin Skinner

Lucy Pascoe

Skill in focus: Listening

Skill in focus: Listening

Skill in focus: Speaking

Abby Blackwell

Sam Bennett

Here we go!

Alternativer Einstieg möglich über **KV 1: The British Isles** (auch einsetzbar auf S. 10).

1 Silky's questions

a) Partner A: You're Silky.
Ask the questions.
Partner B: Answer the questions.

A: What's your name?
B: My name is …
A: Are you …?
…

b) Partner B:
Now you're Silky.

2 Meet your classmates

Talk to different partners.

A: Hi, my name is …
I'm … years old.
What's your name?
B: Hello, I'm …
I'm from …
What about you?
C: Hi, I'm …
I'm from …

3 A card to Silky

Write a card to Silky.

Hello Silky,
My name is Lara. I'm ten years old and I'm from Traunstein in Germany.
I like the colour blue.
What about you?
Lara xxx

xxx steht für "kisses". **xoxo** wäre "hugs and kisses". Beides sind gängige informelle Schlussformeln z.B. bei SMS oder Mails.

TIP
Im **Vocabulary** findest du die neuen Wörter. Es beginnt auf S. 201.

4 Find the words

Find these words in the Vocabulary:

classmate · hill · hometown · meet · near · lots of · tower

→ Workbook 1–2 (p. 2)

Welcome to Plymouth

Alternativer Einstieg möglich über **KV 1: The British Isles**

1 Silky's tour of Plymouth

Grund-schule a) Match the words to the pictures.

girl · river · castle · pool · tower · hill · boy · boat · sea · big wheel

1 - castle, 2 - ...

b) Talk about the map.

A: I can see a boat / a boy / … on the map. And you?

B: I can see …

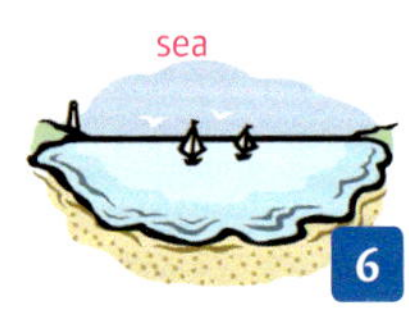

1 02 Grund-schule c) Listen to Silky and look at the places on the map. Listen again and point to the places.

→ **Workbook** *3 (p. 3)*

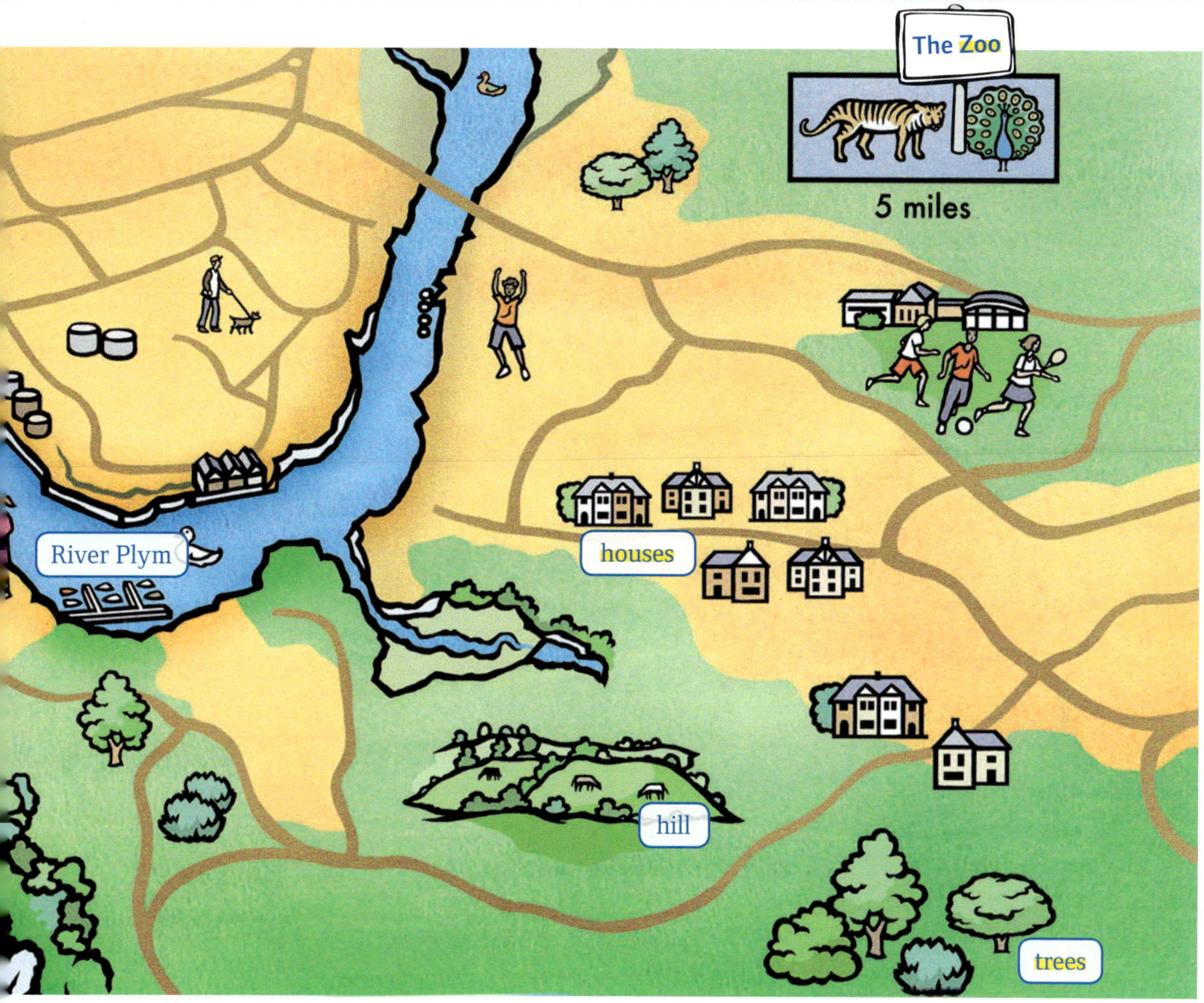

Grund-
schule

2 Silky's song

1 03–04

Listen to Silky's song and sing along.

Chorus: *Let me show you Plymouth Sound,*
It's my hometown! It's my hometown!
Let me show you Plymouth Sound,
Plymouth, Plymouth Sound.

By the sea, there's the Hoe –
Hey, hey Hoe, here we go!
Blue, blue, blue, the Lido Pool.
The water's warm, the kids are cool!

Chorus

Red and white, lots of stripes.
Red and white, tall and bright:
It's the tower, on the Hoe!
Hey, hey Hoe, here we go!

Chorus

Track **1.04** ist die Instrumentalversion.

Die im Song vorkommenden Farben *blue*, *red* und *white* werden nicht als Lernwortschatz eingeführt, sollten den S aber aus der GS bekannt sein. Farben werden auf S. 15 wiederholt/eingeführt.

3 Who is it? What is it?

Answer the questions.

1 Who's Silky?
2 What's Silky's hometown?
3 What's the Lido?
4 What's the Plym?
5 What's blue?
6 What's warm?
7 Who's cool?
8 What's red and white?

1 a seal
2 Plymouth
3 a pool
4 a river
5 the Lido pool
6 the water
7 the kids
8 the tower on the Hoe

Is it Monday, Tuesday, …?
Every day is great in Plymouth!

Box "The days of the week", Voc, S. 206

A week in Plymouth

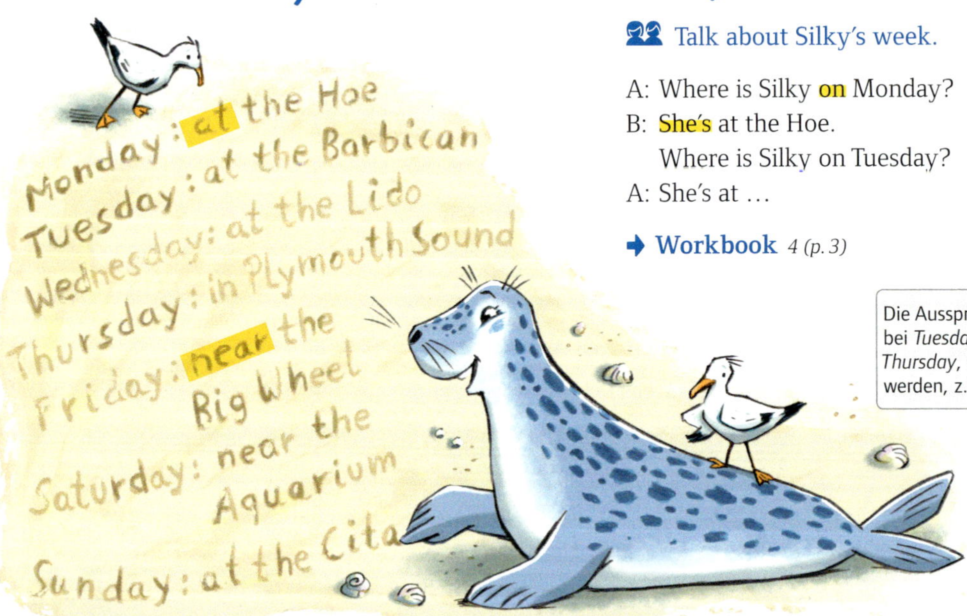

1 Silky's week

Talk about Silky's week.

A: Where is Silky on Monday?
B: She's at the Hoe.
Where is Silky on Tuesday?
A: She's at …

➜ **Workbook** *4 (p. 3)*

Die Aussprache der Wochentage, v.a. bei *Tuesday, Wednesday* und *Thursday*, sollte intensiv geübt werden, z.B. durch ***Chorsprechen***.

2 Plymouth photos

Partner A: Look at pages 12–13.
Partner B: Look at pages 10–11.
Now match the Plymouth photos to places on the map.

A: Photo 1 is Plymouth Sound. Look, it's here on the map.
B: Yes, that's right. And photo 2 is …
A: Yes, … / No, that's wrong. Photo 2 is …

2 the Lido · 3 the Citadel · 4 the Big Wheel · 5 the Aquarium · 6 the Hoe · 7 the Barbican

My favourite day of the week is Sunday. What's your favourite day?

3 Rhyme: The days of the week

1 05

Grundschule

Copy the black lines. Listen and add the green lines. Say the rhyme in class.

Monday, Tuesday, school for you,
Work … Work with a group and a partner too.

Wednesday, Thursday, can you see
… Seals in a boat, one, two, three?

Friday, Friday. Hello! Hi!
… School is over. Say goodbye.

Saturday, Sunday, they're so cool –
… You and your friends at the swimming pool.

Seals in a boat, one, two, three?
Work with a group and a partner too.
You and your friends at the swimming pool.
School is over. Say goodbye.

There are lots of animals in Plymouth. Follow me.

Alternativer Einstieg mit dem Tierquiz auf **KV 2: Animals**.

My favourite animal

ant · bear · bird · butterfly · cat · dog · elephant · frog · giraffe

1 Silky's favourite animal

a) Talk like this:

A: I can see a rabbit / an elephant / …
in the picture. What about you?
B: I can see …

1 06 b) Listen to Silky and the animals.

Grundschule

When you hear an animal, point to it in the picture.
What's Silky's favourite animal?

c) Talk like this:

A: What's your favourite animal?
B: My … What's your favourite …?
A: …

2 Strange animals?

Grundschule

a) Write the letters in the right order.

~~farfeig~~ · ebar · bratib · pelhaten · dirb · tra · ansek · herso · nilo · act · ogd · anugie gip

- farfeig giraffe
- ebar …

giraffe · bear · rabbit · elephant · bird · rat · snake · horse · lion · cat · dog · guinea pig

b) Check with a partner.

TIP
Die **Arbeitsanweisungen** werden auf der hinteren Umschlaginnenseite erklärt.

Zusatz/Differenzierung: Schnelle S denken sich eigene "strange animals" aus und geben sie einem Partner zum Lösen (*bus stop*-Methode).

guinea pig · horse · lion · monkey · pig · rabbit · rat · snake · whale

3 Colours

Box "Colours", Voc, S. 208

Grundschule

a) Copy the names of the colours.

black[4] · blue[9] · brown[7] · green[6] · grey[1] ·
orange[3] · pink[8] · purple[11] · red[5] · white[10] · yellow[2]

Then look at the picture.
Write the number for each colour.

b) Talk like this:
A: Black is number four.
B: Yes, that's right. And blue is …

c) Make groups of three.
- Say a colour.
- Look at the picture.
  Find an animal with the same colour.
- Find a thing in the room
  with the same colour.

Green.

The frogs are green.

My ruler is green.

➔ **Workbook** *5–6 (pp. 4–5)*

4 GAME "I spy with my little eye"

Choose an animal from the picture.
Talk to your group.

A: I spy with my little eye a grey / green / …
animal with two / four / … legs / without legs.
B: Is it a frog / …?
A: Yes, that's right! / No, that's wrong!

5 My favourite colour

Grundschule

Draw animals and other things with your favourite colour. Label your drawing.

More words: ➔ *Wordbank 1 (p. 168)*

➔ *GF 19: The plural of nouns (pp. 194–195)*

A monkey, a guinea pig, an elephant too. I have lots of pets, what about you? Now it's time for an English lesson.

Our English class

1 What's in your classroom?

Grund-schule

a) Copy the words from the box.

> board · cupboard · chair · clock · door · desk · poster · window
>
> +watch *(n)*

b) Talk about the things like this:

A: Board.
B: This is the board. It's black / green / …
B: Chair.
A: This is a chair. It's …

Alternative: KV 3: School things in my room mit einem Wimmelbild, in dem die S Gegenstände suchen und ausmalen können.

2 What's in your school bag?

1 07 a) Listen. Find the things and put them on your desk.

Grund-schule

> book · exercise book · ruler · pen · pencil · pencil case · glue stick · rubber · sharpener

Listen again. When you hear a word, point to the thing and say the word.

b) Talk like this:

A: Let me show you what's on my desk.
This is my ruler. It's white.
Now you.
B: This is my pen. It's blue. And here's my …

3 GAME Simon says

Grund-schule

a) Listen to your teacher. Do only what Simon says.

b) Now you are Simon.
Simon says: put your pen on the desk. /
Talk to the teacher.
Simon says: open the window. / Touch … /
Give me …

➜ **Workbook** *7–8 (pp. 5–6)*

4 The ants go marching 1 08–09

Track **1.09** ist die Instrumentalversion.

Grund-schule

a) Listen and sing along.

The ants go marching one by one,
Hurrah, hurrah!
The ants go marching two by two,
Hurrah, hurrah!
The ants go marching three by three,
The little one stops to climb a tree
And they all go marching
Down … to the ground
To get out … of the rain,
BOOM! BOOM! BOOM!

The ants go marching four by four,
Hurrah, hurrah!
The ants go marching five by five,
Hurrah, hurrah!
The ants go marching six by six,
The little one stops to pick up sticks
And they all go marching
Down … to the ground
To get out … of the rain,
BOOM! BOOM! BOOM!

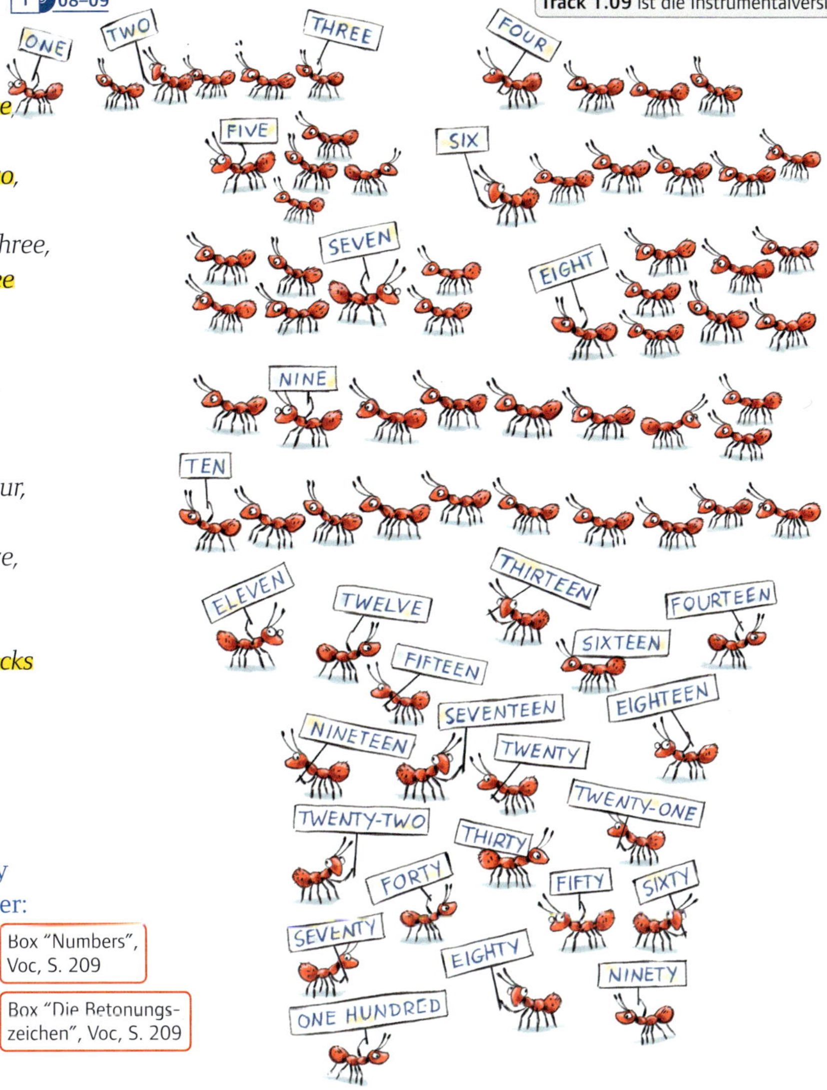

b) Point to the ants and say these numbers to your partner:

1–20
21, 22, 30
40, 50 …100

Box "Numbers", Voc, S. 209

Box "Die Betonungszeichen", Voc, S. 209

5 Telephone numbers

Ask your partner for his/her telephone number. Write it down. Are you right?

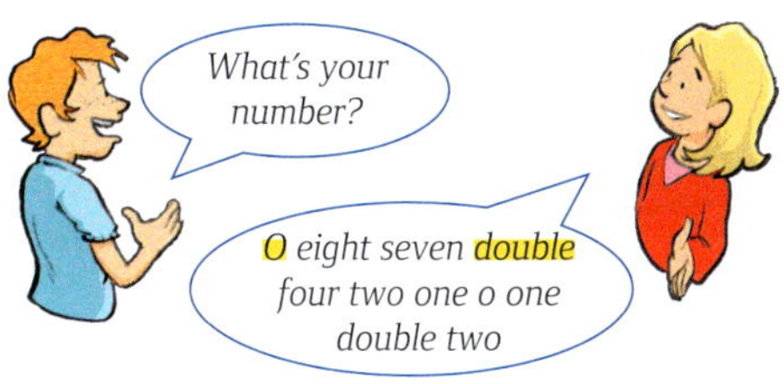

➜ **Workbook** *9–10 (pp. 6–7)*

6 What time is it?

Point to the mobile phones and say the time. Talk like this:

A: What time is it, please? B: It's …
A: Thank you.

ten o'clock | ten fifteen | ten …

half past … | quarter to … | five to …

+quarter past

➜ **Workbook** *11 (p. 7)*

Die Spielregeln

1. Arbeite mit einem Partner.
2. Ihr habt maximal 15 Minuten, um das Ziel der Rally zu erreichen. Beginnt bei Frage 1, folgt der Straße bis Frage Nummer 14.
3. Schreibt eure Antworten auf ein Blatt Papier.
4. Nach 15 Minuten tauscht ihr euer Blatt mit einem anderen Paar.
5. Vergleicht die Ergebnisse mit den richtigen Lösungen auf Seite 167. Für jede richtige Lösung gibt es einen Punkt.
6. Notiert die Punktzahl auf dem Blatt eurer Mitschüler und gebt das Blatt zurück.

Das Paar mit den meisten Punkten hat gewonnen!

1 Die Kapitel deines Englischbuches heißen "Units". Wie viele Units hat dieses Buch? 5 (mit Here we go = 6)

2 Jede Unit enthält mindestens ein Background file zu einem Thema der Unit. Unit 4 hat zwei Background files. Wie heißt das zweite? Grey seals

3 Wie heißen die Seiten, wo du Grammatikregeln nachschlagen kannst? Wo beginnen diese Seiten? Grammar file, ab S. 182

4 Auf einer Übungsseite von Unit 2 findest du das Bild einer Schulbibliothek. Welche Farbe haben die Luftballons dort? grün

5 In einem Teil jeder Unit geht es um die englische Aussprache. Wie lang ist dieser Teil? eine Seite (Pronunciation course)

6

Welche Seiten des Buches enthalten die Wörter, die du von Unit 1 lernen sollst? Schreibe die Seitenzahlen auf.

S. 210–216 (Vocabulary Unit 1)

7

Wie heißt der Teil des Buches, der dir hilft, wenn du Informationen ordnen oder einen kurzen Vortrag halten sollst?

Skills file

8

In einem Bild in Unit 2 steht ein Mann neben einer Uhr. Wie spät ist es dort?

4 o'clock

9

Wie heißt der Teil am Ende einer jeden Unit, der eine längere spannende oder lustige Geschichte enthält?

Text

10

Auf einer Seite jeder Unit dreht sich alles um das Thema „Film". Welche Seite ist das in Unit 1?

S. 33 (The world behind the picture)

11

Wie heißt die Geschichte, die du nach Unit 5 findest?

My home, the zoo

12

Um welches Thema geht es bei der Mediation-Aufgabe in Unit 2 (S. 58)?

Essen bestellen im Restaurant

13

Nach jeder Unit findest du Seiten, die dir bei der Vorbereitung auf Tests helfen. Wie heißen diese Seiten?

Let's prepare for a test

14

Nach jeder Unit gibt es eine Lernaufgabe. Danach kannst du dich selbst einschätzen. Wie heißt diese Seite?

Your task

The first day at school

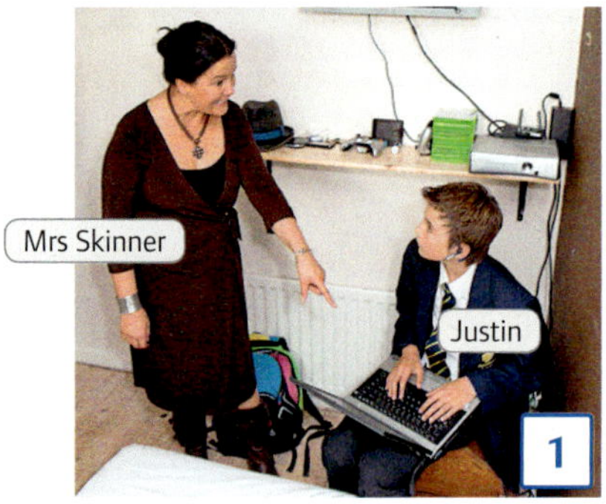

1 Meet the Plymouth kids 1 10–12

Grund-schule

Read texts A, B and C. Then listen and match them to pictures 1, 2 and 3. A 2 · B 3 · C 1

Check with a partner.

A Sunday

Lucy Pascoe and her best friend Maya Sen are eleven. They're at Maya's flat. Monday is their first day at their new schools.

Lucy: Hey, your Coombe Dean[1] uniform is nice! I like black.
Maya: The Plymstock school uniform is nice too.
Lucy: You know the Plymstock uniform?
Maya: My brother Mukesh[2] is at Plymstock.
Lucy: Oh, yes – in Year 9. My sister Holly is in Year 9 too.

[1] [ˌkuːm ˈdiːn] [2] [ˈmukeʃ]

B Monday

Sam Bennett is a student at Plymstock School. But he isn't from Plymouth. He's from London. His mum and dad are in the navy.

Father: Let me look at you. That's a great uniform. Dark blue and grey.
Sam: Your uniform is OK too, Dad.
Father: Thank you, Number One.

C Monday

It's 8:15. Justin Skinner is on Skype with his father in Boston.

Mother: Please, Justin. It's your first day at Plymstock School. And you're late.
Justin: Wait a minute, Mum. I'm on Skype with Dad.
Mother: Hey, what time is it in Boston?

2 Profiles

Start a profile for Lucy, Maya, Justin and Sam.
Get information from page 20. You can add more information later.

Die S sollten im *MyBook* für jedes der Lehrwerkskinder eine neue Seite anlegen, damit sie ausreichend Platz haben, alle Informationen im Laufe des Buches zu sammeln.

Your task

Am Ende dieser Unit wirst du …
… dein *profile* erstellen und dich einem Schüler oder einer Schülerin aus Plymouth vorstellen.

3 Meet Morph

Morph is at Plymstock School too.
The library is his home.

Box "home", Voc, S. 207

Listen to Morph's song and sing along.

1 13–14

Grundschule

Morph's song

I'm Morph, I'm Morph from Plymstock School,
I'm big, I'm °small, I'm °really cool.
°Sometimes I'm blue and sometimes red,
I'm all the colours in your °head.
I can °change my °shape and I can °be
An X, Y, I or J, T, D.
Can you °find me? °Just have a look!
I'm on the °shelf, I'm in a book,
I'm °always in the library.
That's where I am – °come in and see.
I'm Morph, I'm Morph from Plymstock School,
I'm big, I'm small, I'm really cool, I'm Morph.

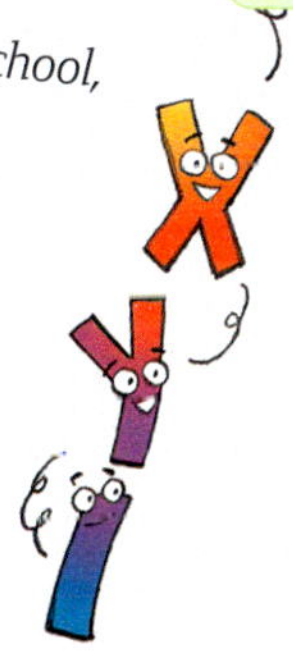

You choose Act out Morph's song.
Or write four more lines for the song:
I'm Morph, I …

Track 1.14 ist die Instrumentalversion.

Neigungsdifferenzierung: Die S haben die Wahl zwischen einer darstellenden Aufgabe und einer kreativen Schreibaufgabe.

→ Workbook *1 (p. 8)*

1 Before school

1 15

Look at the pictures. Who can you see?

Lucy: Hey, Maya!

Maya: Hi, Lucy. My first day at Coombe Dean! It's strange without you.

Lucy: Oh, Maya, my first day at a new school and you aren't there. It's sad.

Maya: Yes, it is. Oh, Lucy, look at the time. It's 8:25.

Lucy: Don't go, Maya. We aren't late. Give me a hug.

Maya: Bye, Lucy.

Lucy: Bye, Maya! Bye!

❖

Lucy: Hey, watch out!

Sam: Oh, sorry! Hey, you're at Plymstock School.

Lucy: So?

Sam: I'm at Plymstock School too.

Lucy: You aren't from Plymouth!

Sam: No, I'm not. I'm new here. I'm from London.

Lucy: OK.

Sam: I'm in Year 7 – in class 7EB. What about you?

Lucy: I'm in 7EB too.

Sam: Hey, that's cool.

Lucy: Is it?

Sam: Yes. Er … my name is Sam.

Lucy: Sam?

Sam: Sam Bennett. What's your name?

Lucy: Lucy. Lucy Pascoe.

Sam: Hi, Lucy. Nice to meet you.

Lucy: Hey, it's 8:30. Hurry up … we're late.

Zusatz: Die S können hier dazu angehalten werden, die betreffenden Textstellen betont (un-)freundlich vorzutragen.

2 Who are they?

Make three or more sentences about Lucy, Maya and Sam. Talk to a partner.

Lucy is …	Lucy is eleven. She's in Year 7. Maya is her best friend …
Maya …	Maya is eleven. She's at Coombe Dean School. Her best friend ist at Plymstock School …
Sam …	Sam is in class 7EB. He's new at Plymstock. He's from London …

Zusatz: Die S formulieren Sätze über andere Lehrwerkskinder oder Mit-S. Die Klasse muss raten, wer gemeint ist.

3 Friendly or not?

Find these phrases in the text and make two lists.

Give me a hug. · Hey, watch out! · So? · Hey, that's cool. · Is it? · Nice to meet you.

friendly	not friendly
Give me a hug. Hey, that's cool. • Nice to meet you.	Hey, watch out! • So? • Is it? …

Listen and check. 1 16

4 At school 1 17

Justin is late. What's Justin's problem?

Background file

There are uniforms at British schools. Look at the kids' different uniforms.

- Who is at Plymstock School? Lucy
  Who is at Coombe Dean School? Maya
- Say which uniform you like.

5 Have a go

What are the students' names? Walk around the classroom. Find two partners and talk like this. Change roles.

School bag, pencil case,
Glue stick too.
First day of school for me,
What about you?

Mit **KV 5: My school uniform** erstellen die S ihre eigene Schuluniform, indem sie die Kleidungsstücke bunt ausmalen. Die KV wird auf S. 25 weiter verwendet.

Looking at language

a) Copy and finish the table. You can find the short forms on pages 22–23.

Personal pronouns and the forms of the verb *be*

Singular		Plural	
long	**short**	**long**	**short**
I am	I'm	we are	we're
you are	you're	you are	you're
he is	he's	they are	they're
she is	she's		
it is	it's		

b) Make a second table for negative forms: I am not, you are not, he ...
Look at pages 22–23 and add the short forms: I'm not, you aren't, he ...

➜ *GF 1: Personal pronouns (p. 183)*
GF 3: The verb (to) be (p. 184)

1 *He, she* or *it?* (Personal pronouns)

Look at the pictures. Talk like this:

A: I spy a *she*. — B: The bag?
A: No, that's an *it*. — B: Justin's mum?
A: That's right. — B: I spy …

2 Plymouth people and things (Personal pronouns)

Finish the sentences with I, you, he, she, it, we or they.

1 Where's Plymouth? – ...'s in England.
2 Lucy and Maya are eleven. ...'re friends.
3 Maya: "I like you, Lucy. ...'re great!"
4 Sam is eleven too. ...'s new in Plymouth.
5 Sam: "...'m in Year 7. What about you?"
6 Maya isn't at Plymstock School. ...'s at Coombe Dean.
7 Lucy: "Maya and I are best friends. But ...'re at different schools."
8 That's the Plymstock uniform. ...'s dark blue.

1 It's • 2 They're • 3 You're • 4 He's •
5 I'm • 6 She's • 7 we're • 8 It's

➜ **Workbook** *2–3 (p. 9)*

3 I'm Maya (*be*: positive statements)

a) Choose the right short forms: 'm, 's or 're.

1 I... from Plymstock in Plymouth.
2 Plymouth? – It... a town in England.
3 I have a big brother. He... OK.
4 My best friend is Lucy. She... great!
5 We... sad – we... at different schools.
6 But I like my new classmates. They... cool.
7 And you? Oh, you... from Germany!

1 I'm • 2 It's • 3 He's • 4 She's • 5 We're ... we're • 6 They're • 7 you're

b) Make sentences like these about yourself. Use short forms of *be*.

4 What's wrong? (*be*: negative statements)

Correct the sentences. Use short forms. Then give the right information.

1 Silky is a snake.
– No, she isn't a snake. She's a seal!
2 Sam is at Coombe Dean School.
– No, he... He's at ...
3 Justin and Sam are in Year 8. – No, ...
4 Plymouth is a town in Germany. – No, ...
5 The sea at Plymouth is red. – No, ...
6 And you? You're in a German lesson now.
– No, I...

2 isn't ... Plymstock School. • 3 they're not ... Year 7 • 4 it's not ... England • 5 it isn't ... blue • 6 I'm not. I'm in an English lesson.

Early finisher Make more wrong sentences and correct them.

5 Who is in the photo? (*be*: positive and negative statements)

Partner A: Go to page 242.

Partner B: Go to page 166.

6 GAME Silly sentences

Make two teams: A and B. In each team there are two students. Play the game like this:

Step 1: Student from Team A:
Say a silly or wrong sentence with five or more words.
"I'm from Plymouth and I'm a giraffe."
Or: "Sam Bennett is a girl."

Step 2: Student from Team B, correct the sentence.
"That's wrong. You aren't from Plymouth and you aren't a giraffe."
Or: "That's wrong. Sam Bennett isn't a girl. He's a boy."

Step 3: Student from Team B, say a new silly or wrong sentence.

➜ Workbook 4 (p. 9)

7 Apostrophe: *'s* and *s'* (The possessive)

a) Match the phrases to the pictures.

1 the girl's dogs C 2 the girls' dogs B 3 the boy's books D 4 the boys' books A

A

B

C

D

b) Draw pictures for these phrases:
1 the kid's ball 2 the kids' ball

Language help

With **people** and **animals** use **'s** or **s'**:
Singular nouns: **apostrophe** + **s** ('s)
*Sam**'s** name, the dog**'s** ball*
Plural nouns ***s'***: apostrophe (') after the s
*the students**'** class, the kids**'** friends*

➜ *GF 4: The possessive form (I) (p. 185)*
➜ **Workbook** *5 (p. 10)*

c) Finish the sentences. Use correct nouns and names with **'s** or **s'**.

1 Sam's name is Bennett.
2 The ... hometown is Plymouth now.
3 ... name is Skinner.
4 The Plymouth ... school is Plymstock.
5 Their ... name is Miss Bell.
6 Sam: My ... names are Justin and Lucy.
7 Lucy: My best ... name is Maya.
8 ... new school is Coombe Dean.

2 Bennetts'
3 Justin's
4 kids'
5 teacher's
6 friends'
7 friend's
8 Maya's

English and German are different

Sam's name. *Sams Name*

More help: Die Wörter sind – ohne Apostroph – in einer Box vorgegeben.

More help ➜ *p. 156*

8 Profiles

1 18

a) There are *four* speakers.
Listen and match each speaker to a picture.
Make a table for your answers.

+(to) speak

Speaker	**Name**
1	...
2	...
...	...

b)
Maya: Plymouth · 11 · Coombe Dean · Lucy
Sam: London · 11 · Plymstock School · Jack
Silky: Plymouth · 2 · Spot
Justin: Plymouth · 12 · Plymstock School · his dad

Say who the speakers are.
Speaker number ... is Justin.
1 Maya · 2 Sam · 3 Silky · 4 Justin

b) Choose a picture from a).
Listen again. Find this information about the speaker in your picture:

hometown · ... years old · school · best friend

c) Find a student with the same picture.
Together write a short profile of the speaker.
This is ...'s profile.
... is from ... in England.
He/She ... years old.
... at ... school.
His/Her best friend ...

Give your text to another pair. Read their text.

➜ *SF 7: Listening (pp. 179–180)*
➜ **Workbook** *6–8 (pp. 10–11)*

9 Don't wear trainers (Imperatives)

Language help

You make positive imperatives like this:

You make negative imperatives like this:

➜ *GF 5: Imperatives (p. 186)*
➜ **Workbook** *9 (p. 11)*

Make imperatives for the pictures.

touch

give

put

open

forget

talk

1 Don't touch the picture. • 2 Give me the pen, please. • 3 Don't put the rat in the bag. • 4 Don't open the window. • 5 Don't forget your bag. • 6 Don't talk in the library.

More help ➜ *(p. 156)*

More help: Die Verben sind im Infinitiv in einer Box vorgegeben und müssen Lückensätzen zugeordnet werden.

10 STUDY SKILLS The Vocabulary

Mithilfe des Vocabulary (ab S. 201) lernst du die neuen Wörter einer Unit kennen.

a) Sieh dir die Seiten 201–242 an und beantworte diese Fragen:

1 Die Zeichen in [ ] zeigen
a) Geheimschrift.
b) Aussprache.
c) Dialekt.

2 Ein rotes Ausrufezeichen (!) weist hin auf
a) gefährliche Wörter.
b) Vokabeltests.
c) mögliche Fehlerquellen.

3 Die rechte der drei Spalten
a) ist für Notizen.
b) enthält Beispielsätze und Verwendungshinweise.
c) soll auswendig gelernt werden.

4 Das Zeichen ◄► steht für
a) Gegenteile.
b) Jahreszahlen.
c) kleiner/größer als.

5 Die blauen Kästen enthalten
a) Hinweise für Lehrer/innen.
b) Bekanntes aus vorigen Units.
c) Übersichten von Wörtern und Wendungen, die du zusammen lernen solltest.

b) Kannst du jetzt diese Fragen beantworten?

1 Was ist das Gegenteil von **new**? (S. 210)
2 Worauf muss man bei der Aussprache von **wrong** achten? (S. 207)
3 Was ist das Besondere am Wort **I** (ich!)? (S. 204)
4 Wie spricht man die englische **Null** in Telefonnummern aus? (S. 209)

1 old • 2 w wird nicht gesprochen • 3 wird immer groß geschrieben • 4 wird wie ein "o" ausgesprochen

Study skills

Das Vocabulary ist nicht der einzige Weg, wie du Vokabeln lernen kannst.
Weitere Methoden zeigt dir das **Skills File**.

➜ *SF 1: Learning vocabulary (pp. 174–175)*

1 A game with Miss Bell 1 19

The students meet their new teacher and play her game. Look at the pictures. What's the game?

Miss Bell: Good morning. I'm Miss Bell, your class teacher. It's your first day at Plymstock School, so …
Justin: Sorry I'm late, Miss.
Miss Bell: OK. Come in, please.
Justin: Yes, Miss.
Miss Bell: Now, let's start with a game. Here's a ball. Throw the ball and ask a question. Catch it and answer the question. OK?
Class: Yes, Miss.
Miss Bell: Here we go. Are you in a football team?
Sam: No, I'm not.
Miss Bell: And now, please, say your name and one or two things about yourself.
Sam: I'm Sam Bennett and I'm from London. My birthday is in September. I do kung fu and I like …
Miss Bell: Thank you, Sam. Now throw the ball.
Sam: OK. Are you from Plymouth?
Justin: Yes, I am. My name is Justin Skinner. I live with my mum at 14 Dean Street. My dad is from the USA. Er … Is your dad from the USA?
Lucy: No, he isn't. My name is … oops!
Sam: Lucy.
Miss Bell: Are you Lucy?
Sam: No, I'm not, Miss.
Miss Bell: Then please don't answer Lucy's question. OK, Lucy, start again.
Lucy: My name is Lucy Pascoe. And my favourite animals are rabbits …

❖

Miss Bell: Now, here are your timetables. And at 11 o'clock it's time for …

2 Who is it?

Read a sentence from the text in 1 to your group. Can the others guess who it is?

A: "Sorry I'm late, Miss."
B: That's Justin!
B: "Come in, please."
C: That's …

3 Have a go

Ask and answer questions like this:

A: Are you in class 5b / in a football team / …?
B: Yes, I am. / No, I'm not.
B: Is your mum from England / the USA / …?
A: Yes, she is. / No, she isn't.

EXTRA Play Miss Bell's game in your class.

Grundschule

Das Spiel sollte in Gruppen von 6–8 S gespielt werden. Pro Gruppe wird ein Ball benötigt.

Looking at language

a) Copy the table and finish the ***yes*** answers. You can find examples on p. 28.

Are you …?	Yes, I …	No, …
Is he …?	Yes, he is.	
Is she …?	Yes, she …	
Is it …?	Yes, it is.	
Are you …?	Yes, we …	
Are they …?	Yes, … are.	

b) Add negative forms to the table:
No, I'm not. No, he …

TIP
Don't answer *Yes* or *No*.
Say *Yes, I am* or *No, I'm not*.

1 Yes, I am (*be*: questions and short answers)

a) Partner A: Ask the questions.

1 Are you in Year 5?
2 Is Sam from London?
3 Are you and your friends in Plymouth now?
4 Are your books in your pencil case?

1 Yes, I am. • 2 Yes, he is. • 3 No, we aren't. • 4 No, they aren't.

Partner B: Ask the questions.

5 Are you nine years old?
6 Are Lucy and Maya friends?
7 Is your English book in your school bag?
8 Is Miss Bell a student?

5 Yes, I am. / No, I'm not. • 6 Yes, they are. • 7 No, it isn't. • 8 No, she isn't.

b) Make more questions for your partner.

A: Is your best friend in our class?
B: – Yes, she is. / No, she isn't.
B: Are your shoes red? …

More help → p. 156
→ GF 3: The verb (to) be (p. 184)
→ Workbook 10 (p. 12)

More help: Einige Ideen für Fragen sind vorgegeben.

2 THINKING ABOUT LANGUAGE Talking to people

1 20–21

Read A and B. In which dialogue is James friendly? What's different? Find phrases for your answer.

A

Marc: Hi. I'm Marc. What's your name?
James: James.
Marc: Are you at Plymstock too?
James: Yes.
Marc: Are you in Year 7?
James: No. Year 8. But I have a sister in Year 7.
Marc: Oh! Is she in 7EB? That's my class.
James: No. 7AP.
Marc: Are you from Plymouth?
James: No.
Marc: Oh, where are you from?
James: London.
Marc: Hey, that's cool!

B

Marc: Hi. I'm Marc. What's your name?
James: Oh, hi, Marc. I'm James.
Marc: Are you at Plymstock too?
James: Yes, I am.
Marc: Are you in Year 7?
James: No, I'm not. I'm in Year 8. But I have a sister in Year 7.
Marc: Oh! Is she in 7EB? That's my class.
James: No, she isn't. She's in 7AP.
Marc: Are you from Plymouth?
James: No, we aren't. We're new here.
Marc: Oh, where are you from?
James: We're from London.
Marc: Hey, that's cool!

3 WORDS School subjects

Box "School subjects", Voc, S. 213

a) Look at the school subjects. Can you understand the words?

- English
- German
- French
- history
- geography
- art
- maths
- science
- ICT
- music
- religion
- PE
- design and technology

1 22 b) Listen to Lucy and Maya. What subjects do they like? What are their favourite subjects?
Lucy likes Geography and History. Her favourite subject is Design and Technology.
Maya likes Maths, Science, German and Religion. Her favourite subject is ICT.

www 1.3

4 WORDS The students' timetable (The school day)

a) Look at the students' timetable. Then finish the text below. You need these new words:

hour · lunch · break

Lesson	Monday	Tuesday	Wednesday	Thursday	Friday
9:00 – 10:00	Design and Technology	English	History	Science	Maths
10:00 – 11:00	Music	Geography	French	Maths	Design and Technology
BREAK 11:00 – 11:20					
11:20 – 12:20	PE	ICT	English	German	German
12:20 – 1:20	English	Learning to Learn	Science	History	Science
LUNCH 1:20 – 1:55					
1:55 – 2:55	Maths	Art	PE	Religion	English

At Plymstock School, there are … lessons every day.
Lessons are one … long.
The first lesson is at …
There's a short … at 11:00.
The … break is at 1:20.
It's … minutes long.
It's time to go home at …

five · hour · 9:00 · break · lunch · 35 · 2:55

More words: ➜ *Wordbank 2 (p. 168)*

b) Talk about the students' timetable like this:
A: What is lesson 1 on Monday?
B: Lesson 1 on Monday is design and technology.

➜ **Workbook** *11–13 (pp. 12–13)*

5 A German timetable

Schaue dir den Stundenplan an und beantworte Lucys Fragen auf Englisch. Verwende Redewendungen aus Aufgabe 4.

	Montag	Dienstag	Mittwoch
8.00-8.45	Mathe	Deutsch	Englisch
8.45-9.30	Sport	Reli	Musik
PAUSE			
9.45-10.30	Deutsch	Mathe	Mathe
10.30-11.15	N+T	Geo	Deutsch
PAUSE			
11.30-12.15	Englisch	N+T	Sport
12.15-13.00	Englisch	N+T	Sport

1 When's the first lesson every day? 8:00
2 What's the first lesson on Monday? Maths
3 When are the breaks? 9:30 + 11:15
4 When's PE? Wednesdays at 11:30
5 When's science? Monday at 10:30, Tuesdays at 11:30
6 When is it time to go home? 1 o'clock

More words: ➜ *Wordbank 2 (p. 168)*

➜ *SF 10: Mediation (p. 181)*

6 Apostrophes

Write correct sentences. Don't forget the apostrophes.

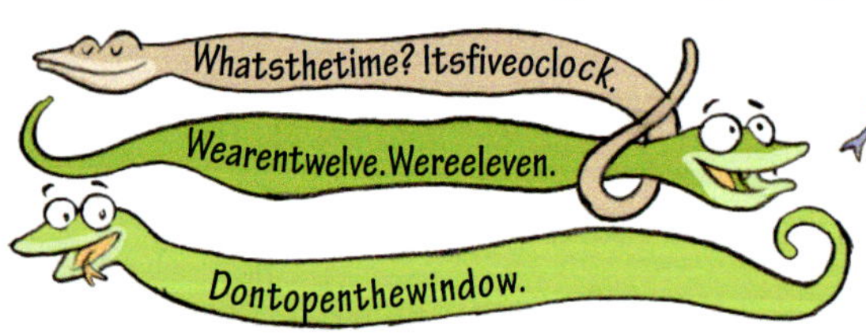

➜ *SF 9: Writing – Check your spelling (p. 181)*

➜ **Workbook** *14 (p. 14)*

Zusatz: Die S machen eigene Buchstabenschlangen und tauschen sie untereinander aus.

What's the time? It's five o'clock. • We aren't twelve. We're eleven. • Don't open the window. • There's a break at eleven o'clock. • Who's that? It's Miss Bell. She's nice. • Let's play a game. Don't go.

7 WORDS My birthday is in … (The months)

Box "The months", Voc, S. 213

1 23

a) On a card, write the month of your birthday.

January · February · March · April · May · June · July · August · September · October · November · December

Alternative: Sollten die Monatsnamen den S bisher unbekannt sein, liest L diese zunächst vor und die S sprechen im Chor nach.

b) Listen. When you hear your month hold up your card and say "My birthday is in …".

Grund-schule

➜ Workbook 15 (p. 14)

Zusatz: Die S basteln aus den Karten einen Geburtstagskalender.

8 WORDS My birthday is on … (Ordinal numbers)

1 24–25

Grund-schule

a) Listen and say the dates. Put up your hand when you hear the date of your birthday.

1st	**first**	12th	**twelfth**
2nd	**second**	13th	thirteenth
3rd	**third**	14th	fourteenth
4th	fourth	…	
5th	**fifth**	20th	**twentieth**
6th	sixth	21st	twenty-first
7th	seventh	22nd	twenty-second
8th	**eighth**	23rd	twenty-third
9th	**ninth**	…	
10th	tenth	30th	**thirtieth**
11th	eleventh	31st	thirty-first

Box "Numbers", Voc, S. 214

➜ Workbook 16 (p. 14)

b) Ask other students.

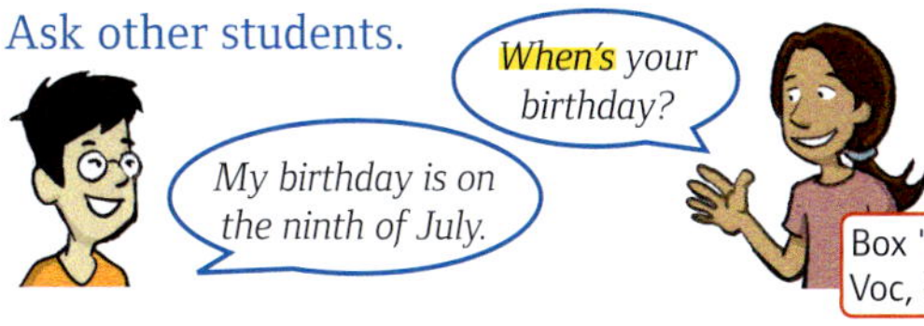

Box "Birthdays", Voc, S. 214

c) Listen to the kids. When are their birthdays? Make a table like this:

Name	Date
Will	13th March
Zoe	
Harry	
Grace	

Zoe: 15th October
Harry: 22nd May
Grace: 13th April

TIP

You say	You write
the second of April	2nd April
the ninth of July	9th July

9 *a* [ə] or *an* [ən] ?

1 26

Listen. What presents would the kids like? Write them in the correct column – a or an?

Name	*a*	*an*
Will		
Zoe		
Harry		
Grace		

Will: a football · an English book
Zoe: a DVD · an orange pen
Harry: a giraffe · an elephant
Grace: a uniform for Teddy · an MP3 player

DVD · elephant · English book · football · giraffe · MP3 player · orange pen · uniform for Teddy

➜ Workbook 17 (p. 15)

10 Come to my party! (Prepositions)

a) Finish the invitation. Use these words:

at (2x) · in · on · to

b) Write an invitation to your party.

Early finisher ➜ p. 164 **Early finisher**: Rätsel

➜ SF 9: Writing – Check your spelling (p. 181)

1 Where's Justin? 1 27

It's 11 o'clock – time for the Plymstock School °Discovery Quiz. Sam, Lucy and Justin are in Team 3.

Sam: What's the first question?
Lucy: "Where are your geography lessons? Find the room and count the maps."
Justin: Here's the geography room – room HU3.
Lucy: Are there any maps?
Sam: Yes, there's a map of England, a map of China …
Lucy: Is there one "n" or two in "China"?
Justin: I can spell it. It's C - h - …

❖

Lucy: OK, second question: "Where can you work with computers? Count the computers there."
Justin: The computer room. Here it is!
Sam: Wow! There are lots of computers! Two, four, six, …, 11, 12!

❖

Lucy: Good. Third question: "Where can you read a book, watch a DVD and fall asleep?"
Justin: I can do that at home, in my room.
Sam: Is your room at Plymstock School, Justin?
Justin: Er … no …
Lucy: You're silly, Justin.
Justin: I'm not silly! The answer is the library. I know that.

Lucy: Yes, but the big question is: "When is this place open?"
Sam: When *is* the library open?
Lucy: I don't know. Let's go and look.

❖

Sam: OK, the library times are here. I can read them for you.
Lucy: OK … Hey, where's Justin?
Sam: I don't know. Er … What's the fourth question?
Lucy: "Where can students meet and eat? What colour are the chairs there?"
Sam: That's the canteen – it's near the gym. Hurry up!

❖

Lucy: OK, the chairs are red and yellow.
Sam: We're finished! Now, where is Justin?
Lucy: I don't know. Can we go back now?
Sam: No, we can't – not without Justin.
Lucy: Then we can't win. Sam, can we find him?
Sam: Yes, we can. Let's go!

2 Right or wrong?

Check with a partner.

1 In the geography room, Justin is with Lucy and Sam.
2 He isn't with them in the computer room.
3 He isn't with them at the library door.
4 Sam and Lucy can go back to the classroom without Justin.

1 Right. • 2 Wrong. He is with them. •
3 Right. • 4 Wrong. They can't go back without him.

3 The winners are … 1 28

a) Listen and correct the sentences.

1 Miss Bell is in the canteen.
No, she isn't. Team 5 are in the canteen.
2 Justin is in the library.
3 There is a map of Plymstock in the geography room.
4 Team 2 are the winners of the quiz.

b) Check your partner's answers.

2 No, he isn't. Justin is in the geography room. • 3 No, there isn't. There's a map of England. • 4 No, they aren't. Team 3 are the winners.

1 The Plymstock School Discovery Quiz

a) Look at the photo of the three students. Then watch the film. Say "Stop!" when you know the names of all three students.

b) Watch the film again. You see these places:

A the canteen
B classroom HU3
C classroom HU6
D a computer room
E the library

Put them in the right order.

The first place is C, classroom HU6.

The second place ...

2 the canteen • 3 the library • 4 classroom HU 3 • 5 a computer room

c) Check with a partner. Then watch the film again. Are you right?

d) Make two lists about the school like this:

☺ I like	☹ I don't like
the uniform	the computer room
...	...

e) Look at a partner's lists. What's the same? What's different?

2 EVERYDAY ENGLISH Classroom English

Für den Einsatz ohne DVD finden Sie die Audiodatei zu dieser Übung auf *www.cornelsen.de/access-bayern*

a) Finish the sentences from an English classroom.

1 Please ... your workbooks at page 15.
2 Can you ... with Paul, please?
3 ... I'm late.
4 What ... are we on?
5 Miss, can I open the ...?
6 I can't ... number 3.
7 Paul, ... you help Lisa, please?
8 Can I ... to the toilet, please?
9 ... for homework?
10 Can you ... "Scotland", please?

1 open • 2 work • 3 Sorry • 4 page • 5 window • 6 do • 7 can • 8 go • 9 What's • 10 spell

More help ➜ *p. 157* **More help:** Die passenden Wörter sind in einer Box vorgegeben.

b) Compare your sentences with a partner.

c) Watch the film and check your answers.

d) Make classroom ladders.

➜ *Classroom English (p. 271)*

1 At Plymstock School *(there is / there are)*

Make sentences and write them down.

There's a … / There are …	but there isn't a … / there aren't any …
uniforms for the students,	swimming pool.
Discovery Quiz for Year 7,	maps.
map of China in room HU3,	Discovery Quiz for Year 8.
18 computers in the computer room,	map of Mexico.
library at the school,	uniforms for the teachers.

Early finisher Make sentences about your pencil case, desk, …
There are three pencils in my pencil case, but there isn't a rubber.

Language help

There's + singular:
- There's a book on my desk.

There are + plural:
- There are two pens on my desk.

English: There aren't any …
German: Es gibt/sind keine …

English: Are there any …?
German: Gibt es …? / Sind …?

➜ *GF 6: There is … / There are … (p. 186)*

2 What's different? *(there is / there are*: questions and short answers)

a) What's different in pictures A and B? Take turns to find and say eight things.
In picture A there are books on the desks. In picture B there aren't any books on the desks.

A

B

b) Take turns to ask your partner about these things at your school:
swimming pool, library, computers, canteen, gym, English students, seals, monsters.
A Is there a swimming pool at our school? … ?/ Are there any …?
B Yes, there is. / Yes, there are. / No, there isn't. / No, there aren't.

➜ **Workbook** *18–20 (pp. 15–16)*

3 I can do it! *(can)*

a) Make correct sentences.
1 can – I – "cupboard." – spell
2 can't – I – French. – speak
3 you – it – in German? – Can – say
4 I – with – work – Lisa? – Can
5 I – What – can – do – now?

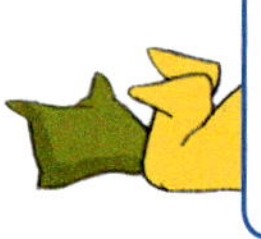

English and German are different
I **can see** *Morph.*
Ich **kann** *Morph* **sehen**.

L sollte an dieser Stelle darauf hinweisen, dass hinter *can* immer ein Vollverb stehen muss.

b) Ask a partner four questions with can. Answer with Yes, I can or No, I can't.
Can you swim like Silky? - Yes, I can./ No, I can't.

➜ *GF 7: can (p. 187)* ➜ **Workbook** *21 (p. 16)*

1 I can spell "cupboard". • 2 I can't speak French. • 3 Can you say it in German? • 4 Can I work with Lisa? • 5 What can I do now?

1 The alphabet song

a) Listen and sing along. 1 29–30

A [eɪ] B [biː] C [siː] D [diː] E [iː] F [ef] G [ʤiː] H [eɪtʃ] I [aɪ] J [ʤeɪ]

K [keɪ] L [el] M [em] N [en] O [əʊ] P [piː] Q [kjuː] R [aː]

S [es] T [tiː] U [juː] V [viː] W ['dʌbljuː] X [eks] Y [waɪ] Z [zed]

Track 1.30 ist die Instrumentalversion des Songs.

1 31 b) Here the alphabet is in sound groups. Say the letters. Listen and check.

AHJK BCD EGP TV FLM NSXZ IY QUW O R

1 32 c) Listen to Morph. Write the words he spells.

school · isn't · aren't · canteen · favourite

Now you know the ABC you can write these words for me.

➜ **Workbook** *22 (p. 17)*

2 You say ... the [ʃ], [tʃ] and [dʒ] sounds

1 33–34

a) Listen and repeat.

1 [ʃ]: she English
2 [tʃ]: chair catch
3 [dʒ]: Justin page

TIP
Look at the list of **English sounds** on page 272!

b) Now match the sounds and the words. Can you hear sound 1, 2 or 3?

British China gym subject watch show

1: British · show
2: China · watch
3: gym · subject

c) Match.

1 F · 2 C · 3 D · 4 E · 5 A · 6 B

1 ['tiːtʃə]	4 [dʒu'laɪ]	A lunch	D language
2 [ʃɔːt]	5 [lʌntʃ]	B German	E July
3 ['læŋgwɪdʒ]	6 ['dʒɜːmən]	C short	F teacher

d) Say and write more words with the sounds [ʃ], [tʃ] and [dʒ]. Check with your partner.

3 How to link words in sentences

1 35–36

Look!
1 consonant + vowel sound
2 vowel sound + vowel sound!
*Read about the **Bindebogen** on page 209 too!*

a) Listen and repeat.

1 **an**‿**e**lephant a bi**g**‿**e**lephant a grou**p**‿**o**f‿**e**lephants
2 tw**o**‿**e**lephants thre**e**‿**e**lephants twent**y**‿**e**lephants

b) Copy Morph's text into your exercise book. Link words with ‿ as in a). Then listen, practise and check with your partner.

I think there's an elephant in our school! But where is it? Let's look in my library!

➜ **Workbook** *23–24 (pp. 17–18)*

Chaos at the corner shop

1 37

Look at the pictures. Say who's in the story and who's new. Follow the numbers and read the story.

1 Right or wrong?

Correct the wrong sentences.

1 Maya is in the Broadway before Lucy.
2 Sam is Lily's big brother.
3 Sam is good at kung fu.
4 Maya is Sam's sister.
5 Maya isn't a good swimmer.
6 Sam is in the shop with his sister.

1 Lucy is in the Broadway before Maya. • 4 Lily is Sam's sister. • 5 Maya is the best swimmer in Plymstock. • 6 Sam is with Maya and Lucy.

2 Feelings

Choose a picture in the story. Match the smileys to the people in that picture and talk about them.

Picture 10/smiley 3: Lucy and Maya are angry.

3 Act it out

Grundschule

Every student gets a speech bubble from the story. Act out your speech bubbles in the right order.

KV 7: Chaos at the corner shop enthält die Sprechblasen für die S zum Ausschneiden und Ordnen.

4 The next picture

You choose Do a) or b).

a) Draw the next picture for the story.

b) What's next? Write speech bubbles for one or more of these people:

Sam – Maya – Lucy – the man from the shop +woman

Show your picture or speech bubbles to your classmates. Say which ideas you like.

Neigungsdifferenzierung: Die S haben die Wahl zwischen einer künstlerisch-gestalterischen Aufgabe und einem kreativen Schreibauftrag. Beide befassen sich inhaltlich mit der gleichen Thematik und können gemeinsam oder in PA ausgewertet werden.

→ Workbook 25–26 (pp. 18–19)

Workbook Checkpoint 1 (pp. 20–23)

1 Your task

Die unit-übergreifende Lernaufgabe führt die erworbenen Kenntnisse und Kompetenzen der Unit zusammen. Sie führt zu individuellen Ergebnissen der S, die stichprobenartig im Unterricht besprochen werden können. Die eigentliche Bearbeitung kann zu Hause stattfinden.

My profile

Tell one of the Plymouth kids about yourself.

STEP 1 Choose your Plymouth kid.

STEP 2 Write your profile: name, hometown, how old you are ... Look at Morph's ideas.

STEP 3 Add the names of your school, class/year, friends. Write your favourites (school subjects, day, colour, animal). Write what you don't like.

STEP 4 In front of your group, tell your Plymouth kid about yourself. Use your profile and speak in complete sentences.

Profile

Name:	Mr Morph
Hometown:	Plymouth, England
How old:	Erm
Birthday:	???
Brother/sisters:	Erm
Pets:	NO!
...	
I like ...	books!
I don't like ...	the school cat!

Der zweite Teil der Seite dient der Selbsteinschätzung durch die S, sollte aber bei diesem ersten Vorkommen zunächst im Unterricht besprochen werden. Das ist v.a. dann wichtig, wenn die S noch keine Erfahrung mit Selbsteinschätzung haben.

Wie gut warst du?

Wie schätzt du dich selbst ein? Schreibe die Sätze unter *Words*, *Grammar* und *Speaking* in dein Heft ab und ordne dir für jede Frage eine Ampelfarbe zu.

- (rot) Das lief nicht gut, ich muss mehr üben.
- (gelb) Das war OK, aber ich könnte besser werden.
- (grün) Das habe ich gut geschafft.

Words

Konntest du dich gut an Wörter und Phrasen für dein *profile* erinnern? Wusstest du, wie man sie ausspricht?

Grammar

Wie war es mit *be*? Konntest du Lang- und Kurzformen problemlos benutzen?

Speaking

Konntest du mithilfe deines *profiles* vor deiner Gruppe mehrere englische Sätze sagen?

Wie kannst du besser werden?

Dort, wo du dich rot oder gelb eingeschätzt hast, helfen dir folgende Tipps.

Words

Wörter der Unit: S. 210–216,

➔ *Wordbank 1 u. 2, S. 168*

➔ *SF 1 Learning vocabulary S. 174–175*

Bei der Aussprache hilft dir die phonetische Umschrift:

➔ *English sounds S. 268*; ➔ *Pronunciation course S. 35*

Grammar

➔ *GF 3 The verb (to) be S. 184*

➔ *LaL S. 24, Übungen S. 25*; ➔ *Workbook S. 9*

Speaking

Arbeite S. 25 Übung 3 nochmal durch.
Übe dein *profile* mit einem Partner und mehrere Male allein.

A

1 What is when?

Write full sentences.

1.	Ma
2.	Geo
3.	Reli
4.	Fr
5.	D & T
6.	Sci

The first lesson is maths.
The ...

2 geography · 3 religion · 4 French · 5 design & technology · 6 science

2 Pairs

a) Match the words.

1 exercise — A break
2 lunch — B book
3 school — C friend
4 best — D bag

2 A · 3 D · 4 C

b) Match the verbs and nouns.

1 throw — A a window
2 spell — B a game
3 play — C a ball
4 open — D your name

1 C · 2 D · 3 B · 4 A

c) Write four sentences: two with pairs from a) and two with pairs from b).

3 At home

Finish the dialogue.

Lucy: Hi, Maya! I'm at *home* now. Let's talk. Plymstock is cool! The **k**... in my **c**... are nice and our teachers are **f**... (kids · class · friendly)
What about you? Are you happy?

Maya: Yes! Coombe Dean is great too! There are 26 kids in my class, twelve boys and fourteen girls. Our **t**... is OK. There are two or three new **s**..., like ICT. (teacher · subjects · lessons)
There are five **l**... every day.

Lucy: Like Plymstock. Our first lesson on **M**... is design and **t**... That's new. (Monday · technology)
And **l**... are new too. There's **F**... and **G**... Our teacher is Miss Bell, and there's a game with a ball in her lesson on the first day. The game is like this: (languages · French · German)
T... the ball and **a**... a question. **C**... the ball and **a**... it. It's cool. There's a Discovery Quiz on the first day too. There are **b**... at eleven o'clock and at one-twenty. (Throw · ask · Catch · answer · breaks)

Maya: Is there a good **c**... for the **l**... break? (canteen · lunch)

Lucy: Yes, there is. The chairs are red and yellow. There's a big **l**... too with lots of books and DVDs and a great **g**... for PE. And what's for **h**...? (library · gym · homework)

Maya: That's the best thing. There's no homework on the first day!
Lucy, come to our **f**... and we can talk **a**... lots of school things. (flat · about)

4 My timetable

Talk to a partner about your timetable, your subjects and your favourite lessons.

Our timetable is OK. On Mondays/Tuesdays ... the first lesson is ...
My favourite subjects are ... and I like ... too. ... is on (days) at (times).

5 New friends (Personal pronouns, *be*: short forms and short answers)

a) Justin meets Jack. Put in *I'm, you're, he's* …

Justin: Hello, Jack! … at Coombe Dean now, right? This is Sam. … in my class at Plymstock.
Jack: Hi, Sam. Plymstock. … a good school.
Justin: Oh, look! Here's Lucy with Maya. … best friends. Hi, Lucy! Jack, this is Lucy. … at Plymstock too.
Maya: And … Maya. … at Coombe Dean. … at different schools now. … sad.

You're • he's • It's • They're • She's • I'm • I'm • We're • We're (I'm)

b) Write Justin's short answers.

1 Are you twelve, Justin? - Yes, …
2 Are you in Year 8? - No, …
3 Are Lucy and Maya twelve? - No, …
4 Are the two girls from Plymouth? - …
5 Is Sam from Plymouth? - …
6 Is Maya your friend too? - Yes, …
7 Is your timetable OK? - Yes, …
8 Are you and Sam good friends? - …

1 I am.
2 I'm not.
3 they aren't.
4 Yes, they are.
5 No, he isn't.
6 she is.
7 it is.
8 Yes, we are.

6 What's wrong? (The possessive forms)

Write the sentences with *'s* or *s'*.

1 Silky's • 2 students' • 3 Maya's • 4 Sens' • 5 friends' • 6 teacher's

1 Silkys home is Plymouth Sound.
2 The students class is 7EB.
3 Is Mukesh Mayas brother?
4 The Sens flat is near Plymstock School.
5 What are your friends names, Sam?
6 What's your teachers name?

7 At school

There's a new student from England in your class. Ask him/her questions. Here are his/her answers. Write your questions.

1 I come from London.
2 No, I can't speak German. Sorry.
3 German students at my school? Yes, there are.
4 My uniform is blue and grey.
5 My school is old. It isn't new.
6 My favourite subject is maths.

1 Where are you from? • 2 Can you speak German? • 3 Are there German students at your school? • 4 Which colour is your uniform? • 5 And your school, is it new or old? • 6 Can you help me with this question?

8 MIXED BAG Lucy's exercise book

Lucy and her mum are at home. Finish the dialogue.

Lucy: Mum, … my German exercise book? I … find it. It … in my school bag. … you help …? where • can't • isn't • Can … me
Mum: Mmm. Let's look in … room. Oh! Phh! It's warm in here. … the window, …, Lucy. Now, … colour is your exercise book? your • Open • please • what
Lucy: It's pink. And … a nice picture of … elephant on it. there's • an
Mum: … a minute. There … lots … books on the chair, and are there … books in your cupboard? Wait • are • of • any
Lucy: No, … …. Oh, no! … time is it? there aren't • What
Mum: It's … past eight. … up! … be late! half • Hurry • Don't
Lucy: But where's my German exercise book. I … go to school … it. can't • without
Mum: But Lucy, … Saturday! … is no school. It's time to meet Maya … the Broadway! it's • There • at

B

9 Meet Jenny

1 38

a) Listen to Jenny. Are the statements right or wrong? Correct the wrong sentences.

1 Jenny is twelve years old.
2 Her birthday is on the thirtieth of January. 13th
3 Jenny's mum is from Germany.
4 Jenny's sister is thirteen. 14
5 Rachel can speak German.
6 Jenny's brother's name is Jasper. Josh
7 Her brother is eight.
8 He can't swim. is a great swimmer
9 Jenny's rabbit is black and white. brown
10 Jenny and Rachel are at different schools.
11 Jenny's uniform is dark blue and grey. black
12 Tuesday is Jenny's favourite day.

b) Listen again and look. Which is Jenny's timetable, A or B?

A

	Monday	Tuesday	Wednesday	Thursday	Friday
1.	Maths	ICT	D&T	English	English
2.	French	Maths	Maths	History	English
3.	Science	Art	Geography	D&T	ICT
4.	English	Science	History	Science	PE
5.	German	Religion	Music	German	PE

B

	Monday	Tuesday	Wednesday	Thursday	Friday
1.	Maths	ICT	German	English	English
2.	French	Maths	Maths	History	English
3.	Science	Art	Geography	Religion	Science
4.	English	Science	History	PE	ICT
5.	German	D&T	Music	PE	D&T

Jenny has PE on Thursdays.

C

10 About you

1 Write to Jenny. Tell her about you and your school, year, class, teachers. Write 70-80 words.

Ideas: classrooms, students, canteen, library, computer room, music room …

Hello, Jenny!
My name is... and I'm at ... school in .... in Germany.
I'm in Year ... My school is old, but it's ...
There's a ... , but there aren't any ...
...
Bye!

2 Write to a Plymouth kid. Tell him or her about your school day, your subjects and your timetable. Write 70-80 words.

Ideas: number of lessons every day, subjects, time of first lesson and sixth lesson, breaks, time to go home, your favourite day and favourite subjects …

Hello, Maya/Justin ...!
Let me tell you about my school day. There are ... lessons ... Our subjects are ...
I like ... but I don't like ...
...
Bye!

GB and the UK

1 Morph's map

1 39

Read and listen to Morph. What are the countries on his map? Look at the map at the front of your book for help.

GB? What's that? And the UK? What's that? Let's see. Ah! It says here: GB is short for Great Britain. That's England, Scotland and Wales. And the UK is short for the United Kingdom. That's England, Scotland, Wales and Northern Ireland too! OK? So here we go!

1 England · 2 Scotland · 3 Wales · 4 Northern Ireland

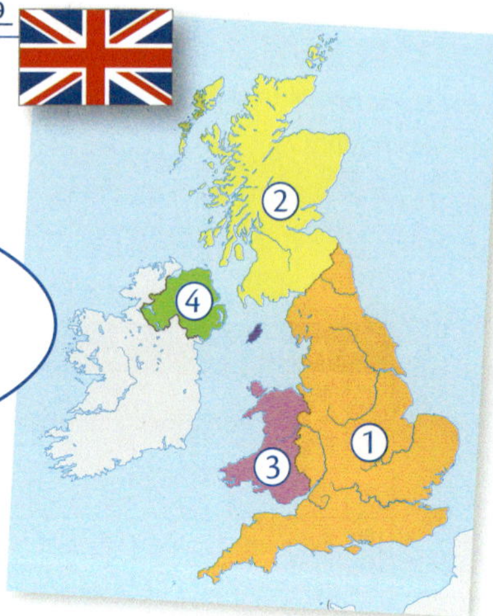

2 Where are they from?

1 40

a) Listen and read along. Match the photos (A-D) on page 43 to the students. 1 C · 2 D · 3 B · 4 A

1

Hi! My name is Masood. I'm from England. There are 54 million people in my country. I'm from London. It's my hometown. It's the capital too. There are people from lots of different countries here, and on the streets of London there are 300 different languages! Which is my photo? A,B,C or D?

3

My name is Shauna. I'm from Northern Ireland in the UK. Belfast is our capital and my hometown. It's a big port, so you can see big ships here. You can see the famous Titanic Museum here too. Which is my photo?

2

Good morning! I'm Angus from Scotland. There are five million people in Scotland. Edinburgh is the capital, but it isn't my hometown. I'm from a little place near Loch Ness. In summer there are lots of people here. There are boat tours on the loch. Can you see Nessie, our monster?

4

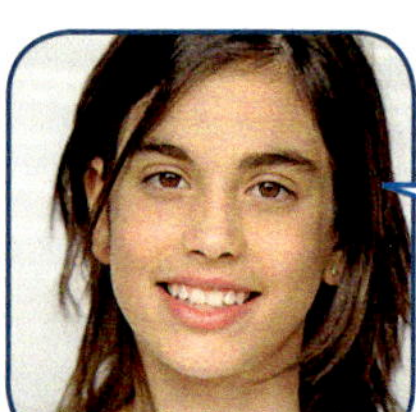

Croeso I Gymru! Welcome to Wales! I'm from Cardiff, that's the capital. My name is Megan. Wales isn't a big country, but it's great. There are three million people in Wales. There are lots of old castles – and lots of history. You can see Cardiff Castle in my photo. People in Wales speak Welsh and English. Welsh is a school subject. Which is my photo? A, B, C or D?

b) Look at pictures A-D. What can you see? Say a sentence or more for each picture.

ATC.1

Wales/Cardiff

A

Northern Ireland/Belfast

B

England/London

C

Scotland/Loch Ness

D

3 The UK

Finish the sentences.

1 The capital of Wales is …
2 There are 54 million people in …
3 Belfast is the capital of …
4 People in … speak Welsh too.
5 There are five million people in …
6 Is there a monster in …?
7 There are three million people in …
8 There are 300 different languages in …

1 Cardiff
2 England
3 Northern Ireland
4 Wales
5 Scotland
6 Loch Ness
7 Wales
8 London

4 Partner quiz

Without your book, ask a partner three questions about countries and places in the UK. Take turns.

What's ... Where's ...?
Is there/Are there...?

5 EXTRA The UK in your classroom

Make a poster with pictures and text about England, Scotland, Wales or N. Ireland.
Write three sentences about the country. You can put the best posters up in your classroom.

6 Your country

Ask a partner four questions about his/her country.

What's ...? Is there/Are there...? How big is ...?

→ **Workbook** *p. I*

Leistungsmessung Unit 2 · KV 8

Homes and families

I live in Beach Road in Wembury, near Plymouth. This is my house.

Box "Straßennamen mit und ohne Hausnummern", Voc, S. 217

Abby Blackwell is in Year 7 at Plymstock School.

1 WORDS Our house

a) Look at the house on page 45. Which rooms are upstairs? Which rooms are downstairs?

b) Find these things in the house on p. 45.

armchair · bed · book · chair · clock · cupboard · desk · door · football · lamp · photo · picture · poster · shelf · sofa · table · toilet · toy · TV · window

+(to) watch TV

Alternative Erarbeitung mit **KV 8: Things you can find in a house.**

2 01 c) Listen and say the numbers from the picture on page 45.

Grund-schule

There's a big table in the dining room.

That's number 12.

d) Ask and answer like this:

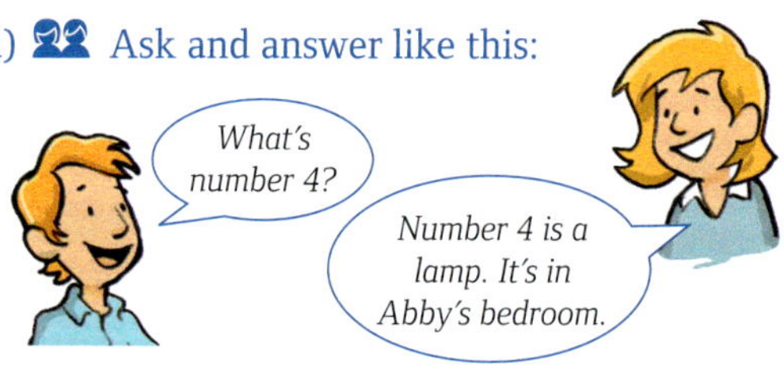

2 02 e) Now listen to Abby and point to the things in the house.

2 My bedroom

a) Take turns and tell your partner three things about your bedroom.

My bedroom is small, but nice. I have …
From my window, I can see … What about you?

b) Draw a picture or plan of your bedroom. Label the things in it.

Alternative: Die S werden gebeten, Fotos mitzubringen.

Get more words if you need them.

→ *Wordbank 3 (p. 169)*

Show your picture or plan to your partner. Then you can put it into your My Book.

Your task

Am Ende dieser Unit wirst du …

… einem Schüler oder einer Schülerin aus Großbritannien dein Haus oder deine Wohnung vorstellen.

→ **Workbook** *1–2 (p. 24)*

My room is small,
My things aren't new,
My bed is old,
My cupboard too.
My shelves are green,
My lamp is blue.
I ♥ my room,
What about you?

1 poster · 2 shelf · 3 book · 4 lamp · 5 desk · 6 toy · 7 toilet · 8 bed · 9 photos · 10 armchair · 11 window · 12 table · 13 chair · 14 clock · 15 TV · 16 pictures · 17 door · 18 sofa · 19 football

1 My day at home 2 03

Read what Silky and her friends do every day.

Alternative: Die Bilder und Bildunterschriften befinden sich ungeordnet auch auf **KV 9**. Die S schneiden sie aus, ordnen sie einander zu und bringen sie in die richtige Reihenfolge.

I wake up at 6 o'clock every morning.

My friends wake up too.

Then I have breakfast – a big plate of crabs.

After breakfast, my friends and I swim and swim and swim …

We play football in a pool in the afternoon.

In the evening, we catch fish for dinner.

I sit on my rock after dinner.

I text my friends or read a book. And then I fall asleep.

Box "in the morning", Voc, S. 218

Box "(to) have breakfast", Voc, S. 218

2 Now you

Talk about your day.

have breakfast · go to school · go home · meet… · play…

3 Write about your day

Write at least five sentences about your day. Use the words and phrases from exercise 2.

4 At the Blackwells' house

2 04

Abby has a new friend, Maya. She knows her from Wembury Sailing Club. Maya is at Abby's house.

Abby: Let's go into the kitchen. I can make a cup of tea for you.
Maya: A cup of tea? Yes, please.
Abby: Oh no, it's Saturday. Dad is in the kitchen. He always reads the paper there at the weekend. Let's go into the living room.

❖

Maya: Who's that?
Abby: Mink, our cat.
Maya: She likes the sofa!
Abby: It's her favourite place. She plays at night. And then she sleeps on the sofa in the morning.
Maya: Wow, you have lots of games!
Abby: Yes, Dad likes games. We play at weekends.
Maya: That's nice. We watch TV.
Skip: Woof, woof!
Maya: There's a dog at the door.
Abby: That's Skip. I feed him in the morning. Then he plays in the garden.
Maya: Can he come in?
Abby: No … please! No dogs in the living room, Mum says. Skip! Go to the kitchen door.
Skip: Woof, woof!
Abby: OK, we can go upstairs.
Maya: Can Skip come with us?

Abby: Of course … he sleeps in my room. His basket is on the floor near my bed.
Maya: Hey, you have a nice bedroom.
Abby: Thanks.
Maya: And you have lots of sailing trophies!
Tim: Yes, look at Abby's trophies! She's the star of Wembury Sailing Club.
Abby: Tim! This is my room. You can't come in here. Go away. Now!
Tim: Help! A mad sister …
Skip: Woof, woof!
Tim: … and a mad dog!
Abby: Oh, Tim thinks he's so cool. Maya, let's go for a walk with Skip.

5 Abby's home

a) What can you say about Abby and her family? Make three sentences.
Are they right or wrong?
Check with a partner.

b) What can you say about the Blackwells' pets? Make three more sentences.
Are they right or wrong?
Check with a partner.

→ Workbook 3–5 (pp. 25–26)

6 Have a go

Make sentences.

who	what	where
My father	eats	in the bedroom.
My mother	sleeps	in the kitchen.
My brother	…	…
My sister		
My cat/dog		

Looking at language

a) Copy and finish the table.
The text on page 47 can help you (lines 10–25).

Singular	Plural
I play football in the afternoon.	We … at weekends.
You play basketball.	You play in the park.
He … in the garden.	They play at home.
She … at night.	
It plays DVDs.	

b) Look at the 3rd person singular (he/she/it). What's different?

➜ *GF 9: The simple present (p. 187)*

1 I wake up in the morning (Simple present: positive statements)

2 05–09

a) Who sings this song? Silky

I wake up in the morning,
Then I eat my crabs,
Then I eat my crabs,
I wake up in the morning,
Then I eat my crabs.

b) Finish the songs for the other singers.
Use these lines:

Then I text my friends, Maya
Then I read a book, Morph
Then I feed the dog, Abby

c) Listen and sing along.

Grund-schule

d) **EXTRA** Write your morning song and sing it.

Als Hintergrund für die Songs der S steht eine Instrumentalversion zur Verfügung (Track 2.09).

2 We have a big breakfast (Simple present: positive statements)

a) Abby talks about the weekend. Make five or more sentences for her.

I Skip and I We My mum and dad They	have a big breakfast play games read books go for a walk …	in the living room/garden/… on the sofa/the Hoe. with my friends/… …

We have a big breakfast in the dining room.

b) Now write five sentences about your weekend.

Early finisher ➜ p. 164

3 The seal and the crab (The "s" sound: [s], [z] or [ɪz])

2 10

a) Read and listen to the poem.

b) Copy the table. Then listen to Morph. Put all the verbs in the right place.

[s]	[z]	[ɪz]
wakes ... thinks, waits, counts, puts, makes	comes ... has, finds, swims, says, runs	watches ... catches

c) Read the poem out loud to your partner.

A seal comes home at half past eight,
And watches a crab on a rock.
The crab wakes up and thinks, "I'm late!
Oh, no! It's nine o'clock!"

The crab has breakfast and finds his pen,
And swims away to school,
The seal waits a minute, she counts to ten,
Then catches the crab in a pool.

The seal puts the crab on her breakfast plate.
Then she makes a cup of tea.
The crab says, "Thanks, but I can't wait",
And runs into the sea.

4 Before school, after school (Simple present: positive statements)

a) Say what the kids do before school.

feed · have · read · text

1 Abby … her dog Skip before school.
2 Maya … Lucy before school.
3 Sam … a big breakfast before school.
4 Lucy … her emails before school.

1 feeds · 2 texts · 3 has · 4 reads

b) Say what the kids do after school.

1 Abby goes for a walk with Skip after school.
2 Maya … her mum in the kitchen after school.
3 Sam … TV after school.
4 Lucy … a cup of tea after school.

2 helps
3 watches
4 has

More help → p. 157

c) Say what you do before and after school.

More help: Die gesuchten Verben sind im Infinitv vorgegeben.

5 Saturdays

a) Tell a partner what you and your family do on Saturdays. Take turns. Say five or more sentences each. The ideas in the box can help you.

b) Tell the class about your partner's Saturdays.

feed the dog/cat/… · go shopping · make breakfast/lunch/… · play football · sleep · watch TV

→ Workbook 6–9 (pp. 26–27)

6 Where and when (Word order)

Write correct sentences.

1 like - their school - the Plymstock students
2 go - at 8.30 - to school - they
3 have - in the canteen - lunch - they – at 1.20.
4 Lucy and Maya - on Saturdays - to the Broadway - go
5 computer games - after school - in his room - plays - Justin

Language help

The word order in English statements is:
S(ubject) – V(erb) – O(bject)
We play football.
Phrases of time usually come after S-V-O, sometimes before:
(In the afternoon), we play football in the afternoon.
Place comes before time:
We play football in the park in the afternoon.

→ Workbook 10 (p. 28) 1 The Plymstock students like their school. · 2 They go to school at 8.30. · 3 They have lunch in the canteen at 1.20. · 4 Lucy and Maya go to the Broadway on Saturdays. · 5 Justin plays computer games in his room after school.

7 STUDY SKILLS Learning words with mind maps

a) How can you learn new words? One way is to make groups and find the umbrella word. Find the umbrella word in these lists:

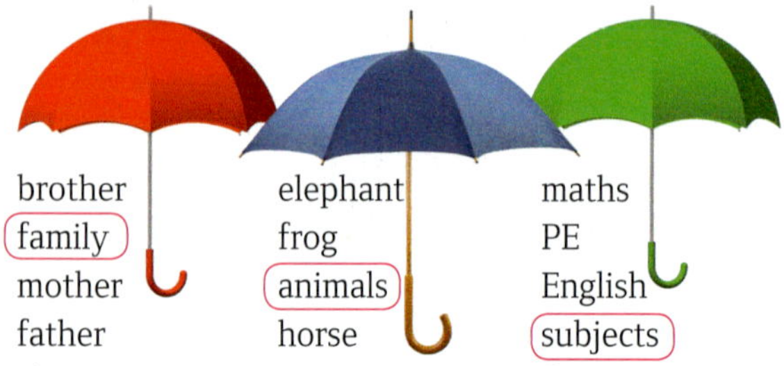

brother	elephant	maths
family	frog	PE
mother	animals	English
father	horse	subjects
sister	rat	German

b) Find umbrella words for these word groups:

1 boy · girl · man · woman
2 blue · orange · purple · red
3 April · June · August · October
4 kitchen · bedroom · dining room · bathroom
5 classmate · timetable · lessons · teacher

1 people
2 colours
3 months
4 house
5 school

More help → p. 157

More help: Die *umbrella words* sind in einer Box vorgegeben.

Check with a partner.

c) A mind map can help you to make groups of words.
What umbrella words can you see in this mind map? What are the missing umbrella words?

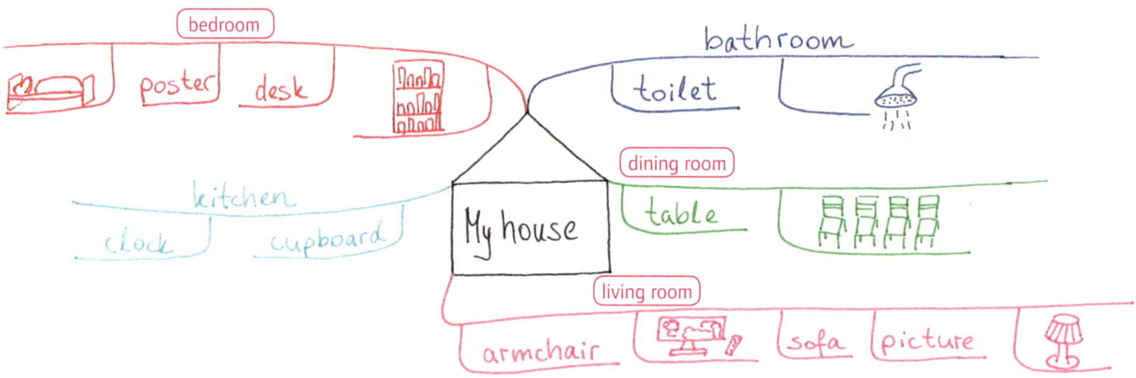

Study skills

Mind maps

1 Du kannst Wortschatz oder Ideen in einer Mindmap ordnen. Schreibe das Thema (**topic**) in die Mitte.
2 Schreibe deine Oberbegriffe (**umbrella words**) auf die Hauptäste deiner Mindmap. Verwende verschiedene Farben, Symbole und Zeichnungen. So kannst du dir die Wörter bessser merken.
3 Ergänze weitere Begriffe, Symbole und Zeichnungen auf Nebenästen.

→ *SF 2: Collecting information (pp. 175–176)*

d) Make a mind map for your house or flat. The study skills box can help you. Use words from pages 44–45.

→ *Wordbank 3 (p. 169)*
→ *SF 1: Learning vocabulary (pp. 174–175)*
→ **Workbook** *11–12 (p. 28)*

1 You say … the *th*-sounds ([θ] and [ð])

a) [θ] is the sound in "three", "thing" and "birthday". [ð] is the sound in "this", "with" and "brother". Practise the sounds and words with your partner.

c) Now practise these phrases:
- my three brothers
- their thirteenth birthday
- the fourth thing
- the twelfth month
- Thelma and Arthur Smith

2 12 Listen and check.

b) Listen. Can you hear [θ] or [ð]? Check with your partner. 2 11

d) Now say Morph's tongue-twister: 2 13

On Thursday the twelfth, it's Thelma and Arthur Smith's thirteenth birthday.

➜ **Workbook** *13 (p. 29)*

2 You say … the [uː] sound

a) [ː] means that a vowel sound is long: here the [uː]-sound. You hear the [uː]-sound in the word "sch<u>**oo**</u>l". Say the words for the pictures and find the words with an [uː]-sound.
2 14 Then listen and check.

b) Say the words. How many words with an [uː]-sound are there: 8, 9 or 10?

cool · do · door · double · floor · glue · go · group · Hoe · look · Lucy · no · out · room · rubber · ruler · so · to · too · touch · who

2 15 Listen and check.

c) Practise with a partner:
- Who has my ruler, my glue and my books?
- Lucy is in our group too, in Room 202.
- Two students are new. And who are you?

3 Word stress

a) Word stress is important for meaning. Dictionaries show you correct word stress, for example ['bedruːm], [fə'get]. Word stress is often different in German and English.
Say these words. Where is the stress?

April · August · elephant · geography · July · minute · music · profile · religion · student · toilet

2 16 b) Listen and check. Then write the words in a) again and show the stress like this: 'April, Ju'ly.
'April · 'August · 'elephant · ge'ography · Ju'ly · 'minute · 'music · 'profile · re'ligion · 'student · 'toilet

+aunt ['æmə, 'ʌmə]

1 Uncle Amar comes to dinner

2 17

It's Saturday evening. Uncle Amar is at Maya's flat.

Uncle: So Mukesh, you go to a sports school!
Mukesh: Yes, Uncle, Plymstock is a sports school near here.
Uncle: And what's your favourite sport? Cricket?
Mukesh: No, I don't like cricket, Uncle, I …
Uncle: What? You're an Indian boy, and you don't like cricket!
Mukesh: I'm not an Indian boy. I'm British.
Mr Sen: Mukesh has lots of homework. He doesn't have time for sport, Amar.
Maya: No, Uncle, he only has time for computer games.
Mrs Sen: Maya! Ssshhh!
Uncle: So, Mukesh goes to a sports school, but he doesn't do sport!
Mr Sen: Maya does lots of sport, Amar.
Maya: Yes, I often go sailing, and I like …
Uncle: So Plymstock is the right school for you!
Mukesh: She doesn't go to Plymstock, Uncle.
Maya: No, I go to Coombe Dean. It's a maths and ICT school.
Uncle: Maya is our next Albert Einstein.
Mukesh: Ha, ha, ha …
Mrs Sen: Mukesh! Ssshhh!
Maya: Uncle, can I ask you a question?
Uncle: A question?
Maya: Yes, my English homework is: "Write about your family". But I don't know about our family. So, can you …?

Uncle: Ah, Maya, I can tell you all about the Sens. We're a big family, you know.
Mr Sen: And we don't all live in India and Britain. Your Uncle Dasan … ['dæsæn, 'dʌsən]
Uncle: Yes, your Uncle Dasan and Aunt Priya ['pri:ja: 'pri:jə] live in South Africa. And your cousins Dilip and Sanjay …
Mukesh: … live in South Africa too.
Uncle: No, they don't live in South Africa now. Dilip lives in New York and Sanjay lives …

2 Who is it?

Find the answers in 1 and finish the sentences.

1 … comes to dinner.
2 … goes to a sports school.
3 … doesn't like cricket.
4 … goes to a maths and ICT school.
5 … knows all about the Sens.
6 … is Maya's uncle in South Africa.

1 Uncle Amar • 2 Mukesh • 3 Mukesh • 4 Maya • 5 Uncle Amar • 6 Dasan

3 Have a go

a) Mukesh says "I don't like cricket". Think of five things you don't like. Write them down.
- I don't like computer games.
- I don't like …

b) Tell your partner what you don't like.

c) Tell the class one thing about your partner.
- Alex doesn't like computer games.

Looking at language

a) Copy and finish the table.
The text on page 52 can help you.

Singular	Plural
I don't like cricket.	We … all live in India.
You … like cricket.	You don't like maths.
He … do sport.	They … live in South Africa.
She … go to Plymstock.	
It doesn't play DVDs.	

➜ *GF 9: The simple present (p. 187)*

b) How do you make negative sentences?
When do you use don't?
When do you use doesn't?

1 Abby doesn't go to Coombe Dean (Simple present: negative statements)

a) Uncle Amar is at Maya's flat. Finish the dialogue. Use negative verbs: *have, know, like, live*.

Uncle: Is your friend Abby in your class?
Maya: No, Uncle, Abby doesn't go to Coombe Dean.
Uncle: What about Abby's flat? Is it near here?
Maya: Abby … in a flat. The Blackwells have a big house – in Wembury. They … in Plymouth.
Uncle: Tell me about the Blackwells.
Maya: I … Abby's family, Uncle.
Uncle: But she has brothers and sisters?
Maya: She … a sister, but she has a brother, Tim. But he isn't so nice.
Uncle: You … her brother!
Maya: I like Abby, Uncle. She's my friend. I … Tim and he … me.
Uncle: OK, Maya, what about your friend Lucy?

doesn't live · don't live · don't know · doesn't have · don't like · don't know · doesn't know

18 b) Listen and check.

c) Practise the dialogue with a partner.

2 At Grandma's farm (Simple present: positive and negative statements) Box "grand-", Voc, S. 219

Sam asks Lucy about her Grandma's farm. Finish the dialogue. Use positive and negative verbs.

feed (3x) · go (2x) · have (2x) · make · sleep · wake up (2x)

Sam: Tell me about a weekend at the farm.
Lucy: Well, we wake up at 6 o'clock. Then we … the dogs and the rabbits.
Sam: You and your sister Holly?
Lucy: No, Holly … at 6 o'clock, so she … the animals. On the farm we … horses and pigs and cows.
Sam: What about elephants?
Lucy: No, Sam. Don't be silly. We … elephants. The farm is in England, not in India.
Sam: OK, so you … the animals – and then?
Lucy: Then Grandma … breakfast. And after breakfast we … for a walk.
Sam: And Holly too?
Lucy: No, Holly … with us. She … till twelve o'clock.

feed · doesn't get up · doesn't feed · have · don't have · feed · makes · go · doesn't come · sleeps

More help ➜ p. 157

More help: Negative Verben sind rot, positive Verben sind grün gedruckt.

3 A weekend in the library (Simple present: positive and negative sentences)

2 19

a) Listen to Morph and correct the sentences.

1 Morph lives in a house.

He doesn't live in a house. He lives in a library.

2 Morph sits on chairs.

3 Morph has a bed.

4 The Plymstock students see Morph every day.

5 Morph sleeps at night.

6 The Plymstock students go to school at weekends.

7 Morph reads French books at weekends.

Correct:
2 sits on books · 3 has lots of books · 4 see the teachers · 5 sleeps in the day · 6 Monday to Friday · 7 reads English books

b) Compare and check your sentences.

4 The weekend

a) Talk about the Plymouth kids.

		1 Abby	2 Justin	3 Lucy	4 Maya	5 Sam
do homework	A	✓	✗	✗	✓	✓
go sailing	B	✓	✗	✗	✓	✓
play basketball	C	✗	✗	✗	✗	✓
read books	D	✗	✓	✓	✓	✗
watch TV	E	✗	✓	✓	✓	✓
wear a uniform	F	✗	✗	✗	✗	✗
write emails	G	✗	✓	✓	✓	✗

b) Talk about your weekends.

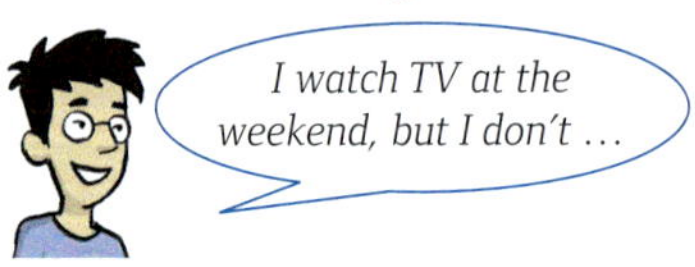

5 They've got a house in Wembury (have got)

Box "German "haben"", Voc, S. 219

Rewrite the text about the Blackwells.
Use have/has got or haven't/hasn't got.

The Blackwells have a house near the sea. They like sailing, but they don't have a boat. Abby has lots of sailing trophies. Tim doesn't have any trophies in his room, but he has lots of great computer games. The Blackwells have two pets. They don't have a guinea pig or a rabbit. They have a cat and a mad dog.

have got · haven't got · has got · hasn't got · has got · have got · haven't got · have got

→ **Workbook** *14–18 (pp. 29–30)*

Language help

For German 'haben, besitzen' you can also use **have got**:
*They **have** a house.* Or: *They **have got** a house.*
*Abby **has** a dog.* Or: *Abby **has got** a dog.*

Short forms:
I've got, you've got, he's/she's/it's got, we've got, they've got
I haven't got, you haven't got, he/she/it hasn't got, we haven't got, they haven't got

*She**'s got** two brothers. She **hasn't got** a sister.*
*We**'ve got** a house, but we **haven't got** a boat.*

→ *GF 11: have got „haben" (p. 190)*

6 WORDS Family

Alternative: Die S festigen mit **KV 10** die *family words* in einer kommunikativen Übung.

The Tizzards ['tɪzəd] — **LUCY PASCOE'S FAMILY TREE** — The Pascoes

a) Look at Lucy's family tree.

Partner A: Point to a person and say the name.
Partner B: Say "That's Lucy's …".

grandfather · grandmother · father · mother · uncle · aunt · brother · sister · cousin

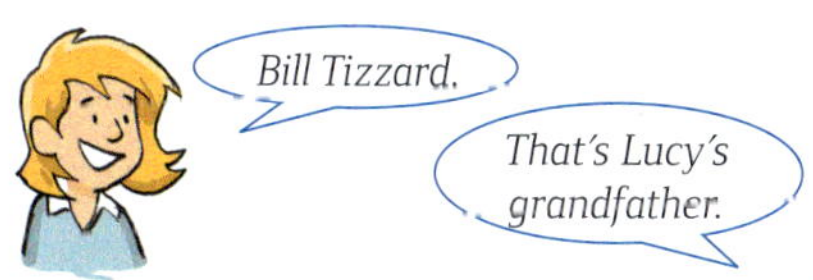

➜ *GF 4: The possessive form (I) (p. 185)*

b) Match the words to the symbols.

dead · divorced · married · single · twins

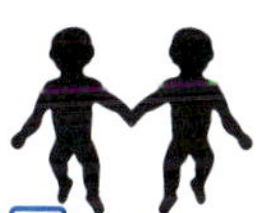
twins
1

single
2

married
3

divorced
4

dead
5

7 Lucy's family

2 20

Lucy talks to Sam about her family tree. Listen and finish the sentences.

1 Lucy's mum and dad are …
2 Grandma Pascoe is …
3 Uncle Jim is …
4 Melissa is Lucy's and Holly's …
5 Uncle Steve is … to Aunt Lynn.
6 Lewis and Lloyd are …

1 divorced
2 dead
3 single
4 cousin
5 married
6 twins

➜ **Workbook** *19–21 (pp. 30–31)*

8 Your family

Make your family tree. Draw people or use photos.

➜ *Wordbank 4 (p. 169)*

EXTRA Tell other students about your family.

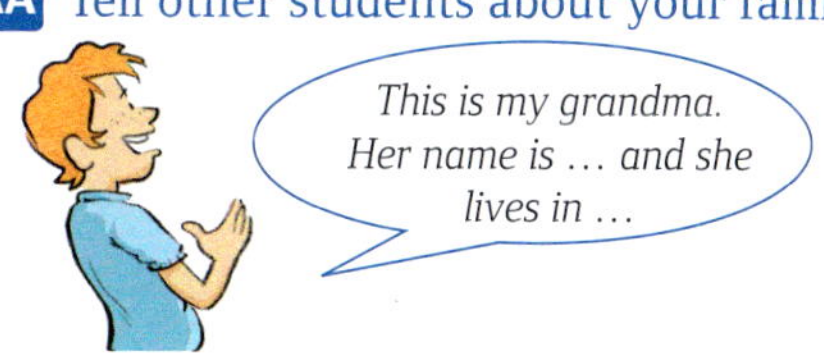

You can put your family tree into your MY BOOK.

1 Sunday lunch

2 21

It's 12:45 on Sunday. The Bennett family is at home. Sam is in the kitchen with Mr Bennett.

Sam: What's for lunch, Dad?
Mr B: Your favourite.
Sam: My favourite? Roast beef with roast potatoes? Yummy!
Mr B: And we start with your mother's yummy vegetable soup.
Sam: Oh, no soup for me, thanks. I don't like vegetable soup.
Mr B: No soup, no roast beef.
Sam: Oh, Dad! Well, what's for dessert?
Mr B: Fruit salad.
Sam: And ice cream, right?
Mr B: No, wrong. No ice cream.
Sam: Oh, Dad!
Mr B: But we can make scones after lunch. And then we can have cream tea at 4 o'clock.
Sam: Cream tea? Great!

Mrs Bennett is in the dining room with Lily.

Ms B: OK, you two. It's time for your lunch. What would you like, Lily?
Lily: Soup, soup, soup! I'd like soup.
Sam: Er, Dad, the soup is …
Mr B: Well, little girl, we have your mum's yummy vegetable soup here.

Sam: Er, Mum, the soup …
Mr B: Sam, put the soup on the table please!
Sam: But Dad, …
Mrs B: Hurry up, Sam. It's time for nice, hot soup.
Sam: But that's it, Mum. The soup – it isn't hot. It's cold!

+What would you like to eat?

2 What's for lunch?

a) Finish the sentences.

1 Sam's favourite is for lunch. It's … with …
2 Sam doesn't like …
3 There's … for dessert, but Sam would like …
4 Mr B says mum's vegetable soup is …
5 Sam says the soup is …

b) What would you like for lunch at the Bennetts' house?

I'd like …

a) 1 roast beef · roast potatoes · 2 vegetable soup · 3 fruit salad · 4 yummy · 5 cold

Background file

Cream tea

People in Britain drink lots of tea. It's always time for a "nice cup of tea". And in the afternoon, at 4 or 5 o'clock, people often have their tea with sandwiches, cake or scones.

+drink (n)

+marmalade

1 WORDS Food and drink

a) What is it? Match the words to the pictures.

biscuits · bread · cheese · cornflakes · fruit · meat · milk · pizza · potatoes · salad · sandwich · soup · spaghetti · vegetables · water · yoghurt

b) Put the words from a) in groups.

breakfast	lunch	dinner
· cornflakes!	·	·
·	·	

➔ Wordbank 5 (pp. 170–171)

c) Talk about your breakfast, lunch and dinner.

Let's have breakfast. What would you like?

I'd like bread and …

1 sandwich · 2 cornflakes · 3 milk · 4 yoghurt · 5 water · 6 cheese · 7 fruit · 8 bread · 9 potatoes · 10 meat · 11 spaghetti · 12 pizza · 13 vegetables · 14 soup · 15 biscuits · 16 salad

More words: ➔ *Wordbank 5 (pp. 170–171)*

➔ **Workbook** *22 (p. 31)*

2 THINKING ABOUT LANGUAGE Food and drink in other languages

a) Some "food and drink" words look or sound similar in many languages, for example salad. Make word stars on the board. Write the English word in the centre. Then add your word, your language and your name, like this:

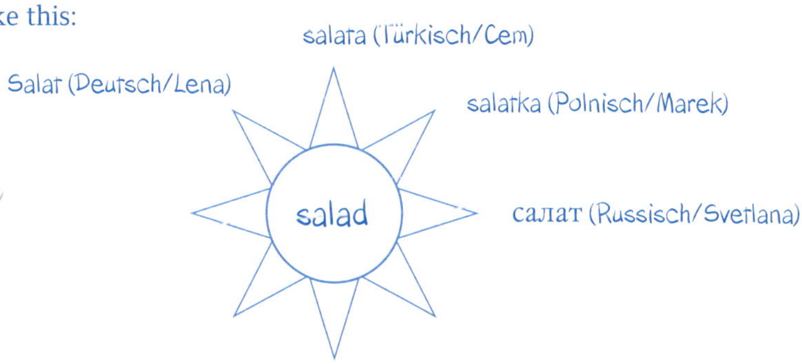

b) Make a table for your words from a). Then write stars on the board for milk, water, soup, yoghurt and put them in the table too.

English	German	Other languages
salad	Salat	salata, …
milk	Milch	…

More words: ➔ *Wordbank 5 (pp. 170–171)*

3 What is there to eat?

Du bist mit deiner Familie und einer/einem englischen Freund/in in einem Restaurant. Sage ihr/ihm auf Englisch, was es zu essen gibt. Sie/Er ist hungrig, mag keinen Fisch, aber Nachtisch sehr gerne. Übersetze nicht und verwende nur Wörter, die du kennst.

You can have soup. There's vegetable soup or … Or there are sandwiches with … Then there's roast beef with … For dessert there's … And what would you like to drink? There's …

Restaurant am Domplatz

Mittagskarte: täglich von 11 bis 15 Uhr

Suppen	Für den kleinen Hunger	Hauptgerichte	Nachspeisen	Getränke
Tomatensuppe	*Belegte Brote (m. Käse, Schinken, Tomate, Ei)*	*Forelle m. Reis u. Salat*	*Gemischtes Eis*	*Kaffee*
Gemüsesuppe	*Weißwurst m. Brezen*	*Rinderbraten m. Kartoffeln u. Gemüse*	*Frischer Obstsalat*	*Tee*
Flädlesuppe	*Kleiner gemischter Salat*	*Pizza (Salami od. Schinken)*	*Apfelstrudel m. Sahne*	*Apfelsaft*
		Großer gemischter Salat	*Schokokuchen*	*Mineralwasser*
			Käsekuchen	*Cola*
				Spezi

➔ **Workbook** *23 (p. 32)*

4 I feed my bird *(my, your, his, …)*

a) Copy the rhyme. Put in the words from the box.

her · his · my · our · their · your · your

I feed my *bird*
You feed … cat
He feeds … snake
She feeds … rat

We feed … frog
You feed … horse
They feed … dog
With meat, of course.

your · his · her · our · your · their

b) Learn the rhyme. Say it to your partner.

c) Tell the class about pets in your family or a friend's pet.
Then write four sentences.
We have two cats. Their names … My friend/aunt has a dog. His …

5 My class *(my, your, his, …)*

a) Sam talks to his dad about his class and his friends. Finish the sentences with my, your, …

1 Sam: "I really like my new class."
2 Dad: "And what about … new teachers?"
3 Sam: "We like … class teacher. … name is Miss Bell. She's nice."
4 Dad: "And who are … friends?"
5 Sam: "… friends? … names are Justin and Lucy."
6 Sam: "Justin lives with … mum. Lucy lives with … mum too."
7 Lucy's grandma and grandpa have a farm. They have lots of animals on … farm – but no elephants."

2 your · 3 our … Her · 4 your · 5 My … Their · 6 his … her · 7 their

More help ➔ *p. 158*

More help: Es sind je zwei Optionen pro Lücke vorgegeben.

b) Talk to a partner about your friends.
My friend … has a brother/sister. His/Her name is … Their house/flat is in our street …

➔ **Workbook** *24–25 (pp. 32–33)*

1 My house, your house

a) Look at the picture. What time of day is it?
Does Lucy live in a house or a flat?
morning or afternoon • a small house

b) Watch the film.
Partner A: Find the photos of Ruby's home. 1, 5, 6
Partner B: Find the photos of Jack's home. 2, 3, 4

Then answer the questions for your photos.
1 What rooms can you see?
2 Is their home a house or a flat?

Jack's flat: bathroom, kitchen, Jack's room
Ruby's house: Ruby's room, kitchen, living room

c) Tell your partner about the photos.

2 EVERYDAY ENGLISH Time for lunch

Für den Einsatz ohne DVD finden sie eine Audiodatei für diese Übung auf *www.cornelsen.de/access-bayern*

a) Watch the film. Match the names to the people (1–5): Katy, Luke, Oliver, Mrs White and Mr White. 1 Mrs White • 2 Luke • 3 Mr White • 4 Katy • 5 Oliver

b) Correct the sentences.
1 Katy likes fish.
2 There's only milk to drink.
3 There's only fruit salad for dessert.

1 lots of potatoes • 2 milk and water • 3 fruit salad and ice cream

c) Who says these things?
1 What's for lunch?
2 What would you like?
3 No fish for me, thanks.
4 What would you like to drink?
5 I'd like milk, please.
6 There's ice cream or fruit salad.

1 Oliver
2 Mrs White
3 Katy
4 Mr White
5 Luke
6 Mrs White

Watch the film again and check.

d) Make a dialogue like the one in the film.

Saturday in Plymouth

What places in Plymouth can you remember?

I can remember the Hoe.

2 22 It's Saturday. Justin and his mum are at the Barbican in Plymouth. Justin has a new video camera – a present from his dad in Boston.

"OK, Justin, let's go to that nice café. Sarah is there – and they have good cream teas."
"I don't like cream teas, Mum."
"That's OK, Justin. Then you can have an ice cream or a sandwich."
"But I don't like cafés. And you and Sarah talk, talk, talk."
"OK, OK, Justin. You win. Let's meet here in an hour. Look at your watch. It's 3:45 now. So meet me here at 4:45. And don't be late! OK?"
"Thank you, Mum!"
Mrs Skinner goes to the café. Justin starts to film.
"Hi, Dad. It's 3:46 on Saturday, and I'm in town. I'm at the Barbican. Here you can see Sutton Harbour."
There are lots of seagulls at the harbour. Justin starts to film them. "Can you see the seagulls, Dad?"

2 23 Then he films a man near the harbour. The man shouts: "Boat tours! Boat tours! See all the navy ships! Next tour in 15 minutes …"
He films a boy and a girl. The girl has a big ice cream. Suddenly, a seagull comes down and takes it from her.
"Wow! That's so cool!" Justin says. "Look! I have it on camera!"
The girl's friend doesn't think it's cool – he's angry. "Don't film us," he shouts. Justin runs away.
There are lots of boats in the harbour. Justin starts to film them. One is a big sailing boat.
"This is my favourite boat, Dad. Maybe it can take me to the USA – to Boston and to you."
Near it is an old sailing boat. Justin films the boat and its name, *Blue Bird*. A small boy in a red T-shirt jumps onto the boat.
"Wow!" Justin thinks. "His family has a sailing boat."

2 24 Justin looks at his watch. "Time to go back to the café," he thinks. Then he sees a group of people with a police officer. They look worried.
Box "look", Voc, S. 221
"Please find him!" a woman shouts. "He can't swim."
"How old is the boy?" the police officer asks.
"He's five years old. He has brown hair, and … he can't swim!"
Box "plural words", Voc, S. 221
"And what about his clothes?"
"He has a red T-shirt, jeans and white trainers. Here's a picture of him," says the woman and takes a photo from her bag. "His name is Tom."
"A red T-shirt … five years old … brown hair! Wait a minute …" Justin thinks. He finds the *Blue Bird* on his video camera.
"Is this Tom?" he asks.
The woman and the police officer look at the picture on Justin's video camera.
"Yes!" shouts the woman. "That's Tom."
"Can you take us to the boat, please?" asks the police officer.

2 25 Justin takes them to the *Blue Bird*. The woman shouts, "Tom! Tom, where are you?"
The police officer jumps onto the boat. After a minute or two, he comes back with the boy.

"Oh, Tom!" the woman says. "Hey, Mum," Tom answers. "This is a great boat. It's so cool. Why is the police officer here?" "Never do that again!" she says and gives the boy a hug. "Do what?" he asks.

Justin looks at his watch. "Uh-oh … it's 4:47! I'm late!" Then suddenly he sees his mother. Her friend Sarah is with her. Mrs Skinner sees Justin with the police officer. "Oh, no, Sarah, Justin is in trouble. Hurry up!"

➜ *SF 8: Reading (p. 180)*

KV 11: Saturday in Plymouth enthält einen Multiple-Choice-Quiz zum Text.

1 The story in pictures

a) Put the pictures in the right order. Check with your partner. B · C · D · A · F · E

b) Find the six scenes in the text. Take turns and read them out.
A: ll.45–55 · B: ll. 1–14 · C: ll. 22–24 · D: ll. 39–43 · E: ll. 77–80 · F: ll. 69–74

2 Tom's mum

Look at lines 44–73. Find sentences that show that Tom's mother is

a) worried

b) happy

worried:
Please find him!
He can't swim.
Tom! Tom, where are you?

happy:
Oh, Tom!
Never do that again!

3 Act it out

a) Make groups of three students. Find the scene below in the text.

– Tom's mother talks to the police officer. Justin shows them the picture on his video camera. They run to the boat.

Choose your role and write down your sentences. Then act the scene.

b) Add information about Justin to his profile in your My Book.

➜ *SF 8: Reading (p. 180)*

➜ **Workbook** *26 (p. 33)*

Workbook Checkpoint 2 (pp. 34–37)

A tour of my home

One of the Plymouth kids visits you. Show him or her your home and talk about your family.

STEP 1: Choose your Plymouth kid.

STEP 2: Talk about the rooms in your home. Your mind map from page 50 can help you.

STEP 3: Talk about your family. Your family tree from page 55 can help you.

STEP 4: In front of your group, tell your friend from Plymouth about your home and your family.

Wie gut warst du?

Wie schätzt du dich selber ein? Schreibe die Sätze unter *Words, Grammar, Mind map* und *Speaking* in dein Heft ab und ordne dir für jede Frage eine Ampelfarbe zu.

Das lief nicht gut, ich muss mehr üben.
Das war OK, aber ich könnte besser werden.
Das habe ich gut geschafft.

Words

- Fielen dir die meisten Wörter schnell ein oder gab es Lücken? Bei welchen Wortfeldern hattest du Schwierigkeiten?

Grammar

- Konntest du die Formen des *simple present* problemlos bilden? Hast du bei *he/she/it* das *s* immer angehängt?
- Hast du Fehler bei *my, your, his, …* gemacht?

Mind map

- Hat dir deine Mindmap bei der Vorbereitung geholfen?

Speaking

- Konntest du gut vor deiner Gruppe auf Englisch sprechen? Welche Probleme hattest du dabei?

Wie kannst du besser werden?

Wenn du dich eher rot oder gelb eingeschätzt hast, helfen dir folgende Tipps beim Wiederholen und Üben.

Words

Die wichtigsten Wörter von Unit 2 findest du hier:

➔ *S.216–222* ➔ *Wordbank 3 (S. 169)*
➔ *Workbook S. 24, 31*

Grammar

Die Grammatik kannst du auf diesen Seiten wiederholen:

➔ *GF 9: The simple present (p. 187)*
➔ *LAL S. 48, S. 53, Übungen S. 48–49, S. 53–54*
➔ *Workbook S. 27, 29*

Mind map

Hier im *Skills File* findest du alle wichtigen Angaben zu Mindmaps:

➔ *SF 2: Collecting information (S. 175–176)*

Speaking

Du kannst dir Vortragskarten mit Stichworten anfertigen. Übe deinen Vortrag ein paar Mal vor dem Spiegel. Sprich deutlich, nicht zu schnell und drücke dich einfach aus.

A

1 Words in groups

a) Find three more umbrella words. Then write the other words in four lists. Three words don't go in the groups.

aunt · armchair · bathroom · bedroom · biscuit · brother · cheese · cupboard · family · food · grandma · hair · harbour · jam · kitchen · meat · rooms · shelves · ship · things at home · TV · uncle · vegetables

1 Things at home: armchair, ...
2 ... 1 ..., cupboard, shelves, TV
3 ... 2 rooms: bathroom, bedroom, kitchen
3 family: aunt, brother, grandma, uncle
4 ... 4 food: biscuit, cheese, jam, meat, vegetables

not in groups: hair • harbour • ship

b) Which word is different?

1	2	3	4	5
afternoon	milk	bread	aunt	farm
evening	water	cheese	twins	harbour
morning	cup	meat	grandpa	café
weekend	tea	plate	cousin	present

1 weekend: The other words are times of the day.
2 ...

2 One word or two?

a) Find pairs with the words in the two boxes. Write them as one word or two words.

dining · down · family · fruit · ice · living · roast

beef · cream · room (2x) · salad · stairs · tree

b) Use the words from a) in these sentences.

1 The Blackwells have dinner in the dining room.
2 They watch TV in the …
3 Abby's cat, Mink, likes to sleep on the sofa …
4 Sam likes … for Sunday lunch.
5 For dessert he likes …, not …
6 Lucy has a … of the Tizzards and the Pascoes.

2 living room • 3 downstairs • 4 roast beef • 5 ice cream ... fruit salad • 6 family tree

3 Sundays

Abby talks about Sundays. What are the missing words from Unit 2?

Sunday mornings are cool. I wake up at nine, but my brother Tim always sleeps ... ten. First I ... Skip. He eats ... and dog biscuits and he ... lots of water. There's always a pool of water on the ... in the kitchen. Dad reads the ... and I ... my friends. Tim ... music in his room - and Mum ... 'Breakfast'. Then we ... in the ... room and ... a big breakfast. I love Sunday lunch too. There's hot vegetable ... - Dad's favourite. After that there's Tim's favourite - ... beef with potatoes, and ... salad for ... - that's Mum's favourite. After lunch I go for a ... with Skip. For Sunday tea we make ... with jam and ... . Yummy! That's *my* favourite!

till • feed • meat • drinks • floor • paper • text • plays • shouts • go • dining • have • soup • roast • fruit • dessert • walk • scones • cream

4 Weekends are great

Tell your partner what you and your family do at weekends. Say six or more sentences.

Saturdays are great! I ... In the afternoon/evening I ... On Sundays we ... My mum ...

5 Lucy and her mum *(there, they're, their, you're, your; his, he's, its, it's)*

a) Put in *there*, *they're* or *their* and *you're* or *your*.

Lucy Mum, look! Can you see the two boys over ...? In Plymstock uniform?
Mum Oh, yes, OK. What about them?
Lucy ... my new friends.
Mum Oh, that's nice. What are ... names?
Lucy Sam and Justin. ... cool.
Mum ... friends are always nice, Lucy. So ... all in Miss Bell's class, right?
Lucy Yes, we are.

there • They're • their • They're • Your • you're

b) Put in *his* or *he's* and *its* or *it's*.

Mum ... nice that you have friends in your class. So who's who?
Lucy Well, Justin is the boy with dark hair. ... dad lives in the USA.
Mum Oh, what's the name of the town?
Lucy I can't remember ... name. Boston, I think. Yes, ... Boston. And Sam is new in Plymouth. ... from London. ... mum and dad are in the navy here.

It's • His • its • it's • He's • His

6 Abby and Tim *(German 'sie')*

Put in the right pronoun.

Tim Where's my school bag? I can't find ... ... isn't in my room.
Abby Ask mum. Maybe ... knows.
Tim Mmm. That's right. Where is ... ? I can ask ... And the meat sandwiches for tea. I can't find ... Where are ...?
Abby In the kitchen?
Tim Ha ha! ... aren't there. Well, I can't see ...
Abby Erm, where's Skip? He likes meat sandwiches.

it • It • she • she • her • them • they • They • them

7 Maya and her mum *(my, your, ...)*

Finish the sentences.

Maya Abby is ... new friend. The Blackwells live in Wembury. ... house is in Beach Road. Abby has sailing trophies in ... room. She has a brother. ... name is Tim. They have a nice cat but I can't remember ... name.
Mum Maybe Abby can come here next week. You can show her ... flat and ... bedroom.
Maya Yes. I can show her ... family tree too. Mukesh can show her ... new computer games. And can we have ... beef curry?

my • Their • her • His • its • our • your • our • his • your

8 On Saturdays (Simple present: positive statements)

Look at the pictures and find the right order.
Then make sentences about Maya.

1 Maya wakes up ... at 9 o'clock.
2 Then she ... has breakfast.
3 After that ... goes shopping.
4 In the afternoon ... she plays volleyball with a friend.
5 In the evening ... watches TV with her brother.

9 MIXED BAG Evenings at home (Simple present: positive and negative statements)

Put in the missing words.

After homework, Abby ... for a ... in the park with Skip. Kids often ... football in the park, so Skip runs and takes ... ball. After the walk there's ... and cake at home. Skip ... eat cake. Mrs Blackwell ... it isn't good for him. Mr Blackwell ... home at half past five. He reads his ... and ... Mum about his day. The kids do their ... in their ...
After homework, Abby ... her mum in the kitchen. The Blackwells like meat for dinner, but they ... meat every day. Skip is sad ... they have fish. He ... fish, but ... Mink's favourite. After dinner, Mr Blackwell ... TV on the sofa with Mink, and Mum ... in ... favourite armchair with a good book.

goes • walk • play • their • tea • doesn't • says • comes • paper • tells • homework • rooms • helps • don't eat/have • when • doesn't like/eat • it's • watches • sits • her

B

10 Mink and Skip

a) Read the text and correct these sentences.

1 The Blackwells wake up at half past six. seven
2 The kids are never late for school. late
3 Mr Blackwell reads the paper ~~every morning~~. doesn't have time to read
4 Mum takes the kids to school at 8.15. Dad
5 Skip doesn't like cat food. likes
6 Tim's desk is near his door. the window

Hello! I'm Mink, the Blackwells' cat. They have a dog too. Tim says he's a mad dog, but he's OK. We all live in a big house. Every morning at half past seven it's chaos. People run upstairs and downstairs – Skip too. Music plays in every room. The kids can't find their things and they're late for school. Mum shouts "Hurry up!"
Skip takes the paper to Dad and he gives him a dog biscuit. But Dad doesn't have time for the paper. Skip eats lots of biscuits. He often eats my cat food too. Dad takes the kids to school at quarter past eight. At half past eight Mum goes to the shops. Skip often goes with her – and I can sleep again.
It's nice without the family. Our house has lots of places where I can sleep. In the mornings I sleep on the sofa downstairs – my favourite place. Skip can't come in there, so that's good for me. But Abby's bed is nice too. I often sleep there. Mrs Blackwell doesn't like that, but she doesn't know.
I often sit on Tim's desk near the window. From his window I can see the birds in the garden. I often fall asleep on the desk - on Tim's homework, and suddenly his pencils are on the floor. That's a nice game. When Tim sees me on his desk he shouts "Silly cat! Go away". I don't know why he's angry. He always says he doesn't like homework.

b) Write three sentences about Mink or three sentences about Skip.

C

11 Write an email

Write an email to a Plymouth kid about a) two people in your family, or b) about your pet. Say what they often do and what they like (food, music, sports). Remember to use *and, but, in the mornings/..., at the weekend, often, always*. Write about 100 words and use your computer.

Hello, Lucy/Justin...!
Let me tell you about my... and my ...

Special days

1 Merry Christmas!

Box "Christmas", Voc, S. 222

2 26 a) Read and listen to Morph.

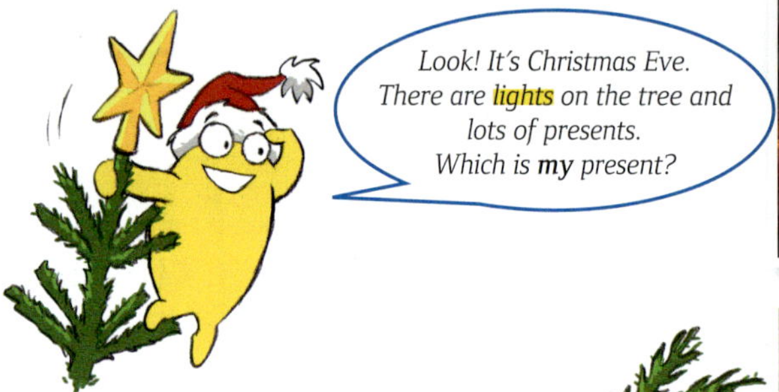

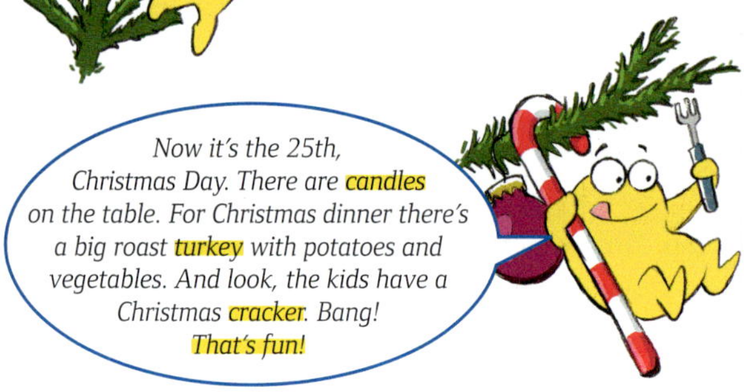

2 27 b) Listen to Jake.
How is Christmas in Germany different?
Say two or more things.
In Germany, we (don't) ...
... we don't open presents in the morning • ... we don't have Christmas crackers • ... we open presents on Christmas Eve, not Christmas Day • ...

c) Tell a partner what you and your family do on Christmas Eve and Christmas Day.
On Christmas Eve we/I ...

Grundschule

d) **EXTRA**
British people send lots of Christmas cards.
Make a Christmas card for your mum and dad or for a friend. Write a greeting in English.

paper hat

turkey

Christmas pudding

cracker

candles

Christmas cake

2 Happy birthday!

a) What can you see in the pictures? Name six things or more.

2 28 b) Listen to Emma. She talks about her birthday. Correct the wrong sentences.

1 Emma has a birthday party every year.
2 She writes invitations for her friends.
3 Emma's birthday isn't in summer.
4 English kids don't have candles on their cakes.
5 You tell everybody your wish.
6 After tea, the kids go home.

1 doesn't have · 2 right · 3 it's in summer · 4 there are candles on the cake · 5 you don't tell · 6 after tea, the kids play funny games

c) Make a double circle and say:
- when your birthday is (date)
  My birthday is on the ... of ...
- who comes on your birthday (friends, cousins, grandma and grandpa)
- what you have to eat and drink
- what you do with your friends (games, quiz, music, DVDs).

d) What would you like for your next birthday? Write down two presents.
Write down two things you would like to do with your family and friends.

For my next birthday I'd like a book about ...
I'd like to have .../go to ...

e) **EXTRA** Make a mind map about birthdays in your My Book.
Draw pictures of party food and presents.
Label the things.

→ **Workbook** *p. I*

Clubs and hobbies

1 Plymstock clubs

a) Work in groups of five.
Each student reads a different text about a club. Tell your group about your club.

– My club is the Samba / … club.
– It's on Monday/Tuesday / … / It's every day … at … / from … to …
– You can …

b) Now listen to the five clubs. Match the sounds to the clubs.
Check your answers with a partner.

2 29–33

Grundschule

A: Number 1 is …
B: Yes, that's right. / No, that isn't right. Number 1 is …

1 Quiet Reading · 2 Samba Club · 3 Basketball · 4 Gardening Club · 5 Film Making

– CLUBS FOR YEAR 7 STUDENTS –

Here are some of the great clubs at Plymstock School! Join one or more.
Look on the school website for information about more clubs, or talk to club teachers.

Basketball

With Miss Taylor
Where: Gym
When: Thur 3–4.30 pm
Play basketball and have fun with us in the gym. For boys and girls. Don't forget your PE kit!

Play an instrument, sing or dance.

Samba Club

With Mr Willis
Where: Music area
When: Mon lunchtime

It's like Rio here in Plymstock!

Quiet Reading

With Mr Wood
Where: Library
When: Mon–Fri lunchtime
We tell you about the best books for young people.
You choose one, find a chair and … read, read, read.

Einige der neuen Wörter auf diesem Aufschlag bringen eine hohe Komplexität in Bezug auf **Aussprache** mit sich *(join, grow, quiet, choose)*. L sollte hier großen Wert auf Nachsprechen der Wörter legen.

2 Your clubs

Talk about a club at your school or in your area. Tell the class what you can do there.

- There's a … club at school/near our house.
- You can do sport/sing/play … there.
- I go there every Tuesday/…

More words: ➜ *Wordbank 6 (pp. 172–173)*

➜ **Workbook** *1–4 (pp. 38–39)*

Your task

Am Ende dieser Unit wirst du …
… für einen Gast aus Plymouth ein spannendes Programm für drei Nachmittage zusammenstellen.

1 In the school canteen 2 34

It's the lunch break. Lucy and her friends talk about school clubs.

Sam: What's grey and never gets wet?
Abby: We don't know, Sam. Tell us.
Sam: An elephant with an umbrella.
Abby: Ha, ha – very funny.
Lucy: Do you know any good jokes, Sam?
Sam: Do I know any good jokes? Yes, of course. What's big and …
Lucy: Look, there's Justin!

Sam: Hey, Justin! Come and sit here. Er … Abby, do you know Justin?
Abby: No, I don't. Hi, Justin – I'm Abby.
Justin: Er … hi …
Sam: Hey, do you play basketball, Justin? I'm in the Basketball Club. You can come with me.
Justin: Er … basketball?
Sam: Yes, on Thursday afternoons.
Justin: Sorry, I can't.
Sam: Why not?
Justin: Because I'm in the Film-Making Club and it meets on Thursdays too.
Lucy: Film-making? Cool! Do you have a camera?
Justin: Yes, I do.
Sam: That's soooo cool!
Lucy: What about you, Abby? Do you go to any clubs?
Abby: Yes, I do. I go to the °Trampoline Club. And I'm in a sailing club too – at home in Wembury.
Lucy: Wembury Sailing Club? My best friend Maya is in that club.
Abby: Oh, do you know Maya too? She's very nice. I often see her at weekends.
Lucy: Really?
Abby: Yes, she sometimes comes to my house.
Lucy: Oh?
Abby: And what about you, Lucy, are you in a club?
Lucy: No, I'm not. Er … I have to go now.
Sam: Why, Lucy? What's the matter?
Lucy: I have to do my maths homework.
Sam: What? Do we have maths homework?
Lucy: Sorry, but I have to go.

2 Which clubs are they in?

Copy and finish the table.

	Abby	Justin	Lucy	Maya	Sam
Film-Making		X			
Basketball Club					x
Trampoline Club	x				
Wembury Sailing Club	x			x	

Add the information to the character profile in your My Book.

Zur Zeitersparnis kann L ein Arbeitsblatt mit der Tabelle erstellen, damit die S diese nicht abschreiben müssen.

3 Do you play basketball?

Make questions and ask a partner.

Do you …

play	football? tennis? …	Yes, I do.
know	Lukas? any good jokes? …	No, I don't.

Alternative: Die S füllen **KV 12: Do you play basketball?** aus und befragen in einer *Milling around activity* ihre Mit-S. Jede/r S sollte ca. 6 Mit-S befragen.

4 At Lucy's house

2 35

Lucy: I have to join a club, Maya. Everyone at Plymstock is in a club.

Maya: Everyone?

Lucy: Yes, Sam goes to basketball. Justin is in the Film-Making Club. And … and Abby is in the Trampoline Club.

Maya: Abby Blackwell? I know her.

Lucy: Yes, she's in your sailing club. What's she like?

Maya: You know her too. She's at your school.

Lucy: Well, she isn't really my friend. But you visit her at weekends.

Maya: Yes, sometimes.

Lucy: Does she live in a nice house?

Maya: Yes, she does. It's great. You can see the sea from her window.

Lucy: Oh, nice. Er … what about her family? Does she have any brothers or sisters?

Maya: Yes, she does. Two brothers. And she has a dog, a cat and …

Lucy: What about her brothers? Do they go sailing too?

Maya: Yes, they do. They all love the sea.

Lucy: And does she visit you at your house?

Maya: No, she doesn't … Hey, Luce, what's the matter? Why all the questions?

Lucy: Nothing, nothing. Let's forget it. I have to choose a club.

Maya: OK. Well, you like tennis. Does Plymstock have a tennis club?

Lucy: No, it doesn't.

Maya: Hmmm, there's a Computer Games Club on the list. My brother is in that.

Lucy: Mukesh? Does he like it?

Maya: Yes, he does. It's the best club, he says.

Lucy: But I don't like computer games so …

Maya: No, you don't. There's a Science Club …

Lucy: No! No science. I don't want more school work. I want to have fun.

Maya: Well, what about Quiet Reading, or the Samba Club …?

Lucy: Samba? That sounds fun. Maybe I can make new friends there.

5 Lucy, Maya and Abby

a) Finish the sentences.

1 Lucy and Maya talk about … .
2 Maya tells Lucy about Abby's … .
3 Maya's brother is in the … .
4 Maya helps Lucy to … .

b) Is Lucy happy? Say what you think.

I think Lucy is happy because …

I think Lucy isn't happy because …

1 … Abby • 2 … family. • 3 … Computer Games Club. • 4 … choose a club.

6 Have a go

Lucy asks questions about Abby:

Does she live in a nice house?
Does she have any brothers or sisters?
…

Think of more questions about Abby. Can your partner answer them?

Does Abby go to Coombe Dean School?

No, she doesn't.

Looking at language

a) Copy the table and finish the questions. The texts on pages 70–71 can help you.

	Singular	Plural
1st person	Do **I** know any good jokes?	Do … have … **we** … maths homework?
2nd person	Do … know … **you** … any good jokes?	Do **you** all like the sea?
3rd person	Does … live … **she** … in a nice house?	Do … **they** go sailing?

Early finisher Find more examples of the third person singular on pages 70–71.

b) What is different in the third person singular?

➔ *GF 12: The simple present (II): questions and short answers (pp. 190–191)*

1 Yes or no? (Simple present: questions and short answers)

Make six questions. Then ask your partner.

Do	you you and your friend Abby and Maya cats	go to Plymstock School? live in Germany? make films? play basketball? play an instrument eat fish?
Does	Sam Lucy Justin your friend	

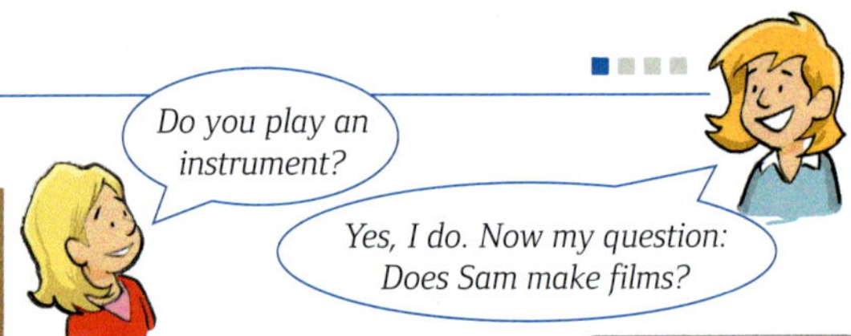

Yes,	I he / she	do. does.
No,	we they	doesn't don't.

Alternative: Die S befragen sich im Plenum. S1 wirft einen Ball und stellt eine Frage. Wer den Ball fängt, antwortet, stellt eine neue Frage und wirft den Ball weiter.

➔ **Workbook** 5–6 (pp. 39–40)

2 WORDS Go, play or do?

Grund-schule

a) Match the words to the pictures.

basketball · chess · the drums · gymnastics · kung fu · sailing · skating · swimming · yoga

b) Make a table. Add the words from a).

go	play	do
swimming riding	… cards · football · the piano	… judo

c) Add these words to your table:

cards · football · the piano · riding · judo

Early finisher ➔ p. 165

Early finisher: Die S können ein Rätsel lösen.

➔ **Workbook** 7 (p. 40)

go	play	do
swimming 1 	basketball 2 	kung fu 3 
skating 4 	chess 5 	yoga 6 
sailing 7 	the drums 8 	gymnastics 9 
Activities with -ing	Team sports, games, instruments	Other sports and activities

Box "Sports and other activities", Voc, S. 224

Alternative: Die S ordnen auf **KV 13: Go, play or do?** den entsprechenden Verben Wörter zu.

3 Activities (Simple present: questions)

a) Use words and your activities table from exercise 2. Take turns to ask and answer six questions with *go, play* and *do*:

b) Ask your partner about his/her best friend and/or family.

4 GAME Guess who!

Partner A: Choose a name from the list. Don't tell your partner the name.
Partner B: Ask questions. Guess the name.

Abby	Morph
Justin	Sam
Lucy	Silky
Maya	

A: Guess who!
B: Is it a he?
A: Yes, it is.
B: Does he live in the library?
A: No, he doesn't.
B: Does he make films?
A: Yes, he does.
B: Then it's Justin!
A: Right! Now you choose a name.

More help → p 158

More help: Als Hilfe sind einige weitere Fragen vorgegeben.

Zusatz: *Who am I?* Ein S überlegt sich einen Star. Die Mit-S müssen durch Erfragen von Eigenschaften den Namen erraten.

→ Workbook 8–9 (p. 41)

5 They have to join a club

Finish the sentences with a form of *have to*.

1 The friends ... choose a school club.
2 Lucy says she ... go because she ... do her maths homework.
3 Abby and her brothers can go sailing on Sunday because they ... help at home.
4 Morph is happy because he ... do homework.

1 have to • 2 has to ... has to • 3 don't have to • 4 doesn't have to

Language help

have to do sth. *(etw. tun müssen)*

I, you, we, they	have to	don't have to
he, she, it	has to	doesn't have to

British students have to wear uniforms.
Justin doesn't have to clean his room today.

6 At home (*have to*)

a) Say two things that you *have to do* at home today, and two things that you *don't have to do*.

b) Tell your class what your partner *has to do* and *doesn't have to do* today.

→ Workbook 10 (p. 41)

7 STUDY SKILLS Collecting information

Maya has to talk about her free time in class. How can she collect information about her free-time activities? Her teacher asks her to try a mind map and a table.

2 36 a) Look at Maya's mind map. What are the missing umbrella words? Listen to Maya and check.

b) Copy Maya's table.
2 37 Now listen to Maya and add the missing information.
Check with a partner.

	Monday	Tuesday	Wednesday	Thursday	Friday
activity	computer club	guitar lesson	skating	guitar lesson	sailing
time	3:15–4:00	5:00–6:00	3:30–5:00	5:00–6:00	4:00–6:00
place	at school	at home	the park	at home	Wembury beach
what I need	computer	guitar	inline skates	guitar	sailing boat

Neigungsdifferenzierung: Die S wählen zwischen Mindmap und Tabelle.

c) Collect information about your hobbies.
You choose Make a mind map or a table.
The study skills box can help with the table.

- Say what you do, where you do it and when you do it.
- Say what you need (clothes / skates / a ball / …) for your hobby.

More words: ➜ *Wordbank 6 (pp. 172–173)*

EXTRA Give a one-minute talk about your hobbies.

- Before class, practise with a partner.
- When you speak in class, use your mind map or your table.
- Show the class what you need (clothes / skates / a ball / …).

➜ **Workbook** *11 (p. 42)*

Study skills

Making a table

1 Überlege zuerst, wie du die Tabelle aufbaust:
In die linke Spalte kommen die Überschriften für die waagerechten Tabellenzeilen (im Beispiel: **activity**, **time**, **place**, …).
– In die obere Zeile kommen die Überschriften für die senkrechten Tabellenspalten (im Beispiel: die Namen der Wochentage).

2 Dann fülle die einzelnen Felder der Tabelle aus. Du kannst auch Symbole und Zeichnungen verwenden.

➜ *SF 2: Collecting information (pp.175–176)*

1 Plymstock school clubs

a) Who can you see in the photos? Oliver • Jack
What clubs are they in? Samba Club • Trampoline Club

b) Watch the film without sound and choose the right answer.

1 Oliver's club meets at lunchtime / after school.
2 They meet in the canteen / in the music area.
3 Oliver plays the guitar / the drums.
4 Jack's club meets at lunchtime / after school.
5 They meet in the gym / outside. +inside
6 You can / can't wear trainers.
7 Jack and Abby do three / six different jumps.

c) Now watch the film with sound and check.

d) Which club does Ruby like?
Which club do you like? Why?
Ruby likes the Samba Club because she likes music.

Für den Einsatz ohne DVD finden sie eine Audiodatei für diese Übung auf *www.cornelsen.de/access-bayern*

2 EVERYDAY ENGLISH How can we join the club?

a) Watch part one of the film.
Where do Oliver and Luke want to go?
What do they want to do?
They want to go to the Life Centre. They want to go swimming.

b) Now watch part two and match the questions (1–5) to the right answers (A–E). 1 F • 2 D • 3 A • 4 B • 5 C

1 What can we do here?
2 When is the pool open?
3 Are there any kung fu classes?
4 Can we go swimming now?
5 How can we join the club?

A No, sorry, we don't have kung fu classes, but you can do karate.

B Sorry, but you have to join the club before you go to the pool.

C We need a letter from your mum and dad.

D It's open every day from 8 am to 10 pm.

E Well, we have lots of activities.

c) You want to join a sports / music / ... club. Make a dialogue like the one in the film. Act it out for your class.

1 On Skype with Dad 2 38

Box "much ("viel") – many ("viele")", Voc, S. 225

Justin skypes with his dad, but his dad has a lot of work, so he can't answer many questions. +much

Justin: Mum, Dad is on Skype. Can I talk to him?
Mum: OK, Justin, but don't forget to finish your homework.
Justin: Come on, Dad, answer … please.
Dad: Hey, Justin!

Box "listen", Voc, S. 225

Justin: Hi, Dad. How are you?
Dad: Listen, Justin. This isn't a good time. I work in the afternoon. You know that.
Justin: Sorry, Dad.
Dad: And I don't have much time. I have a new job, you know, and …
Justin: A new job? Where do you work now?
Dad: Near Boston harbour. In a TV studio.
Justin: Wow! Er … what do you do there?
Dad: I edit TV programmes.
Justin: What programmes do you edit?
Dad: Justin, I really can't talk now. Let's talk later.
Justin: When do you finish work?
Dad: I finish at 7 o'clock, Justin. That's midnight in England – much too late.
Justin: OK, Dad. Maybe at the weekend?
Dad: Yes, the weekend is good.
Justin: When do you get up?
Dad: Try Saturday at 10 o'clock. That's 3 o'clock in England.
Justin: OK, Dad. Thanks. Oh, and thanks for the video camera.
Dad: Oh, yes, right. How do you like it?
Justin: It's great, Dad! I have a video for you. It's about a seagull.
Dad: OK, Justin, send it to me.
Justin: And I want to make a video about Plymouth for you.
Dad: Oh, good idea. You can tell me all about it at the weekend.
Justin: OK, Dad. I can tell you about school too. I'm in the Film-Making Club now. And I have new friends – Lucy, Sam and …
Dad: Talk to you at the weekend, Justin.
Justin: Right, bye, Dad.
Mum: Justin, don't forget your homework.
Justin: Oh yes, my homework. Er … Mum, why does Dad work so much?
Mum: Because he loves his work, Justin.

2 Justin's dad

What can you say about Justin's dad?
Collect information from the text in 1.
Write at least five sentences.

Mr Skinner …
He …
…

Check your sentences with a partner.

3 Have a go

a) Justin asks his dad two questions with *when*.

When do you finish work, Dad?
When do you get up?

Write four questions for your partner with *When do you …?*

b) Take turns. Read out questions and answer them.

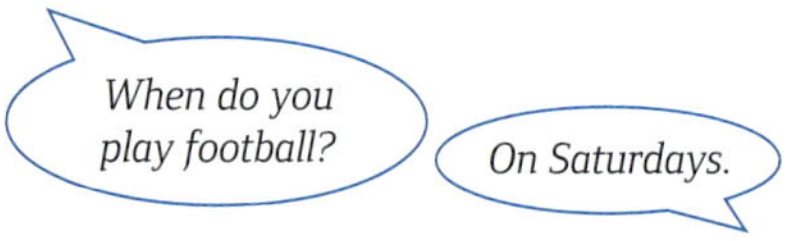

Looking at language

a) Finish the questions. Use the right question word: *what, when, where, why* or *how*.
You can find the questions in the text on page 76.

Where do you work now?	Near Boston harbour.
What do … you do there?	I edit TV programmes.
When do … you finish work?	I finish at 7 o'clock.
How do … you like it?	It's great, Dad.
Why does … Dad work so much?	Because he loves his work.

b) What word do you use after the question word?
What's different in the third person singular?

➜ *GF 12: The simple present (II): questions and short answers (p. 190–191)*

1 Where does Morph live?

(Simple present: questions with question words)

Write questions.

1 does – where – live – Morph
Where does Morph live?
2 work – does – Justin's father – where
3 Justin's father – do – does – what
4 next lesson – does – start – when – our
5 we – go to school – why – do – have to
6 at weekends – you – do – what – do

2 Where does J.'s father work? • 3 What does J.'s father do? • 4 When does our next lesson start? • 5 Why do we have to go to school? • 6 What do you do at weekends?

Early finisher Find a partner.
Ask and answer the questions.

Box "listen – hear", Voc, S. 226

2 Sorry, I can't hear you

(Simple present: questions with question words)

It's very noisy. You can't hear your partner.
Ask questions with *what, when, where* or *why*.

1 I play football.
Sorry, what do you play?
2 On Saturday morning, I help my mum.
Sorry, …?
3 On Sundays I get up at 10 o'clock.
4 Then I go to the swimming pool.
5 I like it there because I meet my friends.
6 My friends all like swimming.

2 …, when do you help your mum? • 3 When do you get up on Sundays? • 4 Where do you go then? • 5 Why do you like it there? • 6 What do your friends like?

More help ➜ *p. 158*

More help: Die Fragewörter sind bereits angegeben.

3 What sport does Abby like? (Simple present: questions with question words)

a) Read the answers. Then finish the questions.

Question	Answer
1 … sport … Abby …? *What sport does Abby like?*	She likes sailing.
2 … food … Silky …?	She eats fish and crabs.
3 … games … you …?	I play computer games.
4 … shoes … Plymstock students …?	They wear black shoes.
5 … films … you …?	I watch James Bond films.
6 … subjects … you …?	I like French and geography.

2 What food does Silky eat? • 3 What games do you play? • 4 What shoes do Plymstock students wear? • 5 What films do you watch? • 6 What subjects do you like?

More help ➜ *p. 159*

English and German are different

Was für Bücher liest du?

What books do you read?

b) Ask and answer questions. *What books/films/food …?*

➜ **Workbook** *12 (p. 42)*

More help: Die Fragen sind als Lückensätze vorgegeben, denen die passenden Objekte aus einer Box zugeordnet werden müssen.

4 Do you know your partner? (Simple present: mixed questions)

a) Copy the table.
Then finish the questions.

b) Ask your partner the questions and write the answers in the table.

c) Now write the answers on a card, like this:

(This boy/girl lives in ...)
He/She has/doesn't have ....
His/Her mum and dad ...
He/She plays/doesn't play ...
...

Questions	Answers
Where do you live?	
... have any brothers or sisters?	
Where ... your mum and dad come from?	
How ... come to school?	
... subjects ... like?	
... music ... like?	
... play an instrument?	
... hobbies ... have?	
... clubs ... go to?	

d) Swap cards round the class.
Read your new card out loud.
Can the class guess the student's name?

Alternative: Zur Zeitersparnis bearbeiten die S **KV 14: Do you know your partner?**

More help → p. 159 **More help:** Als Hilfe sind weitere Redemittel angegeben.

→ Workbook 13–14 (p. 43)

5 There isn't much time *(a lot of, much, many)*

Finish the text with a lot of, much or many.

Justin doesn't have ... homework today, so he phones his dad in Boston. His dad has a new job, so he has ... work. Does Justin have ... questions about the job? Yes, he does, but his dad can't give him ... information today. He can't answer ... questions because there isn't ... time to talk. Justin wants to tell his dad about his new friends, but there isn't ... time to talk. Today Justin's phone call isn't ... fun, but he can phone his dad again at the weekend.

After the phone call, Justin goes to the kitchen. Oh, great! His mum's scones! There aren't ... and there isn't ... jam, but there's ... cheese for a sandwich and there's ... milk too.
Now it's homework time, but Justin is good at maths, so he doesn't need ... help from his mum.

much • a lot of • many • much • many • much • much • many • much • a lot of • a lot of • much

Language help

1 In **positive** statements, *use* ***a lot of/lots of***:
Justin has ***a lot of/lots of*** *ideas for videos.*

2 In **negative** statements and **questions**, use ***much*** (viel) and ***many*** (viele).

Use ***much*** with words like *time, homework, fun, information, music,* and with food words like *milk, cheese, meat*. These words have no plural form because we cannot count them.

Justin ***doesn't have much*** homework today.
Does he have much time for hobbies and clubs?
There ***isn't much*** milk.
Do you eat much meat?
But:
Justin ***isn't*** in ***many*** clubs.
Are there many kids in the Film-Making Club?

→ *GF 14: a lot of/lots of – much – many (p. 192)*

→ Workbook 15–16 (pp. 43)

6 Who knows Morph? (Subject and object questions)

Language help

Who and **what** can be the **subject** or the **object** of a question:

Subject

Who **knows** Morph?
Wer kennt Morph?
What **happens** in the library?

When **who**/**what** is the **subject**, make the question **without do**/**does**.

Object

Who **does** Morph know?
Wen kennt Morph?
What **does** he do every day?

When **who**/**what** is the **object**, make the question **with do**/**does**.

a) Match the questions about Lucy and Abby.

1	Wen kennt Lucy?	A	Who does Abby visit?
2	Wer besucht Abby?	B	Who knows Lucy?
3	Wer kennt Lucy?	C	Who does Lucy know?
4	Wen ruft Lucy an?	D	Who phones Lucy?
5	Wen besucht Abby?	E	Who visits Abby?
6	Wer ruft Lucy an?	F	Who does Lucy phone?

a) 1 C • 2 E • 3 B • 4 F • 5 A • 6 D

b) Write these questions in English.

1 Was lernt Justin im Film-Club?
2 Wer macht Kung Fu?
3 Wen kennt Maya im Segelclub?
4 Was machen Schüler im Samba-Club?
5 Wer erzählt Witze?
6 Wen besucht Maya am Wochenende?

➜ *GF 15: Subject and object questions (p. 193)*

➜ **Workbook** *17 (p. 44)*

b) 1 What does Justin learn in the Film Club? • 2 Who does kung fu? • 3 Who does Maya know in the Sailing Club? • 4 What do students do in the Samba Club? • 5 Who tells jokes? • 6 Who does Maya visit at the weekend?

7 Lucy likes him too (Object pronouns)

a) Copy the table and add the missing pronouns. Look at p. 76 again.

Subject	Object
I	… me
you	… you
he	… him
she	her
it	… it
we	us
… you	you
they	them

b) Use pronouns for the underlined words.

1 Sam likes Mr Wood. Lucy likes <u>Mr Wood</u> too.
2 Lucy can join the Samba Club, and Sam can join <u>the Samba Club</u> too.
3 Maya: Here are some photos of the Sailing Club. Would you like to see <u>the photos</u>?
4 Maya: You can see Abby and me in this photo. You can see <u>Abby and me</u> in this photo too.
5 Ask Miss Bell about the Reading Club, and ask <u>Miss Bell</u> about the Music Club too.
6 Morph can see the kids, but <u>the kids</u> can't see <u>Morph</u>.

1 him • 2 it • 3 them • 4 us • 5 her • 6 they … him

c) Write three more sentence pairs like b), but with a gap (…) for the object pronouns. Your partner has to put in the correct pronouns in your sentences.

➜ *GF 16: Personal pronouns: object forms (p. 193)*

➜ **Workbook** *18–20 (pp. 44–45)*

1 At the Hoe

2 39

Look at pictures 1-4 in 2.
What do you think the text is about?

On Saturday afternoon, Lucy and Maya ride their bikes to the Hoe.

"Hey, Lucy, wait for me!" Maya shouts. But Lucy doesn't wait. She rides to Smeaton's Tower and waits there.

"Let's stop for a minute," Maya says.

"Are you tired?" Lucy asks.

"I'm thirsty," Maya answers. "Would you like some water?"

"No, thank you," Lucy answers.

"I have some chocolate too," Maya says.

"No, thank you."

"Oh come on, Lucy! You usually love chocolate."

❖

Justin is at the Hoe too. He turns on his camera.

"Hi, Dad, this is the Big Wheel at the Hoe. You can see all of Plymouth from here."

Suddenly someone is behind Justin. "Boo!"

+something

+in front of

Justin jumps and turns around.

"It's OK, I'm not a ghost," says Sam.

"Hey, you can film me with your video camera."

Sam does a kung fu move and shouts, "Kung Fu Master Wu is ready for action."

❖

Lucy and Maya hear the two boys.

"They're very loud," Lucy says.

"Hey, they're your school friends!" Maya says.

"That's right – Sam and Justin."

Sam sees the girls and shouts, "Hey, Lucy, Maya – we're here! Justin wants to film me, Master Wu."

"I don't want to film you, Sam," Justin says.

"I want to make a video of Plymouth for my dad."

2 What's in the picture?

Find sentences in the text for pictures 1–4. Read the sentences to a partner. Do you have the same sentences? Are they right?

1 ll. 20–23 • 2 ll. 15–16 • 3 ll. 3–5 • 4 l. 17

1

2

3

4

3 A good idea 2 40

Grund-schule

a) Listen **once** to the rest of the story.
Which of these words do you hear?

Barbican · film · ghost · harbour · monster · scary · ship · snake · streets · time travellers +(to) travel

What is the good idea? a scary film about time travellers, with ghosts in it

b) Correct the wrong sentences.

1 ~~All the kids~~ like action films. Sam
2 Maya wants to make a film about time travellers.
3 ~~Justin~~ wants to make a film about ghosts. Lucy
4 ~~Lucy says~~ Abby can be in the film. Maya and Sam say
5 Lucy says she has some ideas for a story.

Background file

Old Plymouth – the Barbican

The old part of Plymouth, near the harbour, is called the Barbican. With its small streets, old houses, shops, tea rooms and restaurants, it's a great place for walking, shopping and eating. Visitors' favourites are the boats and the seals.

There's a museum in the Barbican too, in New Street. The name of the museum is the Elizabethan House. Visitors can learn about the history of the house – a former sea captain's home – on a short tour. The seven rooms of the house are on three floors. Downstairs there's a kitchen – with food. Upstairs there's the dining room, and on the second floor the bedrooms.

Can you imagine life in 1580? Children's tickets are only £1.50, so come along and see!

a) Read the text and take notes.
→ *SF 5: Taking notes (p. 178)*

b) Use your notes to tell your partner about Old Plymouth.

1 The Elizabethan House

Du bist mit deinen Großeltern in Plymouth. Ihr wollt das Elizabethan House besuchen. Lies die Informationen und beantworte die Fragen deiner Großmutter.

1 Wo ist eigentlich das Elizabethan House?
2 Ist es überhaupt mittwochs auf?
3 Wie sind die Öffnungszeiten?
4 Wie alt ist das Haus überhaupt?
5 Was gibt es da alles zu sehen?
6 Wer hat denn dort gelebt?
7 Gibt es so etwas wie eine Familienermäßigung?
8 Wieviel würde es denn für uns drei kosten?

➜ *SF 10: Mediation (p. 181)*

➜ **Workbook** *21 (p. 46)*

1 32 New Street, The Barbican • 2 Ja. • 3 Di.-Sa., 10-17 Uhr • 4 Das Haus ist aus dem 16. Jh. • 5 man kann z.B. die Küche, alte Möbel und den Garten sehen • 6 in dem Haus hat ein Kapitän gelebt • 7 Ja • 8 £8.50

2 The rooms of the house (Possessive forms)

a) Write phrases with *'s*, *s'* or *of*.

1 the rooms – house: *the rooms of the house*
2 a sea captain – life: *a sea captain's life*
3 a tour – museum:
4 the end – street:
5 the streets – town:
6 Justin – film:
7 the history – museum:
8 Maya – photos:
9 the kids – ticket:
10 the sea captain – home:

3 a tour of the museum
4 the end of the street
5 the streets of the town
6 Justin's film
7 the history of the museum
8 Maya's photos
9 the kids' ticket
10 the sea captain's home

Language help

Possessive form with ***of***
With nouns for **people** and **animals** use **'s** or **s'**:

Singular nouns: *Sam's name, the dog's basket*
Plural nouns: *the students' class, the kids' friend*

With nouns for **things**, use the possessive form with ***of***: *the rooms of the house, the name of the museum*

b) Choose three phrases from a) and use them in three sentences.

The rooms of the house are small and dark.

➜ *GF 17: The possessive form (II) (p. 194)*

➜ **Workbook** *22 (p. 46)*

3 THINKING ABOUT LANGUAGE small letters, CAPITAL LETTERS

TIP

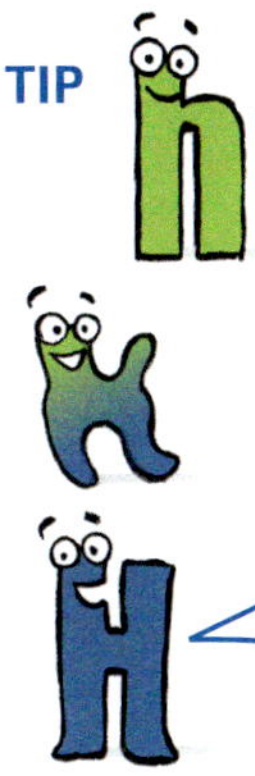

Use small letters for nouns – camera, club, house, etc.

an old house
ein altes Haus

Read the tips about CAPITAL LETTERS. What's the same in German? What's different?

Use **CAPITAL LETTERS** for:

- the word "I": My friend and I like basketball.
- days and months: Monday, January
- names of schools, clubs: Plymstock School, Wembury Sailing Club, …
- countries, cities, streets: Germany, Boston, New Street, the Barbican
- rivers and places: the Plym, the Hoe, the Elizabethan House
- languages: German, French
- country adjectives: an English car

a) Read the text on the right and copy it. Use capital letters where you need them.
Hi! My name is Josh. I come …

b) Check a partner's text.

Early finisher Say sentences with names, days of the week, etc. Your partner has to write your sentence. Is it correct?

hi! my name is josh. i come from wembury near plymouth and i go to plymstock school in church road. i like sport. i do judo and i play football at wembury football club on fridays.
i like germany because my mum is german. she comes from augsburg. in july or august we visit my german uncle there.

➜ **Workbook** *23 (p. 47)*

Hi! My name is Josh. I come from Wembury near Plymouth and I go to Plymstock School in Church Road. I like sport. I do judo and I play football at Wembury Football Club on Fridays. I like Germany because my mum is German. She comes from Augsburg. In July or August we visit my German uncle there.

4 How often? (Word order: adverbs of frequency)

a) Copy the line. Then add the missing words: often, sometimes, usually.

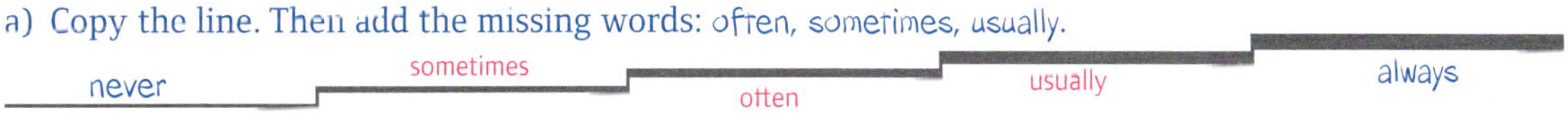

b) Put the words in the right order.

1 goes – always – Sam – on Thurdays. – to a club
Sam always goes to a club on Thursdays.
2 doesn't – Lucy – eat – always – in the canteen.
3 sometimes – Justin and Sam – on the Hoe. – meet
4 doesn't – Justin – see – often – his dad.
5 goes – swimming – at the Lido. – often – Maya
6 does – kung fu – usually – Sam – at weekends.
7 in Plymstock Library. – Morph – sleeps – always
8 cornflakes – eats – for breakfast. – never – Silky

More help ➜ *p. 159* **More help:** Die S fügen die Adverbien an der richtigen Stelle im Satz ein.

Early finisher Write another sentence with often, always … about Silky or Morph. Draw a picture for your sentence.

c) Play this game in groups of four.

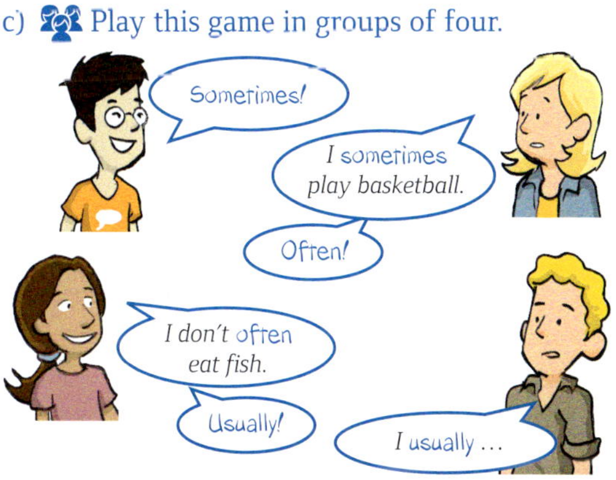

English and German are different

I sometimes play chess.

Ich spiele manchmal Schach.

➜ *GF 18: Word order (II): Adverbs of frequency (p. 194)* ➜ **Workbook** *24 (p. 47)*

3 Justin and Sam sometimes meet on the Hoe. • 4 Justin doesn't often see his dad. • 5 Maya often goes swimming at the Lido. • 6 Sam usually does kung fu at weekends. • 7 Morph always sleeps in Plymstock Library.

5 Baskets, boxes and butterflies (The plural of nouns)

2 41

a) Listen to the plurals of these words.
Do you spell them with s or with es?

action · address · basket · beach · bed · box · boy · bus · map · month · sandwich · watch

b) Choose words from the box in a).
Ask your partner to spell the plural.
Take turns.

Language help

1 You usually add **s** to make a noun plural:
street – street**s** [s], club – club**s** [z].

2 You add **-es** after -s, -x, -sh, -ch:
box – box**es** [ɪz], beach – beach**es** [ɪz]

3 For consonant + **y** the ending is **ies**:
family – famil**ies** [iːz], stor**y** – stor**ies** [iːz],

But after a vowel + **y**, add only **s**:
boy – **boys** [z]

c) Which words have the plural ending ies?

boy · butterfly · day · hobby · library · monkey · party · smiley · story · toy · trophy

➔ *GF 19: Plural of nouns (p. 194)*
➔ **Workbook** *25 (p. 47)*

a) -s: actions · baskets · beds · boys · maps · months
-es: addresses · beaches · boxes · buses · sandwiches · watches

6 MIXED BAG Anna calls

Lucy and Holly's cousin Anna calls. Put in the missing words.

Lucy: Oh, hi, Anna. ... you want ... speak to Holly?
Anna: I'd like to ask her to my party ... Saturday. And you too, of ... .
Lucy: A party. Great! Thanks. We really like ... . Holly is at school.
Anna: Oh, ... she go ... a club?
Lucy: Yes, she ... . She ... to the Computer Games Club ... Tuesdays.
Anna: And what ... they do there? ... games do they play?
Lucy: I ... know. I don't like computer games. I think they're silly.
... you go to any clubs?
Anna: I'm in a photo club. Taking photos is one of my favourite ... .
Lucy: I ... ... choose a club too. Maybe I can ... the Samba Club.
I love music and dancing.
Anna: Samba. Cool! That ... fun. But ... me about your new classmates.
Who are your friends?
Lucy: Well, there's Sam. He ... kung fu and he tells silly ... . Then there's Justin.
Anna: Sam and Justin. Two ...! What about girls? ... Maya go to Plymstock?
Lucy: No, ... She's at Coombe Dean.
Anna: Do you see ... at weekends?
Lucy: Yes, we often meet. But Maya ... a new friend now. ... name is Abby.
Maya sometimes ... her in Wembury. They ... sailing.
Anna: Oh! You can go with ... . It's a cool sport.
Lucy: Erm, no thanks. Sailing is cool, but you ... wet!

➔ **Workbook** *26 (p. 48)*

Do · to · on · course · parties · does · to · does · goes · on · do · What · don't · Do · hobbies · have to · join · is · tell · does · jokes · boys · Does · she doesn't · her · has · Her · meets · go · them · get

1 You say ... the [f]-, [v]- and [w]-sounds

2 42 a) Listen to the words.

1 [f] is the sound in 'forget', 'photo' , 'shelf'.
2 [v] is the sound in 'very','never', 'have'.
3 [w] is the sound in 'want', 'which', 'someone'.

Practise the sounds and words with a partner.

b) Listen and repeat. 2 43

Can you hear sound 1, 2 or 3?

Check with a partner.

[f] (father) · [w] (wet) · [v] (visit) · [w] (what) · [v] (travel) · [w] (sandwich) · [f] (off) · [v] (of) · [v] (live) · [f] (life) · [f] (four) · [v] (vegetable)

c) Practise with a partner:

- fruit, vegetables, sandwiches and water
- Where's Val's funny video?
- Welcome to Wales in winter!
- Will wants to work with Victor.
- Visit Wembury in November!

2 44 Listen and check.

d) Say Morph's tongue-twisters:

Forty-five wet frogs and twelve friendly whales.

We want to watch TV and a DVD.

When we visit Will and Victor every week, it's never very wet.

Listen and check. 2 45

2 You say ... the [ɔː]-sound

a) [ɔː] is the sound in 'sport' and 'walk'.
Look at the six pictures. Find five words with an [ɔː]-sound. Then listen and check. 2 46

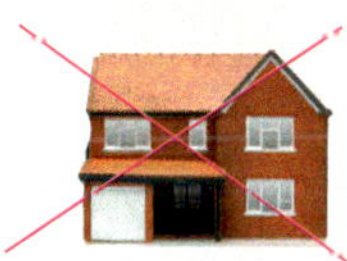

b) How many words with an [ɔː]-sound can you find in the box: 8, 9 or 10?

boat · course · fall · floor · food · form · group · hour · more · short · small · talk · throw · water · your

3 Word stress: What's different in German and English?

a) Say these words. Then write them and mark the stressed syllable[1].

activity · chocolate · cousin · information · instrument · person · programme

2 47 Listen and check.

b) Think of three sentences. Use one or more words from a) in each sentence. Say your sentences to a partner.

➜ **Workbook** *27 (p. 48)*

1 stressed syllable [strest'sɪləbl] *betonte Silbe*

The captain's ghost

Do you like ghost stories? Look at the pictures. Who's in the story and where does it take place?

1 2 48

Abigail and her friend May are at Abigail's house. "What's that funny sound?" asks May. "Oh, it's Skipper," says Abigail. "My dog – he's in the attic. He catches rats there." "Let's go to the attic, then," says May. "It's boring here." In the attic, they see Skipper. He has a book in his mouth. "Here Skipper, give it to me!" says Abigail. "What is it?" asks May. "It looks like a diary. And there's a name and a year: Captain Justin Pascoe, 1581." "1581. Wow! That's *old*," says May. "And here's an address: New Street, Plymouth." "Hey!" May shouts. "That's in the Barbican." The two girls look at the diary. "What's on that page there?" Abigail asks. "It's a map – a map of a house," answers May. "And look, it shows where Captain Pascoe has his gold." "Gold!" Abigail shouts. "Wow!" Then she sees a letter in the diary. She takes it and reads:

10th February 1581
Dear Father,
Mother is very sick. We don't have any money.
We can't eat. Please come home. Please help us!
Lucille

"How sad," says May. "I hope the girl finds her father's gold." "Oh, no!" Abigail shouts. "Skipper has a bottle in his mouth!" She takes the bottle from him and opens it. "That smells funny, Abigail," says May. "Oooh, I'm so tired …" "Yes, me too," says Abigail.

2 2 49

May wakes up. She looks out of the attic window. There are horses, and people in strange clothes. She calls Abigail and Skipper. "Look! The street looks different." They all run out of the house. Abigail shouts to a boy, "Sorry, but are we in Plymouth?" "Well, we aren't on the moon," says the boy. "And what year is it?" asks May.

"What year? 1581, of course." "The year of the diary!" Abigail shouts. "Your clothes are very strange," the boy says. "Sorry," says May, "but we have to find a girl. Her name is Lucille Pascoe. Do you know her? "Of course. Lucille is my friend. I can show you her house."

3 2 50

They walk along New Street. The boy stops at a house and shouts: "Lucille! Lucille!" Lucille opens the door. "Oh, it's you, Samuel," she says. "But who are they?" "I'm May, and this is Abigail. Can we come in?" "Er … yes, but what do you want?" "We want to help you," says Abigail. "Help me? How?" Lucille asks. "Your father," May says. "We have his …" "My father is dead. Now go, I have work to do." "No, wait please," says May. "Look at this." Lucille looks. "This is a map of my house!" "Yes," says May. "And it shows where your father's gold is." Suddenly, the door behind Lucille opens. Skipper barks. They hear loud steps and then a loud voice.

"Stop! Thieves!" it says. "Give me back my book! You can't have my gold!"
A hand touches Abigail. It throws her onto the floor.
"Help, a ghost!" she shouts. Skipper barks again.
"Come on, old ghost. I'm ready to fight!" shouts Samuel.
"Luci-i-i-ille," the voice says.
"Father? Is that you?" asks Lucille.
"Yes, it's me. Stop them! They have the map."
"But they say they can help me," Lucille answers.
"Help you?" the voice asks. "But how?"
"Here, Lucille," May says. "The map is for you."
Lucille takes the map. "Father," she says. "Maybe they're really our friends? … Father?"
But the ghost doesn't answer.

4 2 51

Lucille is quiet for a minute. Then she speaks:
"Let's go upstairs."
They all follow her.
"Here, this is the place," says Samuel. "There's a little door in the floor. Open it, Lucille. Open it!"
Lucille opens the door. "Yes, it's here! The gold is here!" she shouts. "Lots of gold coins." She takes a coin. "This is for you, May."
"Hey! I'm thirsty," says Samuel.
"Let's go and drink some tea," Lucille says.
They go downstairs.

"This tea tastes funny," May says.
"Oh, no, I'm tired again … so tired."
"Yes, me too," says Abigail.

"Woof, woof!"
The girls wake up.
"Abigail," says May, "we're back in your attic!"
"What's that in your hand?" Abigail asks.
May looks in her hand and sees an old gold coin.

5 2 52

"And that's the end of my dream," says Lucy.
"Wow, that's a great story," says Sam.
"Yes, it's perfect for our film," says Maya.
"Let's tell Justin about it," says Sam.
"But we need Abby," says Maya. "Let's call her."
"Yes," says Lucy, "and we need her dog too!"

1 Understanding the story

Choose titles for the five parts of the story.
Or write your own titles.

It's 1581!
A great story
The sea captain's diary
Thieves or friends?
Lucille finds gold
Is this Plymouth?
Skipper finds an old book

2 New words

Find these new words in the story.
Is it easy to understand them? Why?

captain (l. 13) · gold (l. 21) · moon (l. 44) · thieves (l. 72) · dream (l. 109)

➜ SF 4: Understanding and looking up new words (pp. 177–178)

3 The captain's ghost

Neigungsdifferenzierung: Die S haben die Wahl zwischen einer künstlerischen Aufgabe und einer kreativen Schreibaufgabe.

You choose Do a) or b).

a) Make a film poster for "The captain's ghost". Who is in the film? What are their roles?
– Draw one or more scenes from the film on your poster.
– Hang up the posters in your classroom. Walk around and look at the posters. Make notes about what you like and don't like about them.

b) Write a dialogue for part 1, 2 or 3 of the story.
– Act it out for the class.

EXTRA Work with other groups and act out the whole story as a play.

➜ Workbook 28 (p. 49)

Workbook Checkpoint 3 (pp. 50–53)

3 Your task

Step 1 und **2** können als vorbereitende Hausaufgabe bearbeitet werden. In der Folgestunde erfolgt dann die Gruppenarbeit in **Step 3**. **Step 4** und die **Selbsteinschätzung** können wieder zu Hause erfolgen.

What can we do this week? ✎

Your friend from Plymouth is in your town. What can you do with him or her? Make plans for three afternoons, like Morph.

STEP 1 Make a table for three afternoons. Add activities and times. Look for ideas on pp. 68–74.

STEP 2 Prepare to talk about your ideas. Words and phrases from 2 on page 72 can help.

STEP 3 Talk about your ideas with a partner.

STEP 4 Text your British friend about your best ideas. Work alone.

Wie gut warst du?

Wie schätzt du dich selbst ein? Schreibe die Sätze unter *Words*, *Speaking* und *Writing* in dein Heft ab und ordne dir für jede Frage eine Ampelfarbe zu.

- Das lief nicht gut, ich muss mehr üben.
- Das war OK, aber ich könnte besser werden.
- Das habe ich gut geschafft.

Words

Fielen dir Wörter und Phrasen für Freizeitaktivitäten ein, z. B. mit *go*, *play* und *do*? Wusstest du, wie man sie ausspricht?

Speaking

Konntest du im Partnergespräch über deine Vorschläge für Freizeitaktivitäten sprechen? Konntest du nützliche Redewendungen benutzen?

Writing

Konntest du Notizen zu den Ideen deines Partners/deiner Partnerin machen? Konntest du dann in deiner Nachricht für drei Nachmittage drei Vorschläge machen?

Wie kannst du besser werden?

Dort, wo du dich rot oder gelb eingeschätzt hast, helfen dir folgende Tipps.

Words

Suche in Unit 3 und den Wordbanks Wörter für Freizeitaktivitäten. Bei der Aussprache hilft dir die phonetische Umschrift.

➜ *Wordbank 6, S. 172–173*

Speaking

Lerne diese Redewendungen auswendig. So kannst du Vorschläge machen, annehmen und ablehnen:

Let's …, What about …? We can …, Would you like to … Good idea. Sorry, I don't like …, I don't think that's a very good idea because …

Writing

Tausche deine Nachricht mit deinem Partner/deiner Partnerin aus. Überprüfe die Rechtschreibung und die Redewendungen mit *go*, *play*, *do*.

A

1 Clubs and activities

be quiet • get wet • have fun • join a club • make a joke/new friends/fun • play the guitar • ride your bike • tell a joke

a) Match verbs from the orange box with words from the green box.

be · get · have · join · make · play · ride · tell

your bike · a club · a joke · new friends · fun · the guitar · quiet · wet

b) Finish the sentences with words from a). 1 join • 2 have • 3 ride • 4 make

1 Plymstock students have to … a club.
2 The Film Club is great. We all … fun.
3 You can … a bike, so come to the Bike Club!
4 Clubs are cool. You can … new friends there.

2 Jo and his family

Jo talks about his family's sports and hobbies. Finish the text with a form of *go*, *play* or *do*.

In our family we all … lots of sport. I'm in our junior football team. We … on Fridays after school. I … kung fu too. My sister … judo and she … riding on Sundays. Mum and Dad … tennis. Mum … gymnastics too, and in summer we all … swimming. Hobbies? Well, Dad … chess in a club and I … the trumpet. I think it's cool – but Mum isn't too happy.

do • play • do • does • goes • play • does • go • plays • play

3 A club for Ed

Read the dialogue between Jo and Ed to the end. Then put in the missing words.

Jo: Hi, Ed! You look worried. What's the **m**…?
Ed: **N**… I'm OK. But I **h**… to **j**… a club, and I don't know **w**… club to **c**…
Jo: Well, you can read the **i**… on the school **w**… . It tells you about all the clubs. I go to the **G**… Club on Wednesdays. It's **f**… 3.15 to 4.15 with Mrs Hobbs. I like it.
Ed: **R**… ? But it's **b**… Nothing happens. Gardening isn't for me. **W**… do you like it?
Jo: Well, I like it **b**… it's **q**… in the school garden. All the other clubs are inside, so it's nice to be **o**… – when it isn't cold.
Ed: And Mrs Hobbs? What's she **l**…?
Jo: She's nice. We **g**… tomatoes and potatoes and then we can **s**… them. What do you do in your **f**… time? Do you have any **h**…?
Ed: Music is my hobby. Maybe I can join the **D**… Club and learn breakdance or hip hop.
Jo: Well, that **s**… fun. But I think you have to dance with girls in the school club.
Ed: Oh, really? So that's boring too. Erm, when does the Gardening Club **m**…?

matter • Nothing • have • join • which • choose • information • website • Gardening • from • Really • boring • Why • because • quiet • outside • like • grow • sell • free • hobbies • Dance • sounds • meet

4 About you

Talk to a partner about your free time. Take turns to ask and answer questions.
Ideas: after school, at weekends; at home, in town; friends, books, computer, music, pets, TV, shops

What do you do after school? What books do you read?
When/Where do you …? I sometimes go/do/play/…

5 Sports (Simple present: mixed questions)

a) Write questions.

1 a sport – do – do – you ?
2 sport – you – do – do – what?
3 play – Justin – does – basketball?
4 does – go – Maya – swimming – when?
5 Abby and Tim – where – do – sailing – go?
6 do – does – Lucy – how often – gymnastics?

1 Do you do a sport? • 2 What sport do you do? • 3 Does Justin play basketball? • 4 When does Maya go swimming? • 5 Where do Abby and Tim go sailing? • 6 How often does Lucy do gymnastics?

b) Write six questions about sport and hobbies for a class questionnaire.

Do you ...? What hobbies .../
When/Where/How often do you ...?

6 Plymstock school clubs (Simple present: questions with question words)

Read the answers. Then write the questions with the correct question words.

1 Sam joins <u>the Basketball Club</u>.
What club ...?
2 The Cricket Club meets in the gym <u>at 3.15</u>.
3 The Science Club meets <u>in Room 203</u>.
4 At the Food Club you learn <u>how to make party food</u>.
5 Justin joins <u>the Film-Making Club</u>.
6 Abby joins the Trampoline Club <u>because it's fun</u>.

1 What club does Sam join? • 2 When does the Cricket Club meet? • 3 Where does the Science Club meet? • 4 What do you learn at the Food Club? • 5 What club does Justin join? • 6 Why does Abby join the Trampoline Club?

7 Free time (Word order: adverbs of frequency)

In which sentences is the word order right? Correct the four wrong sentences.

1 Lucy and Maya ride their bikes often to the Hoe.
2 Sam doesn't do homework usually at weekends.
3 Weekends are always cool. There's no school!
4 Mukesh plays never cricket.
5 The friends don't go often to a museum.
6 Justin sometimes is in town with his camera.

1 Lucy and Maya often ride their bikes to the Hoe. • 2 Sam usually doesn't do homework at weekends • 4 Mukesh never plays cricket. • 5 The friends don't often go to a museum.

8 MIXED BAG Justin's new film

Here's Justin's email to his dad. Read the text to the end. Write the missing words and phrases.

Arial 11 F K U T

Hi, Dad!
Do I love my video camera? Yes, … …! Film-making is my favourite activity, and I have an **i**… for a new film! I **s**… go for a walk in the Barbican. There's a **v**… old house in New Street, it's **o**… 400 years old. It's a museum now. When you **v**… its old rooms, you can **i**… life in Plymouth in 1580. So, Dad, what **a**… a scary story in the old house - with a **g**…? Here it is. Four kids are in the dark house at night. It's **s**… because they **h**… strange **s**… . They have a map … the house and they find lots of gold **c**… **u**… a little door in the floor. Suddenly a man's **v**… says: "Stop! It's my gold. Give it to … ." Then they see an old man – but he's a ghost. He's **a**… because he **w**… his gold back. A hand touches Abigail and … throws … to the floor. So the kids **f**… with the ghost. … wins? Well, you … to see the film! So that's the story. … do you like it? Sam wants to be the ghost. He … want … be one of the kids. But … ghosts do kung fu?
And now your new job: … is it like? … do you work? In a big, famous studio? … TV **p**… do you edit? And … do you work so much? You're never at home! Let's talk on Saturday!

I do • idea • sometimes • very • over • visit • imagine • about • ghost • scary • hear • sounds • of • coins • under • voice • me • angry • wants • it • her • fight • Who • have • How • doesn't • to • can/do • What • Where • Which • programmes • why

B

9 Molly and Max

2 53

a) Listen to Molly. Which photo shows Molly? Which photo shows her brother? Say why. Molly: 2 Max: 3

b) Copy the table. Add information about Molly and Max when you listen again.

	Molly	Max
age	…11 yrs	… 13
sports and activities	sailing, chess	football, basketball, swimming
clubs and teams	Chess Club	school swimming team
when	Tuesdays and Fridays at lunchtime	Monday and Friday evenings

c) Are the statements right or wrong?
The information in your table can help you.

1 Molly is eleven. right
2 The Bartons live in Plymstock. wrong
3 Molly goes sailing with her brother. wrong
4 The Chess Club meets after school. wrong
5 Mrs Barton plays chess. right
6 Molly often meets a friend on the beach. wrong

d) Put in the words.

1 Bella is … dog. the Bartons'
2 Molly and Anna … to the same school. don't go
3 … isn't Max's favourite sport. Sailing
4 Max is in the school … team. swimming
5 Max has training on … and … evenings. Monday · Friday
6 When Molly talks about Sophie, Max usually … gets angry.

C

10 Hi, …!

Write an email to a new friend in England.
Tell him/her about your sports, hobbies and school clubs.
Ask him/her about free time too, about school clubs, activities, friends, what he/she does after school and on Saturdays.

Write questions with Do/Does and questions with What/When/Where/Why/How often … do/does …
Use your computer and write about 100 words.

Shopping

1 British money: pounds and pence!

Britain has pounds and pence. Is it the same in your country?

Box "British money", Voc, S. 229

a) Read what Morph says.
Then answer his question.

You write:	You say:
1p	one p [piː] (= penny)
20p	twenty p (= pence)
£1.50	one (pound) fifty
£5	five pounds
£6.90	six (pounds) ninety

2 54 b) How much are these things? Listen and write. Then check with a partner.

1 £6.75 2 £ … 2 £19.49 · 3 £149.95 · 4 £45.99 · 5 £145 · 6 £12.95 each · 7 £65.35 · 8 £59.50

1

2

3

4

5

6

7

8

c) Use your answers from b). Ask and answer questions about pictures 1–8.

Partner A: How much are the felt pens, please?
Partner B: They're six pounds seventy-five.
How much is the football, please?
Partner A: It's …

How much is a shoe, please?

ATC.2

2 When are the shops open?

2 55 a) Listen to Morph and read along.

In Britain, shops are open from 10 am to 6.30 pm from Monday to Saturday. Shopping centres are usually open till 8 pm. In big towns, big shops, like clothes and food shops, are open for six hours on Sundays too! Some big supermarkets are open 24 hours, but not so long on Sundays. All shops are closed on 25th December, 1st January and Easter Sunday. So happy shopping!

b) When are the shops open where you live? What's different? Say three or more sentences.

3 Who says what?

56 a) Jake needs some new felt pens. Write his dialogue with the shop assistant in the correct order. Then listen and check.

- Let me see. They're £2.75 each.
- Well, what colours do you have?
- Yes, we do. What colour do you want?
- Yes. Do you have felt pens, please?
- We have red, blue, black, green, pink …
- How much are they?
- Hello. Can I help you?
- £2.75 is OK. So, I'd like red, green and blue, please.

b) Learn the dialogue and act it out.

Assistant: Hello. Can I help you? • Jake: Yes. Do you have felt pens, please? • Assistant: Yes, we do. What colour do you want? • Jake: Well, what colours do you have? • Assistant: We have red, blue, black, green, pink … • Jake: How much are they? • Assistant: Let me see. They're £2.75 each. • Jake: £2.75 is OK. So, I'd like red, green and blue, please.

4 In a shoe shop

57 a) Jake is in a shoe shop with his mum. Listen and correct the wrong statements.

1 Jake needs ~~new shoes~~ for school. new trainers
2 His mum thinks he needs size 5.
3 Jake wants ~~black~~ trainers. red
4 Jake thinks black and white trainers are boring.
5 The black and yellow trainers are ~~£89.50~~. £89.95

b) Answer the questions.

1 Does Jake like the yellow trainers? No, he doesn't.
2 Which trainers does he like? the red and blue ones
3 Which size does Jake need? size 6
4 Do they take the red and blue trainers? Yes, they do.
5 What does Jake have to do at home? clean his room

c) Write another dialogue.
Ask and answer questions about one of the things in exercise 1b).
Practise your dialogue and act it out for the class.

*Do you like my cool new trainers? No? Hmmm! Well, what trainers **do** you like?*

d) **EXTRA** Draw a picture of Jake, his mum and the assistant in the shoe shop. Give each person a speech bubble. Write one or two sentences in each bubble. You can put your picture in your My Book.

→ **Workbook** p. II

Weekends

1 In the picture

a) Who is in the pictures? Where are they?
Maya, Abby and Tim are in a garage.
Silky …

b) Find these things in the pictures.

basketball · birthday invitation · bottle · box · life jacket · magazine · mobile phone · note · rock · sand · shorts · trainers

c) Talk to a partner about what you can see where.

A: I can see Sam's shorts and his trainers in picture D.
B: And there's some sand in picture B.
A: Yes, and there's/there are …

2 Weekend plans

3 01–04

a) Listen and match the four dialogues to pictures A–D. 1 D · 2 B · 3 A · 4 C

Grund-schule

b) Listen again. Which sentence is correct?

Sam wants to … win his basketball match.
help his dad in the kitchen.
Silky wants to … break a bottle on a rock.
go to a seals' party.
Abby wants to … phone her brother.
sail to Ivy Island.
Lucy wants to … go to the Wheel of Plymouth.
play a game.

1 a) … and Spot are at the beach. · Lucy and Maya are in Lucy's room. · Sam and his dad are in the Bennetts' kitchen.

1 b) Picture A: bottle · box · life jacket · magazine · mobile phone · trainers · Picture B: bottle · birthday invitation · note · rock · sand · Picture C: note · Picture D: basketball · shorts · trainers

3 Your weekends

Zur Zeitersparnis erarbeiten die S die Übung anhand der Tabelle auf **KV 15: Your weekends**.

a) Tell a partner what you do at the weekend. Then ask your partner what he/she does.
The words in the boxes can help.

A I sometimes ride my bike with a friend or we go to the cinema. What do you do?
B On Saturdays, I often … (too).

b) Tell the class one thing that is the same for your partner and you, and one thing that is different.

A We sometimes go to the cinema with friends.
B I …, but my partner doesn't …

→ **Workbook** *1–3 (p. 54)*

Your task

Am Ende dieser Unit wirst du …
… ein Spiel anfertigen und mit deiner Gruppe spielen.

PLACES
cinema · home · lake · library · museum · my friend's flat · my grandparents' garden · park · shopping mall · zoo · …

+parents

ACTIVITIES
go shopping · listen to … · see · play · read · ride a bike · visit · watch · …

Remember to add information about the Plymouth kids to the profiles in your My Book.

1 Where were you? 3 05

It's 9 am in Boston. Justin's dad is on Skype.

Dad: Justin? Are you there?
Justin: Hi, Dad! I'm here. Can you see me?
Dad: Wait a minute … Oh, yes, there you are. Hi, Justin. How are you?
Justin: Well, I was sick yesterday.
Dad: Oh, I'm sorry.
Justin: But I'm OK today. What about you, Dad?
Dad: Oh, I'm fine.
Justin: Dad, where were you last weekend?
Dad: Er … I'm sorry about last Saturday, Justin. I was busy at the weekend, so I wasn't at home.
Justin: Yeah, you weren't on Skype.
Dad: No … sorry, I was at the studios all day. But listen, thank you for that video.
Justin: The video of the seagull, at Sutton Harbour?
Dad: Right.
Justin: Was it OK?
Dad: It was really good! And the part with the seagull and the ice cream was fantastic.
Justin: Thanks, Dad.
Dad: And where were you last weekend?
Justin: I was at the Barbican with my friends. We were in a film, Dad!
Dad: What film was it?
Justin: No, Dad, we weren't at the cinema. It was our film. We were the actors.
Dad: That sounds exciting.

Justin: Yes, it was about a girl in old Plymouth and her father's ghost.
Dad: So, were you the cameraman?
Justin: Yes, and guess what, Dad – I was the ghost too!
Dad: Really? So, when can I see the film?
Justin: I still have to edit it, Dad.
Dad: OK, maybe I can help you when you come to Boston in the summer.

2 On Skype

a) Collect information about Justin's dad from the text in 1.
Write at least four sentences.

Justin's dad … was busy last weekend • was at the studio all day • thinks Justin's video was really good • thinks that the part with the seagull and the ice cream was fantastic • …
…

b) What do Justin and his dad talk about?
Write down two things.

They … … talk about Justin's video of the seagull • … talk about Justin's film about the girl in old Plymouth • …
…

3 Chain game

Grund-schule

Play the game twice: in groups of three or four students, then in groups of five or six students.

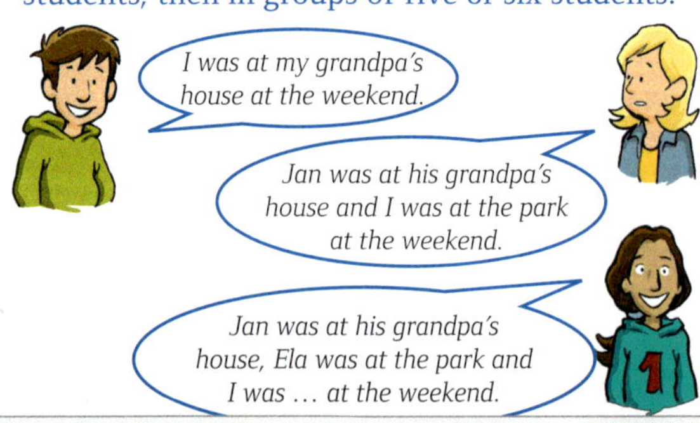

Zur Erhöhung der individuellen Sprechzeit empfiehlt es sich, die Übung in Kleingruppen (5–6 S) über mehrere Runden durchzuführen.

Language help

The simple past of the verb *be*:

	Positive / Negative	Question	
I he she it	was / wasn't	Was	I he she it
you we they	were / weren't	Were	you we they

➔ *GF 21: The simple past of (to) be (p. 195)*

1 Dad wasn't at home

(Simple past of *be*: statements)

Finish the sentences.
Use positive (+) or negative (-) forms of *be*.

1 Justin: "Dad (-) at home last weekend. He (+) at the TV studios."
2 Lucy: "I (-) at home last Sunday. I (+) at Maya's flat. Mukesh (+) there, but Mr and Mrs Sen (+) at the cinema."
3 Sam: "I (-) at home yesterday afternoon either. I (+) at my basketball club. It (+) great."
4 Mr and Mrs Bennett: "We (-) at home last Saturday. We (+) in London with Lily. But Sam (-) with us. He (+) at a basketball match."
5 Abby: "Maya, you (-) at home yesterday!"
Maya: "No, I (+) at Lucy's house."

1 Dad wasn't at home last weekend. He was at the TV studios. • 2 I wasn't at home last Sunday. I was at Maya's flat. Mukesh was there, but Mr and Mrs Sen were at the cinema. • 3 I wasn't at home yesterday afternoon. I was at my basketball club. It was great. • 4 We weren't at home last Saturday. We were in London with Lily. But Sam wasn't with us. He was at a basketball match. • 5 Maya, you weren't at home yesterday! – No, I was at Lucy's house.

2 Was it fun?

a) Read the dialogue between Jack and Ruby.
Fill in the gaps with a word from the box.

boring · cold · exciting · funny · long · sad · scary · silly · strange · warm · wet

Ruby: I was at the pool on Saturday.
Jack: At the Lido? Was it fun?
Ruby: Yes, it was. The water was really (...). What about you?
Jack: I was at the cinema.
Ruby: Was the film good?
Jack: Yes, it was. It was really (...).

3 06 b) Listen to the dialogue.
Then practise with your partner.

c) Make your own dialogue about Saturday.
You can use words from the box in a).

More help ➔ p. 160

More help: Ein Dialoggerüst und weitere Adjektive sind vorgegeben.

TIP
Remember how you make short answers:
Was it fun? – Yes, it was.
Was it good? – No, it wasn't.

Unit 4 bietet viele Partnerübungen. Mit Hilfe der **KV 16: Appointment partners** kann L die *Appointment*-Methode einführen und im Laufe der Unit immer wieder verwenden.

3 How was your weekend?

(Simple past of *be*: question words)

Read the dialogue between Jack and Oliver.
Finish it with question words from the box and *was* or *were*.

how · how · when · where · who · why

Jack: Hey, Oliver! *How was* your weekend?
Oliver: Great, thanks.
Jack: Cool! ... ... you?
Oliver: At a party.
Jack: Whose party ... it?
Oliver: My cousin Katy's party.
Jack: Oh, and ... ... you there?
Oliver: I ... there because it was her birthday.
Jack: And ... ... the party?
Oliver: On Sunday afternoon.
Jack: Oh, and ... ... there?
Oliver: Abby with her friend Maya, and lots of other kids ... there. And what about you? ... ... your weekend?
Jack: It ... cool, thanks. No homework!

Where were • was • why were • was • when was • who was • were • How was • was

More help ➔ p. 160

More help: Textstellen, die auf das richtige Fragewort deuten, sind hervorgehoben.

➔ Workbook 4 (p. 55)

1 The basketball match 3 07

On Saturday morning, Plymstock School played against Devonport High School in the Plymouth Schools' Basketball Final. Sam was really excited.

❖

Later, on the way to Lucy's party, he talked to Justin about the match.

Wörter wie *minibus, final* oder *half* sollten vor dem Lesen nicht semantisiert werden, sodass die S sie sich durch die Nähe zur deutschen Sprache oder den Kontext erschließen. Diese Strategien werden im Verlauf der Unit wieder aufgegriffen.

2 Sam's match

a) Put the five sentences into the correct order.
Check with a partner. C · A · D · E · B

A Plymstock scored 16 points in the first half.
B Sam showed his dad his medal.
C Sam played in a basketball match on Saturday.
D In the second half, Plymstock was better.
E Sam's team won the match.

b) Make two more sentences about the match.

3 Have a go

Look at the pictures of Morph.
Use the verbs to write about his Saturday morning.

cleaned · learned · listened · finished

On Saturday morning, Morph … English in bed.
Then he … his room.
Later he … to music.
After that he … his book.

learned · cleaned · listened · finished

Looking at language

a) Look at the simple past form of the verb *play*. Then go to 1 on pages 98–99. Find the simple past forms of the other verbs. Make a table.

	Past
play	played
talk	… talked
score	… scored
shout	… shouted

	Past
stop	… stopped
jump	… jumped
arrive	… arrived

What is the simple past ending of regular verbs?

b) Look at the simple past form of the verb *go*. Then go to 1 on pages 98–99. Find the simple past forms of the other verbs. Make a table.

	Past
go	went
come	… came
have	… had
win	… won
see	… saw

Uh-oh. I have to learn the past forms of irregular verbs.

➔ *GF 22: The simple past (I) (p. 196)*
➔ **Workbook** *5–6 (p. 56)*

1 Morph's Saturday evening (Simple past: positive statements, regular verbs)

Finish what Morph says about Saturday evening. Use the simple past form of these verbs: *arrive, dance, jump, look, shout, want, wait, walk.*

After dinner I walked around the library.

I was happy. I … danced between the shelves.

I … to find a new book. wanted

Suddenly a cat … in the library. arrived

She … at me – and she wasn't friendly. looked

"Help!" I …. shouted "She wants to eat me."

I … onto a shelf between two books. jumped

I … there till the silly waited cat … away. walked

2 What's right? (The *-ed* sound: [d], [t] or [ɪd]) 3 08–09

a) Listen to the -ed sounds of the verbs in the story about Morph's Saturday evening. Put them in a table like this:

[d]	[t]	[ɪd]
arrived	walked	wanted
…	…	…
a) – b) answered · called · listened · played · showed · turned	a) danced · looked · jumped b) asked · touched · watched · liked	a) started · shouted · waited b) visited · needed

b) Listen to the -ed sounds of these verbs. Add them to your table.

answered · arrived · asked · called · liked · listened · needed · played · showed · touched · turned · visited · watched

c) Compare your table with a partner. Read the verbs out loud.

Hier kann wieder **KV 16: Appointment partners** zum Einsatz kommen.

3 A visit from London (Simple past: positive statements, regular and irregular verbs)

Tom is Sam's friend from London. Read about his visit to Plymouth.

a) Put the verbs into the simple past.

1 Last month Tom (come) came to Plymouth for a weekend.
2 He (arrive) ... on Friday afternoon.
3 After dinner, Sam and Tom (play) ... chess.
4 Tom (win) ... two games; Sam (win) ... one.
5 Then Sam (want) ... to play computer games, but Tom was too tired.
6 So Tom (go) ... to bed and Sam (watch) ... a DVD.

Early finisher → p. 165

Early finisher: Die S lösen einige Rätsel.

→ **Workbook** 7–8 (pp. 56–57)

2 arrived • 3 played • 4 won (2x) • 5 wanted • 6 went … watched

b) Fill in the simple past forms of these verbs:

go (2x) · like · see · show · visit · walk · want

On Saturday, the boys ... (1) into Plymouth by bus. Sam ... (2) Tom the Hoe and then they ... (3) swimming at the Lido. Later, Tom ... (4) to see old Plymouth, so they ... (5) around the Barbican for an hour. They ... (6) lots of old houses and they ... (7) the museum in the Elizabethan House. Tom really ... (8) his day in Plymouth.

More help → p. 160

More help: Die Verben sind bereits im *Simple past* vorgegeben.

1 went • 2 showed • 3 went • 4 wanted • 5 walked • 6 saw • 7 visited • 8 liked

4 Dave's day in London

Partner B: Go to p. 166.

Partner A:

a) Dave was in London. He talked to his grandma about his day there.
Tell your partner your picture story: *Dave was in London last Saturday. In the morning he went to ...*

b) Listen to your partner's story.
Then say how the two stories are different.
A: In my story he talked to his grandma.
B: In my story he talked to his classmates.
And in my story he went …

c) Why do you think Dave's stories were different? Which story do you think is true?

EXTRA Imagine you are Dave. Write about your great day in London.

1 Party at the Hoe 3 10

Where are the students? Sam doesn't look happy. What do you think is the matter?

Box "Unregelmäßige Vergangenheitsformen", Voc, S. 232

Mum: Are you all ready to go on the Wheel?
Sam: I'm ready!
Justin: Yes, me too!
Lucy: Hey, Mum! We still have to wait for somebody. Remember?
Maya: Look, there's Abby!
Lucy: Hi, Abby. I'm … er … It's great that you're here.
Abby: Hi – sorry I'm late! I missed the bus.
Lucy: That's OK. Let's go.

❖

After the ride, Lucy, Maya, Justin and Abby ran over to the birthday picnic. Sam didn't run. He walked. He didn't look happy.
Dad: Come on, everybody! Sit down. I want to hear all about your ride.
Lucy: It was really good, Dad! Plymouth Sound looked fantastic …
Maya: … and we saw the Barbican and Sutton Harbour. The boats were really small.
Abby: I saw our school in Plymstock.
Lucy: *I didn't see* Plymstock School – it was too far away.
Dad: What about you, Sam? Sam, are you all right?
Sam: I'm OK, Mr Pascoe.
Lucy: Sam didn't like the ride, Dad.
Dad: Oh, I'm sorry, Sam. What was the problem?
Lucy: It was too high.
Maya: Sam didn't like that.
Justin: And he didn't look out.
Mum: So you didn't see any sights. I'm sorry about that.
Sam: It's OK. I know all those places.
Dad: Yes, of course.
Sam: And today is a great day too. We won our match against Devonport!
Maya: And it's Lucy's birthday!
Dad: Right. Where's the cake? It's time to make a wish, Lucy.

2 The missing word

Can you remember the missing word? Who was the speaker?

1 "Sorry I'm late! I … the bus."
2 "The … were really small."
3 "I saw our … in Plymstock."
4 "Sam didn't like the …, Dad."
5 "Oh, I'm sorry, Sam. What was the …?"
6 "We won our … against Devonport!"

1 missed (Abby) • 2 boats (Maya) • 3 school (Abby) • 4 ride (Lucy) • 5 problem (Lucy's dad) • 6 match (Sam)

3 Have a go

Tell your partner what you *didn't* do last weekend.
You can use ideas from the box.

I didn't go on a big wheel last weekend.
I didn't …

go on a big wheel · see my best friend · go to a birthday party · do my homework · get up early · play football

Box "Unregelmäßige Vergangenheitsformen", Voc, S. 232

Looking at language

a) Finish these sentences from 1 on page 102.

Sam ... run. He walked. He ... look happy. didn't (3x)
I ... see Plymstock School – it was too far away.

b) Find more sentences with *didn't* in 1.
Write them down.

c) How do you make negative sentences in the simple past?

➜ *GF 23: The simple past (II) (pp. 196–197)*

positive	negative
I played basketball.	I didn't play tennis.
He went swimming.	He didn't go sailing.

don't play
doesn't play
didn't play

Aha ... after didn't you use the infinitive too and with he/she/it you use didn't!

1 Maya didn't read her book

(Simple past: negative statements)

Last weekend Maya had a long list of things to do. But she only did three things.
Look at her list. Say what she didn't do.

Last weekend Maya didn't read her book. She didn't ...

- read my book
- find a birthday present for Lucy ✓
- go shopping
- call Sam and Justin
- do my maths homework
- go to Lucy's party ✓
- ride my bike
- go sailing with Abby and Tim ✓
- write to my cousin Dilip
- visit Uncle Amar
- watch a video

didn't read her book • didn't go shopping • didn't call • didn't do her maths homework • didn't ride her bike • didn't write to her cousin • didn't visit • didn't watch a video

2 I played ... I didn't play ...

(Simple past: positive and negative statements)

a) Think about last week. Write two positive and two negative sentences about what you did.

More help ➜ p. 161

More help: Enthält eine Anzahl von Anregungen/Redemitteln.

b) Make a double circle. Tell your partner what you did and what you didn't do. Then ...

🔴 stay in your place.

🔵 move one place to a new partner.

I played with my dog.
I didn't play computer games.

I went to bed early.
I didn't read in bed.

Hier kann wieder **KV 16: Appointment partners** zum Einsatz kommen.

3 I think that's true

Make two sentences about your last weekend – one positive and one negative.
Only one sentence is true. Can the others guess the true sentence?

Last weekend I touched an elephant.
I didn't go shopping.

You didn't go shopping:
I think that's true.

➜ **Workbook** *9–13 (pp. 57–59)*

4 Seal saves hurt dog

a) Answer the questions.

1 Where was Charles Hacker on Saturday evening?
2 What did he hear and see?
3 Why couldn't the dog swim?
4 Who helped the dog and how?
5 Who called the police?
6 What happened when the police arrived?

b) Write two more questions.
Answer and check with a partner.

c) Write another story with an animal hero.
Use the simple past, positive and negative.
Write about 100 words.

a) He went for a walk on the beach. • 2 He heard a strange sound and saw a small grey dog. • 3 Because it was hurt. • 4 A seal helped the dog to swim back to the beach. • 5 Mr Hacker called the police. • 6 The police took the dog to an animal help centre.

Devon News

Seal saves dog in South Devon

At 8:15 on Saturday evening, Charles Hacker went for a walk on the beach in Exmouth, Devon. Suddenly, he heard a strange sound. Then he saw a small grey dog, it was hurt. When Mr Hacker came near, the dog jumped off the rocks into the water. But because the dog was hurt, it couldn't swim. Mr Hacker saw that the dog had a problem. He wanted to help, but he didn't know how. Then he saw a seal in the water. The seal started to swim around the dog. Then it swam behind the dog and pushed it onto the beach. Mr Hacker called the police. The police came and took the dog to an animal help centre.

"I didn't save the dog," said Mr Hacker later in an interview. "It was the seal."

Background file

Devon – an English county

Devon is a county in the south-west of England. Its biggest city is Plymouth, with 260,000 people. Dartmoor is the biggest area of wild country in the south of Britain. It is the setting for lots of famous detective stories.

Wild ponies on Dartmoor, Devon

Devon's north and south coasts have lots of sandy beaches. Swimming, surfing and fishing are very popular with holidaymakers.

Woolacombe Beach, Devon ['wʊləkəm]

Devon is one of the warmest places in Britain. You can find lots of palm trees there!

Torquay Gardens, Devon [ˌtɔːˈkiː]

Write a short text. Say why you would / wouldn't like to go to Devon.

More help → p. 161

More help: Sprachliche Hilfen werden strukturiert vorgegeben.

Zusatz: KV 17: Welcome to sunny Torquay! enthält einen weiteren Lesetext zu Devon.

1 Consonants at the end of words

3/11 a) Listen to the words. What sound do you hear at the end of each word? [p] or [b], [t] or [d], [k] or [g]? First, make a table (1-8) in your exercise book. Then tick [√] the sound that you hear.

	[p]	[b]	[t]	[d]	[k]	[g]
1			√			
2						

2 [d] (had) · 3 [g] (frog) · 4 [b] (web) · 5 [d] (loud) · 6 [g] (leg) · 7 [p] (top) · 8 [b] (club)

3/12 b) Listen to the words. Do you hear the green word or the red word?

1 sat / sad   2 hurt / heard   3 plate / played   4 kid / kit
5 clap / club   6 bag / back   7 shop / job   8 pig / pick

2 You say ... the [e]-sound and the [æ]-sound

3/13 a) Listen to the sounds.
Then practise the words with a partner.
[e] is the sound in 'bed', 'said', 'men'.
[æ] is the sound in 'bad, 'sad', 'man'.

b) What do you hear? a) or b)? 3/14

1 a) and   b) end   2 a) bed   b) bad
3 a) dad   b) dead   4 a) sad   b) said
5 a) man   b) men   6 a) ate   b) at

c) Say the words for the pictures. Which words have an [æ]-sound? Are there 3, 4 or 5?
3/15 Listen and check with your partner.

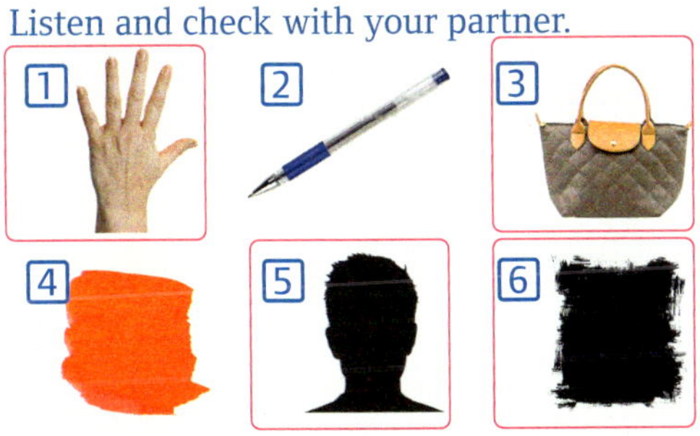

d) Practise with a partner.
1 Jack's black cat has jam for breakfast.
2 Ed's dad has a red crab in his bag.
3 Ed's cat is black and its bed is red.
4 Ben never has rabbits, cats and ants on his desk in his flat.

Listen and check. 3/16

3 Intonation

3/17 a) Listen. How is the intonation of sentences 2 and 4 different from the intonation of sentences 1 and 3? Why? 1+3: voice goes down (statement) · 2+4: voice goes up (question)

1 Ruby was at the pool.
2 Was it fun?
3 Abby and her brothers go sailing.
4 Did they go sailing yesterday?

b) Now say sentences 1-8. Does your voice go up or down at the end?

1 Sam does kung fu. down
2 He started when he was nine. down
3 Can Lucy do kung fu? up
4 No, she can't. down
5 Does Justin edit films? up
6 Yes, he does. Ask him about it. down
7 Did Sam's team win the match? up
8 Was it exciting? up

3/18 Listen and check.

→ Workbook 14 (p. 59)

1 Sailing on Sunday 3 19

Abby talks about a scary sailing trip.

Abby walked into the canteen and saw Lucy.
"Hi, Lucy. Can I sit with you?" she asked.
"Of course," said Lucy.
Abby sat down. "Hey, your party was great. Thanks again for the invitation!"
Lucy smiled. "Did you have a good Sunday?"
"Yes, I did," Abby answered. "I went sailing with Maya and my brother Tim. Did Maya tell you about it?"
"No, she didn't. Where did you go?"
"Well, we sailed to a beach near Ivy Island."
"That's nice," Lucy said.
"Yes," said Abby. "And guess what we saw!"
"Tell me," Lucy said, "what did you see?"
"Seals!" said Abby. "There was a big group of seals on the beach."
"Wow!" said Lucy. "That sounds exciting."
"Yes," said Abby. "But it was scary too. Seals can bite, you know."
"So what did you do?" Lucy asked.
"We were very quiet," Abby answered. "We just walked around the beach and looked. And then we wanted to go back to the boat, but we couldn't."
"Why not?"
"Because there was a big seal in front of it."
"Oh no!" said Lucy, "what did you do?"
"We waited, but the seal didn't go away. Then the sea came in and took our boat."
"Oh no! What did you do then?"
"We went into the water and swam back to the boat. Some of the seals followed us, but we were OK."
"Seals can be scary. I didn't know that," said Lucy.
"Yes," said Abby. "Big seals can be scary, but not baby seals."
"Did you see baby seals on Sunday too?" asked Lucy.
"No, I didn't," said Abby. "But when I was nine … oh, that's a long story."
"Tell me," said Lucy. "Please … "
"Well," said Abby, "I went sailing with my two brothers – Tim and Will – and …"
"Uh-oh," said Lucy. "There's the bell."
"OK," said Abby. "I can tell you the story later."

Die hier angedeutete Geschichte wird im **Text** ab S. 112 erzählt.

Background file **Grey seals**

Grey seals are white at birth, but they soon become grey or brown with dark spots. Seals can weigh over 200 kg. They are wild animals and can bite, so seal-watchers mustn't go too close to them on the beach.
Grey seals can swim 70 metres down into the sea. They eat about 5 kilos of fish and crabs a day, but they needn't eat every day. They needn't drink because they get enough water from their food. Box "get", Voc, S. 233
A seal's first year is very hard. A baby seal mustn't go too far away from its mother. It needs her milk to grow.
Seal mothers leave their babies after only three weeks, so young seals must learn to catch fish very soon. Like kids, they must practise, practise and practise. Box "must", Voc, S. 233

Close the book. Tell your partner three things about seals.

2 Abby's story

Look at these scenes from Abby's story. Find sentences in 1 for each picture.

1 We went into the water and swam back to the boat. (ll. 32–33) / Some of the seals followed us, but we were OK. (ll. 33–34)
2 I went sailing with Maya and my brother Tim. (ll. 8–9) / Well, we sailed to a beach near Ivy Island. (l. 12)
3 There was a big group of seals on the beach. (ll. 16–17)

Early finisher

a) Choose a sentence or two from the story in 1 and draw a picture.

b) Find a partner and show your picture. Can he/she find the lines in the text?

3 Lucy's questions

Here are Abby's answers to some of Lucy's questions.
Find the questions in 1 and write them down.

1 "Yes, I did," Abby answered. "I went sailing with Maya and my brother Tim."
2 "Seals!" said Abby. "There was a big group of seals on the beach."
3 "We waited, but the seal didn't go away. Then the sea came in and took our boat."
4 "No I didn't," said Abby. "But when I was nine ..."

1 Did you have a good Sunday? • 2 What did you see? • 3 What did you do? • 4 Did you see baby seals on Saturday too?

4 Your weekend

Take turns to ask and answer the questions.

1 Did you have a good weekend?
Yes, I did. / No, I didn't.
2 Did you stay at home?
Yes, I did. / No, I didn't.
3 Where did you go?
I went to .../visited .../ ...
4 What did you do?
I saw ... / I played ... / I met ... / ...
5 Who visited you?
My friend/aunt/...
6 Who did you visit?
I/We ...

➜ **Workbook** *15 (p. 60)*

Language help

In the simple present, you use Do or Does + **infinitive** to make questions.
Do you go sailing in the summer?
Does Abby go sailing on Sundays?

In the simple past, you use Did.
Did you go sailing at the weekend?
Did Abby go sailing with Maya?

Remember how you make short answers:
Did you …? Yes, I **did**. / No, I **didn't**.

➜ *GF 24: The simple past (III) (p. 197)*

1 Did you see an elephant yesterday? (Simple past: questions)

Ask questions from the table below and answer them. Take turns.

Did you	see	an elephant / the moon / …	yesterday?
	go	swimming / skating / … to the park / to a party / …	last week?
	play	football / tennis / chess / … the piano / the drums / …	last month?
	visit	your grandma / friend / …	last year?

Early finisher Think of more questions with Did you …? for your partner. Can you make funny questions too?
Did you go to the moon yesterday?

Hier kann wieder **KV 16: Appointment partners** zum Einsatz kommen.

2 Holidays

a) Make a double circle.
Ask what your partner did in the last holidays.

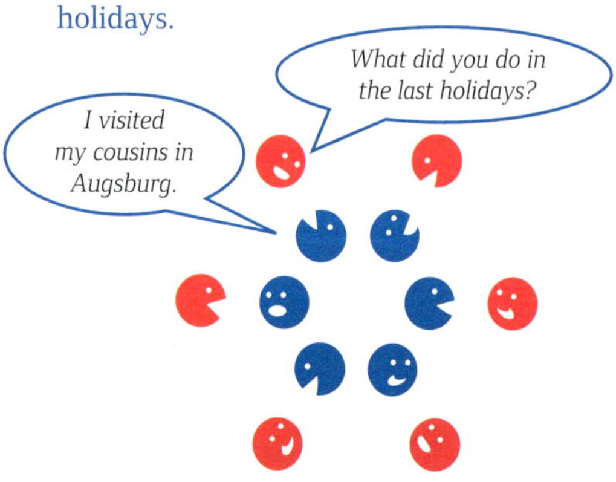

b) What can you remember about your classmates' holidays?

➜ **Workbook** *16–19 (pp. 60–61)*

Language help

Must, **needn't** and **mustn't** have only one form: *I/you/he/she/… must/needn't/mustn't*

must	(müssen):	*Baby seals must learn to catch fish.*
needn't	(nicht müssen/nicht brauchen):	*They needn't drink water.*
mustn't	(nicht dürfen):	*They mustn't leave their mother.*

→ *GF 25: must, needn't, mustn't (p. 197)*
→ **Workbook** *20 (p. 62)*

3 Abby knows about seals *(must, needn't, mustn't)*

Complete the dialogue with must, mustn't and needn't.

Box "hurt", Voc, S. 234

Abby: Seals can be scary. You … run away when you see them because they don't hurt you. But you … watch out. They sometimes come near your boat. You … touch them because they can bite. I sometimes see groups of seals on the beach when I'm with Skip. You … shout or make noise when you're near seals, but Skip barks all the time. Oh, it's four o'clock, but I … go till 4.30. I can tell you more about seals and their babies, so you … go on the internet.

Sam: Thanks, Abby, but no. I … be late for my kung fu class. It starts at 4.30. I … forget what you told me about scary seals when I write my project.

needn't • must • mustn't • mustn't • needn't • needn't • mustn't • mustn't

English and German are different

🇬🇧	*you mustn't*	*you needn't*
🇩🇪	*du darfst nicht*	*du musst nicht*

4 At a pony club

Auf einem Ponyhof begegnest du einer englischen Familie. Das Mädchen stellt dir ein paar Fragen. Beantworte sie auf Englisch. Verwende can, needn't, must oder mustn't in einigen deiner Antworten.

1 Are there riding lessons for children?
2 My little sister is only five. Can she have lessons too?
3 I don't have a riding hat. Must I wear one for lessons?
4 Can I wear shorts and trainers?
5 We have a dog. Can I bring him too?
6 What do I do if I can't come to a lesson?
7 Is there anything to eat and drink here? Do you have to bring snacks with you?
8 Can you feed the ponies?

Box "German "bringen"", Voc, S. 234

→ **Workbook** *21–23 (pp. 62–63)*

PONYHOF WIESER

Willkommen auf unserem Ponyhof im Tölzer Land!

Gäste werden gebeten, Folgendes zu beachten:

- Unsere Ponys dürfen ohne Erlaubnis des Reitpersonals nicht gefüttert werden. Bitte keinen Zucker mitbringen!
- Ponys mögen keinen Lärm. Bitte verhalten Sie sich in der Nähe der Ponys ruhig.
- Gehen Sie bitte nicht in den Stall. Unsere Ponys benötigen Ruhepausen.
- **Reitunterricht:** Wir bieten Reitunterricht für Kinder und Erwachsene in Gruppen- und Einzelunterricht. Für kleine Kinder (ab 5 Jahren) gibt es unseren Zwergerlkurs. Alle Preise und Informationen erhalten Sie auf Anfrage im Ponyhof Café.
- Für Reitstunden brauchen Sie keine besondere Ausrüstung. Es ist jedoch Pflicht, einen Helm zu tragen. Helme können kostenlos ausgeliehen werden. Reitstiefel sind nicht Vorschrift. Tragen Sie aber bitte feste Schuhe.
- Bitte beachten Sie, dass bei Kindern Reiten ohne Führung grundsätzlich nicht erlaubt ist.
- Wenn Sie eine Reitstunde absagen müssen, bitten wir Sie, uns zwei Tage vorher zu informieren.
- Beachten Sie bitte unsere Öffnungszeiten (s. Broschüre).
- Hunde müssen leider zu Hause bleiben.

1 Yes, children can learn to ride. • 2 Yes, she can. • 3 Yes, you must wear a helmet but you needn't have your own. • 4 Yes, you can. • 5 You mustn't bring your dog. • 6 You must tell the Ponyhof. • 7 There is a café. • 8 You mustn't feed the ponies.

KV 18

KV 18: Putting a page together enthält diese SB-Seite zum Ausschneiden, sodass die S die einzelnen Elemente hin- und herschieben können.

5 STUDY SKILLS Putting a page together

Plymstock School News is the school paper at Plymstock. Imagine you work for it.
Last week you asked Abby for a story and now you have to put a nice page together.
Here are the four paragraphs from Abby's story, and two titles, two drawings and two captions.

A

1 It was dark when we arrived back in Wembury. And I was so happy to be at home!

2 I live in Wembury, so I often go sailing at the weekend. Last Sunday, I went sailing too, but it was different.

3 My friend Maya, my brother Tim and I sailed to a small beach near Ivy Island. There was a big group of seals on the beach. We walked around the beach and looked.

4 Later, we went back to the boat, but there was a big seal in front of it! We waited, but the seal didn't go away. Then the sea came in and took our boat. We swam back to the boat and some of the seals followed us, but we were okay.

B

Seals at Ivy Island

The sea took our boat

C

D

Back to the boat!

On the way to the beach

a) Match these labels to the letters A, B, C and D:

Captions D	Drawings C	Paragraphs A	Titles B

b) Read the Study skills box. Then:

1 Put the paragraphs in the right order. 2 · 3 · 4 · 1
2 Choose one of the titles for the story, or think of another title.
3 Choose one of the drawings, or make another.
4 Choose one of the captions, or think of another caption.
5 Arrange all the parts of the text on a page and put it into your My Book.

c) Compare your page with another group.

– Are the paragraphs in the right order?
– Do the titles tell you what the story is about?
– Do the captions go with the pictures?

➜ *SF 3: Putting a page together (p. 176)*

Study skills

Putting a page together

Wie gestaltet man eine gute Seite mit Text und Bild, z. B. für eine Schülerzeitung?

1 Ein guter Text hat eine kleine Einleitung, einen längeren Hauptteil und einen Schluss.
2 Der Text braucht eine Überschrift und evtl. auch Zwischenüberschriften. Überschriften verdeutlichen, worum es im Text geht.
3 Bilder liefern weitere Informationen – auch in den Bildunterschriften.

➜ **Workbook** *24–25 (p. 64)*

1 Plymouth, my hometown

a) In the film, the girl shows us her hometown. Watch the film. What did she show us? Choose A or B.

In the film I saw ...

A	B
a gym	a swimming pool
an ice cream	a pizza
boats	buses
a museum	the Aquarium

b) Watch the film again. What other things and places can you see in the film? Make a list. a girl • a restaurant • sailing boats • a police boat • a shopping mall • shops • the Hoe • ...

c) Compare your list with your partner. Agree on three places or things for a weekend in Plymouth.
– My top place is ... I also like ...

Für den Einsatz ohne DVD finden sie eine Audiodatei für diese Übung auf *www.cornelsen.de/access-bayern*

2 EVERYDAY ENGLISH A present for Ruby

a) Watch the film. What are Jack and Oliver's ideas for Ruby's present? What do they give her? Their ideas are: a bag, a T-shirt and a book. In the end they give her a bell for her bike.

b) Match the sentences below with sentences from the box.

So, together we have £10.
– That's enough to buy a good present.
Do you have any ideas? → What about a bag?
– W...
How much is it? → It's £16. That's too much.
Let's buy her a T-shirt. → No, that's a boring present.
Does she have any hobbies? → Well, she rides her bike.

~~That's enough to buy a good present.~~
It's £16. That's too much.
What about a bag?
Well, she rides her bike.
No, that's a boring present.
It's £9.99.

c) Watch the film again and check.

d) What presents can you buy for a friend? Talk to your partner and make a list.

e) Write a dialogue like in the film and act it out.

Hier kann wieder **KV 16: Appointment partners** zum Einsatz kommen.

Der Text beschäftigt sich mit dem auf S. 106 bereits angedeuteten Segelausflug von Abby und ihren Brüdern.

A baby seal

3 20 **15 October, a beach near Ivy Island, not far from Wembury.**

A baby seal with bright eyes moved over the sand and into a small pool of water. Then another little seal came … and another and another. But the pool was small, too small. So the seal with the bright eyes went back over the sand to the group of big seals on the rocks. She called and listened. She called again. Her mother called back. The baby seal was hungry and pushed her head against her mother's body. She drank the milk. It was so good. The morning sun touched the baby seal's body, and she fell asleep. When she woke up, she called her mother again. But her mother wasn't there.

The sun went down. The baby seal was hungry and called her mother. Her mother didn't come.

Box "Unregelmäßige Vergangenheitsformen", Voc, S. 235

The baby seal shouted at the sea. The sea didn't answer.

The morning came and the baby seals were ready to play after their milk breakfast. But not the seal with the bright eyes. She was too tired to play, and too tired to swim. When the sea came in, she moved back over the sand – away from the dark water.

18 October, near Ivy Island on the open sea. 3 21

Abby looked at her two brothers.

"Why can't I steer the boat?" she asked.

"Because you're only nine!" said Tim. +(to) be wrong

"Tim's right," said Will. "You're too young, Abby."

"That isn't fair," shouted the girl. She went to the front of the boat and sat down. "I can sail too! I won a trophy this year from Wembury Sailing Club!"

"Yeah, yeah. We know, Abby. Everybody in Wembury knows that!" said Tim.

Abby looked away, over the water. There was a small beach not far away. She looked again and saw something white.

"Hey look, what's that?" she asked.

Her brothers didn't look.

"Stop! I can see something," she shouted.

"We can't stop the boat, Abby," said her brother Will.

"But it's an animal – maybe a seal!" she said.

"It's only a rock, Abby," said Tim.

"No, it isn't," she shouted. "You didn't look. Stop the boat! We have to go back. Please!"

"Oh, OK," said Will. "Let's turn around, Tim!"

1 Did you get it?

Choose the right ending for each sentence. 1 c · 2 e · 3 a · 4 f · 5 g · 6 d · 7 b

1 The baby seal came out of the pool …
2 She was too tired to swim …
3 The boys didn't let Abby steer the boat …
4 Abby wanted to sail back to the beach …
5 Will called the rescue centre …
6 The baby seal's mother is dead …
7 Abby called the baby seal Silky …

because

a she wasn't old enough.
b she looked very soft.
c there were too many other seals there.
d she swam too near a ship.
e she didn't get any milk from her mother.
f she saw a seal there.
g the baby seal needed help.

"Aye, aye, Captain Blackwell!" They turned around and sailed to the beach.

"We're too near the rocks, Tim!" Will shouted. "Steer the boat away."

But Tim was too slow. The boat hit the rocks and threw Will into the water.

"Will! Are you OK?" shouted Tim.

"Yeah, yeah – I'm wet, but I'm OK!" said Will.

He and Tim pulled the boat onto the sand. Abby jumped down and ran to the animal.

"I *was* right! It *is* a seal!" she shouted.

"Be careful, Abby. Don't go too near it. Seals can bite."

"But I think it's sick," said Abby. "Call Mum, please …"

"I can't. My phone is wet."

"Here, Will, take my phone," said Tim.

The two men put the baby seal into the cage.

❖

22 "And don't touch the seal!" said Mum. "Call the rescue centre. Here's the number."

Will called the centre. The woman asked him lots of questions.

"Now just wait for us … and please, don't go too near the seal," said the woman.

They waited. Tim was hungry. Will was cold. Abby watched the baby seal.

"Please don't die," she said again and again.

The rescue team came by boat. "They're here, they're here!" shouted Abby. Two men and a woman pulled their boat onto the sand. They had a cage.

"Poor little seal," said the woman. "She needs food. She didn't get enough milk from her mother."

"They usually fight," said the woman. "But this little baby is too tired and hungry."

"Where's her mother?" asked Abby.

"Well, yesterday, we found a dead seal not far from here."

"Oh, no!" said Abby.

"Yes, the poor girl swam too near a ship's propeller."

"That isn't fair," said Abby.

"No, it isn't. But you found her baby before it was too late. That's good."

"We're ready," said one of the men. "It's time to go." He looked at Abby and said, "You found her – so you can give her a name."

Abby thought for a minute. "She looks so soft," she said. "I know! Call her Silky."

2 New words

Here are some new words from the story:

body *(l. 10)* · fair *(l. 32)* · front *(l. 33)* · steer *(l. 54)* · cage *(l. 80)* · propeller *(l. 92)* · before *(l. 94)* · soft *(l. 99)*

Did you understand them
- from the pictures?
- because they are like German words?
- because they are like other English words?

Or did you check them in the Dictionary?

➔ *SF 4: Understanding and looking up new words (pp. 177–178)*

3 On the rescue team

Neigungsdifferenzierung: Die S wählen je nach Neigung eine der kreativen Aufgaben aus.

You choose Do a) or b).

a) In groups of four (Will, Abby, woman and man from rescue team) act out the story of the rescue.

b) Imagine you were the woman on the rescue team. Tell the story of the rescue to the paper Devon News. Write about 100 words.

A boy called the rescue centre. His name was Will Blackwell. There was a problem with a baby seal …

➔ **Workbook** 26 (p. 65)

Workbook Checkpoint 4 (pp. 66–69)

Step 1–4 sollten wegen der Gruppenarbeit im Unterricht durchgeführt werden. Es bietet sich aber auch an, die Selbsteinschätzung ausführlich mit den S im Plenum zu besprechen.

A memory game

Make a memory game and play in your group.

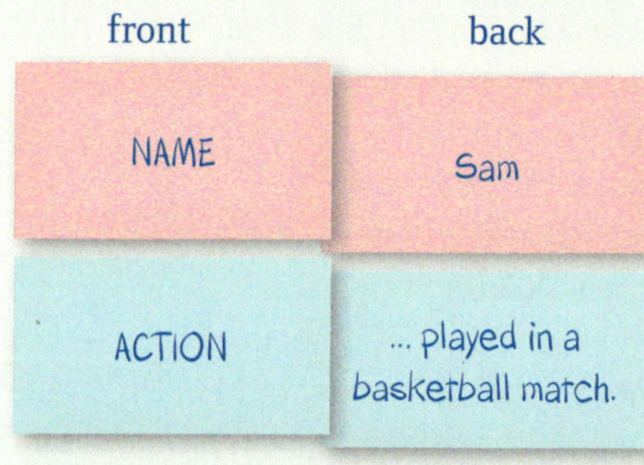

STEP 1 Make 12 NAME cards for characters in your book.

Write NAME on one side and a name (Sam, Lucy, Silky ...) on the other. You can use names twice.

STEP 2 Make 12 ACTION cards, one for each name card. Write ACTION on one side and a typical action for the person on the other side. Use the simple past.

STEP 3 Check the spelling and simple past forms on the cards. Correct mistakes.

STEP 4 Swap your set of cards with another group. Play 'Memory'. Find correct pairs of NAME and ACTION cards. Who has the most? You can use these phrases:

Whose turn is it?[1] · It's my/your/Maria's turn.[2] · Yes, that's right. · Those cards go together. · No, that's wrong. · They don't go together. · Great, I get these two cards. · That's the end of the game. · Count your cards. · Maria is the winner.

Wie gut warst du?

Wie schätzt du dich selbst ein? Schreibe die Sätze unter *Words, Grammar* und *Speaking* in dein Heft ab und ordne dir für jede Frage eine Ampelfarbe zu.

- (rot) Das lief nicht gut, ich muss mehr üben.
- (gelb) Das war OK, aber ich könnte besser werden.
- (grün) Das habe ich gut geschafft.

Words
Konntest du dir nützliche Wörter für 'actions' schnell ins Gedächtnis rufen und fehlerfrei schreiben?

Grammar
Hattest du Schwierigkeiten beim Gebrauch der unregelmäßigen Verben?

Speaking
Konntest du beim Spielen einige der Redewendungen zu Step 4 spontan anwenden?

Wie kannst du besser werden?

Dort, wo du dich rot oder gelb eingeschätzt hast, helfen dir folgende Tipps.

Words
Suche im *Vocabulary* (z. B. Units 3–4) und in den Wordbanks Wörter für Aktivitäten/Handlungen.

➜ *Wordbank 6 S. 172–173*

Grammar
Hilfe bei der Bildung und der Verwendung des *simple past* findest du hier:

➜ *GF 22–24:* simple past *(pp. 196–197)*
➜ *List of irregular verbs (pp. 269–270)*
➜ *Exercises: 1, 2 (p. 100), 3, 4 (p. 101)*

Speaking
Lerne die Redewendungen in dem Kasten zu Step 4 auswendig.

1 Whose turn is it? [huːz 'tɜːn] *Wer ist dran?* 2 It's my/your/Maria's turn. *Ich bin / Du bist / Maria ist dran.*

A

1 Opposites

a) Find and say pairs.

boring · bright · buy · cold · dark · early · exciting · hard · hot · late · pull · push · sell · soft

boring – exciting · bright – dark · buy – sell · cold – hot · early – late · hard – soft · pull – push

b) Write four sentences with a pair of opposites from a) in each sentence..
I like **bright** colours, not **dark** colours.

2 Lucy's birthday cake

Read the text to the end. Then put in the missing words.

'Oh, no. We don't have **e**... eggs for Lucy's birthday cake', **s**... Mrs Pascoe from the kitchen.
'I need four, but we have only two. Holly, can you go **s**... to the corner shop, please? I don't have time because I'm very **b**... with the party food.'
'OK, Mum. How **m**... eggs do you need?' Holly asked.
'Here's some money. **B**... a box of six, please, large eggs. You needn't buy more.
Kids are always **h**... so let's make lots of sandwiches too. And hurry up, please. The corner shop is only open till 6 o'clock today. Take your bike, but be **c**... with the eggs. You musn't **b**... them.'
On the **w**... to the shop, Holly **s**... her best friend, so she stopped. They talked and talked for **h**... an hour.
Holly **f**... the time – and the shopping for her mum too.
'Oh, you're back, Holly. Good. Did you get the eggs?' asked her mum.
'Erm, well, I'm **s**... about the shopping, Mum, but there **w**... a small **p**... You see.'

enough · shouts · shopping · busy · many · Buy · hungry · careful · break · way · saw · half · forgot · sorry · was · problem

3 A great day

Choose words from the box in the correct form to complete the text. You don't need all the words. First, read the text to the end.

bell · cage · cinema · excited · grandparents · holidays · invitation · life jacket · magazine · mobile phone · picnic · ride · sights

On Saturday, all Lucy's friends had an … to her party. She had a … on the Hoe with some great food, and all her friends were … when they went for a … on the Wheel. Lucy got some presents too: two music …, some … tickets from Holly, books and DVDs and a new … from her parents and… . That was cool, but her best present was a big surprise from Maya and Abby: an orange … so that she can go sailing with them.

invitation · picnic · excited · ride · magazines · cinema · mobile phone · grandparents · life jacket

4 Last weekend

Tell a partner about last weekend.
Say where you went, what you saw and did, who you met.
Use time phrases: *On Saturday morning/… In the afternoon,…*
Ideas: *stay at home/in bed, visit friends/family, go to the shopping mall/cinema/zoo/…*

On Sunday after breakfast, I went to Scotland. At lunchtime, I was in Wales and in the evening I had an invitation to Buckingham Palace in London! And you?

5 Saturday (Simple past: positive statements)

Put in verbs from this unit in the simple past.

Last Saturday ... the day of Sam's basketball match against Devonport. The teams ... very excited. In the second half, it was noisy because the Plymstock fans ... a lot. Sam ... two points in the last minute, so Plymstock ... the match. Great! Mr Taylor, their teacher, ... up and down.
In the afternoon, all the kids ... to the Hoe for Lucy's birthday party. Abby ... late because she ... the bus. After a ride on the Wheel they ... a great picnic. Mr Pascoe ... Sam lots of questions about the basketball match, and Sam ... all the kids his medal.

was • were • shouted • made • won • jumped • went • was • missed • had • asked • showed

6 Sam's 'to do' list (Simple past: positive and negative statements)

- stay in bed till 10'o clock ☺ ✓
- make bed ☹ ✗
- have a big breakfast! ☺ ✓
- clean bike ☹ ✗
- meet friends! ☺ ✓
- do English homework ☹ ✗
- buy a sports magazine! ☺ ✓
- throw away old music magazines ☹ ✗

a) Look at Sam's 'to do' list for Sunday. What did he do? What didn't he do? Write three more sentences like the example sentence. Use positive and negative forms in each sentence.
1 He stayed in bed till 10 o'clock, but he didn't make his bed.
2 He ...

b) Find four things on Sam's list that you didn't do last Sunday. Write four sentences.

7 Sorry, what did you say? (Simple past: mixed questions)

On the phone, Sam tells you about the weekend with Tom from London. You don't understand some things because it's noisy. Ask Sam questions with *what, where, when, why* or *how*. Sam said:

1 Tom arrived on Friday afternoon.
Sorry, when did Tom arrive?
2 After dinner, we played chess.
Sorry, what ...
3 Tom went to bed early because he was tired.
4 On Saturday, we went to the Barbican by bus.
5 I showed him the Elizabethan House.
6 We had an ice cream at the harbour.
7 Tom liked the Wheel and the Hoe.
8 Later, we went swimming at the Lido.
9 We went home at 6 o' clock.
10 After dinner, we watched a DVD

2 What did you play? • 3 Why did Tom go to bed early? • 4 How did you go to the Barbican? • 5 What did you show him? • 6 Where did you have ice cream? • 7 What did Tom like? • 8 Where did you go swimming? • 9 When did you go home? • 10 When did you watch a DVD?

8 MIXED BAG Sam's visit to London

Put in the missing words. Write verbs in the simple past.

Sam ... to London ... bus. He ... on Friday evening. 'Hi! Welcome back to London!' Tom ... .
'... you have a good bus **r**...?' ... his dad. 'Yes, ..., thanks. But it's a long ... from Plymouth'.
'Well, we can see all the London **s**... and we can go ... the **c**... . There's a new Will Smith film ... the Odeon,' said Tom. 'What's the film **a**...?' asked Sam. 'It's an **e**... action film,' answered Tom. 'But I **n**... tell you the story now. I can do that later. How about an XXL pizza? You **m**... be hungry.'
On Saturday they ... around town. They **l**... in sports shops and Sam **b**... two sports **m**... to read on the bus. They **s**... for a sandwich at a café and later they ... computer games in a computer shop. Sam was **e**... because he was back in London. He **l**... London at 3 o'clock ... Sunday afternoon. Tom and ... mum ... him to the bus. Sam was sad, Tom too.
... home in Plymouth Sam said, 'Hi! I'm back. And **g**... what, London is **s**... really cool.'

went • by • arrived • said • Did • ride • asked • I did • way • sights • to • cinema • at • about • exciting • needn't • must • walked • looked • bought • magazines • stopped • played • excited • left • on • his • took • Back • guess • still

B

9 Justin's cousin

a) Read Justin's story and answer the questions.

One weekend in May, Justin's cousin from Liverpool came to visit. Before Katie arrived, Mrs Skinner said to Justin, 'Katie is 15. I'm sure you can think of some nice places to show her. You can go to a museum. You needn't stay there all day. Then you can have an ice cream at the harbour.'
'But Mum, I don't know her. I saw her once when I was five. And I want to meet my friends.'
'Well, this weekend you can do something with Katie. You mustn't be unfriendly. Aunt Emily was always nice to you when you were little.' So Justin made a plan for Saturday.
After breakfast, he and Katie took a bus to the Hoe. Katie didn't want to go on the Wheel, but they went up Smeaton's Tower. Then they walked to the harbour. Katie didn't want to go on a boat trip, so they just watched the boats and the seals. They didn't talk much.
At home, Justin said, 'Mum, Katie and I don't have much to talk about. She wasn't very excited about the Plymouth sights. But I think she likes shops. She was in a shopping mall most of the time.
I just waited outside and texted my friends. Maybe she thinks I'm just a kid, and she doesn't really want to be friends.'
'Or maybe she's just quiet. Why don't you show her your video camera and tell her about your film-making?' asked his mum. Suddenly Katie came into the kitchen.
'Video camera? You have a video camera, Justin? Film-making is my favourite hobby!' she said.
'What? It's my favourite hobby too! Why didn't you tell me?' answered Justin, very surprised.
'Well, you didn't ask. And I'm very unhappy because I couldn't find my camera yesterday. I think I left it on a bus. Mum and Dad gave it to me for my birthday, so I couldn't tell them. I looked at new video cameras in the shopping mall today, but I can't buy one. What can I do? I'm really worried.'
'Oh, so that's why you were ...,' said Justin. 'Well, come on. You can see my films, and you have to tell me about your films. Do you want to see my scary film about a ghost? It's fun. My Dad works in a film studio in Boston and he shows me how to edit and do some really great things and ...
They talked and talked.
On Sunday after lunch, Katie took the train back home. Justin said, 'It was great with Katie, Mum. Can she come again in summer?'

1 When did Katie visit the Skinners?
2 Are Justin and Katie the same age?
3 Was Justin happy about Katie's visit?
4 What did they do on Saturday? Say three things.
5 What was Mrs Skinner's good idea?
6 Did Katie like the Plymouth sights?

b) Katie was quiet when she was in town with Justin. Say why in a few sentences.

a) 1 She came one weekend in May. • 2 Katie is older than Justin. (15) • 3 No, he wasn't. • 4 They took a bus to the Hoe/went up Smeaton's Tower/watched the boats and the seals/ ... • 5 She tells Justin to show Katie his video camera. • 6 She wasn't very excited about the sights.

C

10 A nice weekend visit

Imagine a cousin came to visit you for a weekend. Write an email to an English friend about where you went, what you saw and did with your cousin. Use your computer and write about 120 words.
Use some words from Unit 4: *shopping mall, cinema, magazine, mobile, exciting, boring ...*
Use time phrases: *On Saturday morning,... /First,/After that, ... In the evening, ...*

Last weekend, my cousin ... from ... came to visit us. He's/She's ...and he/she likes ..., so we went ...
We didn't ... because ...

Access to cultures

London

1 Here we go – to London!

3 23 a) Listen to Morph and read along. Answer his questions.

I have lots of books about London in my library, with some great pictures. I'd love to go there. What do you know about London? How many people live there? I know that Queen Elizabeth lives there! She has a very nice house. What's its name? Do you know?

2 Young people in London

3 24–27

a) Listen and read along. Which sights do the young people talk about? Write a list of the names

A: Buckingham Palace • Tower of London
B: Houses of Parliament & Big Ben • River Tham
Natural History Museum
C: London Eye • Hyde Park
D: Tower Bridge

A

I live in Philadelphia in the USA. It's cool – but London is very cool. This is my second visit. I just love Buckingham Palace. I did the tour there. Wow! And the Tower of London is a 'must see'. There's so much history and tradition.

C

We're from Sydney, Australia. This is our first time in London. Yesterday we went on the London Eye. You can see for miles from the top. It was fantastic! We love Hyde Park too. We were at a concert there last night. People just sit on the grass and listen. Great bands! London rocks!

B

I come from India. This is my first visit to see my aunt and uncle and cousins here. Last week they showed me some great sights, like the Houses of Parliament and Big Ben. Then we went on a boat trip on the River Thames. We visited the Natural History Museum too. There's a great dinosaur there – dead, of course! It's a really cool place for kids. I have to go there again.

D

I live in London. I'm a student here. I think people from all countries of the world live here! There are lots of places to see, but I love the parks, the churches and the museums because it's quiet there. I often sit in the sun and read. Tourists often ask me about places to see. I always tell them to go to Tower Bridge. It's cool when it opens to let a ship sail through, but we have some great markets, theatres, discos and sports centres too. And the shopping is fantastic! London is never boring.

b) Look at the photos. Match them to the sights on your list from 2a).

I think that's Hyde Park because ...
Yes, that's right. And that must be ...
I don't know what number ... is. Do you know?
...

1 Tower of London · 2 Natural History Museum · 3 Tower Bridge · 4 London Eye · 5 London Buses · 6 Homeless people in London · 7 Prince William and Kate · 8 Buckingham Palace · 9 Hyde Park · 10 Houses of Parliament/Big Ben

1

2

3

4

5

6

7

8

9

10

c) Choose a picture from 2 b) and describe it to your group. They have to guess the number of your picture. You can use these words and phrases: *on the right/left, in the middle/ background/ foreground, behind, next to, in front of.*

In my picture there's ... on the right. In the middle there are ...   I know. That must be picture ...

Box "left – right", Voc, S. 237

3 A London quiz

Write eight questions for a class quiz about London.
Ask about places, sights and people. Ask your questions in class.

Who is/are/lives/.... Where/What/When/How... do/does/can/... ? How many people ...?
What's the name of ...

4 What about you?

a) Would you like to go to London? Tell a partner what you would like to see and do there. Say five or more things.

b) Tell a partner three things about the capital city of your country.

➜ **Workbook** *p. III*

By the sea

Cawsand Beach, near Plymouth

1 Cawsand Beach

a) Look at the photo of the beach.
What can you see in it?
Write down as many words as you can.

b) Compare your list with a partner's.
Add words to your list.

2 At the beach

3 28

a) Now imagine you are at Cawsand Beach.
Listen and write down what you hear.
Think about what you can feel, and write that down too.
I can hear a seagull. I can feel the sun on my face.

b) In a group, talk about Cawsand Beach.
Say what you would like to do there.
A: I'd like to swim in the sea and look for Silky.
B: I'd like to go sailing and catch fish.

Box "Unregelmäßige Vergangenheitsformen", Voc, S. 237

3 One, two, three, four, five

3 29–30

Listen and learn the rhyme. Then sing along.

Grund-schule

Track 3.30 ist die Instrumentalversion.

One, two, three, four, five,
Once I caught a fish alive.
Six, seven, eight, nine, ten,
Then I let it go again.

Why did you let it go?
Because it bit my finger so.
Which finger did it bite?
This little finger on the right.

Your task

Am Ende dieser Unit wirst du …
… Argumente für einen Urlaub in Bayern sammeln.
Dann wirst du deinen englischen Cousin mit deinen Argumenten überzeugen, dich im Sommer zu besuchen.

→ Workbook *1 (p. 70)*

1 An afternoon in Cawsand

Last weekend, Justin, Lucy, Maya, Abby and Sam went to Cawsand Beach.
Justin made a film of their trip for his dad.

A 3 31
Hi, Dad, it's Saturday, 11:36. I'm at Sutton Harbour with my friends. We want to take the ferry to Cawsand Beach. Lucy is late. Can you see her? She's wearing a pink top. And she's running. Maya and Sam are calling her. Abby is on the ferry too, but you can't see her. She's inside.

B 3 32
Hey, Dad, we're at the beach now. It's 12:30. Sam is running after the girls. They're playing °tag and Sam is "it". But he's much too slow.
Hey, come on Sam – you aren't running fast enough.

C 3 33
Now it's time for a group photo. Look, here's Abby with her new camera. She's smiling at the others, but uh-oh – they aren't smiling at her. They're making silly faces.

D 3 34
The others are swimming now. I'm not swimming. It's too cold for me. At the moment, I'm looking at °rock pools. You can see all kinds of sea life there.
Hey, what's that sound?
It's coming from my rucksack. Oh, it's my mobile. Somebody is calling me. … Sorry, Dad, that was Lucy. It's time for our picnic.

E 3 35
Hi, Dad. The picnic is over.
Hey, Maya! That's my …
Hi, Mr Skinner. This is Maya. Justin isn't filming now. I'm filming! So now you can see Justin with his friends – Sam, Lucy and Abby.

F 3 36
Hey, Dad. We're on the ferry now. Look at the girls. They're all laughing. Sam is telling jokes again. It's almost 5 o'clock – we're going back home. It was a really great day.

2 Justin's film

Read text A. Match it to the right picture (1–6). Then read texts B–F and match each one to a picture.

A4 · B2 · C5 · D6 · E1 · F3

KV 19: Justin's film bietet *Right/wrong-statements* zur Überprüfung des Textverständnisses.

3 Have a go

a) What are the kids doing? Choose the right phrase from the box.

making silly faces · playing °tag with the girls · running to the ferry · ~~smiling at the camera~~ · telling jokes

In photo 1, Abby, Justin, Sam and Lucy are smiling at the camera.
In photo 2, Sam is ...
In photo 3, Sam is ...
In photo 4, Lucy is ...
In photo 5, Maya, Sam and Lucy are ...

2 … playing tag with the girls.
3 … telling jokes.
4 … running to the ferry.
5 … making silly faces.

b) Play the game 'I spy …'.
Take turns to ask and answer like this:

Abby
Justin
Sam
Lucy
1

Maya
2

3

4

5

6

Looking at language

a) The table shows how you make the present progressive. Copy it and write in more examples from the text on p. 122. Look at the spelling of the ing-forms.

➜ *GF 26: The present progressive (p. 198)*

b) How do you make negative sentences in the present progressive? Check p. 122 for examples.

Subject + form of *be*	-ing form	
I'm	looking	for crabs
You're	eating	my sandwiches.
Sam is	tell…	jokes.
She's	wear…	a pink top.

English and German are different

In German there are no progressive forms:

Sam is telling jokes.

Sam erzählt gerade Witze.

1 Reading, writing and running (*-ing* forms)

KV 20: Reading, writing and running enthält die Tabelle sowie ein Wimmelbild, das die S schriftlich beschreiben.

a) Look at the table. What is different about the spelling of the -ing form in groups 2 and 3?

Group 1	Group 2	Group 3
read > reading	write > writing	run > running
…	…	…

➜ *GF 26 b: The present progressive (p. 198)*

b) Copy the table from a). Add these words to the right group:

arrive · come · get · give · go · laugh · play · sit · sleep · swim · take · win · work

Early finisher ➜ *p. 165* **Early finisher:** Die S lösen Rätsel.

Group 1 (unverändert): go, laugh, play, sleep, work · Group 2 (letzter Buchstabe verschwindet): arrive, come, give, take · Group 3 (letzter Buchstabe verdoppelt): get, sit, swim, win

2 At Cawsand Beach (Present progressive: positive statements)

Silky and Spot are at the beach. Finish the sentences with a form of *be* and the -ing form of these verbs: *come, catch, film, look, move, sit, smile*.

1 It's 4:50. Silky and Spot are swimming in the sea near Cawsand Beach.
2 They … for some crabs for dinner.
3 The ferry … . Lots of kids … on it.
4 It … very fast.
5 Silky: There's a boy with a camera. He … and he … us.
6 Spot: And we … fish. Hurry up!

2 are looking · 3 is coming … are sitting

4 is moving · 5 is smiling … is filming · 6 are catching

➜ **Workbook** *2 (p. 71)*

3 After the picnic (Present progressive: positive statements)

a) Say what is happening in the picture. Take turns. You can use the verbs in the box.
The dog is smelling …

eat · film · listen · play · read · sleep · ~~smell~~ · text · walk

b) Write five sentences about the picture.

➜ **Workbook** *3–4 (pp. 71–72)*

The dog is smelling Justin's rucksack. · Justin is filming a seagull. · The seagull is eating a worm. · Maya is reading a book. · Maya is listening to music too. · Lucy is texting. · Abby and Sam are playing chess. · Three crabs are walking on the beach. · A seal is sleeping.

4 I'm not laughing. I'm singing.
(Present progressive: positive and negative statements)

3 37 a) Listen. What sounds do you hear? Make two sentences for each sound: one positive and one negative.

1 I ... (laugh). I ... (sing).
I'm not laughing. I'm singing.
2 He ... (read). He ... (sleep).
3 She ... (walk). She ... (run).
4 They ... (play) tennis. They ... (swim).
5 We ... (eat). We ... (watch) TV.
6 She ... (play) the guitar. She ... (play) the piano.
7 I ... (feed) the dog. I ... (feed) the cat.
8 They ... (speak) English. They ... (speak) German.

2 isn't reading / is sleeping · 3 isn't walking / is running · 4 aren't playing / are swimming · 5 aren't eating / are watching · 6 isn't playing / is playing · 7 I'm not feeding / I'm feeding · 8 aren't speaking / are speaking

b) Make positive and negative sentences about the people in the picture. More help → p. 162

More help: Die korrekten Verbformen müssen in Lückensätze eingetragen werden.

5 Today is different (Simple present and present progressive)

Finish the sentences with the right form of the verbs in brackets.

1 Silky usually (eat) ... crabs for breakfast, but today she (eat) ... fish.
Silky usually eats ..., but today she's ...
2 Justin often (drink) ... milk for breakfast, but this morning he (drink) ... tea.
3 Sam often (walk) ... to school, but today he (ride) ... his bike.
4 Sam and Justin usually (sit) ... together in the canteen, but today Sam (sit) ... with Oliver.
5 Lucy and Maya often (ride) ... their bikes to the Hoe, but today they (go) ... by bus.

1 eats / is eating · 2 drinks / is drinking · 3 walks / is riding · 4 sit / is sitting · 5 ride / are going

Language help

Use the simple present to talk about routines.
In the summer, Lucy often **swims** at the Lido.
Sam **plays** basketball at 3 pm on Thursdays.
Justin usually **talks** to his dad at the weekend.

Use the present progressive to say what somebody is doing now.
Lucy and Maya **are swimming** at the Lido now.
At the moment, Sam **is playing** basketball.
It's 3 o'clock on Saturday. Justin **is talking** to his dad on Skype.

6 A phone call (Simple present and present progressive)

a) Write a dialogue for a phone call. Use the simple present with signal words (usually, always, at the weekend/...) and the present progressive with signal words (now, at the moment, today/...), like this:

A Hi! It's me. I'm sitting at home at the moment. It's boring. I usually meet my best friend on Saturdays, but today he/she is visiting an aunt. My brother/sister ... . What about you?
B Well, I often ... at the weekend, but at the moment ... . My mum/brother/sister ...

TIP Signal words
With the simple present you can use: *always, often, usually, sometimes, never, every week/ Sunday, on Saturdays, at weekends*

With the present progressive you can use: *now, today, at the moment*

b) Learn your phone call and act it out for the class.

→ Workbook 5–6 (p. 72)

1 On Lucy's phone 3 38

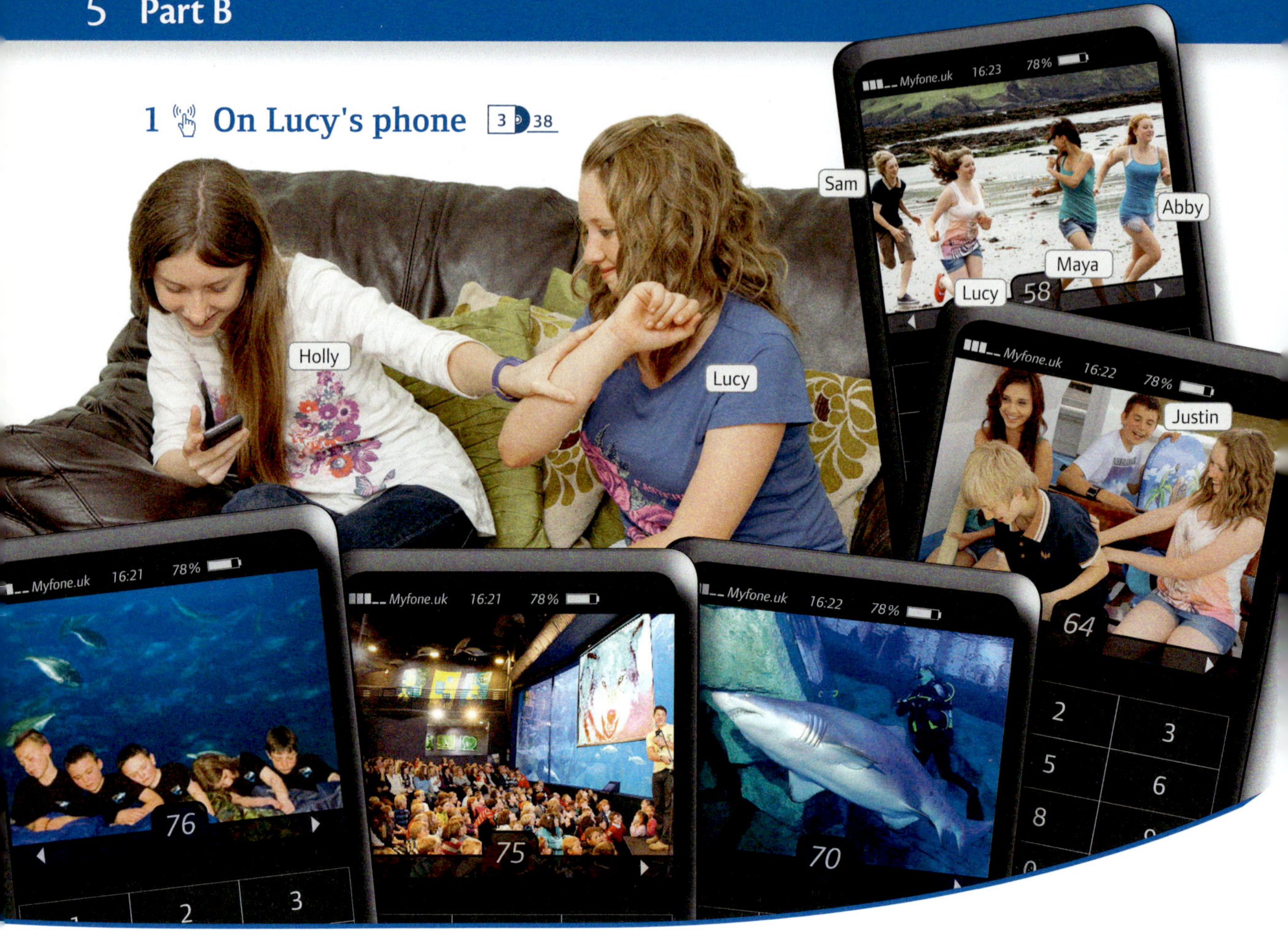

Holly: Hi, Luce, do you want to play cards?
Lucy: I can't. I'm working on a mini-talk for school.
Holly: No, you aren't. You're looking at your mobile.
Lucy: Yes, silly. My talk is about the sleepover at the aquarium. And my sleepover photos are on my mobile.
Holly: Let me see. Here, give me your mobile. Right. Are those kids really sleeping?
Lucy: Yes, they are. They're sleeping in front of an aquarium window.
Holly: What's this? Are you watching the fish?
Lucy: No, we aren't. We're watching a film about fish.
Holly: How was it?
Lucy: It wasn't bad.
Holly: But where are the sharks? At the sleepover, you sleep with sharks, right?
Lucy: Right.
Holly: But there aren't any sharks.
Lucy: Of course there are sharks! Look.
Holly: At last! A shark! What's that diver doing?
Lucy: It's feeding time, so he's feeding the sharks.
Holly: That's a scary job! Now, wait a minute, what's this? Why are you pushing that boy?
Lucy: What boy?
Holly: That blond boy. Are you fighting with him?
Lucy: No, I'm not. That's my friend Sam. Abby took that photo. We're …
Holly: Is that at the sleepover?
Lucy: No, it isn't. Give me back my phone!
Holly: No, let me look at these photos first. Oh, now you're running away from that boy.
Lucy: Give me back my phone, Holly.
Holly: No, these photos are fun. Here you're running away from that *blond* boy. And then you're pushing him onto the floor. Mum! Come and look at Lucy's photos! They're really interesting!

2 Did you get it?

a) Find lines in the text that go with the photos on Lucy's mobile.

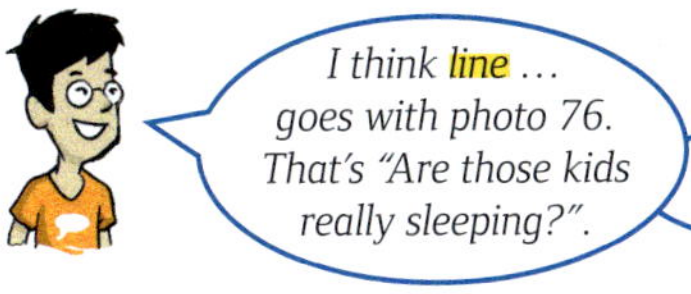

b) Look at the photo of Lucy and Holly. Find a line in the text that goes with it.

c) Does Lucy want to show Holly her photos? Why? / Why not? How is she feeling: angry, happy, worried, …?

Background file

The aquarium in Plymouth

The National Marine Aquarium in Plymouth is the biggest in the UK.
It has four zones:

- **Plymouth Sound:** Sea life in the Plymouth area
- **British Coasts:** Sea life in all parts of Britain
- **Atlantic Ocean:** Sharks and Caribbean sea life
- **Blue Planet:** Sea life from every ocean and from Australia's Great Barrier Reef

Children at the National Marine Aquarium

The aquarium has a learning centre for children. Students are welcome at the centre.

Children between 6 and 12 can have birthday parties at the aquarium.

There are four sleepovers (Sleeping with sharks) every year.

Sleeping with sharks – the programme

- Arrive at 7 pm
- Watch a 4D film
- Aquarium tour – see what fish do at night
- Games
- Midnight snacks
- Breakfast in the aquarium café
- Sleepover finishes at 9 am
- Price: £35

You choose Do a) or b):

a) What would you like to see and do at the aquarium? Write a short text.

b) Would you like to go to the sleepover with sharks? Why/why not? Write a short text.

Neigungsdifferenzierung: Die S wählen aus zwei Aufgaben diejenige aus, die sie mehr anspricht.

3 At the aquarium

Nach der Schule erzählst du einem/einer Freund/in über das Aquarium. Vervollständige den Dialog.

You: Es gibt vier Abteilungen, zum Beispiel über das Meeresleben in der Gegend um Plymouth.
Friend: Geht's da nur um Plymouth?
You: Nein, … es gibt auch Abteilungen über den Atlantik, die britische Küste oder das Great Barrier Reef.
Friend: Bieten sie etwas Besonderes für Kinder?
You: Sie haben ein Schülerzentrum und Geburtstagspartys. Und nachts kann man da schlafen.
Friend: Eine Übernachtung im Aquarium? Wie geht das?
You: … Das heißt "Sleeping with sharks", weil man da nachts Haie beobachten kann.
Friend: Und das kann man jede Nacht machen?
You: Nein, nur in den Ferien.
Friend: Und was macht man da genau?
You: … Man kann einen Film in 4D gucken oder eine Tour machen.

More help → p. 162, → SF 10: Mediation (p. 181)

More help: Die S finden hier deutschsprachige Hilfen.

→ Workbook 7 (p. 73)

Language help

In the present progressive, you use the verb *be* in questions and short answers.

Am I		Yes, I am. /No, I'm not.
Are you	waiting?	Yes, you are. / No, you aren't.
Is he/she/it	leaving?	Yes, he/she/it is. No, … isn't.
Are we	swimming?	Yes, we are. / No, we aren't.
Are they		Yes, they are. / No, they aren't.

Why are you laughing? *Are you telling silly jokes?*
What is Lucy doing? *Is she having fun?*

➔ *GF 26 c: The present progressive (p. 198)*

1 Is he drinking? (Present progressive: questions)

KV 21: Are you fighting? bietet Bildkarten zu *Miming activities*.

Partner B: Go to page 167.
Partner A: Ask what's happening in pictures 1–3.
You can use verbs from the box.

A: In picture 1, is the boy drinking?
B: No, he isn't.
A: Well, is he …?

dance · drink · eat · look for · make · play · read · sing · text · write

1

2

3

Partner A: Go to page 242. Partner B: Ask what's happening in pictures 4–6.

4

5

6

2 Where is he going? (Present progressive: questions)

Sam and his sister Lily are watching a film. Lily has lots of questions. Finish them.
Use *Where*, *What* and *Who*.

Sam: That's Captain Goldfinger, Lily. He's bad! He's going to the harbour now.
Lily: Sorry Sam, (go) …?
Where is he …?
Sam: To the harbour. And look! A policeman is following Goldfinger.
Lily: (follow) … Goldfinger?
Sam: A policeman. Hey, there's Goldfinger's team. They're meeting on that boat.
Lily: (meet) …?
Sam: On the green boat.
Lily: Oh no, it's Goldfinger, Sam. (give) … them?
Sam: A CD – with important information. Hey! The policeman is swimming to the boat.
Lily: (swim) …?
Sam: To the boat. Oh, Lily, it's 8 o'clock – time for you to go to bed.

Where is he going? • Who is following Goldfinger? • Where are they meeting? • What is he giving them? • Where is he swimming?

More help ➔ *p. 163*

More help: Die Fragewörter sind vorgegeben.

➔ **Workbook** *8–9 (pp. 73–74)*

3 What's happening?

Write a question in the present progressive about each picture.
Take turns to ask and answer your questions.

1 
2 
3 

A: In picture one, what is the man doing?
B: I think he's … /Maybe he's …

4 WORDS Adjectives

a) Finish the sentences with the opposites of the underlined words.

1 fast • 2 interesting • 3 bad • 4 same • 5 bright

1 Lucy: Little fish are usually slow, but sharks are really … .
2 Holly: Was the information about sharks boring? – Lucy: No, it wasn't. It was very … .
3 Holly: Was the film at the aquarium good? – Lucy: Well, it wasn't … .
4 Lucy: At the aquarium there are different kinds of sharks. They aren't all the … .
5 Lucy: Some fish had only dark colours, but I liked the fish with lots of … colours best.

b) Find the opposites of these adjectives. Then make sentences with the adjective pairs.

blond · late · loud · sad · soft

1 blond – dark: Sam has blond hair, but Justin's hair is dark.
… 2 late – early • 3 loud – quiet • 4 sad – happy • 5 soft – hard

5 Sea Life in Munich

Du hast Gäste aus London zu Besuch, die gerne ins Sea Life in München gehen würden. Du schaust nach Informationen im Internet und machst dir Notizen. Verwende die Notizen unten, um die Fragen deiner Gäste auf Englisch zu beantworten.

- im Olympiapark
- geöffnet täglich 10-19 Uhr
- über 4.500 Meerestiere - Haie, Quallen, Riesenschildkröten
- Berührungsbecken - Krebse, Seesterne
- viele verschied. Hai-Arten, auch Gitarrenhaie
  Fütterung Mo-Fr 14.30,
  Sa-So 11.30-12.30
- Unterwassertunnel → tolle Fotos
- Kindergeburtstage - Feier mit Spielen, Schatzsuche, Geschenk-Freikarte f. 1 Jahr
- Eintritt EUR 12,50 (bis 14 J.), online EUR 9,50, auch Familienkarten
- Imbissstube u. Souvenirshop

1 yes (over 4,500 sea animals) • 2 at Olympiapark • 3 touch crabs/see sea turtles/celebrate birthday/… • 4 €12.50 per child (up to 14 yrs) • 5 yes (lots of different sharks) • 6 yes (snack bar) • 7 yes (at the souvenir shop) • 8 10am–7pm (daily)

→ **Workbook** *10–12 (pp. 74–75)*

1 Partners

Box "Unregelmäßige Vergangenheitsformen", Voc, S. 239

3 39

After lunch on Thursday, Sam walked to the next lesson with Justin.

"What's your poster about?" he asked.

"Poster?" said Justin. "What poster?"

"We have to make a poster about our favourite place by the sea – and give a mini-talk! Remember?"

"Oh, that poster," Justin said. "Er … I don't know yet."

"Miss Bell says we can work with a partner," Sam told him. "Do you want to be my partner?"

"OK. Let's give a talk about Cawsand then," Justin said. "I really liked it there."

"Good idea," Sam agreed, "Cawsand and smugglers …"

+(to) agree on sth.

"Smugglers?" Justin asked.

"Yes, there were lots of smugglers in Cawsand. I know that because I saw a sign about it in the village."

"But I know nothing about smuggling," Justin said.

"That's all right, Justin. I have a book about smuggling at home," Sam said. "We can work at my house on Saturday."

"Saturday? Yes, why not?"

❖

On Saturday, Justin and Sam looked at Sam's book. Justin pointed to a picture of a woman. "She looks funny. How can she be so fat?"

"She isn't really fat. She looks fat because she's smuggling something under her clothes," Sam explained.

"That's clever. Let's use that picture then," said Justin.

"Well, maybe," said Sam. "But what can we talk about? We have to know what our mini-talk is about before we make the poster."

"All right," said Justin. "But we have to use that picture on our poster. It's so good. Or draw a picture like it."

"OK," Sam said. "So let's work on our talk first. Then …"

"… then we make a poster for the talk," Justin went on, "and find more good pictures for it."

2 The boys' project

a) Finish the sentences.

1 Justin wants to give a talk about Cawsand because … .
2 Sam knows about smugglers in Cawsand because … .
3 Sam has a book about smuggling, so … .
4 The boys have to work on their talk before … .
5 The woman in the picture looks fat because … .

1 … he really liked it there. • 2 … he saw a sign about it in the village. • 3 … they met at Sam's house. • 4 … they make a poster for the talk. • 5 … she's smuggling something under her clothes.

b) Write two more sentences about the text like in part a) for a partner. Your partner has to finish them.

Remember to check!

3 The poster

CAWSAND

Our favourite place by the sea

Cawsand today

- Cawsand is a village near Plymouth with a great beach.
- Lots of tourists go there by ferry. It's only 30 minutes from the Barbican.

- 18th and 19th centuries: lonely villages like Cawsand were great places for smuggling.
- Smugglers' ships arrived with tea, pepper and other expensive goods.
- Smugglers sold their goods in Plymouth.

+cheap

Smugglers often hid goods in their clothes.

Cawsand – a really cool place!

4 Poster check

+(to) check

a) Say what you like about Sam and Justin's poster.

b) Now use this list to check Sam and Justin's poster. What is good? How can they make it better?

Almost everything is there. They forgot the names of the authors.

A good poster has:
- a title
- a subtitle
- important information only
- different colours
- pictures with captions
- names of authors

OK, there's a title.

Yes, the title is CAWSAND.

5 The mini-talk

3 40

a) In their mini-talk, Sam and Justin give extra information about Cawsand. Listen. Which of these points do they talk about? Write down the numbers.

1 what you can see on Cawsand Beach
2 what tourists do at Cawsand
3 where you can eat at Cawsand
4 how often smugglers came to Cawsand
5 how smugglers took their goods to Plymouth
6 why smugglers smuggled tea and pepper

b) Say which numbers you wrote down and why.
Justin talks about number 1. He says ...

Then listen again and check.

1 STUDY SKILLS Preparing and giving a mini-talk

You have to prepare a mini-talk about your favourite character from this book or your favourite film/ sports or pop star. Follow these steps:

a) Collect information about your character.
Use the profile in your MyBook and think about these things:
- your character's home
- age
- family and friends
- likes and dislikes
- hobbies, activities, clubs
- school

➜ SF 2: Collecting information (pp. 175–176)

b) Make a poster about your favourite character.
- Give your poster a title.
- Use the information from a) and write about your character (keywords only).
- Write in big letters so that everyone can read the poster.
- Look through the book. Choose and copy your favourite pictures of your character.
- Write captions for your pictures.
- Put the title, texts, pictures and captions on your poster.

➜ SF 3: Putting a page together (p. 176)

c) Give a mini-talk for one minute about your favourite character to your group. Your poster and the box on the right can help you.

You can use these phrases:
- My favourite character is ...
- I like him/her because ...
- It was funny/interesting/exciting/sad/... when he/she ...
- I was angry/happy when ...

Study skills

Giving a (mini-)talk
1 Steh auf, atme tief durch und zähle bis 3, bevor du anfängst.
2 Schau deine Zuhörer an, wenn du sprichst.
3 Sprich langsam, laut und deutlich.
4 Wenn du den Faden verlierst, schau schnell in deine Notizen.

➜ SF 6: Giving a mini-talk (p. 179)

d) Make a copy of the table and fill it with smileys: ☺ 😐 ☹. Say what you liked about the mini-talks and what your partners can do better next time. Then listen to your partners' feedback.

	You looked at us when you talked.	We could hear you.	Your talk was interesting.	Your talk was easy to understand.
Lukas	☹	☺	😐	☺
Cem	😐			
Lena				

e) Who is your group's favourite character? Tell the class.

➜ **Workbook** 13 (p. 76)

2 They smuggled pepper because ... (Word order)

Language help

The word order in English statements is:

S(ubject) – V(erb) – O(bject)
They smuggled pepper.

! The word order in English sub-clauses is also S-V-O:

They smuggled pepper because they needed money.
Sie schmuggelten Pfeffer, weil sie Geld brauchten.

➜ GF 27: Word order (III) (p. 199)

a) Join the sentences with the word in brackets. Sometimes the sub-clause can come first.

1 Justin wanted to give a talk about Cawsand. He really liked it there. (because)
Justin wanted to give a talk about Cawsand because he really liked it there.
2 Sam knew a lot about smugglers. He had a book about them at home. (because)
3 The boys were nervous. They started their talk. (before)
4 The students asked questions. Sam and Justin finished their mini-talk. (when)
5 Their mini-talk was over. The boys were happy. (after)

2 ... because he had a book about them at home. • 3 ... because they wanted to work on the poster. • 4 ... when Sam and Justin finished their mini-talk. • 5 ... when their mini-talk was over.

b) Write the sentences in the right word order.

1 Morph – lives – in the library, – where – he – lots of books – read – can.
2 He – likes – English – because – it – a – cool language – is.
3 The Plymstock students – never see – Morph – because – he – in the day – sleeps.
4 He – gets up – when – the students – at home – are.
5 He hides – when – he – the school cat –sees.

Early finisher Write a sentence from the text in the wrong word order. Find a partner. Can he/she put the words in the right order?

➜ **Workbook** 14 (p. 77)

b) 1 Morph lives in the library, where he can read lots of books. • 2 He likes English because it is a cool language. • 3 The Plymstock students never see Morph because he sleeps in the day. • 4 He gets up when the students are at home. • 5 He hides when he sees the school cat.

3 THINKING ABOUT LANGUAGE English nouns in other languages

a) Think about the nouns in the box. Which do you use in German with the same sound and meaning? Which noun from the box do we not use in German?

hobby · jeans · job · mobile (phone) · smiley

b) Use the Vocabulary (pp. 199–238) and find more English nouns like in a). How many can you find? z.B.: tip • tour • pool • house • song • photo • elephant

c) Do you use the nouns from a) and b) in other languages? Make word stars on the board with your language and/or your name, like this:

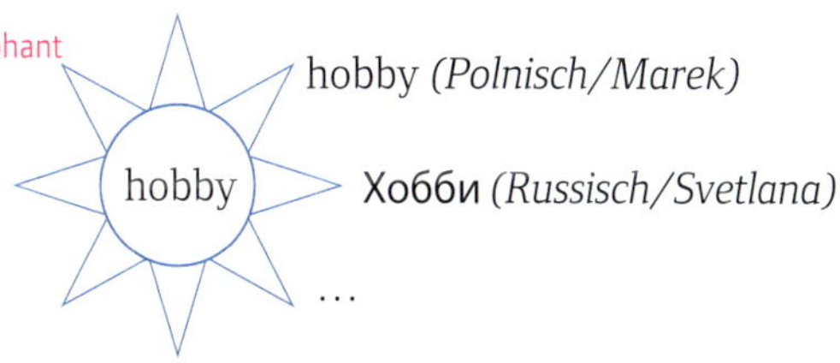

d) Make a table for your words in a) - c), like this:

English	German	Other languages
hobby	Hobby	hobi, hobby, Хобби, ...
jeans	Jeans	...

KV 17: Welcome to sunny Torquay bietet einen weiteren Lesetext zu Devon und kann hier eingestzt werden, wenn das noch nicht auf S. 104 geschehen ist.

Background file

Box "First, Second, Third …", Voc, S. 240

Devon for tourists

There are many reasons why families like to go on holiday to Devon. It has something for everyone.

First, it has some beautiful °sandy beaches. Second, you can walk or ride your bike for miles along the coast with fantastic sea views.
Third, tourists like to drive along the coast roads and visit the old °fishing villages. There are lots of tours, so you can go there by bus too. Some of the villages, like Clovelly on the north coast, were smuggling villages in the 18th and 19th centuries, so you can hear exciting stories about smugglers.
Devon is perfect for walking and climbing too. There aren't any high mountains in Devon, but there are some high hills. Dartmoor National Park is very popular with tourists. There aren't any dangerous animals on Dartmoor, but there are some small snakes in the hills. They can bite, so dogs must be careful.

Devon has everything. There are national parks, old castles full of history, museums, some fun parks, great shopping, excellent °seafood – and Devon cream teas too!

Clovelly

°Hillwalking on Dartmoor

Do you think Devon is a great place for a family holiday? What would you/your family like to see and do there? Tell a partner.

4 A holiday in Devon *(some and any)*

The Bennetts are talking about holidays.
Put in some or any.

Mum: Let's stay in Devon. We can go on some day trips.
Dad: Good idea. There are … great places on the coast. We don't know … tourist places on the south coast, like Torquay. There are °palm trees there.
Sam: But there aren't … interesting things for kids.
Dad: You're wrong, Sam. There are … great hillwalks and farms on Dartmoor. There are … very good museums and old castles too.
Sam: Are there … scary castles with ghosts? And are there … fun parks with cool rides?
Mum: Well, we can look for …
Lily: Are there … dangerous animals in Devon?
Sam: Of course there are, Lily. But they're in the zoos, silly!

some · any · any · some · some · any · any · some · any

Language help

For German *'einige, ein paar'* use **some** in positive statements and **any** in negative statements and questions:

*There are **some** great beaches.*
*There aren't **any** high mountains. ('keine')*
*Are there **any** snakes in Devon?*

➜ GF 28: some and any (p. 199)

5 Let's go to Cornwall! (*some* and *any* and compounds)

The Bennetts are still talking about holidays. Complete their conversation with *some, something, somebody* and *any, anything, anybody*.

Dad: Well, what about a holiday by the sea in Cornwall? ... told me that there are ... great surfing beaches.
Does ... know ... about surfing?
Mum: Sorry, I don't know ... about it. But Cornwall is a good idea. I know ... in Bude. Maybe we can visit them.
Sam: Mum, it's a holiday. We don't want to visit ... in Bude. We want to do ... exciting.
Mum: Well, ... ideas?
Sam: Are there ... old castles with ghosts in Cornwall?
Dad: Well, there's Pengersick Castle. It has the most ghosts in the UK.
Sam: Oh yes, let's go there!

Somebody · some · anybody · anything · anything · somebody · anybody · something · any · any

TIP
Look at Language help (***some*** and ***any***) on p. 134 again.

Use ***something/somebody*** in positive statements and ***anything/anybody*** in negative statements and questions.

Someone and ***anyone*** are the same as ***somebody*** and ***anybody***.

➔ *GF 28: some and any (p. 199)*

More help ➔ *p. 163*

More help: Die S wählen aus zwei Formen die korrekte aus.

➔ **Workbook** *15–16 (pp. 77–78)*

6 WORDS What's correct? (*go, drive, ride*)

a) Read the Background file on page 134 again and look for sentences with the verbs *go, drive* and *ride*. Write them down and think about what they mean in German. Check with a partner.

b) Now complete the dialogue with go, drive or ride in the correct tense and form.

Sam: We usually ... to Wales on holiday, but last year we ... to Scotland.
Maya: Did you ... by car or by bus?
Sam: We ... by car. Mum usually ... .
Maya: My brother wants to learn to ... , but he's too young. He ... his bike to school.
Sam: I ... my bike to school too, but when it's wet mum sometimes ... me.

go · went · go · went · drives · drive · rides · ride · drives

7 WORDS Get it right!

For some German words there are two English words. Which word do you need?
Some English words look like German words, but do they mean the same?
Complete the sentences with correct words from the box.

become · card · finished · game · get · get up · happy · hour · lake · lesson · lucky · match · ready · sea · stand up · ticket

1 Maya: We sometimes go for a picnic to a big ... in a park.
2 Sam: On Saturday I had to ... early. It was the day of the basketball ... .
3 Holly: I think fish in aquariums are ... . They don't have to look for food.
4 Justin: I like chess. It's a really good ... .
5 Sam: On Mum's birthday, Dad bought theatre ... . Mum was really ... .
6 Lucy: It's my cousin Melissa's birthday soon. I must send her a ... .
7 Justin: Why did some people in Cawsand ... smugglers?
8 Lucy: At Plymstock there are five ... every day.
9 Abby: Did you ... a nice birthday present from your grandma?
10 Holly: That was the last question. Now I'm ... . I can get ... to go to the party.

➔ **Workbook** *17 (p. 78)*

lake · get up · match · lucky · game · tickets · happy · card · become · lessons · get · finished · ready

1 A ferry trip to Cawsand

a) You're on the ferry to Cawsand.
What can you see?

b) Watch the film and put photos A–F in the right order. D · F · C · E · A · B

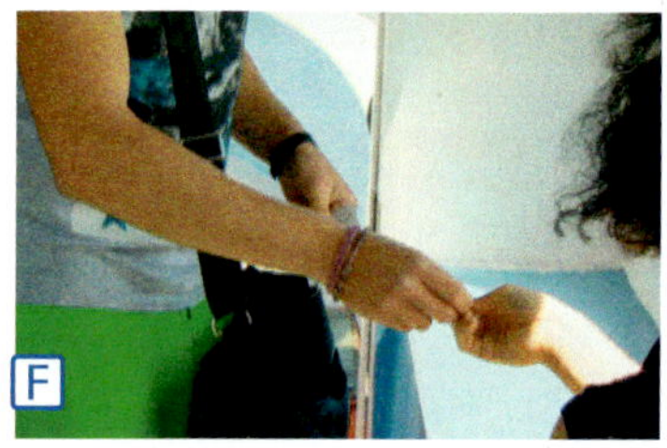

c) Match the photos with these captions:

D Welcome to Cawsand ferry! · F Buy your ticket on the ferry. · C Cawsand Beach from the ferry

A A walk in Cawsand village · B Hello Plymouth! · E Be careful when you get off!

2 EVERYDAY ENGLISH Making plans

Für den Einsatz ohne DVD finden sie eine Audiodatei für diese Übung auf *www.cornelsen.de/access-bayern*

a) Watch the film.
What are the children's ideas for a trip?
Where do they decide to go?
- Jack wants to go ...

Jack: Lido first, then Cawsand Beach; doesn't want to go to Wembury Beach · Ruby: Wembury Beach · Oliver: doesn't want to go to the Lido

They decide to go to Wembury Beach.

b) **Think**: Write the name of two fun places in your hometown. Say why you would go there and what you would do there.

Pair: Talk to a partner. Give reasons why you like or don't like the different places. Agree on one place. Use the phrases in the box.

What about ...? · I agree. · I don't agree with you. · Yes, you're right. · I like / love swimming / sailing / playing / ... · How do we get there? · That isn't a good idea. · That's a great idea. · OK, let's go to ...

EXTRA **Share:** Work in groups of four. Agree on one place. Tell the class where your group wants to go.

1 You say ... the [əʊ]- or the [ɒ]- sound

3 41–44

a) Listen to the words.
1 [əʊ] is the sound in 'most', 'old', 'photo'. 2 [ɒ] is the sound in 'soft', 'top', 'copy'.

b) Which sound do you hear? Listen to the ten examples and write down the number of the sound. Then say the words aloud.

c) Look at the pictures. How many words with an [əʊ]-sound can you find? 3, 4 or 5? Listen and check.

1
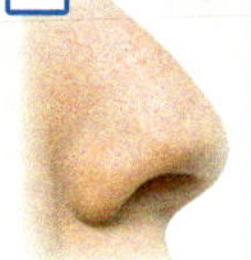
2

3

4

5

6

d) Practise with Morph. Write Morph's sentence with [əʊ] or [ɒ] after seven of the words.

Oh [əʊ], no [əʊ]! There's a frog [ɒ] on [ɒ] my nose [əʊ] and it's so [əʊ] cold [əʊ]!

2 Sounds and symbols

3 45

Match the words and the symbols. For help look at **English sounds** on p. 268. Listen and check.

1 live	A [liːv]	5 at	E [et]	9 shoes	I [tʃuːz]
2 H	B [eɪdʒ]	6 called	F [kɔːld]	10 choose	J [ʃuːz]
3 age	C [eɪtʃ]	7 cold	G [kəʊld]	11 word	K [wʊd]
4 leave	D [lɪv]	8 ate	H [æt]	12 would	L [wɜːd]

1 D • 2 C • 3 B • 4 A • 5 E • 6 F • 7 G • 8 H • 9 J • 10 I • 11 L • 12 K

3 Intonation (Questions)

3 46

a) Listen to the questions. How many kinds of questions can you hear? What's different?

1 What are the kids talking about? down
2 What are their ideas for a trip? down
3 Does Jack want to go to Cawsand? up
4 Do you get there by ferry? up
5 Where do they decide to go? down
6 How do they get there? down
7 Do they know how much ferry tickets are? up
8 Can you see seals from the ferry? up

b) Read the questions to a partner. He/She must check if your voice goes up or down. Take turns. Then listen again and check.

c) Write a dialogue about ideas for a trip.
Use statements, yes/no questions and Wh-questions.
Remember where your voice goes up and down at the end of sentences.

A Where can we go on Saturday?
B I don't know. Do you have any good ideas?
A What about ...? Do you know it?
B ...

d) Learn your dialogue and act it out for the class.

→ Workbook 18 (p. 79)

PLAY The pepper smugglers

Scene 1: 3 47

There are three smugglers at the Red Lion in Cawsand. Molly's brother Flynn wants to join them. Molly is worried.

Molly: Cook! Come and look! There are three smugglers in the dining room!

Cook: Don't be silly, Molly! They're just poor farmers. I know them: that's Tom White, and the others are Jack Hill and Old Bill.

Molly: But look, they're drawing maps and plans. They're pepper smugglers, Cook, and my brother Flynn wants to work with them.

Cook: They *were* farmers, Molly. But they had to sell their farms to Mr Collings.

Molly: Yes, but …

Cook: And then Mr Collings took away your parents' farm too! Now he's rich and we're all poor.

Molly: But …

Cook: That isn't right, my girl. That isn't right.

(Flynn comes in. He looks excited.)

Flynn: Come, sister, dance with me! *(They dance.)* Soon you can have your new dress.

Molly: But I don't want a new dress! You can't go with those men, Flynn! Please …

Flynn: I have to go, Molly – I don't want to be poor all my life. We have a great plan. But there isn't much time. Please come and help me.

Molly: But …

Cook: Go and help your brother! I don't need you here. Good luck!

(Molly and Flynn go out.)

Scene 2: 3 48

Cawsand Beach at night. Tom, Jack, Flynn and Old Bill wait for the ship with their pepper. Mr Collings watches from a hill.

Flynn: Tom, someone is watching us.

Tom: *(He holds up his lamp.)* Where?

Flynn: On the hill there. *(He points.)*

Tom: Where? There's no one on the hill, Flynn. Your eyes are playing games with you.

Jack: Look! Did you see the blue light from the sea?

Tom: Yes, that's the sign. The ship from France is here with our pepper.

Jack: Come on, then, let's go!

(They go to the ship in their boat. Men from the ship throw bags to Flynn and Tom.)

Tom: This is hard work, my boy. But we can sell the pepper for lots of money in Plymouth.

Bill: Hurry up, boys! Put the bags in the cart.

(They take the bags of pepper to the cart.)

Jack: Come on, boys! Morning is coming.

Tom: OK, Jack, that's the last bag.

Bill: Good. Now to Tom's house!

Scene 3: 3 49

In Tom's kitchen. Molly and Flynn put the bags of pepper into boxes.

Flynn: Now hide the pepper under these potatoes. Like that, yes.

Molly: *(She hides the bags.)* Mr Collings was at the Red Lion last night. And he knows about your plans.

Flynn: Oh, that's silly, Molly. Mr Collings never goes to the Red Lion.

Molly: But it's true! Collings wants to stop you. He's dangerous, Flynn, and he has a sword.

Flynn: Don't try to stop me, Molly, please!

(Jack arrives.)

Jack: The others are ready, my boy. Take the boxes outside.

(Five minutes later.)

Flynn: This is the last box. Goodbye, Molly.

(He tries to give Molly a hug. Molly pushes him away and runs outside.)

Scene 4: 3 50

Tom's boat at Cawsand Beach. Molly arrives. She hides in the boat. Flynn and Tom arrive. They carry the boxes of potatoes onto the boat.

Tom: Flynn, are you ready? We're going to the market in Plymouth.

Flynn: I'm ready.

Tom: OK, let's go.

(Mr Collings arrives with his sword and points it at Flynn.)

Mr C: No, you can't go to Plymouth – it's prison for you! I know what's in the boxes. You're smugglers! Now move! Out of the boat!

Flynn: Mr Collings! So, *you* were on the hill yesterday! Tom, what can we do?

(Molly throws potatoes onto the deck. Mr Collings falls. He gets up again. He still has his sword. Molly gets up and throws pepper into his face.)

Molly: Your family took away our farm, but you can't take more away.

Mr C: Ah – ah – aaaah – choo!

(Mr Collings sneezes and Tom takes his sword.)

Flynn: Now you get off our boat!

(Mr Collings jumps off the boat. Tom throws the sword after him.)

Tom: What you can't do with a sword, you can do with pepper.

(They all laugh. Flynn gives Molly a hug.)

Flynn: To the market! Let's go to Plymouth!

A year later, Collings and his men caught the smugglers on Cawsand beach. They had to go to prison for a long time …

1 New words

Here are eight new words. Find them in the play.

farmer · rich · good luck · light · market · sword · deck · sneeze

l. 7 • l. 17 • l. 33 • l. 43 • ll. 82, 106 • ll. 69, 94, 99, 102, 103 • l. 93 • l. 99

Are they like any German words you know?

Farmer • reich • (viel) Glück • Licht • Markt • Schwert • Deck • niesen

2 The four scenes

a) Choose the best title for the first scene.

1 Look, Cook, look!

2 A new dress for Molly

3 At the Red Lion

b) Now write titles for the other three scenes.

c) Make a programme for the play. List your titles for each scene. Give information about the story and the characters.

KV 22: A theatre programme bietet eine Mustervorlage für ein Theaterprogramm.

3 Your play

Neigungsdifferenzierung: Die S wählen zwischen zwei unterschiedlichen kreativen Übungen.

You choose Do a) or b).

a) Make a group of seven students. Choose your actors. Learn the play.

Think about each scene. What can you use as a kitchen, the beach, the smugglers' boat, …? Act out the play for your class.

b) Draw a comic strip for each scene in the play. Use speech bubbles and captions to show the story.

Es bietet sich an, im Anschluss an die Arbeit mit dem SB mit den S eine **Lektüre** zu lesen.

➜ **Workbook** *19 (p. 79)*

Workbook Checkpoint 5 (pp. 80–83)

Step 1–4 können als vorbereitende Hausaufgabe durchgeführt werden, an die sich in der Folgestunde die Partnerarbeit in **Step 5** anschließt. Es bietet sich aber auch an, die Selbsteinschäzung ausführlich mit den S im Plenum zu besprechen.

Holidays in Bavaria

Du möchtest, dass dein englischer Cousin dich in den Sommerferien besucht. Gib ihm Touristeninformationen über Bayern.

STEP 1 Schau dir den Flyer an und suche Informationen heraus, die für deinen 13-jährigen Cousin interessant wären.

STEP 2 Sammle die Informationen in einer Mindmap oder einer Tabelle: z. B. Orte, Sehenswürdigkeiten, Aktivitäten, Sport.

STEP 3 Überlege, wie du deinem Cousin auf Englisch über die großartigen Aktivitäten und Sehenswürdigkeiten in Bayern berichten kannst. Übersetze nicht und verwende deine eigenen Worte.

STEP 4 Stell dir vor, dein/e Partner/in ist dein englischer Cousin. Erkläre ihm, warum ein Besuch in Bayern in den Sommerferien eine großartige Idee ist.

BAYERN *ist:*

Berge und Seen, Burgen und Schlösser, Bauernhöfe, Brauchtum, Blasmusik und Bayrisch Creme, Geschichte und Gastfreundschaft, Action und Erholung, Sport, Spiel und Spaß, die Metropole München und das größte Volksfest der Welt! Bayern bietet auch 1.200 Museen und Kunstgalerien, 40 Theater und Opernhäuser! Und diese vielen Attraktionen genießen über 31 Millionen Besucher pro Jahr! Hier einige Touristen-Highlights für jung und alt:

- *z. B. eine erholsame Bootsfahrt auf dem smaragdgrünen Königssee, im Herzen des Nationalparks Berchtesgaden.*

- *Bei jedem Wetter ein Foto wert: das Märchenschloss Neuschwanstein vom bayerischen König Ludwig II. Danach eine leckere Brotzeit in der Füssener Altstadt!*

- *Ein Freizeitparadies für die ganze Familie finden Sie im Bayern Park: über 80 Attraktionen wie z. B. abenteuerliche Wasserfahrgeschäfte und Achterbahn!*

- *Auch der Sport kommt nicht zu kurz: Radtouren und Wanderungen im Frankenwald, Angeln und Wassersport jeder Art an kristallklaren Seen, Bergsteigen und Klettern, im Winter Skifahren, Snowboarden und Rodeln.*

Wie gut warst du?

Wie schätzt du dich selbst ein? Schreibe die Bereiche *Organizing information* und *Mediation* in dein Heft ab und ordne dir für die Fragen eine Ampelfarbe zu.

- (rot) Das lief nicht gut, ich muss mehr üben.
- (gelb) Das war OK, aber ich könnte besser werden.
- (grün) Das habe ich gut geschafft.

Organizing information

Welche Organisationsform hast du verwendet: Mindmap oder Tabelle? Wie gut hat das geklappt?

Mediation

Wie einfach war es, nur die wichtigsten Informationen auf Englisch mit eigenen Worten wiederzugeben?

Wie kannst du besser werden?

Wenn du dich eher rot oder gelb eingeschätzt hast, helfen dir folgende Tipps beim Wiederholen und Üben.

Organizing information

➜ *SF 2: Collecting information (S. 175–176)*

➜ *Study skills in Unit 3 (U3, S. 74)*

Mediation

Wähle vorher aus, was du an Informationen weitergeben möchtest. Überlege, wie du diese Inhalte in einfachen Sätzen mit bekannten Vokabeln auf Englisch ausdrücken kannst.

➜ *SF 10 Mediation (S. 181)*

Schau dir auch die Mediation-Aufgaben in allen Units noch einmal an:

➜ *S. 30, 58, 82, 109, 127, 129*

A

1 One word or two?

a) Find pairs of green and orange words.
Do you write them as one word or as two words?
ferry ticket, ... grandparents • ice cream • life jacket • mobile phone • sleepover • shopping mall

ferry · grand · ice · life · mobile · sleep · shopping

cream · jacket · mall · over · parents · phone · ticket

b) Look for more words like ferry ticket in the Vocabulary (pp. 199–238) Write them down.
school bag, ... swimming pool • guinea pig • pencil case • corner shop • living room • police officer • boat trip • phone call • ...

2 Have fun!

a) What goes together? Find words in the box that go with verbs 1-6. Write a list.
1 do 2 get 3 go 4 have 5 make 6 take
1 do judo, do ...

angry · a wish · breakfast · for a walk · friends · fun · judo · photos · shopping · sport · turns

a) 1 do the shopping, do sport • 2 get angry, get breakfast • 3 go for a walk, go shopping • 4 have breakfast, have friends, have fun • 5 make a wish, make breakfast, make friends, make fun • 6 take photos, take turns

b) Use your list from a) and write a sentence with each verb.

c) Think of more words that go with the verbs. How many can you find?
do your homework/..., get cold/ ...do the dishes/... • get off the bus/get ready/get up • go down/go home/go on/go on a boat trip/go together/go with sth./... • have lunch/ have dinner/ have a go/have a look/... • make sth. better/make a mistake/... • take place/take care of sb./sth./...

3 A day out

Read the text to the end. Then put in the missing words.

It was a hot Saturday in July. Jeff and Max wanted to go on a **t**..., but they couldn't agree ... a good place to visit. 'Let's have a day ... the sea. We can take the **f**... to Cawsand,' said Jeff. Max agreed ... his friend that Cawsand was a good idea because his dog, Sammy, loved the beach too.
An hour later, they arrived ... Cawsand beach. Sammy got ... the ferry **f**... , and the boys followed. Sammy saw another dog, and he ran ... it.
'Oh, look, I think Sammy is looking ... crabs. Dogs have good noses. Maybe he can **s**... some crabs under the rocks, ' said Jeff.
'I know, he often finds crabs. But crabs can bite. They can be **d**... , but I can't **e**... that ... Sammy,' Max went ... .
Suddenly, Sammy started ... bark. 'Max, look ... Sammy! He's running up and ... the beach, ... a mad dog. What's the matter ... him?' asked Jeff.
'Oh, no! Poor Sammy! I think he found a crab - again.' *(Vocabulary pp. 233–238)*
trip • on • by • ferry • with • at • off • first • towards • for • smell • dangerous • explain • to • on • to • at • down • like • with

4 By the sea

Talk to a partner. Ask and answer questions about holidays by the sea.
Do you like beach holidays? Say why or why not.
Think about a beach holiday that you had.
Say where you went, what you saw and did, who you met.

A Do you like beach holidays?
B Yes, I do.

A What do you like to do best?
B ...

5 Justin's mail (Present progressive)

Finish Justin's email with some of the verbs in the box. Use the present progressive.

come · do · drink · film · have (2x) · phone · read · run · sit · smile · swim · take · wait · win · write

Hi , Dad!
It's nice today, so I'm at the Lido with my friends. Sam and Maya … in the pool. Oh, it's a race, and Maya … because she's better. Lucy … near me . She … postcards. Oh, now Abby … a photo of us, so we … at her. Big smiles! Sam and Maya … out of the pool now. Maybe it's too cold.
They … towards us now, and Abby … them. We … lots of fun!
What … you … today, Dad? It's 9 am in Boston, so maybe you … breakfast now.
Till next week, Justin

are swimming • is winning • is sitting • is writing • is taking • are smiling • are coming • are running • is filming • are having • are … doing • are having

6 Today is different (Simple present or present progressive)

Put in the missing verb forms.

After the first break on Wednesdays, class 7 EB usually … an English lesson, but today the students … a DVD with Miss Bell. They usually … English books or … exercises, but now they … because the DVD is funny. In Maya's class it's the music lesson, but today the students (not) … any work. They … loud pop songs in class, and one boy … (dance) on his desk. His friends … photos of him on their mobiles. Some other kids … to music on their MP3 players or they are … silly jokes. The students never … these things on other days. All the Plymouth students … lots of fun today, but why … they … mad things? Why is today different? Maybe it's because it's the last day of school before the holidays!

have • are watching • read • do • are laughing • aren't doing • are listening to/singing • is dancing • are taking • are listening • telling • do • are having • are … doing

7 Because … (Word order)

Read 'The pepper smugglers' (pp. 138–139) again.
Complete the sentences with *because*, *when* or *after* and a sub-clause.

1 The farmers are poor …
2 Molly is unhappy …
3 The men go to the ship in their boat …
4 Mr Collings is dangerous …
5 Collings falls on the deck …
6 Collings sneezes …

1 … because they had to sell their farms to Mr Collings. • 2 … because/when her brother wants to join the smugglers. • 3 … because they saw the blue light from the sea. • 4 … because he knows about the smugglers' plans and wants to stop them. • 5 … because Molly throws potatoes onto the deck. • 6 … when Molly throws pepper into his face.

8 MIXED BAG A phone call

A friend phones Justin. First, read what Justin says. Then put in the missing words.

"Oh! Hi Pete! Just now I … in the sun at the Lido. I … an exciting book about **s**… in Cornwall. In the 18th and 19th **c**…, lots of people were **f**… . They … in small **v**… on the **c**… of Devon and Cornwall. But **r**… men … away their farms, so then they were **p**… . They didn't have … money, … they **s**… goods from France, like tea and **p**… and other **e**… things. Then they … the goods at the **m**… . Smuggling was very **d**… . Smugglers often had to … the goods under their **c**…, so they … fat. My friend Sam … a lot … smugglers. He … me this book to read. Well, in the story, one night a **s**… is just … from France. Three friends … to the French ship in their little boat. But they are worried … they think **s**… is watching them from the hill. It's really exciting. Erm, can you phone me later maybe?"

am sitting • am reading • smugglers • century • farmers • lived • villages • coast • rich • took • poor • any • so • smuggled • pepper • expensive • sold • market • dangerous • hide • clothes • looked • knows • about • gave • ship • arriving • go • because • someone

B

9 Tourists in Plymouth

3 51–56

a) Paul Hill, his parents and his 7-year-old sister are tourists in Plymouth. Listen to six short scenes. What are the Hills talking about? Where are they? Put pictures A-F in the correct order. D · E · F · B · A · C

A

B

C

D

E

F

1 I think they are at ... because .... That's picture ... 2 ...

b) Listen again. Are the statements right or wrong? Correct the wrong statements.

1 The Hills start the day on the Hoe. right
2 Paul and his ~~mum~~ climb the tower. dad
3 They go to the Barbican before lunch. right
4 Paul wants to see the ~~Elizabethan House~~. sharks at the Aquarium
5 Paul ~~doesn't like shark~~s. thinks sharks are exciting
6 The boat trip is ~~two hour~~s long. about an hour

c) Answer the questions about scenes 4–6.

1 What does Lisa never want to do?
2 When is the Lido open for an evening swim?
3 Does Lisa want to go to the Lido or to a beach?
4 Why does Paul want to go to the shops?
5 What does Lisa want to see on Dartmoor?
6 What would Lisa like to eat in the café?

c) 1 She never wants to do a sleepover with sharks. · 2 It's open on Wednesdays till 7.30pm. · 3 She wants to go to a beach. · 4 He wants to look at video games. · 5 She wants to see the Dartmoor ponies. · 6 She would like a big ice cream.

C

10 Holidays: on a beach, in a city

a) Talk about one of the pictures for one to two minutes. What can you see? What are the people doing? First make notes.

1

b) Person A was on holiday in the place in picture 1. Person B was on holiday in the place in picture 2. Ask and answer questions about what you did and saw there, what you liked and didn't like. First make notes.

2

The USA and Canada

1 Welcome to the USA!

3 57 **a)** Listen to Morph and read along. Then answer his questions.

This is my map of the United States of America. It's a very big country. About 320 million people live there. Do you know how many states there are? Do you know the name of the capital? And what's the name of the big country north of the USA?

There are 50 states in the USA. • The capital is Washington D.C. • The country north of the USA is called Canada.

b) Now find these cities on the map:
New York, Washington D.C., San Francisco, Los Angeles, Miami.

Find Boston on the map. In the school holidays, Justin is going to visit his dad there. They're going to see lots of great places.

c) Think of US states, more cities, rivers and sights, for example the Grand Canyon. Make a list. How many places can you think of?

d) Take turns to name cities and states.

A: Where's Dallas?

B: It's in Texas.

ATC.3

2 Great places to visit!

In groups of three or four, talk about the pictures and match them to the cities in 1b). Which picture shows a city in Canada? Tell the class your answers.

A Well, picture number … is … because ….
Do you agree with me?
B Yes, that's easy. I think we all agree on that.

C But what about picture number …?
…
D I think picture … shows Canada.
What about you?

1 Miami (beach) • 2 Los Angeles (Walk of Fame) • 3 Washington, D.C. (White House) • 4 Ottawa/Canada (Canadian Flag, Mounties) • 5 San Francisco (Golden Gate Bridge) • 6 New York (Statue of Liberty)

1

2

3

4

5

6

3 My city

3 58

Listen to Dexter. He is talking about where he lives in the USA.
Which city does he live in? How do you know? Make notes.

(I think) Dexter lives in … because he talks about … He says … too.
Then he tells us about …

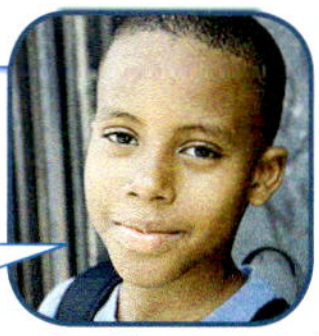

(I think) Dexter lives in New York because he talks about all the tourists. He says that over 8 million people live there too. Then he tells us about Central Park and other parks. He also talks about musicals on Broadway and skyscrapers. The One World Trade Center is one of the biggest ones. He mentions the Statue of Liberty as well.

4 A class quiz

Make eight questions for a quiz about the USA.
Ask about states, cities and famous sights. Exercises 1-3 can help you.

What/Where is…? What/Where can you see…?

5 A visit to the USA

Would you like to visit the USA? Why or why not?
Which city would you like to visit first? Say why.

Yes, I would really like to visit the USA. First, I'd like to … because …

→ Workbook p. IV

English as a world language

1 Morph's map

3 59 **a)** Read and listen to Morph. Look at the map.

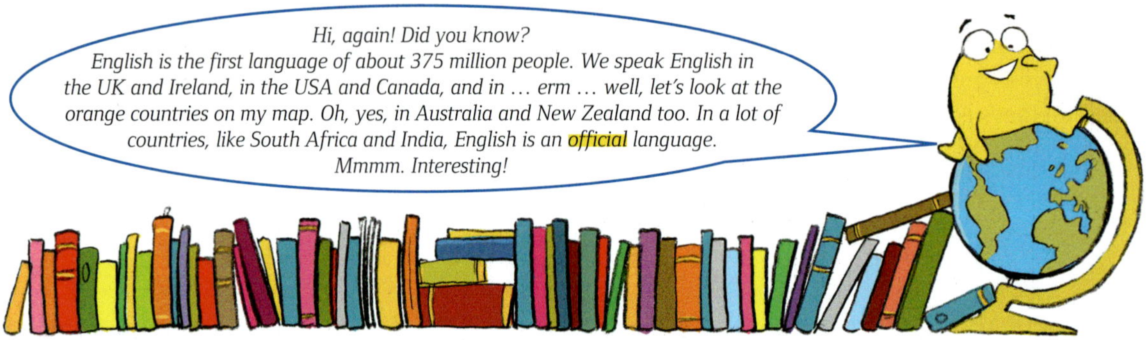

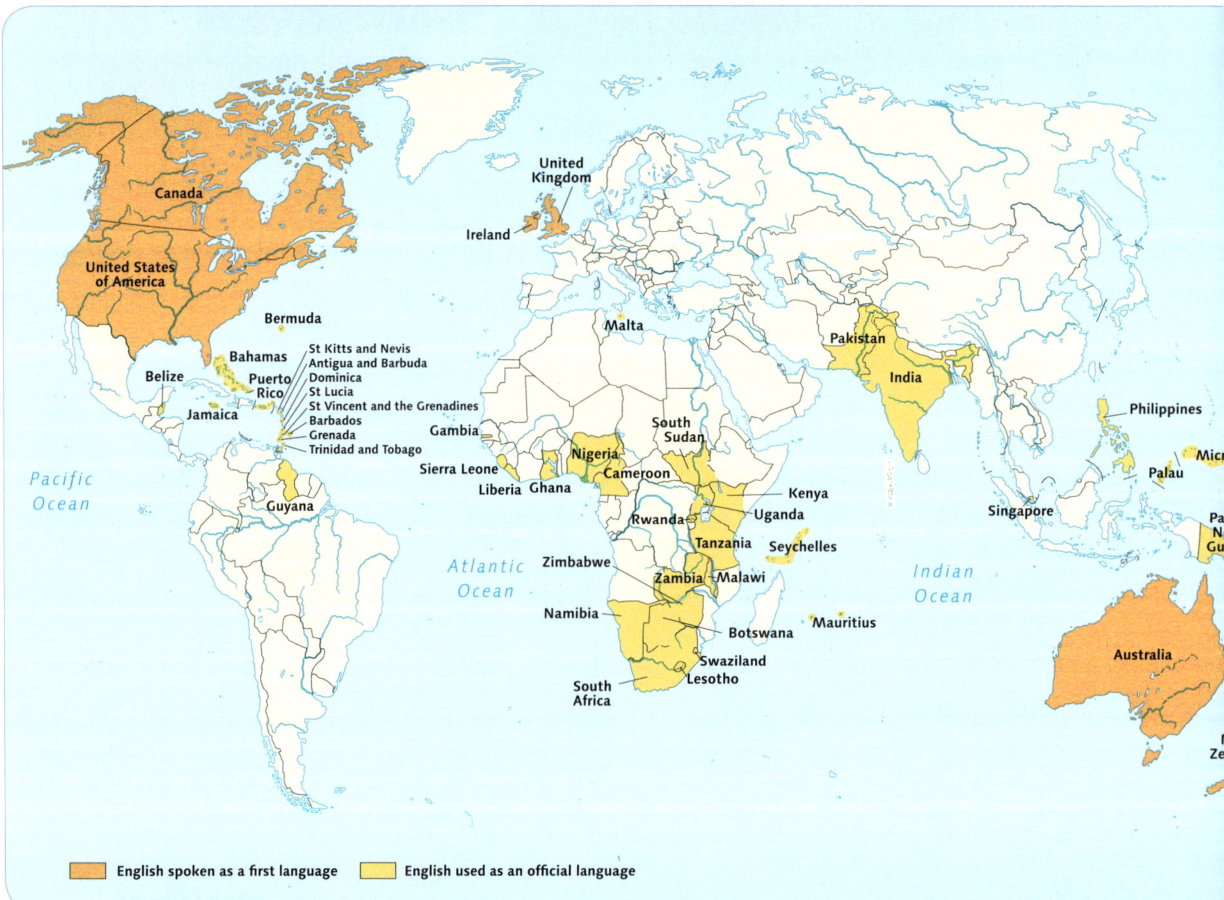

b) Look at the map. Name four countries where most people speak English as their first language. Name two countries where English is an official language.

First language: Australia, Canada, USA, Ireland, …
Official language: South Africa, Namibia, Nigeria, India, …

2 Where are they from?

a) Listen to students from different parts of the world and read along.

3 60

Hi! My name is Angelina. I'm American. We live in L.A. but my dad is from Mexico. We speak English at home and I learn Spanish in school. Some kids in my class have parents or grandparents from lots of other countries too, but we all speak American English.

My name is Tyler and I'm from Sydney, Australia. English is the first language here. Our English sounds a bit different. It isn't the same as UK or US English. But it's easy to understand. About one per cent of our people are °Aboriginal Australians. They speak many Aboriginal languages.

3 61

3 62

I'm Tamwar from India. I speak Hindi and English, our two official languages. But India is a very big country and so many people live here. There are about 400 Indian languages. Sometimes, we can only understand other Indians through English. I have a friend in the °south of India. He speaks Tamil at home and I speak Hindi, so we speak English together. No problem!

3 63

Hi! My name is S'bu. I'm from South Africa. English is one of 11 official languages here. White people speak English or Afrikaans. I speak Zulu, an African language, but English is important for me too. We need it every day, not only in school. Think about the internet, music and international sport!

3 64

I'm Karo from Bamberg and my friend Maja is from Poland. I can't speak Polish and Maja can't speak German, so we write emails in English. It's important to learn English. You can have friends from different parts of the world. You can understand films and pop songs in English too. That's so cool!

b) Answer the questions.

1 Which students from a) speak English at home? Angelina, Tyler, Tamwar, S'bu

2 Why is English important in the world? Give three or more reasons. English is the first language in lots of countries. • People need it to talk with each other because they don't speak the same language. • Many things on the internet are in English (and lots of music and films are too).

65–67 c) Listen to three speakers. Where are they from? 1 India • 2 USA • 3 Australia

d) People use English words in German too, like *cool*, *shop*, *skateboard*. Think of English words from TV, magazines and the internet. Write a list. Which group can find the most words? You have two minutes.

→ **Workbook** *p. IV*

Die S können die Geschichte sowohl zu Hause als auch im Unterricht lesen. Eine Lesephase im Unterricht ist aber durchaus sinnvoll und hilfreich.

Es gibt Wörter in dieser Geschichte, die du nicht kennst. Das macht nichts – versuch trotzdem erstmal, die Geschichte zu lesen und zu genießen. Vieles wirst du auch so verstehen. Und wenn's gar nicht geht: Einige Wörter findest du unten auf der Seite, alle anderen im Dictionary ab S. 239.

Dieses fakultative Angebot mit der Hauptfunktion des ***Reading for fun*** zielt v.a. auf die zentrale Kompetenz des **extensiven Lesens**. Geübt werden **sinnentnehmendes Leseverstehen**, selbstständiger **Umgang mit Annotationen** und Strategien zum **Erschließen von unbekanntem Vokabular**. Die S können auch üben, eine Geschichte auf wesentliche Informationen zu Handlung und Hauptfiguren hin zu untersuchen.

Unter *www.cornelsen.de/access-bayern* und auf dem UMa befindet sich die **KV Animals in Stockbridge Zoo**, die ein leeres Raster zum Sammeln von Informationen über die Tiere in *My home, the zoo* bietet. Eine Lösungsschablone mit gesammelten Informationen befindet sich auf der zweiten Seite der KV (B).

My home, the zoo

My home

I live in a zoo. No, I'm not a monkey and my mum and dad are people too. We live in a house – we don't live in a cage. But our house is in the middle of Stockbridge Zoo. My name is Luke – Luke Miller – and I'm 11 years old. My dad is the director of the zoo. It isn't an easy job, but he loves animals. We have 75 different animals here. I love animals too … but not all animals. I do *not* like wasps.

In the morning, I usually wake up when my mum comes into my room and touches my hair. "Good morning, Luke," she says. "It's time to wake up!"

I stay in bed. It's so nice and warm. I listen to the different bird songs and match the right bird names to the songs. After ten minutes, Mum shouts: "Luke! Get up, now!"

After I get up, I look out of my bedroom window through my binoculars.

l. 4 **cage** [keɪdʒ] Käfig · l. 10 **wasp** [wɒsp] Wespe · l. 20 **binoculars** *(pl)* [bɪˈnɒkjələz] Fernglas

The monkey area is right behind our house. We have twelve Rhesus monkeys, and they are always very active. They climb trees, they run around and around, they fight, and then they're friends again. Really, they're like the kids at lunch break at my school.

There's also a baby monkey. Her name is Rosie. She usually rides on her mum's back to their little house. I watch them for a long time until my mum shouts, "Come down, Luke! It's 8:15. You're late!"

I run downstairs to the kitchen. I eat my breakfast in 30 seconds. Then Mum takes me to school.

That's my routine every morning.

BUT, sometimes, King Tut wakes me up. No. Wrong. I don't wake up. I hear him and I jump out of bed. King Tut doesn't come into my room – he only roars. King Tut is our lion. We have four lions here, but King Tut is – can you guess? – the king. Everybody listens to him. When he roars, my windows rattle. It's always a good day when he roars. I'm not late for school and Mum is happy.

My secret

I'm in Year 7 at Stockbridge School. Only my best friend Jeff knows my secret.

The other kids in my class don't know that I live in a zoo. Why? There are lots of reasons:

1) *When I say, "Hey, I live in a zoo with lions, tigers and bears," they usually say, "Yeah, right … and I live at Buckingham Palace and my mum is the Queen."*

2) *I can't ask everybody in my class to come to my house. Mum and Dad need money for the zoo. Every visitor needs a ticket to see the animals.*

3) *I don't want the kids to tease me: "Luke Miller lives in a zoo. He looks like a monkey – and smells like one too!"*

4) *I want true friends, kids who are my friends because they like me, not because they want to visit the zoo without a ticket.*

After school, Mum takes me home. Sometimes we meet Tom on the road to our house. Tom is a zookeeper. He takes care of the monkeys, the otters and the big cats. He feeds them, he cleans their cages and takes care of them when they are sick.

l. 23 (to) **climb** [klaɪm] klettern • l. 28 (to) **ride** reiten • l. 28 **back** Rücken • l. 35 **routine** Routine • l. 39 (to) **roar** [rɔː] brüllen • l. 45 **secret** ['siːkrət] Geheimnis • l. 49 **reason** ['riːzn] Grund • l. 58 (to) **tease sb.** [tiːz] sich über jn. lustig machen • l. 66 (to) **take care of sth.** [keə] sich um etwas kümmern

Tom knows a lot and often tells me cool things about the animals. Here's an example: Rhesus monkeys put lots and lots of food into their mouths. But they don't eat it right away. They keep the extra food in their mouths and eat it later on when they are alone.

Every day I ask Mum, "Can I go with Tom today? Please?" She usually says, "What about your homework? Homework comes before the animals, Luke."

Or she says, "OK, Luke, but not in your school uniform."

Tom smiles at me and says, "Meet me at the otters in 15 minutes."

Tom always wears a zookeeper uniform.

Dad says I'm part of the zoo team, and the visitors need to see that. So, I wear special clothes too. I wear a red "SZ" T-shirt and a black cap.

It's feeding time

We have four otters: there's Mickey, Minnie, Pip and Pop. There are otters in the rivers in Britain, but our otters are special. They are from Asia. When they see me, they make a funny sound, a loud 'eeep-eeep, eeep-eeep'.

Then they jump out of their pool and roll around in the sand. Tom usually lets me feed the otters. They eat baby chicks and fish. I throw a baby chick into their pool and they jump into the water and catch it. The otters are Megan's favourite animals.

Megan is my little sister. She's eight years old and is at a different school. Megan plays ball with the otters, but she doesn't like to feed them. The baby chicks and the fish are dead and they don't smell very good. Megan doesn't like to touch dead animals. I don't have a problem with that. I hold my nose with one hand and get a chick with the other.

Then Tom and I go and feed the tigers – Sasha, Igor and Inga. Tom gets the meat and asks me to find a long stick. He puts a piece of meat onto the end of the stick and lets me push it through the fence. The tigers come and one of them gets the meat from the stick.

Sometimes they fight for the food. We have to hurry up and give them more. We can't go over the fence, of course. Tigers have really big teeth. And we don't want to be their lunch.

Mum usually calls me on my mobile phone at five o'clock. She says it's time to come home. I say goodbye to Inga, Igor, Sasha and Tom of course, but before I go home every day, there is one more animal family that I visit: the Indian elephants Raj, Sheba and their son Omar.

I love to watch them. They can suck up 15 litres of water with their trunks and they drink over 150 litres every day!

l. 71 **example** Beispiel · l. 73 **right away** sofort · l. 95 (to) **roll** rollen · l. 98 **chick** Küken · l. 107 (to) **hold** halten · l. 111 **stick** Stock · l. 113 **through** [θruː] durch · l. 113 **fence** [fens] Zaun · l. 118 **teeth** *(pl)* [tiːθ] Zähne · l. 125 (to) **suck up** aufsaugen · l. 126 **trunk** Rüssel

An elephant's trunk can do so many things: it can smell, pull up grass and trees, take fruit from trees, spray water, and hold another elephant's trunk – that's the way they give hugs. Elephants talk to each other in different ways: they move their ears, they make little sounds we can't hear and they trumpet really loud with their trunks. Elephants are the biggest land animals in the world. They eat 250 kilos of food every day.

Dad calls me the elephant expert. One day I want to go to India and ride an elephant in the jungle.

Before my mobile rings again, I run home.

Weekends at the zoo

Sometimes, kids from my school come to the zoo at the weekend with their parents. I wear my red SZ T-shirt, cap and sunglasses all weekend. There's a lot of work to do.

I often help Mum at the Learning Centre. I hold Suzie, our boa constrictor, and Mum tells visitors about her. She tells them what she eats (mice and rats), how she eats (a mouse or rat in one bite) and where she is from (Mexico).

Suzie is eight years old, is three metres long and weighs twelve kilos. It's a bit scary to hold a snake, but I like it.

Then it's feeding time for me! When I help in the Learning Centre, I can have lunch at the restaurant. My favourite food is a roast beef sandwich with salad and chocolate ice cream for dessert.

l.129 (to) **pull up** herausreißen • l.130 (to) **spray** sprühen • l.132 **in different ways** auf verschiedene Weise • l.133 (to) **move** [muːv] bewegen • l.133 **ear** [ɪə] Ohr • l.134 (to) **trumpet** ['trʌmpɪt] tröten • l.145 **sunglasses** *(pl)* ['sʌnglɑːsɪz] Sonnenbrille • l.150 **mice** *(pl)* [maɪs] Mäuse • l.150 **in one bite** [baɪt] mit einem Bissen • l.153 (to) **weigh** [weɪ] wiegen

My birthday!

Kids sometimes have birthday parties at the zoo. They start in the Learning Centre. The birthday kid can touch Suzie, and they learn about other snakes, scorpions and other insects. Tom gives a talk about the big cats. Then the group goes to the Children's Corner. There they can feed the goats and ponies. They also get a yummy lunch at the restaurant and have cake and ice cream. After that, they play party games in the activity area near the restaurant or at the playground.

Today is my birthday. Every year I get a big surprise. Let's see what it is this year.

My birthday party

Well, I did it. I asked twelve kids to my birthday party. I used the Stockbridge Zoo birthday invitation. It has a picture of King Tut on the front and it says, "Come to my birthday party". Inside it says: "Let's have a roaring good time!"

Everybody arrived at 11 am. We met them at the gate. Then Dad took us on a special tour of the zoo. We fed the otters and watched Tom the zookeeper feed the lions. At 12.30, we had lunch at the restaurant: pizza and cola. Tom came out of the kitchen with a big birthday cake. He sang "Happy birthday" and everybody sang along. Then Tom gave me a hug. One of my friends asked, "Is he your uncle or something?"

At the Learning Centre, I held Suzie the boa constrictor without help from my mum. Suzie kissed my face and wrapped her tail around my hand.

"Wow! That snake loves you!" said Jeff.

At the end of the day, I said goodbye to all the kids and gave them party bags with chocolate and cards with photos of different animals.

A girl from my class asked me where I live.

Megan shouted, "We live here, of course! I was born in the zoo!"

Megan pointed to a building.

"See," she said, "that's our house there."

My friends heard her and looked at me in a strange way.

"So it's true," said one girl. "You live in the zoo. That's so cool!"

The surprise

That night Mum made my favourite dinner, beef curry. Tom was there too.

After dinner, Dad said, "Now it's time for your surprise, Luke. Somebody is waiting for you. Come on, let's go."

The zoo wasn't open, but the lights were on. We took the "safari path" between King Tut and the monkeys.

Then I saw him – Raj had a black cloth on his back. On his head were lines of red and gold paint.

We climbed over the fence. Next came the hard part: How could I climb onto Raj's back? It wasn't easy but Raj helped me. He went down onto his knees, and I climbed up one of his legs and then moved over his back and sat just behind his ears.

Raj knew I was ready and stood up. I was so high! Sheba stood by the small pool with Omar. Raj took a few steps and I almost fell down!

---

l.167 **goat** [gəʊt] Ziege · l.173 **surprise** [sə'praɪz] Überraschung · l.182 **gate** [geɪt] Tor · l.193 (to) **kiss** [kɪs] küssen · l.193 (to) **wrap** [ræp] wickeln · l.193 **tail** [teɪl] Schwanz · l.217 **cloth** [klɒθ] Tuch · l.219 **paint** [peɪnt] Farbe · l.223 **knee** [ni:] Knie

"Hold onto his ears, Luke!" Tom shouted. Raj went to the pool and sucked water up through his trunk. First he sprayed water on his son Omar. He sucked up more water and moved his trunk to his mouth for a drink. But, suddenly he had a new idea. He moved his trunk up and sprayed the water onto his back – and onto me! I was wet from head to foot.But I loved it. This birthday present was the best in my whole life.

Everybody knows

I was at school early the next day. I went to my desk and got out my books for the first lesson. Usually everybody is noisy and tells jokes before the teacher comes, but that day, the kids were quiet. They just watched me.

Then Jeff asked, "Can I hold Suzie the next time I come to the zoo?"

Then came more questions:
"How old is the baby elephant?"
"Can I come to your house at the weekend?"
"Yeah, me too?"
"And can I feed the otters?"
"Can you take animals into your house?"

I felt like a celebrity … and I didn't like it at all. But then our teacher came in, and all the kids went back to their desks.

Things were really bad at lunchtime. Kids from other classes heard the news too, and there was a big group around me. They asked so many questions that I had no time to eat my lunch.

The snake gang

The next week, everything was back to normal – or that's what I thought. On Friday afternoon, Mum was late. I played a game on my mobile phone and waited for her at the school gate.

Then four Year 8 boys came towards me.

"Look, it's Tarzan," one of them said. "He lives in the zoo with all the other monkeys. Ha, ha, ha."

I don't like it when people laugh at their own jokes. I knew that boy. It was Robbie, the brother of a girl in my class.

"He likes to hold snakes. Right, Tarzan?" said Robbie.

"Everybody can do it," I said. "Boas don't hurt people. But you have to hold them in the right way, or …"

"Or what?"

"They can strangle you," I said.

"Oh, is that right? You mean … like this?"

Suddenly Robbie's hands were around my neck. A second boy took the mobile phone from me.

"Hey! That's my mobile! Give it back!" I shouted. But the boy threw it to one of his friends. Robbie let me go, but the mobile went from boy to boy.

---

l. 237 **whole** [həʊl] ganze(r, s) • l. 252 **celebrity** [sə'lebrəti] berühmte Persönlichkeit • l. 266 **towards sb.** [tə'wɔːdz] jm. entgegen • l. 270 **own** eigene(r, s) • l. 275 (to) **hurt sb.** [hɜːt] jm. wehtun, jn. verletzen • l. 279 (to) **strangle** erdrosseln

It was an old mobile. I walked away. But they followed me.

"Hey, where are you going, Tarzan?"

"What do you want from me?" I asked.

"We want your s-snake … sss …" he said.

"Snake?" I asked.

"The big s-snake … Suzie … sss," he said. Robbie was not only scary, he was also very strange.

"Why?" I asked.

"For our gang," said one of the other boys. Then they showed me their arms under their jackets. All four boys had a handmade snake tattoo.

"We're the Snakes and we want your snake as our mascot."

"But Suzie isn't my snake. She belongs to the zoo!" I shouted.

"Maybe you didn't hear what I said, Tarzan. We want that snake, OK?"

Then he pushed me onto the ground. Just then, I heard my mother's voice. I got up and cleaned the dirt off my uniform.

Robbie touched me on the back.

"Is this yours? It was on the ground," he said and held out my mobile phone. I took it from him and got into the car.

"See you tomorrow, Luke," Robbie said with a big smile.

"Are you OK?" said Mum. "You're as white as a ghost!"

"I'm fine, Mum," I said.

Robbie and his friends didn't leave me alone. The next day they took my schoolbag. On Wednesday they tried to put worms into my lunch. And on Thursday they took my PE kit. They also left me a note that said, "Bring us Suzie tomorrow, or you're in trouble."

I didn't know what to do, so in the afternoon, I told Tom the whole story.

"He wants Suzie, does he?" said Tom.

Then Tom gave me a really good idea. He said, "Let Robbie meet Suzie. Real snakes are scary. You know all about Suzie, but Robbie doesn't. We can give him a nice surprise."

So on Friday morning, I told Robbie to meet me at the gate of Stockbridge Zoo at 8 pm. "I can show you how to hold Suzie," I said.

"Oh yeah? I know all that already," said Robbie. "I just want that snake."

But he *was* there at 8 pm, with a big box. We went to the reptile room in the Learning Centre. Tom was there too, but he didn't say much. He let me do everything myself. First I took Suzie out of her cage. I wrapped her around my neck. Her tail moved around my hand and she gave me a friendly squeeze. Then she pushed out her black tongue near my face. It tickled.

---

l. 308 **ground** [graʊnd] Boden · l. 310 **dirt** [dɜːt] Dreck · l. 341 **myself** [maɪˈself] selbst · l. 344 (to) **give sb. a squeeze** [skwiːz] jn. drücken · l. 345 **tongue** [tʌŋ] Zunge · l. 345 (to) **tickle** [ˈtɪkl] kitzeln

"Hey, let me try that!" said Robbie. He tried to take Suzie from me. I moved back just before he got her.

"You can't just grab her," I said. "She doesn't like that. Boas sometimes bite!"

I put one hand near her tail and my other hand near her head. Then I said, "OK, Robbie, just put her around your neck like a scarf. Like this." I put her around Robbie's neck. Her little black tongue went in and out near Robbie's face.

At first Robbie thought it was really cool to hold her. But then Suzie moved around Robbie – front and back.

"Hey she's squeezing me! Help! She's squeezing me to death! Take her away from me!"

I went to Robbie and took Suzie back. "She's not really trying to hurt you. She just wants to know that you're not going to let her fall to the ground. It just feels strange the first time. You can try it again."

"No, not now," said Robbie.

"Do you know what boas eat, Robbie?" asked Tom.

"Salad?" said Robbie.

"No, they eat mice and rats," I said.

"We feed her live rats. She only needs one a week. And I have good news: today is feeding day."

I took a rat out of its cage and held it by its tail in front of Suzie's open cage. Suzie waited and then suddenly moved towards it.

But she didn't get it and the rat fell to the ground. I don't know why, but the rat ran up Robbie's leg, around his neck and onto his back. Robbie jumped and shouted and tried to get the rat off his back.

Then he called "Help!". I think it was scary for the rat too because it stayed just there, on Robbie's back, behind his head.So I grabbed its tail and pulled it off.

"Are you all right, Robbie?" I asked.

"Yeah, of course I'm all right. But it's late, and I need to go home. Maybe Mum is worried. And listen, I don't think that I can take Suzie. My room isn't big enough. I also didn't know about the rats. Mum doesn't like rats. She doesn't want them in the house. So, I have to go home now. You can keep the box."

I walked back to the gate with Robbie and said goodbye. There was never any trouble from him again.

The end

KV The snake gang (unter *www.cornelsen.de/access-bayern* und auf dem UMa) enthält *scrambled sentences* zur Sicherung des Textverständnisses.

l. 349 (to) **grab** [græb] greifen • l. 353 **scarf** [skɑːf] Schal • l. 372 **live** [laɪv] lebend, lebendig

1 Part A Practice

7 Apostrophe: 's and s' (The possessive)

p. 26

c) Finish the sentences. Use correct words with 's or s'.

Bennetts · friend · friends · Justin · kids · Maya · Sam · teacher

1 Sam's name is Bennett.
2 The ... hometown is Plymouth now.
3 ... name is Skinner.
4 The Plymouth ... school is Plymstock.
5 Their ... name is Miss Bell.
6 Sam: My ... names are Justin and Lucy.
7 Lucy: My best ... name is Maya.
8 ... new school is Coombe Dean.

English and German are different

Sam's name. *Sams Name*

9 Don't wear trainers (Imperatives)

p. 27

Make imperatives. Finish the sentences for the pictures. Use the words from the box.

forget · give · open · put · talk · touch

1 ... ... the picture.

2 ... me the pen, please.

3 ... ... the rat in the bag.

4 ... ... the window.

5 ... ... your bag.

6 ... ... in the library.

Part B Practice

1 Yes, I am

p. 29

b) Make more questions for your partner. Use ideas from the box.

A: *Is your best friend in our class?*
B: *Yes, she is. / No, she isn't.*
B: *Are your shoes red? ...*

Is	your mum your dad your dog your ...	from Berlin? friendly? at home? sad? British? in our class? in Year 5? red? ...
Are	you your friends ...	

Part C Practice

2 EVERYDAY ENGLISH Classroom English

p. 33

a) Finish the sentences with the words from the box.

can · do · go · open · page · sorry · spell · What's · window · work

1 Please ... your workbooks at page 15.
2 Can you ... with Paul, please?
3 ... I'm late.
4 What ... are we on?
5 Miss, can I open the ...?
6 I can't ... number 3.
7 Paul, ... you help Lisa, please?
8 Can I ... to the toilet, please?
9 ... for homework?
10 Can you ... "Scotland", please?

2

Part A Practice

4 Before school, after school (Simple present: positive statements)

p. 49

b) Say what the kids do after school.

1 Abby (go) goes for a walk with Skip after school.
2 Maya (help) ... her mum in the kitchen after school.
3 Sam (watch) ... TV after school.
4 Lucy (have) ... a cup of tea after school.

7 STUDY SKILLS Learning words with mind maps

p. 50

b) Find umbrella words for these word groups: Check with a partner.

colours · house · months · people · school

1 boy · girl · man · woman
2 blue · orange · purple · red
3 April · June · August · October
4 kitchen · bedroom · dining room · bathroom
5 classmate · timetable · lessons · teacher

Part B Practice

2 At Grandma's farm (Simple present: positive and negative statements)

p. 53

Sam asks Lucy about her Grandma's farm. Finish the dialogue. Use positive and negative verbs.

Sam: Tell me about a weekend at the farm.
Lucy: Well, we (wake up) wake up at 6 o'clock. Then we (feed) ... the dogs and the rabbits.
Sam: You and your sister Holly?
Lucy: No, Holly (wake up) ... at 6 o'clock, so she (feed) ... the animals. On the farm we (have) ... horses and pigs and cows.
Sam: What about elephants?
Lucy: No, Sam. Don't be silly. We (have) ... elephants. The farm is in England, not in India.
Sam: OK, so you (feed) ... the animals – and then?
Lucy: Then Grandma (make) ... breakfast. And after breakfast we (go) ... for a walk.
Sam: And Holly too?
Lucy: No, Holly (go) ... with us. She (sleep) ... till twelve o'clock.

Part C Practice

5 My class *(my, your, his, …)*

p. 58

a) Sam talks to his dad about his class and his friends. Choose the right word to finish the sentences.

1 Sam: "I really like my new class."
2 Dad: "And what about your/their new teachers?"
3 Sam: We like our/your class teascher. His/Her name is Miss Bell. She's nice.
4 Dad: And who are his/your friends?
5 Sam: My/Her friends? Their/His names are Justin and Lucy.
6 Sam: Justin lives with her/his mum. Lucy lives with her/their mum too.
7 Lucy's grandma and grandpa have a farm. They have lots of animals on his/their farm – but no elephants.

3

Part A Practice

4 GAME Guess who!

Partner B (p. 73)

Partner A: Choose a name from the list. Don't tell your partner the name.
Partner B: Ask questions. The questions below can help you. Guess the name.

Abby	Morph
Justin	Sam
Lucy	Silky
Maya	

A: Guess who!
B: Is it a he?
A: Yes, it is.
B: Does he live in the library?
A: No, he doesn't.
B: Does he make films?
A: Yes, he does.
B: Then it's Justin!
A: Right! Now you choose a name.

Does she live in a big house?
Does she have piano lessons?
Does he film people and places?
Does he make jokes?
Does he live in the library?
Does she go to Coombe Dean School?
Does she have one brother?

Part B Practice

2 Sorry, I can't hear you (Simple present: questions with question words)

p. 77

It's very noisy. You can't hear your partner. Ask questions with *what, when, where,* or *why.*

1 I play football.
A: Sorry, what do you play? B: Football!
2 On Saturday morning, I help my mum.
A: Sorry, when …
3 On Sundays I get up at 10 o'clock.
A: Sorry, when …
4 Then I go to the swimming pool.
A: Sorry, where …
5 I like it there because I meet my friends.
A: Sorry, why …
6 My friends all like swimming.
A: Sorry, what …

3 What sport does Abby like? (Simple present: questions with question words)

p. 77

a) Read the answers. Then finish the questions. Use words from the box.

food · films · games · shoes · sport · subjects

Question	Answer
1 What sport does Abby like?	She likes sailing.
2 What … does Silky eat?	She eats fish and crabs.
3 What … do you play?	I play computer games.
4 What … do Plymstock students wear?	They wear black shoes.
5 What … do you watch?	I watch James Bond films.
6 What … do you like?	I like French and geography.

TIP

German: *Was für Bücher liest du?*

English: *What books do you read?*

4 Do you know your partner? (Simple present: mixed questions)

p. 78

a) Copy the table.
Add your ideas about your partner.

b) Ask your partner the questions and write the answers in the table.

c) Now write the answers on a card like this:

This boy or girl lives in a house.
He/She has ... brothers and ... sisters.
His/Her mum/dad ... comes from ...
He/She comes to school by ... .
He/She likes ...
His/Her hobbies are ... and ... .
He/She plays ... .

Questions	Your partner's answers
Where do you live?	
... have any brothers or sisters?	
Where ... your mum and dad come from?	
How ... come to school?	
What subjects ... like?	
What music ... like?	
... play an instrument?	
What hobbies ... have?	
What sport ... go to?	

Part C Practice

4 How often? (Word order: adverbs of frequency)

p. 83

b) Put the adverb in brackets in the right place in the sentence.

1 Sam goes to a club on Thursdays. (always)
Sam always goes to a club on Thursdays.
2 Lucy doesn't eat in the canteen. (always)
3 Justin and Sam meet on the Hoe. (sometimes)
4 Justin doesn't see his dad. (often)
5 Maya goes swimming at the Lido. (often)
6 Sam does kung fu at the weekends. (usually)
7 Morph sleeps in Plymstock Library. (always)
8 Silky eats cornflakes for breakfast. (never)

4 Part A Practice

2 Was it fun?

p. 97

c) Make your own dialogue about Saturday. Maybe you were at a castle, the cinema, a club, a farm, the gym, a museum, a shopping mall, …

You can use these adjectives in your dialogue.

boring · cool · exciting · fantastic · funny · good · sad · scary · silly · strange · …

A: I was at … on Saturday.
B: Was it good/exciting/…?
A: Yes, it was. / No, it wasn't. It was …
Where were you on Saturday?
B: I was at …
A: Was it …?
B: Yes, … / No, …

TIP
Remember how you make short answers:
Was it fun? – Yes, **it was**.
Was it good? – No, **it wasn't**.

3 How was your weekend? (Simple past of *be*: question words)

p. 97

Read the dialogue between Jack and Oliver.
Finish it with question words from the box and was or were.
The words in the box can help you to find the right question words.

how · how · when · where · who · why

Jack: Hey, Oliver! How was your weekend?
Oliver: Great, thanks.
Jack: Cool! … … you?
Oliver: At a party.
Jack: Whose party … it?
Oliver: My cousin Katy's party.
Jack: Oh, and … … you there?
Oliver: I … there because it was her birthday.
Jack: And … … the party?
Oliver: On Sunday afternoon.
Jack: Oh, and … … there?
Oliver: Abby with her friend Maya, and lots of other kids … there. And what about you? … … your weekend?
Jack: It … cool, thanks. No homework!

Part B Practice

3 A visit from London (Simple past: positive statements, regular and irregular verbs)

p. 101

b) Put in these verbs:

liked · saw · showed · visited · walked · wanted · went · went

On Saturday, the boys … (1) into Plymouth by bus. Sam … (2) Tom the Hoe and then they … (3) swimming at the Lido. Later, Tom … (4) to see old Plymouth, so they … (5) around the Barbican for an hour. They … (6) lots of old houses and they … (7) the museum in the Elizabethan House. Tom really … (8) his day in Plymouth.

Part C Practice

2 I played … I didn't play … (Simple past: positive and negative statements)

p. 103

a) Think about last week. Write two positive and two negative sentences about what you did. Here are some ideas:

watch a film on TV · play cards · have ice cream for breakfast · fall asleep at school · see my grandmother · forget my homework · help my dad · write a song · ride my bike to school · text my grandpa · go to Berlin · say "I love you" · win some money · eat a book · make a cake · talk to my brother · …

Background file

p. 104

Devon – an English county

Devon is a county in the south-west of England. Its biggest city is Plymouth, with 260,000 people.

Dartmoor is the biggest area of wild country in the south of Britain. It is the setting for lots of famous detective stories.

Wild ponies on Dartmoor, Devon

Devon's north and south coasts have lots of sandy beaches. Swimming, surfing and fishing are very popular with holidaymakers.

Woolacombe Beach, Devon

Devon is one of the warmest places in Britain. You can find lots of palm trees there!

Torquay Gardens, Devon

Write a short text. Say why you would / wouldn't like to go to Devon.

I would / wouldn't like to go to Devon because …	Plymouth Dartmoor the beaches …	looks look	great. scary. exciting. boring. …
I would / wouldn't like to go to …	Plymouth Dartmoor the beaches …	because	I like / don't like swimming and surfing. I want / don't want to see the palm trees. the wild country looks / doesn't look great. there's lots / there isn't much to do there. …

5 Part A Practice

4 I'm not laughing. I'm singing. (Present progressive: positive and negative statements)

p.125

b) Look at the picture on the right and fill in the gaps.

The man *isn't wearing* a yellow T-shirt.
He *is wearing* a green T-shirt.
The woman ... a green T-shirt.
She ... a blue T-shirt.
The man ... a black watch. He ... a yellow watch.
The woman ... a white watch. She ... a red watch.
The man ... on a table. He ... in an armchair.
The woman ... on a chair. She ... on the floor.
The man ... to music. He ... TV.
The woman ... TV. She ... a book.
The man ... cake. He ... a sandwich.
The woman ... an apple. She ... a biscuit.
The man ... to music. He ... with a cat.
The woman ... with a cat. She ... to music.

Part B Practice

3 At the aquarium

p.127

Nach der Schule erzählst du einem/einer Freund/in über das Aquarium.
Vervollständige den Dialog. Du kannst die Redewendungen im Kasten verwenden.

- Abteilungen über den Atlantik, die britische Küste oder das Great Barrier Reef
- du nachts die Haie beobachten kannst
- ein Schülerlernzentrum und Geburtstagspartys
- einen Film in 4D schauen, oder eine Tour durch das Aquarium machen
- kann man da schlafen
- nur in den Ferien
- vier Abteilungen

A: Es gibt *vier Abteilungen*, zum Beispiel über das Meeresleben in der Gegend um Plymouth.
B: Geht's da nur um Plymouth?
A: Nein, es gibt auch ... .
B: Bieten sie etwas Besonderes für Kinder?
A: Ja, sie haben dort ... . Und nachts ... .
B: Eine Übernachtung im Aquarium?
A: Ja, das heißt „Sleeping with sharks", weil ... .
B: Und das kann man jede Nacht machen?
A: Nein, ...
B: Und was macht man da genau?
A: Du kannst ... .

2 Where is he going? (Present progressive: questions)

p.128

Sam and his sister Lily are watching a film. Lily has lots of questions.
Write her questions with the words in brackets.

Sam: That's Captain Goldfinger, Lily. He's bad! He's going to the harbour now.
Lily: Sorry, Sam, ... (where – go)?
where is he going?
Sam: To the harbour. And look! A policeman is following Goldfinger.
Lily: (Who – follow) Goldfinger?
Sam: A policeman. Hey, there's Goldfinger's team. They're meeting on that boat.
Lily: (Where – meet)?
Sam: On the green boat.
Lily: Oh, no. It's Goldfinger, Sam. (What – give) them?
Sam: A CD – with important information. Hey! The policeman is swimming to the boat.
Lily: (Where – swim)?
Sam: To the boat. Oh, Lily, it's 8 o'clock – time for you to go to bed.

Part C Practice

5 Let's go to Cornwall! (*some* and *any* and compounds)

p.135

The Bennetts are still talking about holidays.
Complete their conversation with the correct word from the brackets.

Dad: Well, what about a holiday by the sea in Cornwall? (Anybody/Somebody) told me that there are (some/any) great surfing beaches. Does (someone/anyone) know (anything/something) about surfing?
Mum: Sorry, I don't know (something/anything) about it. But Cornwall is a good idea. I know (somebody/anybody) in Bude. Maybe we can visit them.
Sam: Mum, it's a holiday. We don't want to visit (somebody/anybody) in Bude. We want to do (anything/something) exciting.
Mum: Well, (some/any) ideas?
Sam: Are there (any/some) old castles with ghosts in Cornwall?
Dad: Well, there's Pengersick Castle. It has the most ghosts in the UK.
Sam: Oh yes, let's go there!

TIP
Look at Language help (***some*** and ***any***) on p. 134 again.

Use ***something/somebody*** in positive statements and ***anything/anybody*** in negative statements and questions.

Someone and ***anyone*** are the same as ***somebody*** and ***anybody***.

1 Part B Practice

What is it?

p. 31, exercise 10

Find the letters and write them in your exercise book. The letters tell you the name of a place.

1 *Uhr* in English: the fourth letter.
2 Justin is from here: the fifth letter.
3 Do only what *he* says: the fourth letter.
4 Maya's brother: the first letter.
5 The third letter of the second month.
6 The sixth letter of Lucy's family name.
7 The pool in Plymouth: the third letter.
8 The seventh letter of the twelfth month.
9 Lucy's favourite animal: the second letter.
10 Sam's sport: the third letter.
11 The first letter of a two-year-old seal.
12 The fourth letter of the third month.
13 Lucy's sister: the first letter.
14 *Geschichte* in English: the fifth letter.
15 Sam is from here: the second letter.
16 The fourth letter of the class teacher's name.

2 Part A Practice

What's different?

p. 48, exercise 2

These photos are different. Look at them for one minute. Then cover photo B with your exercise book.

Here are the things in photo A:

1 ball · 2 books · 3 cards · 1 CD · 1 clock · 1 computer · 2 DVDs · 1 glue stick · 1 lamp · 2 maps · 1 pen · 1 pencil · 1 pencil case · 2 photos · 1 rubber · 1 ruler · 1 sharpener · 2 telephones

What is different in photo B? What is the same?

3 Part A Practice

Go, play or do?

p. 72, exercise 2

Four children do four different activities.
Copy the table.
Then use this information to find out who does what.

a) There is no "k" in Ann's activity.
b) There is no "g" at the end of Leo's activity.
c) Henry's activity has eight letters in it.
d) Leo's activity does not have four letters.

Leo	Henry	Maria	Ann	ACTIVITY
				football
				swimming
				skating
				judo

4 Part B Practice

Think!

p. 101, exercise 3

Can you solve these puzzles?

a) Mary's mum has four children: the first child is called April; the second is called June; the third is called August.
What's the name of the fourth child?

b) You're the driver of a London-to-Plymouth bus. In London, 33 people get on the bus. In Oxford, 5 men get off and 10 women get on. In Bristol, 25 boys get off and 12 girls get on. In Exeter, 4 men get off and 10 boys get on.
What's the driver's name?

c) Think of three days that start with the letter "t".

d) A boat goes from France to Plymouth at 20 km/h. 20 minutes later, a boat leaves Plymouth for France at 25 km/h. Plymouth is 200 km from France. When the two boats meet, which boat is nearer Plymouth?

e) On every day of the week, what's always in the middle of Plymstock?

f) You are in a room with three monkeys. One has a book, one has a bottle, one has nothing. Which animal in the room is the most intelligent?

5 Part A Practice

Remember?

p. 124, exercise 1

Read the sentences and write them down. Can you remember who said them?
Where were the sentences in the book?

1 ARE YOU A BOY OR A GIRL?
– Are you ...
2 'ΓOOHƆ ΓλWSTOCK ꟽOꓤꓞ HꓤꓤO W,I 'HꓤꓤO W,I
3 Hey, hey Hoe, here we go!
4 Go and find the yoghurt, little sister!
5 !YKKU SSƎOTATO TSAO HTI ƎƎƎ TSAO
6 What's grey and never gets wet?
7 Boat tours! See all the navy ships!
8 She looks so soft. Call her Silky.
9 Stop! Thieves! Give me back my book!
10 Help! A m[illegible] u[illegible]ister and a mad dog!

Answers (p. 257)

1 Part A Practice

5 Who's in the photo? (*be*: positive and negative statements) p. 25

Partner B:

a) Listen to your partner. Who is the boy in his/her photo?

b) Say as much as you can about *one* of these girls.
Don't say her name.
Can your partner guess who it is?

You can use these ideas to make sentences.
The girl in my photo is/isn't from Plymouth.
She's …
Her brother/sister is …

4 Part B Practice

4 Dave's day in London p. 101

Partner B:

a) Listen to your partner's story about Dave's day in London.

b) Tell your partner your picture story: *Dave was in London last Saturday. In the morning he went to …*
Then say how the two stories are different.
A: In my story he talked to his grandma.
B: In my story he talked to his classmates. And in my story he went …

Why do you think Dave's stories were different? Which story do you think is true?

EXTRA Imagine you are Dave. Write about your great day in London.

Partner B

5 Part B Practice

1 Is he drinking? (Present progressive: questions)

p. 128

Partner B: Answer Partner A's questions about pictures 1–3.
Use short answers (Yes, he is. / No, he isn't., etc.). Then go back to page 110.

A: In picture 1: is the boy drinking? B: No, he isn't.
A: Well, is he …?

Book rally – answers

1 Das Buch hat 5 Units.
2 Das zweite Background file heißt 'Grey seals'.
3 'Grammar file'. Es beginnt auf S. 182.
4 Die Luftballons sind grün.
5 Der Teil zur Aussprache ist eine Seite lang.
6 Die Vokabeln zu Unit 1 sind auf S. 210–216.
7 Der Teil heißt 'Skills file'.
8 Es ist 4.00 Uhr/16.00 Uhr.
9 Dieser Teil heißt 'Text'.
10 Die 'Film'-Seite in Unit 1 ist auf S. 33.
11 Die Geschichte nach Unit 5 heißt 'My home, the zoo.'
12 Das Thema der Mediationsaufgabe ist 'Essen/Lebensmittel'.
13 Die Vorbereitungsseiten heißen 'Let's prepare for a test.'
14 Die Seite mit der Lernaufgabe heißt 'Your task'.

Wordbank 1: More animals and pets ➔ *Here we go! (p.15)*

cow

goat

one sheep

three sheep

one mouse

three mice

hamster

gerbil

tortoise

turtle

budgie

canary

parrot

lizard

pet [pet] Haustier • **cow** [kaʊ] • **goat** [gəʊt] • **sheep,** *pl* **sheep** [ʃiːp] • **mouse,** *pl* **mice** [maʊs], [maɪs] • **hamster** ['hæmstə] • **gerbil** ['dʒɜːbɪl] Rennmaus • **tortoise** ['tɔːtəs] Landschildkröte • **turtle** ['tɜːtl] Wasserschildkröte • **budgie** ['bʌdʒi] • **canary** [kə'neəri] • **parrot** ['pærət] • **lizard** ['lɪzəd] Eidechse •

Wordbank 2: My timetable ➔ *Unit 1 (p. 30)*

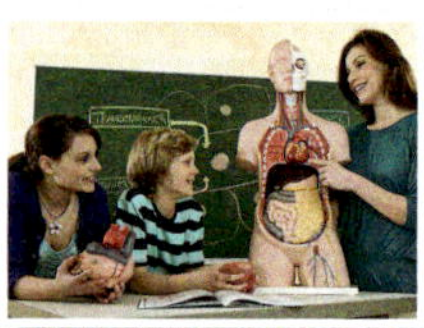
biology

chemistry

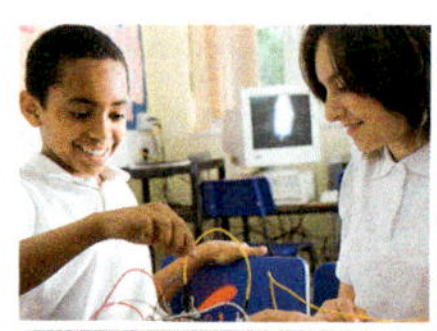
physics

class assembly

Spanish

Italian

Latin

ethics

social studies

drama

extracurricular activities

biology [baɪ'ɒlədʒi] • **chemistry** ['kemɪstri] • **physics** ['fɪzɪks] • **class assembly** [ˌklɑːs‿ə'sembli] Klassenlehrerstunde, Verfügungsstunde • **Spanish** ['spænɪʃ] • **Italian** [ɪ'tæliən] • **Latin** ['lætɪn] • **ethics** ['eθɪks] Ethik • **social studies** [ˌsəʊʃl 'stʌdiz] Gesellschaftskunde, Gemeinschaftskunde • **drama** ['drɑːmə] darstellende Kunst, Schauspiel • **extracurricular activities** [ˌekstrəkəˌrɪkjələr‿æk'tɪvətiz] Arbeitsgemeinschaften u.Ä

Wordbank 3: My bedroom ➔ *Unit 2 (p. 44)*

blinds *(pl)* [blaɪndz] • **cage** [keɪdʒ] • **carpet** ['kɑːpɪt] • **chest of drawers** [ˌtʃest‿əv 'drɔːz] Kommode • **curtain** ['kɜːtn] • **cushion** ['kʊʃn] • **drawer** [drɔː] • **mirror** ['mɪrə] • **printer** ['prɪntə] • **radiator** ['reɪdieɪtə] Heizkörper • **wardrobe** ['wɔːdrəʊb]

Wordbank 4: Families ➔ *Unit 2 (p. 55)*

Me and my parents.

Philip and Laura have two children, a son and a daughter – Tim and Emma. They're my cousins.

My sister Clara. She's Philip and Laura's niece.

My cousin Jasper with his dad and his stepmother.

My grandparents and my grandma's dad. He's my great-grandfather.

child, *pl* **children** [tʃaɪld], [tʃɪldrən] • **daughter** ['dɔːtə] • **grandparents** ['grænpeərənts] Großeltern • **great-grandfather/-mother** Urgroßvater/-mutter • **husband** ['hʌzbənd] Ehemann • **nephew** ['nefjuː] Neffe • **niece** [niːs] Nichte • **parents** ['peərənts] • **son** [sʌn] • **stepmother** ['stepmʌðə] • **wife** [waɪf] Ehefrau

Wordbank 5: Food ➜ *Unit 2 (p. 57)*

FRUIT

apples

pears

oranges

strawberries

cherries

bananas

grapes

plums

VEGETABLES

carrots

tomatoes

peppers

peas

beans

mushrooms

broccoli

cauliflower

cucumber

lettuce

sweetcorn

MEAT AND FISH

grilled steak

lamb chops

roast chicken

sausages

salami

ham

cold cuts

fish fingers

fish filet

bean [biːn] • **carrot** [ˈkærət] • **cauliflower** [ˈkɒliflaʊə] • **cherry** [ˈtʃeri] • **cold cuts** *(pl)* [ˈkəʊld kʌts] Aufschnitt • **cucumber** [ˈkjuːkʌmbə] • **fish fillet** [fɪʃ ˈfɪlət] • **fish finger** [fɪʃ ˈfɪŋgə] • **lamb chop** [ˈlæm tʃɒp] Lammkotelett • **lettuce** [ˈletɪs] • **mushroom** [ˈmʌʃrʊm] • **pea** [piː] • **pear** [peə] • **plum** [plʌm] • **roast chicken** [ˌrəʊst ˈtʃɪkɪn] • **sausage** [ˈsɒsɪdʒ] • **strawberry** [ˈstrɔːbəri] • **sweetcorn** [ˈswiːtkɔːn]

EGGS, POTATOES, PASTA, …

pasta

pasta salad

rice

boiled eggs

scrambled eggs

fried eggs

omelette

mashed potatoes

fried potatoes

chips

potato salad

DRINKS

coffee

hot chocolate

mineral water

orange juice

lemonade

DESSERTS / SWEETS

blancmange

fruit flan with whipped cream

jelly with custard

cupcakes

AND FOR BREAKFAST …

butter

honey

chocolate hazelnut spread

muesli

cereals

rolls

toast

blancmange [blə'mɒnʒ] • **boiled egg** [ˌbɔɪld‿'eg] • **butter** ['bʌtə] • **cereals** *(pl)* ['sɪəriəlz] Getreideflocken, Frühstücksflocken • **chocolate hazelnut spread** [ˌtʃɒklət ˌheɪzlnʌt 'spred] • **custard** ['kʌstəd] • **fried egg** [ˌfraɪd‿'eg] • **honey** ['hʌni] • **jelly** ['dʒeli] • **lemonade** [ˌlemə'neɪd] • **mashed potatoes** *(pl)* [ˌmæʃt pə'teɪtəʊz] • **muesli** ['mjuːzli] • **orange juice** ['ɒrɪndʒ dʒuːs] • **pasta** ['pæstə] • **roll** [rəʊl] • **scrambled eggs** *(pl)* [ˌskræmbld‿'egz] • **whipped cream** [ˌwɪpt 'kriːm]

Wordbank 6: Clubs and hobbies

➔ *Unit 3 (p. 69/p. 74)*

SPORTS

I play ...

badminton

hockey

ice hockey

table tennis

volleyball

I go ...

canoeing

climbing

ice skating

riding

rowing

skateboarding

skating

skiing

snowboarding

windsurfing

I do ...

gymnastics

judo

yoga

badminton racket, shuttlecocks

hockey stick

ice hockey stick, puck

table tennis bat

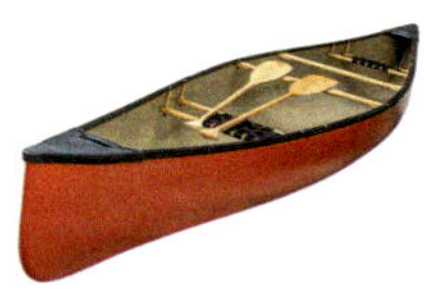
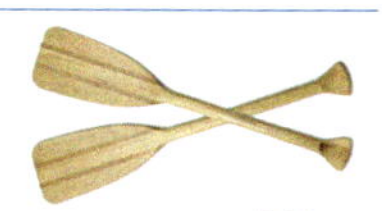
canoe, paddles

rope, climbing gear

saddle, riding boots

(ice) skates

(in-line) skates

skateboard

helmets

pads

skis, snowboard

badminton racket ['rækɪt] • **canoe** [kə'nuː] • **climbing gear** ['klaɪmɪŋ gɪə] Kletterausrüstung • **gymnastics** [dʒɪm'næstɪks] • **helmets** ['helmɪts] • **judo** ['dʒuːdəʊ] • **paddles** ['pædlz] • **pads** [pædz] (Schutz-)Polster, Schützer • **puck** [pʌk] • **riding boots** [buːts] • **rope** [rəʊp] • **rowing** ['rəʊɪŋ] • **saddle** ['sædl] • **shuttlecock** ['ʃʌtlkɒk] • **skiing** ['skiːɪŋ] • **yoga** ['jəʊgə]

MUSIC

I like ...
My hobby is ...

ballet dancing

listening to music

playing in a band

playing in the school orchestra

rapping

singing in a choir

I play the ...

clarinet

flute

recorder

saxophone

trumpet

◄ Wind instruments

String instruments ►

cello

violin

OTHER HOBBIES

I like ...
My hobby is ...

acting

drawing

making models

collecting stamps (comics, stickers, ...)

surfing the internet

taking photos

acting ['æktɪŋ] • **ballet dancing** ['bæleɪ] • **choir** ['kwaɪə] • **clarinet** [ˌklærə'net] • **drawing** ['drɔːɪŋ] • **flute** [fluːt] Querflöte • **model** ['mɒdl] • **orchestra** ['ɔːkɪstrə] • **recorder** [rɪ'kɔːdə] Blockflöte • **saxophone** ['sæksəfəʊn] • **trumpet** ['trʌmpɪt] • **violin** [ˌvaɪə'lɪn]

SF 1 Learning vocabulary

➔ p. 27, p. 50

Vokabeln kann man auf unterschiedliche Weise lernen. Wir stellen dir hier ein paar Möglichkeiten vor. Probiere sie im Laufe des Schuljahres aus, dann kannst du herausfinden, welche Methode für dich die beste ist.

Vokabeln lernen mit dem Vocabulary

Dein erster Weg führt dich zum Vocabulary (ab S. 201). Die wichtigsten Dinge dazu hast du ja schon in Unit 1 gelernt (S. 27).
Und so lernst du damit:

1 Lies die Vokabeln
- Lies das englische Wort in der linken Spalte laut.
- Lies dann die deutsche Übersetzung und den Beispielsatz.

I'm a seal. [aɪm] (= **I am** a seal.)	Ich bin eine Robbe.	! Das englische Wort **I** (= „ich") wird immer großgeschrieben – auch wenn es nicht am Satzanfang steht.
a seal [ə ˈsiːl]	eine Robbe	[iː] ist ein langes „i" wie in „Wien".

2 Teste dich Zeile für Zeile
- Decke die Spalte mit der deutschen Übersetzung ab. Sage die deutschen Wörter.
- Decke die linke und rechte Spalte ab. Sage die englischen Wörter. Versuche auch immer noch die Beispielsätze aus der rechten Spalte zu nennen.

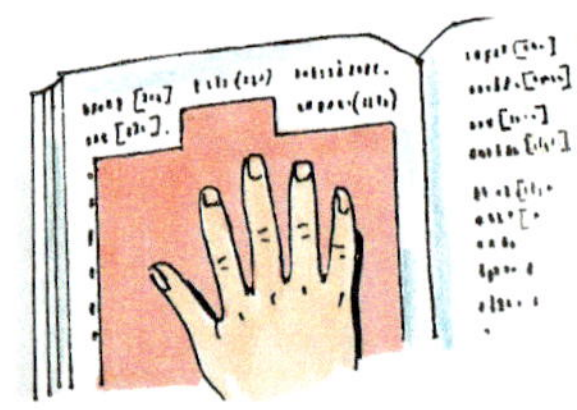

Und so kannst du dir eine Lernhilfe zum Abdecken der Spalten basteln:

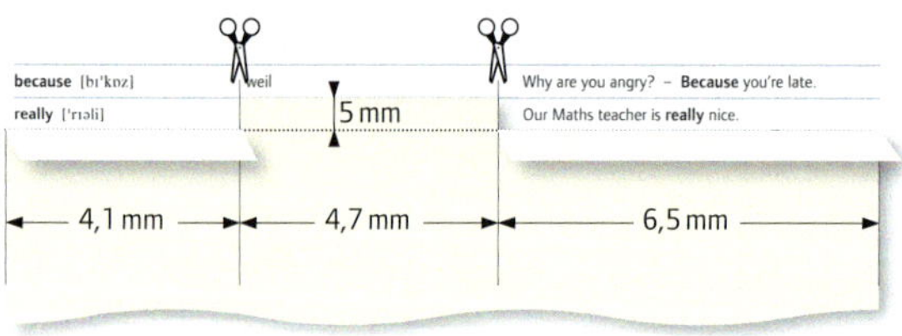

Englisch – Deutsch

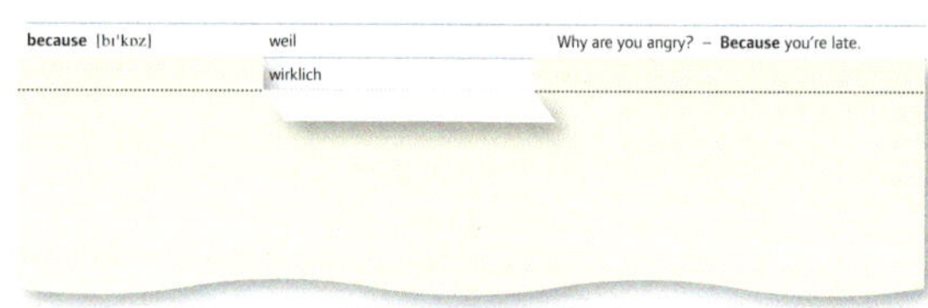

Deutsch – Englisch

> **TIPP**
> - Lerne immer 7–10 Wörter und Wendungen zusammen.
> - Lerne Vokabeln regelmäßig, am besten jeden Tag 5–10 Minuten.
> - Wiederhole die gelernten Vokabeln einmal in der Woche.
> - Lernen mit anderen macht Spaß – und ihr könnt euch gegenseitig abfragen.

Vokabeln lernen mit dem Vokabelheft

Manche lernen Vokabeln besonders gut, wenn sie sie aufschreiben: Dazu kannst du ein Vokabelheft mit drei Spalten anlegen. Schreibe das englische Wort in die linke Spalte, die deutsche Übersetzung in die mittlere Spalte und einen Beispielsatz (z. B. aus dem Vocabulary) in die rechte Spalte. Du kannst auch ein Bild malen. Lies die geschriebenen Wörter noch einmal laut.

Vokabeln lernen mit Merkzetteln

Du kannst Vokabeln, die du dir schwer merken kannst, auf kleine Notizzettel schreiben und zu Hause an Stellen kleben, wo du sie häufig siehst.

Du kannst auch Zettel an Gegenstände in deinem Zimmer kleben und so die englischen Wörter für diese Gegenstände lernen.

Vokabeln lernen mit Karteikarten

Manche können auch mit Karteikarten prima Vokabeln lernen. Und so geht das:

1 Schreibe das englische Wort mit einem Beispielsatz (z. B. aus dem Vocabulary) und evtl. einem Bild auf die Vorderseite einer Karteikarte und die deutsche Übersetzung auf die Rückseite.

2 Lies das englische Wort laut und sage die deutsche Bedeutung dazu. Dann kontrollierst du, ob du richtig gelegen hast. Beim nächsten Durchgang liest du das deutsche Wort zuerst und sagst das englische Wort laut.

Vorderseite *Rückseite*

TIPP

- Vergiss nicht, auch regelmäßig die Wörter zu wiederholen, die du kannst. Erst wenn du die Wörter nach zwei oder drei Wochen immer noch weißt, kannst du die Karten aussortieren.

Vokabeln in Gruppen sammeln und ordnen: Mindmaps

Du kannst neue Vokabeln ordnen und in Gruppen lernen – zum Beispiel mit Mindmaps. Wie das geht, kannst du dir auf S. 176 noch mal ansehen.

Vokabeln lernen mit dem Computer

Vielleicht fällt dir das Vokabellernen auch leichter, wenn du am Computer übst. Du kannst dazu dein e-Workbook nutzen.

SF 2 Collecting information

➜ p. 74

Wenn du einen Text schreiben oder etwas vortragen sollst, hilft es, wenn du vorher alle wichtigen Ideen und Informationen sammelst und ordnest. Dafür gibt es verschiedene Möglichkeiten wie z. B. Listen, Tabellen oder Mindmaps.

Listen

Listen sind die einfachste Art, Ideen zu sammeln. Sie sind gut geeignet, wenn du z. B. nur ein paar Punkte notieren willst.

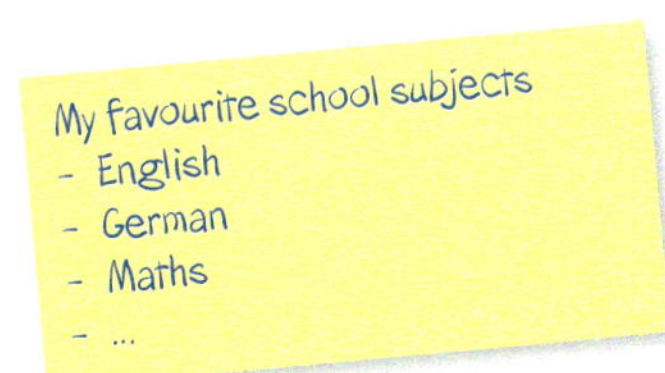

Tabellen

Tabellen sind vor allem dann gut, wenn deine Informationen schon eine gewisse Struktur haben, z. B. wenn du darüber reden willst, wann du was machst. Wie du eine Tabelle aufbauen kannst und worauf du achten solltest, kannst du noch mal auf S. 74 nachlesen.

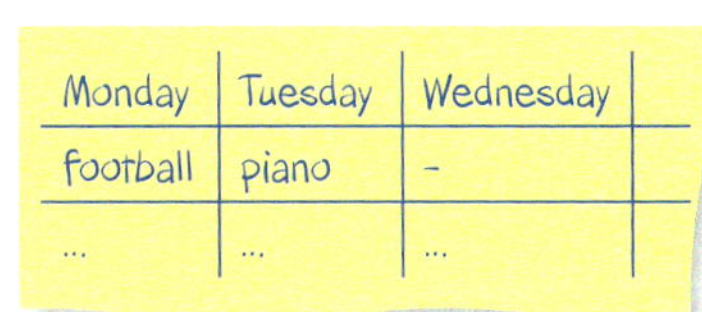

Mindmaps

Mindmaps können dir beim Sammeln und Ordnen von Ideen helfen.

Stell dir vor, du sollst einen Text über deine Schule schreiben. Wenn du nur über deine Fächer reden möchtest, ist eine Liste eine gute Wahl. Wenn es mehr um deinen Stundenplan geht, ist das mit einer Tabelle vielleicht einfacher. Wenn du aber über alles rund ums Thema Schule reden willst, dann eignet sich am besten eine Mindmap.

1 Was brauchst du?

- Ein leeres Blatt Papier, das du quer vor dich legst.
- Stifte in verschiedenen Farben.

2 Wie erstellst du eine Mindmap?

- Schreibe das Thema in die Mitte des Blattes und umrahme es mit einem Kreis oder einer Zeichnung.
- Überlege dir, welche Oberbegriffe *(umbrella words)* zu deiner Sammlung von Ideen passen. Verwende unterschiedliche Farben. Jetzt hat deine Mindmap Hauptäste.
- Ergänze jede Idee, die zu einem *umbrella word* passt, auf einem Nebenast.
- Du kannst statt Wörtern auch Zahlen oder Symbole eintragen und Bilder ergänzen.

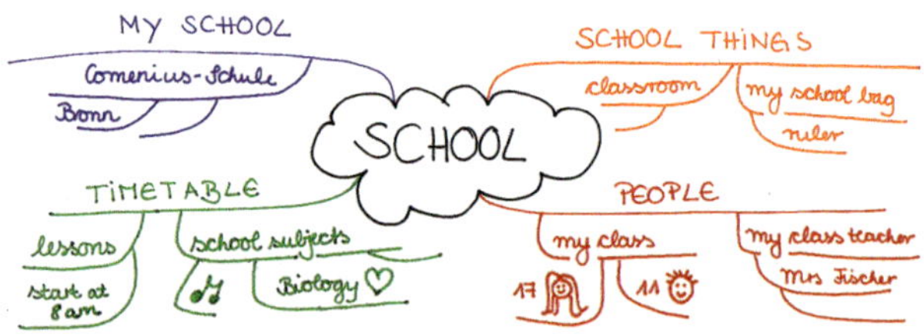

SF 3 Putting a page together

➜ p. 110

Nimm an, du möchtest eine Seite gestalten, z. B. für die Schülerzeitung oder als Poster für einen kleinen Vortrag. Folgende Hinweise können dir dabei helfen.

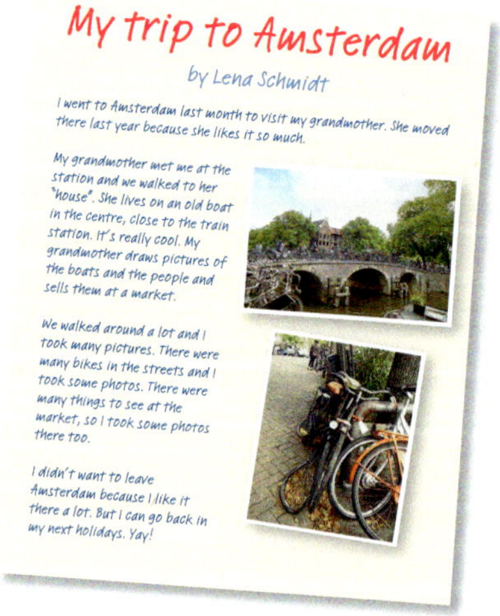

My trip to Amsterdam

by Lena Schmidt

I went to Amsterdam last month to visit my grandmother. She moved there last year because she likes it so much.

My grandmother met me at the station and we walked to her "house". She lives on an old boat in the centre, close to the train station. It's really cool. My grandmother draws pictures of the boats and the people and sells them at a market.

We walked around a lot and I took many pictures. There were many bikes in the streets and I took some photos. There were many things to see at the market, so I took some photos there too.

I didn't want to leave Amsterdam because I like it there a lot. But I can go back in my next holidays. Yay!

Sammle und ordne deine Informationen

- Sortiere die Informationen, die auf der Seite stehen sollen. Wenn du dir nicht mehr ganz sicher bist, wie das geht, sieh noch mal auf S. 74 nach.

Schreibe deinen Text

- Gib deinem Text eine klare Struktur. Die meisten Texte haben drei Teile: eine Einleitung, einen Hauptteil und einen Schluss.
- Beginne einen neuen Absatz für jeden neuen Gedanken, aber nicht für jeden Satz.
- Achte darauf, dass du dich nicht wiederholst und keine überflüssigen Informationen lieferst.

Wähle eine passende Überschrift

- Die Überschrift verdeutlicht, worum es in deinem Text geht. Sie kann auch lustig sein und den Leser neugierig machen auf das, was in deinem Text steht.
- Wenn es in deinem Text um mehrere Themen geht, dann kannst du für einzelne Abschnitte auch Zwischenüberschriften verwenden. Das gibt deinem Text eine klare Struktur und hilft dem Leser, sich schnell zu orientieren.

Suche oder zeichne Bilder für deinen Text

- Die Bilder sollten deinen Text näher erklären und interessant machen.
- Wähle Bildunterschriften, die das Bild kurz erläutern.

Sortiere Text und Bilder auf der Seite

- Achte darauf, dass die Seite nicht zu voll oder halbleer ist.
- Man muss erkennen, welches Bild zu welchem Textabschnitt gehört.

SF 4 Understanding and looking up new words

➜ p. 87

Immer gleich nachschlagen?

Englische Texte enthalten oft Wörter, die du noch nicht kennst. Schlage sie nicht gleich im Wörterbuch nach, denn das kostet Zeit und nimmt dir vielleicht den Spaß am Lesen. Häufig kannst du die Bedeutung dieser Wörter selbst herausfinden. Folgende Punkte können dir dabei helfen.

Was hilft dir, unbekannte Wörter zu verstehen?

1 Siehe dir die Bilder an
Bilder sind eine große Hilfe. Oft zeigen sie Dinge, die du in einem Text nicht verstehst. Was könnte im folgenden Satz mit ***leash*** gemeint sein?

My dog Rocky has a new red leash.

2 Denke an ähnliche Wörter im Deutschen
Es gibt viele englische Wörter, die im Deutschen ähnlich geschrieben werden oder ähnlich klingen, so genannte „verwandte Wörter". Was bedeuten wohl die Wörter in der Box rechts auf Deutsch?

balloon · brilliant · clarinet · combination · private · series · sharp · shine · spray · violin

3 Schaue dir die Wörter genau an
Manchmal stecken in unbekannten Wörtern bekannte Teile.

singer · **friend**ly · un**happy** · **end**less

4 Schaue dir den Satzzusammenhang an
Oft helfen dir auch die Wörter, die in der Nähe des unbekannten Wortes stehen. Kannst du im Beispiel rechts aus dem Zusammenhang heraus verstehen, was mit ***building*** gemeint ist?

The Queen lives in Buckingham Palace. It's a big **building** with over 600 rooms.

Und wenn du doch nachschlagen musst?

Wenn du trotz allem das unbekannte Wort nicht herausfindest und dir der Text Probleme macht, hilft dir das Dictionary (ab S. 243). Es enthält alle Wörter und Wendungen, die im Buch vorkommen.

Das Dictionary zeigt dir zudem auch, wie man die Wörter ausspricht.

Wie benutzt du das Dictionary?

1 Die blau gedruckten Stichwörter (z. B. **fall**, **family**) sind alphabetisch angeordnet (also **f** vor **g**, **fa** vor **fe**, **fla** vor **flo**).

2 Längere Ausdrücke findest du oft unter mehr als einem Stichwort, z. B. **free-time activities** unter **free** und unter **activity**.

3 Aussprache und Betonung stehen in den eckigen Klammern. Du bist bei den Lautschriftzeichen unsicher? Dann schaue dir *English sounds*, S. 272 an.

4 Es ist wichtig, den ganzen Eintrag nach dem Stichwort zu lesen. Oft findest du zusätzliche Hinweise, z. B. auf
- besondere Pluralformen
- längere Ausdrücke (z. B. **the first day**).

5 Die Ziffern 1., 2. usw. zeigen, dass das englische Stichwort mehrere Bedeutungen hat.

fall [fɔːl], *simple past:* **fell** fallen, stürzen; hinfallen 5 (119) **fall asleep** einschlafen 1 (30)
family ['fæməli] Familie 2 (36) **the Blackwell family** (die) Familie Blackwell 2 (36) °**family name** Familienname, Nachname **family tree** (Familien-)Stammbaum 2 (47)

free [friː] frei 3 (62) **free time** Freizeit, freie Zeit 3 (62) ▶ **free-time activities** Freizeitaktivitäten 3 (62)

first [fɜːst] zuerst, als Erstes 5 (108) **the first day** der erste Tag 1 (18) ▶ S. 233 English numbers
fish [fɪʃ], *pl* **fish** Fisch 2 (38)

get [get], *simple past:* **got:** **1.** bekommen 4 (99) **Did you get it?** *(infml)* Hast du es verstanden? / Hast du es mitbekommen? 4 (98) **2.** gelangen, (hin)kommen 5 (116)

SF 5 Taking notes

➜ p. 81

Manchmal liest oder hörst du etwas und willst es dir merken, z. B. um anderen davon zu erzählen. Da hilft es, wenn du dir in Stichworten Notizen machst.

Wie machst du Notizen?

Am besten kannst du das an einem Beispiel sehen. Yasmin soll herausfinden, wie man in England Halloween feiert. Sie hat ihre englische Freundin Sophie gefragt. Schaue dir an, wie sie in Sophies Antwort das Wichtige markiert und sich in Stichworten Notizen gemacht hat.

Dear Yasmin
Do I have a Halloween party? Yes, I do – every year. The party is only for girls – from my football team and from my class. There are no boys at this party. This year I'm a pirate.
The party usually starts at seven o'clock. We play games and then we eat pizza and chocolate cake. My mum always tells a ghost story at the end of the party.
Your friend
Sophie

Sophie: Halloween party ✓
only girls, ~~boys~~
Sophie: pirate
party starts: at 7
play games, eat pizza + choc. cake
end of party: Mum – ghost story

TIPP
- Verwende Ziffern (z. B. „7" statt „seven").
- Verwende Symbole und Abkürzungen, z. B. ✓ („Ja") und + („und") wie im Beispiel oben. Am besten erfindest du eigene Symbole.
- Verwende „not" oder ✗ bei Verneinungen.

SF 6 Giving a mini-talk

➜ p. 132

Oft sollst du Arbeitsergebnisse aus der Hausaufgabe, einem Projekt oder einer Gruppenarbeit in einem kleinen Vortrag präsentieren. Folgende Schritte helfen dir, dich gut vorzubereiten und deinen *mini-talk* interessant zu gestalten.

Wie hältst du einen guten Vortrag?

1 Sammle deine Ideen

- Sammle alle wichtigen Ideen und Punkte und ordne sie, z. B. in einer Liste, Tabelle oder Mindmap. Wenn du Informationen aus einem Buch oder dem Internet benutzt, schreibe dir auf, woher sie stammen.
  ➜ *SF 2: Collecting information (p. 175)*

2 Zeige deinen Zuhörern etwas

- Für deine Zuhörer ist es hilfreich, wenn sie nicht nur zuhören müssen, sondern etwas sehen (Bilder, Folien etc.) oder lesen können (Arbeitsblatt mit kleinen Texten). Wenn du z. B. ein Poster gestaltest, achte darauf, dass es gut lesbar und übersichtlich ist.
  ➜ *SF 3: Putting a page together (p. 176)*

3 Übe deinen Vortrag

- Lerne deinen Vortrag nicht auswendig, lies ihn auch nicht ab, sondern schreibe dir einen kleinen Merkzettel.

4 Während des Vortrags

- Beginne erst, wenn es ruhig ist.
- Schaue deine Zuhörer an.
- Nenne den Titel deines Vortrags und sag kurz, worüber du reden wirst.
- Sprich klar und deutlich und nicht zu schnell.
- Drücke dich möglichst einfach aus.

5 Am Ende des Vortrags

- Erkundige dich, ob es Nachfragen gibt.
- Bedanke dich für die Aufmerksamkeit.

SF 7 Listening

➜ p. 26

Wenn du Leute im Alltag reden hörst, hast du normalerweise eine Menge Informationen, die dir helfen herauszufinden, worum es geht (Gesichtsausdruck, Körpersprache usw.). Im Unterricht ist das schwieriger, weil das Gespräch aus dem CD-Player/aus dem Computer kommt, und meistens musst du auch noch Aufgaben dazu beantworten. Diese Hinweise können dir dabei helfen.

Vor dem Hören

- Schaue dir die Aufgabenstellung vor dem Hören genau an. Was genau sollst du heraushören? Konzentriere dich darauf.
- Wenn es Überschriften und Bilder zu der Höraufgabe gibt, schaue sie dir vorm Hören an und finde heraus, wer in der Aufnahme wohl mit wem spricht, wo die Leute sind und worum es geht.
- Überlege kurz, was du über das Thema schon weißt und welche englischen Begriffe wohl im Gespräch fallen werden.

Während des Hörens

- Höre nicht nur auf die Sprecher, sondern auch auf die Hintergrundgeräusche – ist das Gespräch in einem Laden, am Strand, in der Schule?
- „Hilfe – ich verstehe nicht alles!“ – Keine Panik, das ist völlig normal. Mache dir lieber klar, was du alles verstanden hast; oft ergibt sich der Rest.

Nach dem Hören

- Wenn möglich, vergleiche kurz mit einem Partner, ob ihr das Gleiche verstanden habt. Vielleicht kannst du den Text auch noch ein zweites Mal hören.

SF 8 Reading

➜ p. 61

Vor dem Lesen

Ehe du anfängst, einen Text zu lesen, schaue dir die Überschrift und die Bilder an, die dazu gehören. Was sagen sie dir über den Inhalt des Textes?

Während des ersten Lesens

- Lies den Text einmal am Stück durch und versuche, ihn insgesamt zu verstehen. Lasse unbekannte Wörter erstmal beiseite.

Nach dem ersten Lesen

- Wenn du fertig bist, versuche, die fünf W-Fragen zum Text zu beantworten: „Wer? Wo? Wann? Was? Warum?“ um sicher zu sein, dass du den Text verstanden hast. Noch besser ist es, mit einem Partner zusammen die Fragen zu beantworten.

Während des zweiten Lesens

- Gehe den Text noch einmal genauer durch. Wenn du auf ein unbekanntes Wort triffst, versuche, die Bedeutung zu erschließen. Tipps dafür gibt es in Skills File 4 . ➜ *SF 4: Understanding and looking up new words, p. 177*
- Was dir jetzt noch unbekannt ist, musst du nachschlagen oder erfragen.

SF 9 Writing – Check your spelling

➔ p. 31

Dein Text ist fertig – und jetzt?

Glückwunsch, du hast einen Text geschrieben! Leider bist du noch nicht ganz fertig, denn du solltest ihn noch einmal durchlesen, um Fehler zu korrigieren.

Wenn möglich, lies dir deinen Text laut vor. Das kann helfen, Fehler schneller zu finden. Noch besser: finde einen Partner, mit dem du Texte tauschen kannst. Fremde Fehler sind oft leichter zu erkennen als eigene.

Achte insbesondere auf folgende Dinge:

Laute, die gleich klingen, aber anders geschrieben werden	*their/there/they're* *your/you're*
Schreibung des Apostrophs	*the pupils' books, the pupil's books*
Bildung der Zeitformen der Verben	*stop* → *sto**pp**ing, try* → *tr**ies***
Groß- und Kleinschreibung	*Tom is **B**ritish, I am **G**erman.*
ungewöhnliche Buchstabenkombinationen	*thought, enough*
Wörter, die im Deutschen ähnlich, aber nicht ganz genau gleich sind	*Elefant* → *elephant* *Biologie* → *biology*
Wörter mit Buchstaben, die man nicht spricht	*walk, talk*

Immer die gleichen Fehler?

Versuche herauszufinden, welche Fehler du immer wieder machst. Sieh dir an, was bei deinen Texten oder Klassenarbeiten wiederholt angestrichen ist.

TIPP
Schreibe diese Fehler auf kleine Zettel. Dann helfen sie dir vielleicht, wenn du wieder einen Text schreibst.

SF 10 Mediation

➔ p. 30

Was ist Mediation?

Wenn du zwischen zwei Sprachen vermittelst, also z. B. deutsche Informationen auf Englisch wiedergibst oder umgekehrt, nennt man das *mediation*.

Worauf muss ich achten?

- Übersetze nicht alles wörtlich, gib nur wichtige Informationen wieder. Du kannst Unwichtiges weglassen und Sätze anders formulieren.
- Verwende kurze und einfache Sätze.
- Wenn du ein Wort nicht kennst, umschreibe es oder ersetze es durch ein anderes mit ähnlicher Bedeutung.

Grammar File – Inhalt

Seite

Im **Grammar File** (S. 182–200) kannst du nachsehen,
- wenn du selbstständig etwas lernen oder etwas wiederholen möchtest,
- wenn du Übungen aus dem *Practice*-Teil deines Englischbuches oder aus dem *Workbook* bearbeitest,
- wenn du dich auf einen Test vorbereiten willst.

In der **linken Spalte** findest du **Beispielsätze** und **Übersichten**, z. B.

GF 3 The verb *(to) be* Das Verb *(to) be* („sein“)

a) Statements with *be*

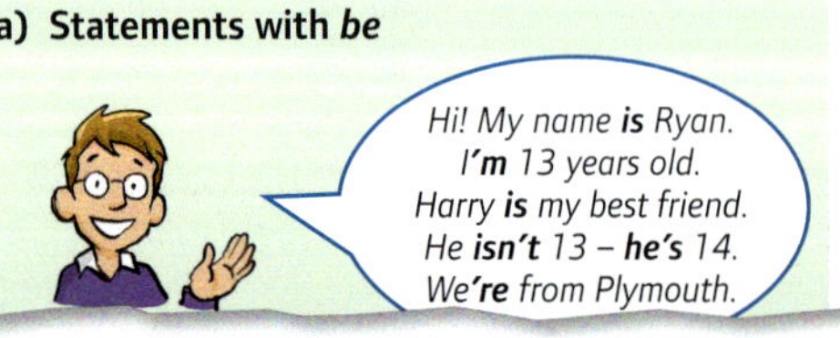

In der **rechten Spalte** stehen **Erklärungen** und nützliche Hinweise (auf Deutsch).

Besonders wichtig sind die Stellen mit den **roten Ausrufezeichen** (!). Sie zeigen, was im Deutschen anders ist, und machen dich auf Fehlerquellen aufmerksam.

Verweise wie ➔ *p. 26, exercise 7* zeigen dir, wo Übungen zum gerade behandelten grammatischen Thema stehen.

Die **grammatischen Fachbegriffe** *(grammatical terms)* kannst du auf den Seiten 199–200 nachschlagen.

Am Ende der *Grammar-File*-Abschnitte stehen kleine **Aufgaben** zur **Selbstkontrolle**. Hier kannst du überprüfen, ob du das gerade behandelte Thema verstanden hast. Auf S. 200 kannst du dann nachsehen, ob deine Lösungen richtig sind.

Unit 1

GF 1 Personal pronouns Personalpronomen

Nomen:	*boy*	*girl*	*pencil*

Pronomen:	*he*	*she*	*it*

Nomen stehen für Lebewesen *(boy, girl, seal, cat)* und Gegenstände *(book, photo, pencil)*, aber auch für alles, was man nicht sehen oder anfassen kann *(name, time, word, love)*.

Auch **Pronomen (Fürwörter)** können für Lebewesen, Gegenstände und Begriffe stehen.
Die Pronomen ***I, you, he, she, it, we, you, they*** nennt man **Personalpronomen**.

You are nice. = Du bist nett. / Ihr seid nett. / Sie sind nett.

! Das englische Personalpronomen ***you*** kann ***du*** oder ***ihr*** oder ***Sie*** heißen.

Personal pronouns

Bei einer männlichen Person – ***he***
Bei einer weiblichen Person – ***she***
Bei einem Gegenstand oder Begriff – ***it***
Bei einem Haustier – ***he*** oder ***she***
Bei einem Tier, das keinen Namen hat – ***it***
Bei mehreren Personen, Gegenständen, Tieren – ***they***

	What colour is …	**Welche Farbe hat …**
	… ***the pencil****?* – ***It****'s green.*	… **der** Bleistift? – **Er** ist grün.
	… ***the bag****?* – ***It****'s blue.*	… **die** Tasche? – **Sie** ist blau.
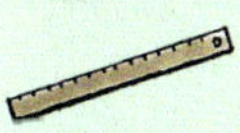	… ***the ruler****?* – ***It****'s brown.*	… **das** Lineal? – **Es** ist braun.

! Das englische Personalpronomen ***it*** steht für alle Gegenstände und Begriffe, kann also ***er*** oder ***sie*** oder ***es*** heißen.

→ *p. 24, exercises 1–2*

Möchtest du überprüfen, ob du alles verstanden hast? Dann löse jetzt diese beiden Aufgaben:

a) Wie viele Personalpronomen enthält diese Liste?

boy · the · it · Silky · she · they · nice · your · you · we · green

b) ***he***, ***she***, ***it*** oder ***they***?

1 *Look, a snake. – …'s big.*
2 *This is my cat Susie. – How old is …?*
3 *And this is my dog Victor. – …'s nice.*
4 *Where are your rabbits? – …'re in my room.*

(Auf S. 200 kannst du nachschauen, ob deine Antworten richtig sind.)

GF 2 Possessive determiners Possessivbegleiter

Possessive determiners

I	– **my room**	*mein Zimmer*
you	– **your room**	*dein/Ihr Zimmer*
he	– **his room**	*sein Zimmer*
she	– **her room**	*ihr Zimmer*
it	– **its room**	*sein/ihr Zimmer*
we	– **our room**	*unser Zimmer*
you	– **your room**	*euer/Ihr Zimmer*
they	– **their room**	*ihr Zimmer*

Die **Possessivbegleiter** ***my, your, his, her, its, our, your, their*** stehen vor einem Nomen.
Sie zeigen an, wem (oder zu wem) etwas gehört.
Sie werden daher auch **besitzanzeigende Begleiter** genannt.

Their *name is Taylor.*	***They're*** *new here.*
Ihr Name …	Sie sind …
Your *dog is nice.*	***You're*** *nice, too.*
Dein/Ihr Hund …	Du bist …/Sie sind …
His *brother is 16, and*	***he's*** *14.*
Sein Bruder …	er ist …
Its *name is Goldie.*	***It's*** *a hamster.*
Sein Name …	Es ist …

! Einige **Possessivbegleiter** kann man leicht mit **Kurzformen von *be*** verwechseln.

GF 3 The verb *(to) be* Das Verb *(to) be* („sein")

a) Statements with *be*

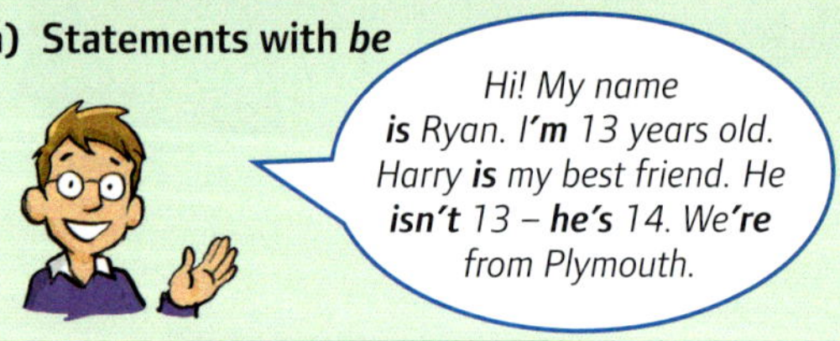

Aussagen mit *be*

Das Verb **be** hat in der Gegenwart *(present)* drei Formen: ***am, are*** und ***is***.

◄ Hier siehst du einige Lang- und Kurzformen von *be*.

be **(present) – Aussagen**

Langformen: bejaht (+)	verneint (–)	Kurzformen: bejaht (+)	verneint (–)
I am	I am not	I'm	I'm not
you are	you are not	you're	you aren't
he/she/it is	he/she/it is not	he's/she's/it's	he/she/it isn't
we are	we are not	we're	we aren't
you are	you are not	you're	you aren't
they are	they are not	they're	they aren't

Beim Sprechen und in persönlichen Briefen werden meist die Kurzformen von *be* verwendet.

➜ *p. 25, exercises 3–5*

b) Questions with *be*

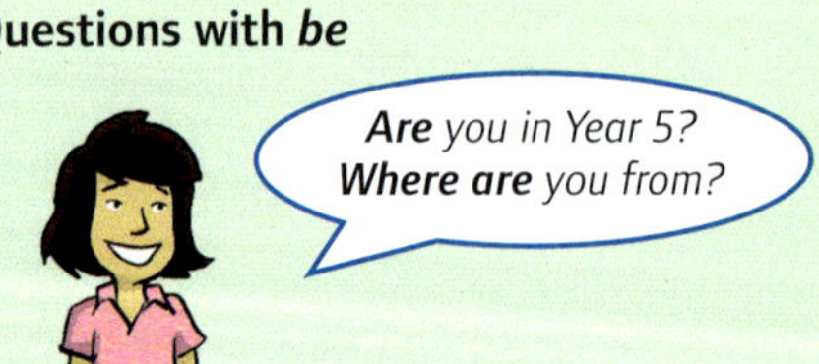

be **(present) – Fragen**

Am I …?	Are we …?
Are you …?	Are you …?
Is he/she/it …?	Are they …?

➜ *p. 29, exercise 1*

Fragen mit *be*

Es gibt zwei Arten von Fragen:

- **ohne** Fragewort: ***Are you 13?*** · ***Is she your friend?***
- **mit** Fragewort: ***Who are you?*** · ***Where are you?***

Nach einem Fragewort wird ***is*** oft verkürzt:

Who's *that?*
Where's *my book?*
What's *your name?*

c) Short answers with *be*

Are you 13? – **Yes, I am.**
Are you from Plymouth? – **No, I'm not.**
Is Emma your sister? – **Yes, she is. / No, she isn't.**

be (present) – Kurzantworten:

+		–	
	Yes, I am.		No, I'm not.
	Yes, you are.		No, you aren't.
	Yes, he/she/it is.		No, he/she/it isn't.
	Yes, we/you/they are.		No, we/you/they aren't.

➡ *p. 29, exercise 1*

Kurzantworten mit *be*

Fragen ohne Fragewort werden meist nicht nur mit *Yes* oder *No* beantwortet – das wäre unhöflich. Du solltest eine Kurzantwort verwenden, z. B. ***Yes, I am*** oder ***No, I'm not***.

! In Kurzantworten mit ***Yes*** darfst du keine Kurzform verwenden.
Also nur
***Yes, I am.* / *Yes, she is.* / *Yes, we are*.**
usw.

Alles verstanden? Dann kannst du jetzt diese Aufgabe lösen:
Wie antwortet man höflich auf die folgende Frage? (Zwei Antworten sind richtig.)

Are you eleven? – **1** *Yes.* · **2** *Yes, I'm.* · **3** *Yes, I am.* · **4** *No.* · **5** *No, I'm not.*

GF 4 The possessive form (I) Der s-Genitiv

Wenn du sagen willst, dass etwas jemandem gehört (oder zu jemandem gehört), benutzt du den **s-Genitiv**.

English:	***Lucy's*** *books*	***Justin's*** *dad*
German:	**Lucys** Bücher	**Justins** Vater

! Anders als im Deutschen steht im Englischen ein Apostroph: *Abby's house*.

Singular: *Maya's backpack is in* ***Lucy's*** *room.*
Mayas Rucksack ist in Lucys Zimmer.

◄ Im Singular wird *'s* angehängt.

Plural: *The cats are in the* ***boys'*** *room.*
Die Katzen sind im Zimmer der Jungen.

◄ Wenn die Pluralform auf **s** endet, wird nur ein Apostroph angehängt.

➡ *p. 26, exercise 7*

Verstanden? Dann beantworte jetzt diese Fragen:
Wie viele Personen sind es? Sind es **ein** oder **mehrere** Brüder, Mädchen, Schüler/innen?

1 *my* ***brother's*** *room*
2 *my* ***brothers'*** *room*
3 *the* ***girls'*** *father*
4 *the* ***students'*** *teacher*
5 *the* ***student's*** *desk*
6 *the* ***girl's*** *family name*

GF 5 **Imperatives** Aufforderungen, Befehle

➜ *p. 27, exercise 9*

Anders als im Deutschen gibt es im Englischen nur eine Befehlsform, egal mit wem du sprichst:

Englisch: ***Open** the window, please.*
Deutsch: ***Öffne / Öffnet / Öffnen Sie** bitte das Fenster.*

Aus Höflichkeit solltest du ***please*** verwenden, wenn du jemanden aufforderst, etwas zu tun.

Bei einer Aufforderung, etwas nicht zu tun (einem verneinten Befehl), steht ***don't*** vor dem Infinitiv:

Don't open** the window.* (Langform: ***Do not open ...)

GF 6 *There is ... / There are ...*

***There's** a desk in my room.*
In meinen Zimmer steht ein Schreibtisch.

***There are** books and school things on my desk.*
Es liegen Bücher und Schulsachen auf meinem Schreibtisch.

***Is there** a clock in your room?*
*– **Yes, there is.** / **No, there isn't.***

***There aren't any** cats in my picture.*
Es gibt keine Katzen auf meinem Bild.

***Are there any** cats in your picture?*
Sind Katzen auf deinem Bild?

➜ *p. 34, exercises 1–2*

Mit ***There is ...*** (kurz: ***There's ...***) und ***There are ...*** drückst du aus, dass etwas vorhanden ist.

Im Deutschen benutzt man meist ***Es gibt ...***, ***Es ist ... / Es sind ...*** oder Sätze mit ***liegen*** oder ***stehen***.

Auf Fragen reagiert man mit einer Kurzantwort:
\+ ***Yes, there is. / Yes, there are.***
– ***No, there isn't. / No, there aren't.***

! Beachte, dass nach ***There aren't*** und ***Are there*** in der Regel das Wort ***any*** steht.

Schaue dir das Bild an und vervollständige die Sätze.
(Vorsicht: In drei Sätzen brauchst du ***any***!)

1 *... a computer on the desk.*
2 *... books on the desk.*
3 *(pencils?) ... on the desk? – Yes, ...*
4 *(ball?) ... on the desk? – No, ...*
5 *(CDs?) ... on the desk? – ...*
6 *(ruler?) ... on the desk? – ...*

GF 7 *can* „können"

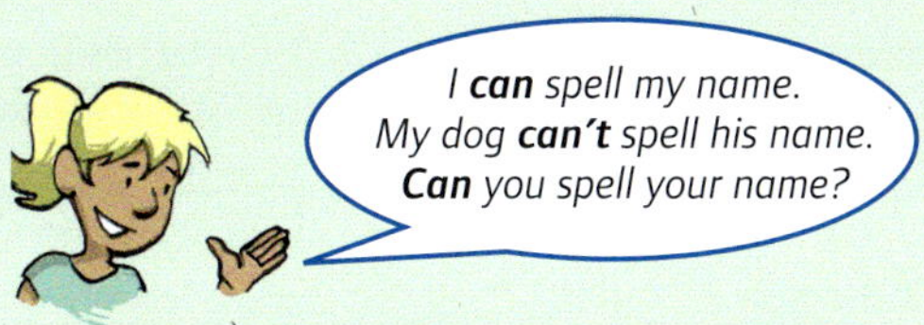

I ***can answer*** ***your question***.
Ich kann **deine Frage** beantworten.

We ***can't help*** ***you***.
Wir können **dir** nicht helfen.

Can *we watch a DVD, please?*
– ***Yes, you can.*** */* ***No, you can't.***

➜ *p. 34, exercise 3*

Mit ***can*** drückst du aus, was jemand tun kann.

Mit ***can't*** (Langform: ***cannot***) drückst du aus, was jemand nicht tun kann.

Die Formen ***can*** und ***can't*** gelten für alle Personen:

I/you/he/she/it/we/you/they ***can*** *spell.*
I/you/he/she/it/we/you/they ***can't*** *spell.*

! Anders als im Deutschen steht das Verb im Englischen direkt hinter ***can*** bzw. ***can't***.

Auf Fragen reagiert man mit einer Kurzantwort:
\+ ***Yes, I can. / Yes, you can.*** usw.
– ***No, I can't. / No, you can't.*** usw.

GF 8 *this, that – these, those*

Die Wörter ***this*** und ***that*** (Singular) und ***these*** und ***those*** (Plural) weisen auf etwas hin. Sie können **vor einem Nomen** oder **allein, anstelle eines Nomens** stehen.

Man nennt sie **Demonstrativbegleiter** *(demonstrative determiners)* bzw. **Demonstrativpronomen** *(demonstrative pronouns)*.

- Wenn etwas **näher beim Sprecher** ist, verwendet man eher ***this*** bzw. ***these***.
- Wenn etwas **weiter entfernt** ist, verwendet man eher ***that*** bzw. ***those***.

Unit 2

GF 9 The simple present (I): positive and negative statements

Die einfache Form der Gegenwart (I): postive und negative Aussagesätze

a) Positive statements

➜ *pp. 48–49, exercises 1–5*

Bejahte Aussagesätze

Der Junge redet darüber, wie jeden Morgen sein Tag beginnt. Er verwendet das *simple present* (die einfache Form der Gegenwart).

Verben im *simple present* haben bei ***I***, ***you***, ***we*** und ***they*** keine Endung:
I/You/We/They ***like*** *games.*

Nur bei ***he***, ***she*** und ***it*** (der 3. Person Singular) wird ein ***s*** angefügt:
He/She/It ***likes*** *games.*

He, she, it –
das **s** muss mit!

! Das Hilfsverb ***can*** hat **kein s** bei *he/she/it*!

Vergleiche: *Our teacher* ***can help*** *us.*
Our teacher always ***helps*** *us.*

Eine kleine Aufgabe? Wo fehlt ein **s**? Schreibe die korrekten Sätze in dein Übungsheft.

1 *I like_ card games.*
2 *My sister like_ football.*
3 *My dog always sleep_ in his basket.*
4 *Susie can_ sleep_ on my bed.*
5 *Seals eat_ fish.*
6 *Silky eat_ crabs too.*

b) 3rd person singular: pronunciation and spelling

3. Person Singular: Aussprache und Schreibung

Der Laut **vor** dem **s** bestimmt, wie das **s** ausgesprochen wird:

1 [s] *Silky **eats** fish.* [-ts]
*Skip **sleeps** in a basket.* [-ps]
*Mr Blackwell **likes** games.* [-ks]

◀ **1** Folgt das **s** auf einen **stimmlosen Konsonanten**, wird es wie das Zischen einer Schlange gesprochen: [s].
Stimmlose Konsonanten sind z.B. [t], [p], [k].

2 [z] *Silky **lives** in Plymouth.* [-vz]
*Dad always **comes** home late.* [-mz]
*Abby **feeds** Skip in the morning.* [-dz]
*Mink **plays** at night.* [-eɪz]
*Abby **knows** Maya.* [-əʊz]

◀ **2** Folgt das **s** auf einen **stimmhaften Konsonanten** oder einen **Vokal**, wird es wie das Summen einer Biene gesprochen: [z].
Stimmhafte Konsonanten sind z.B. [v], [m], [d].

3 [ɪz] *Silky always **catches** lots of fish.* [-tʃɪz]
*Maya **watches** TV at weekends.* [-tʃɪz]
*Our teacher **uses** red pens.* [-zɪz]

◀ **3** Folgt das **s** auf einen **Zischlaut**, wird es [ɪz] gesprochen.
Zischlaute sind z.B. [s], [z], [ʃ], [tʃ], [dʒ].
Nach Zischlauten wird *es* oder *s* angehängt, je nach Schreibung des Infinitivs: *catch – catches* · *use – uses*.

---

*He's late for school, so he **hurries** up.*
Er ist spät dran für die Schule, daher beeilt er sich.

*Sam always **tries** to help his sister Lily.*
Sam versucht immer, seiner Schwester Lily zu helfen.

◀ Bei Verben, die auf **Konsonant** + **y** enden, gibt es eine Besonderheit in der 3. Person Singular: ***y*** **+ *s*** ⟶ ***ies***.

Beispiel: ***hurry*** **+ *s*** ⟶ ***hurries***, ***try*** **+ *s*** ⟶ ***tries***

(Aber: **Vokal** + **y** bleibt unverändert: ***play*** **+ *s*** ⟶ ***plays***)

! Auch bei den Verben ***have, go, do*** und ***say*** gibt es Besonderheiten in der 3. Person Singular:

*Abby **has** a new friend.*

- ***have*** ⟶ *he/she/it* ***has***

*Sam **goes** to Plymstock School.*

- ***go*** **+ *es*** ⟶ *he/she/it* ***goes***

*Abby always **does** her homework in her room.* [dʌz]

- ***do*** **+ *es*** ⟶ *he/she/it* ***does***
  Die Aussprache ändert sich: *do* [duː] – *does* [dʌz]

*Simon **says**, "Put your pens on your desk."* [sez]

- Bei ***say*** ändert sich die Aussprache:
  I say [seɪ] – *he/she/it says* [sez]

➜ *p. 49, exercise 3*

Und hier wieder zwei kleine Aufgaben:

a) Bei welchen Verben musst du bei *he/she/it* die Endung ***-es*** (statt **-s**) anhängen?

watch · write · think · touch · go · play · sleep · catch · put · do

b) Welche Aussprache ist richtig? Ordne die Wörter den Buchstaben **A** bis **C** zu.

1 *helps* · **2** *watches* · **3** *answers* · **4** *goes* · **5** *follows*
6 *touches* · **7** *meets* · **8** *comes* · **9** *asks* · **10** *feeds*

A [s] **B** [z] **C** [ɪz]

c) Negative statements

*I **don't like** cricket.*	Ich mag Kricket nicht.
*He **doesn't have** time for sport.*	Er hat keine Zeit für Sport.

Verneinte Aussagesätze

So verneinst du Aussagesätze im *simple present*:

- bei *I, you, we, they* mit ***don't*** **+ Infinitiv**
- bei *he, she, it* mit ***doesn't*** **+ Infinitiv**.

! Das **s** der 3. Person Singular steckt im Wort ***doesn't***:
*He/She **doesn't live** in Britain.*
(nicht: *He/She doesn't live~~s~~ …*)

Simple present – verneinte Aussagen

I	don't	live	
You	don't	live	
He/She/It	doesn't	live	in Britain.
We	don't	live	
You	don't	live	
They	don't	live	

➜ *pp. 53–54, exercises 1–4*

Vervollständige jetzt diese Sätze in deinem Übungsheft. Vorsicht – ***don't*** oder ***doesn't***?
Beispiel: *We (~~watch TV~~)* don't watch TV *at weekends, we play games.*

1 *Dilip and Sanjay (~~live~~) … in South Africa.*
2 *Uncle Dasan (~~live~~) … in Britain.*
3 *He goes to a sports school, but he (~~do sport~~) …*
4 *Maya (~~go~~) … to Plymstock School.*
5 *My cats (~~sleep~~) … at night – they play.*
6 *I (~~have~~) … a cat, I have a rabbit.*

GF 10 Word order (I): S-V-O Wortstellung (I): S-V-O

Subject	**Verb**	**Object**
Maya's brother	likes	computer games.
He	doesn't like	cricket.
Maya	asks	about her family.
She	has to write	about it.

Die wichtigste Wortstellungsregel im Englischen ist **S–V–O**: ***subject – verb – object***
(Subjekt – Prädikat – Objekt)

Das kannst du dir gut merken, wenn du an die **Straßenverkehrsordnung** denkst.

1 *"Maya, you **can ask** **Uncle Amar**."*
„Maya, du **kannst** **Onkel Amar** **fragen**."

2 *Sam **watches TV** **every Sunday afternoon**.*
Sam **schaut** **jeden Sonntagnachmittag** **Fernsehen**.

3 *Lucy has breakfast **in the kitchen** **every morning**.*
Lucy frühstückt **jeden Morgen** **in der Küche**.

➜ *p. 49, exercise 6*

! Es gibt einige wichtige Unterschiede zwischen dem Englischen und dem Deutschen. Sieh dir die Beispielsätze und die Übersetzungen gut an.

1 Das Objekt (hier: *Uncle Amar*) kann **nicht** zwischen *can* und Vollverb (hier: *ask*) stehen.

2 Zeitangaben (hier: *every Sunday afternoon*) können **nicht** zwischen Prädikat und Objekt stehen. Sie stehen am Ende oder am Anfang des Satzes.

3 Ortsangaben (hier: *in the kitchen*) stehen vor Zeitangaben (hier: *every morning*).

Ort vor Zeit – *wie im Alphabet!*

Schreibe die Sätze mit der richtigen Wortstellung in dein Übungsheft.

1 ***We*** … *(can – cards – play – when – you – home – come)*
2 ***Today*** … *(can – you – your homework – do – in the dining room)*
3 ***My room*** … *(is – too small – so – meet – we – usually – at Emily's house)*
4 ***Justin*** … *(live – doesn't – with his dad – because – his dad – a job – in Boston – has)*
5 ***After breakfast*** … *(I – feed – always – my cat)*

GF 11 *have got* „haben"

*The Blackwells **have got** two pets.*
Die Blackwells haben zwei Haustiere.

*I **haven't got** a pet.*
Ich habe kein Haustier.

*Amy **has got** a lot of sailing trophies.*
*Her brother **hasn't got** any trophies,*
*but he**'s got** lots of computer games.*

Im *simple present* kann ***have got*** für das deutsche „haben", „besitzen" verwendet werden.

Die Form ***have got*** gilt für ***I, you, we, you, they***.
Bei ***he/she/it*** heißt die Form ***has got***.

Oft werden **Kurzformen** verwendet:
- *I**'ve got** a sister, but I **haven't got** a brother.*
  *(= I **have got** … I **have not got** …)*
- *She**'s got** a dog, but she **hasn't got** a cat.*
  *(= She **has got** … she **has not got** …)*

have got

Langformen: +	–	Kurzformen: +	–
I/you **have got**	I/you **have not got**	I**'ve**/you**'ve got**	I/you **haven't got**
he/she/it **has got**	he/she/it **has not got**	he**'s**/she**'s**/it**'s got**	he/she/it **hasn't got**
we/you/they **have got**	we/you/they **have not got**	we**'ve**/you**'ve**/they**'ve got**	we/you/they **haven't got**

***Have** you **got** a pet?*

***When have** we **got** Maths today?*
*And **what have** we **got** now?*

◄ Bei Fragen sind ***have*** (bzw. ***has***) und das Subjekt vertauscht:
- ***Have** you **got** a pet?*
- ***Has** she **got** a rabbit?*

Have you got a pet? – ***Yes, I have. / No, I haven't.***
Have we got Maths today? – ***Yes, we have. / No, we haven't.***
Has your sister got a rabbit? – ***Yes, she has. / No, she hasn't.***

➜ *p. 54, exercise 5*

! Beachte:
- Bei **Kurzantworten** fällt ***got*** weg.
- Nach der **Kurzantwort mit *Yes*** musst du die **Langform** verwenden.

Unit 3

GF 12 The simple present (II): questions and short answers

Die einfache Form der Gegenwart (II): Fragen und Kurzantworten

a) *Yes/No* questions and short answers

Entscheidungsfragen und Kurzantworten

Entscheidungsfragen sind Fragen, auf die man mit „Ja" oder „Nein" antworten kann.

Fragen im *simple present* bildet man mit ***do*** oder ***does***:

- ***do*** bei *I, you, we, they*
- ***does*** bei *he, she, it* (3. Person Singular).

Die Wortstellung in Entscheidungsfragen ist wie beim Aussagesatz. Vergleiche:

Aussagesatz:	*They go sailing.*	*Sie gehen segeln.*
Fragesatz:	***Do** they go sailing?*	*Gehen sie segeln?*

__Does__ Lucy __know__ Abby?
__Does__ Abby __live__ in a nice house?
__Does__ Sam __go__ to basketball?

! Das **s** der 3. Person Singular steckt im Wort ***does***:
***Does** she **live** in a nice house?*
(nicht: *Does she lives …?*)

__Do__ you __like__ sport? – __Yes, I do. / No, I don't.__
__Does__ Justin __have__ a camera? – __Yes, he does.__
__Does__ Lucy __go__ to any clubs? – __No, she doesn't.__
__Do__ Abby's brothers __have__ a hobby? – __Yes, they do.__

Entscheidungsfragen werden meist nicht nur mit *Yes* oder *No* beantwortet, sondern mit einer Kurzantwort:
- ***Yes, I do. / Yes, she does. / Yes, we do.*** usw.
- ***No, I don't. / No, she doesn't. / No, we don't.*** usw.

Simple present – Entscheidungsfragen und Kurzantworten

?			+	–
Do	I	know …?	Yes, you do.	No, you don't.
Do	you	know …?	Yes, I do.	No, I don't.
Does	he/she/it	know …?	Yes, he/she/it does.	No, he/she/it doesn't.
Do	we	know …?	Yes, you do.	No, you don't.
Do	you	know …?	Yes, we do.	No, we don't.
Do	they	know …?	Yes, they do.	No, they don't.

➜ *p. 72, exercise 1 • p. 73, exercises 3–4*

Möchtest du wieder überprüfen, ob du alles verstanden hast? Hier zwei Aufgaben:

a) Stelle Fragen. Frage nach den Personen in Klammern.
Beispiel: *Justin has a camera. (Sam?)* Does Sam have a camera too?

1 *Sam plays basketball. (Lucy?)*
2 *The Blackwells play games at weekends. (Maya?)*
3 *Abby lives in a nice house. (Sam and Lily?)*
4 *Maya visits Abby at weekends. (Lucy?)*
5 *Justin makes video films. (Sam?)*
6 *Abby goes sailing. (Abby's brothers?)*

b) Welche Kurzantwort ist richtig, **A**, **B** oder **C**?

1 *Does Maya have a dog?* **A** *Yes, she does.* **B** *Yes, she don't.* **C** *Yes, she do.*
2 *Does your brother like cornflakes?* **A** *No, they don't.* **B** *No, he doesn't.* **C** *No, he don't.*
3 *Do Maya's cousins live in Africa?* **A** *No, she doesn't.* **B** *No, they doesn't.* **C** *No, they don't.*

b) Questions with question words

Justin: *__Where do__ you __work__, Dad?*
And __what do__ you __do__ there?

__Why does__ Dad __work__ so much, Mum?

➜ *pp. 77–78, exercises 1–4*

Fragen mit Fragewörtern

Fragen mit Fragewörtern *(When, Where, What, Why, How)* bildest du wie Entscheidungsfragen.
Das Fragewort steht am Anfang der Frage, vor *do* bzw. *does*. Vergleiche:

	*They **go** sailing.*
Entscheidungsfrage:	***Do** they **go** sailing?*
Frage mit Fragewort:	***Where do** they **go** sailing?*

Sieh dir die Antwort an, finde das richtige Fragewort und bilde die Frage.
Beispiel: *(… you – have breakfast?)* ***At 7 o'clock.*** ⟶ When do you have breakfast?

1 *(… Maya – visit Abby?)* ***At weekends.***
2 *(… Abby – live?)* ***In a nice house in Wembury.***
3 *(… Abby's brothers – go sailing)?* ***Because they love the sea.***
4 *(… you – do in your free time?)* ***I play hockey.***

GF 13 Das Verb *(to) have to* Das Verb *(to) have to* („müssen“)

*Abby and Tim **have to** feed Skip in the morning.*
*But they **don't have to** take him for a walk.*
Abby und Tim **müssen** morgens Skip füttern.
Aber sie **müssen nicht** mit ihm rausgehen.

*Every evening Justin **has to** help with dinner.*
*But he **doesn't have to** wash the dishes.*

***Do** you **have to** help a lot at home, Maya? – Yes, I do.*
***Does** Mukesh **have to** help too? – No, he doesn't!*

*Why **do*** Mum and Dad ***have to** go out?*

Wenn du ausdrücken willst, was du oder andere tun müssen, verwendest du ***have to***.

In der 3. Person Singular *(he/she/it)* heißt es ***has to***.

! Das ***to*** nach ***have*** und ***has*** muss immer dabeistehen.

◄ Wie du siehst, werden verneinte Sätze, Fragen und Kurzantworten mit Hilfe von ***do/does*** gebildet – wie bei anderen Verben auch.
Schau dir die Beispiele links genau an.

(to) have to

+		–		?	
I/you	have to	I/you	don't have to.	Do I/you	have to ...?
he/she/it	**has to**	he/she/it	**doesn't have to**	**Does** he/she/it	**have to** ...?
we/you/they	have to	we/you/they	don't have to	Do we/you/they	have to ...?

➜ *p. 73, exercises 5–6*

GF 14 *a lot of/lots of – much – many* „viel, viele“

zählbare Nomen (countable nouns):

DVD – DVDs	*idea – ideas*	*teacher – teachers*
DVD – DVDs	Idee – Ideen	Lehrer/in – Lehrer/innen

nicht zählbare Nomen (uncountable nouns):

cheese	*milk*	*music*	*time*
Käse	Milch	Musik	Zeit

Im Deutschen verwenden wir **„viele“** mit dem Plural von zählbaren Nomen:
viele DVDs, Ideen, Lehrer/innen, ...

Bei nicht zählbaren Nomen verwenden wir **„viel“**:
viel Käse, Milch, Musik, Zeit, ...

Auch im Englischen musst du darauf achten, ob es sich um zählbare oder um nicht zählbare Nomen handelt:

*How **many CDs** do you have?*	Wie viele CDs ...?
*– Not **many**. Only ten or twelve.*	Nicht viele.
*But I have **a lot of DVDs**.*	... viele DVDs.

◄ Mit dem **Plural von zählbaren Nomen** verwendest du ***many*** oder ***a lot of/lots of***:
many DVDs, ideas, teachers, ... oder
a lot of/lots of DVDs, ideas, teachers ...

*How **much cheese** do we need?*	Wie viel Käse ...?
*– Not **much**.*	Nicht viel.
*But we need **lots of milk**.*	... viel Milch.

◄ Mit **nicht zählbaren Nomen** verwendest du ***much*** oder ***a lot of/lots of***:
much cheese, milk, music, time, ... oder
a lot of/lots of cheese, milk, music, time, ...

Bejahter Aussagesatz:	We need **a lot of/lots of** scones and **a lot of/lots of** of bread.
Verneinter Aussagesatz:	But we don't need **many** cakes. And we don't need **much** cheese.
Frage:	Do you have **many** parties at home? Do you eat **much** chocolate?

! Beachte:

- In **bejahten Aussagesätzen** wird meist ***a lot of*** (oder ***lots of***) verwendet.
- In **verneinten Aussagesätzen** und in **Fragen** wird dagegen eher ***many*** bzw. ***much*** verwendet.

➜ *p. 78, exercise 5*

Wo brauchst du *much*, wo brauchst du *many*?

1 *We don't eat … meat at home.*
2 *How … hamburgers do you eat every week?*
3 *My brother doesn't have … friends.*
4 *I don't drink … tea.*

GF 15 Subject and object questions Subjekt- und Objektfragen

Mit *who* und *what* kann man nach dem **Subjekt** oder nach dem **Objekt** eines Satzes fragen.

*What **happens** every Saturday morning?*
Was passiert jeden Samstagmorgen?

*Who **has to find** a school club? – Lucy.*
Wer muss eine Schul-AG finden? – …

*Who **goes sailing** with Abby? – Maya.*
Wer geht mit Abby segeln? – …

Kein **do/does**, wenn **who** = **wer**!

◂ **Subjektfragen** sind „Wer oder was?"-Fragen. Subjektfragen im *simple present* werden **ohne *do/does*** gebildet. Die Wortstellung ist wie in Aussagesätzen, das Fragewort ist Subjekt des Fragesatzes. Vergleiche:

	Subjekt	Objekt
Aussage:	*Justin*	*wants to visit his dad.*
Subjektfrage:	***Who*** **Wer** …?	*wants to visit his dad?* Antwort: Justin

*What **does** Lucy have to **find**? – A school club.*
Was muss Lucy finden? – …

*Who **does** Lucy **ask** about clubs? – Maya.*
Wen befragt Lucy zu AGs? – …

*Who **does** Maya **meet** at the weekend? – Abby.*
Wen trifft Maya am Wochenende? – …

◂ **Objektfragen** sind „Wen/Wem oder was?"-Fragen. Objektfragen werden **mit *do/does*** gebildet. Das Fragewort ist Objekt des Fragesatzes.

	Objekt	Subjekt
Objektfrage:	***Who*** **Wen** …?	*does Justin want to visit?* Antwort: his dad

*Who does Justin skype **with**? – His father.*
Mit wem skypt Justin? – …

*What school does Maya go **to**? – Coombe Dean.*
Auf welche Schule geht Maya? – …

! Anders als im Deutschen steht die **Präposition** *(with, to)* in englischen Objektfragen am Ende der Frage.

➔ *p. 79, exercise 6*

GF 16 Personal pronouns: object forms Personalpronomen: Objektformen

*I can't do this exercise. Can you help **me**?*

*You can't see me, but I can see **you**.*

*Look, there's Sam. **He**'s nice. Can you see **him**?*

*And there's Lucy. **She**'s in my class. Do you know **her**?*

*It's a present from my mum. Do you like **it**?*

*We go swimming on Fridays. You can join **us**.*

*Sam and Lily, **you**'re behind the tree. I can see **you**.*

*Lucy and Abby? **They** aren't here. You can't talk to **them**.*

➔ *p. 79, exercise 7*

Bei den **Personalpronomen** muss man **Subjektformen** *(I, he, we, …)* und **Objektformen** *(me, him, us, …)* unterscheiden.

Anders als im Deutschen gibt es für jede Person nur eine Objektform:

*Can you help **her**?*	*Kannst du **ihr** helfen?*
*You can ask **her**.*	*Du kannst **sie** fragen.*

GF 17 The possessive form (II) Die *of*-Fügung

*The **door of room 3** is open.*
Die Tür von Raum 3 ist offen.

*What's the **name of the street**?*
Wie ist der Name der Straße?

*I like the **colour of your T-shirt**.*
Ich mag die Farbe deines T-Shirts.

➜ *p. 82, exercise 2*

Du weißt bereits, dass man den **-s-Genitiv** benutzt, wenn man sagen will, dass etwas jemandem gehört (oder zu jemandem gehört):
Abby's room / my teacher's name / my dog's basket
Abbys Zimmer / der Name meiner Lehrerin / der Korb meines Hundes

Wenn du sagen willst, dass etwas **zu einer Sache gehört**, musst die die ***of*-Fügung** verwenden.

GF 18 Word order (II): Adverbs of frequency Wortstellung (II): Häufigkeitsadverbien

*Lucy and Maya **often ride** their bikes.*
Lucy und Maya fahren oft Rad.

*They **usually ride** to Smeaton's Tower.*
Sie fahren meistens zu *Smeaton's Tower*.

*They **sometimes have** a picnic there.*
Sie machen manchmal ein Picknick dort.

*But they **don't always meet** the boys.*
Aber sie treffen nicht immer die Jungen.

	Objekt		Objekt
*We **often play***	***cards**.*	*But we **never play***	***chess**.*
Wir **spielen oft**	**Karten**.	Aber wir **spielen nie**	**Schach**.

*On Saturdays, Lucy and Maya **are often** on the Hoe.*
*Sam **is always** nice to his sister Lily.*

➜ *p. 83, exercise 4*

In *simple present*-Sätzen stehen oft sogenannte Häufigkeitsadverbien:
always, usually, often, sometimes, never.

Sie drücken aus, wie regelmäßig etwas geschieht oder nicht geschieht.

◂ Häufigkeitsadverbien stehen in der Regel **direkt vor dem Vollverb** (hier: *ride, have, meet*).
Vergleiche die Beispiele links mit ihren deutschen Übersetzungen.

! Anders als im Deutschen stehen Häufigkeitsadverbien **nie zwischen Verb und Objekt**.

! Vorsicht bei den Formen von *be*:
Häufigkeitsadverbien stehen **hinter** *am/are/is*.

Füge die Häufigkeitsadverbien an der richtigen Stelle ein:

1 *(usually)* *Kids like ice cream.*
2 *(often)* *It is very cold in Germany in January.*
3 *(always)* *Sam goes to basketball on Thursdays.*
4 *(never)* *I eat scones for breakfast.*
5 *(sometimes)* *Morph plays cards in the evening.*

GF 19 The plural of nouns Der Plural der Nomen

*a **bag***
(Singular)

*two **bags***
(Plural)

Du bildest den **Plural** (die Mehrzahl) eines Nomens, indem du **s** an das Nomen anhängst.

Singular + s → Plural

Wie beim **s** der 3. Person Singular (vgl. GF 9b auf S. 188) hängt die Aussprache des Plural-**s** vom **vorhergehenden Laut** ab.

1 [s] ***basket*s** · ***biscuit*s** · ***cup*s**
***group*s** · ***bike*s** · ***book*s**

2 [z] ***club*s** · ***bed*s** · ***bag*s**
***girl*s** · ***room*s** · ***cousin*s**
***boy*s** · ***tree*s** · ***camera*s**

3 [ɪz] ***class*es** · ***place*s** · ***bus*es**
***box*es** · ***house*s** · ***wish*es**
***watch*es** · ***page*s**

◀ 1 [s] nach **stimmlosen Konsonanten**.
Stimmlose Konsonanten sind z.B. [t], [p], [k].

◀ 2 [z] nach **stimmhaften Konsonanten** und **Vokalen**.
Stimmhafte Konsonanten sind z.B. [b], [d], [g], [l], [m].

◀ 3 [ɪz] nach **Zischlauten**.
Zischlaute sind z.B. [s], [z], [ʃ], [tʃ], [dʒ].
Nach Zischlauten wird *es* oder *s* angehängt, je nach Schreibung des Singulars:
beach – beaches · *horse – horses*

***activity* + s → activities** | ***diary* + s → diaries**
***family* + s → families** | ***hobby* + s → hobbies**
***party* + s → parties** | ***story* + s → stories**

◀ Bei Nomen, die auf **Konsonant + y** enden, gibt es eine Besonderheit im Plural: *y + s* → *ies*.

(Aber **Vokal + y** bleibt unverändert: ***day + s → days***)

***half* [f] + s → *halves* [vz]** | ***life* + s → lives**
***shelf* + s → shelves** | ***thief* + s → thieves**

◀ Nomen, die auf *-f* oder *-fe* enden, bilden den Plural meist mit *-ves*.

child* → *children | ***fish* → *fish***
man* → *men | ***woman* → *women***

◀ Einige Nomen haben **unregelmäßige Pluralformen**

! Beachte die Bildung der *possessive form* (s-Genitiv) bei unregelmäßigen Pluralformen:
***the children's room, the women's plans, men's clothes*.**

➜ *p. 84, exercise 5*

Unit 4

GF 20 *whose* „wessen"

Whose ***father*** *works in Boston? – Justin's.*
Wessen Vater arbeitet in Boston? – …

Whose ***books*** *are these? And* ***whose*** *are those?*
Wessen Bücher sind das hier? Und wem gehören die da?

Das Fragewort ***whose*** entspricht dem deutschen „wessen".

GF 21 The simple past of *(to) be* Die einfache Form der Vergangenheit von *(to) be*

➜ *p. 97, exercises 1–3*

Beim *simple past* von **be** gibt es nur zwei Formen:

I, he/she/it was ***you, we, they were***

- Die verneinten Formen heißen ***wasn't*** und ***weren't***.
- Fragen bilden man mit ***Was I …?, Were you …?*** usw.
- Die Kurzantworten lauten ***Yes, I was., No, we weren't.*** usw.
- Fragewörter stehen wie immer am Satzanfang.

GF 22 The simple past (I): positive statements

Die einfache Form der Vergangenheit (I): bejahte Aussagesätze

a) Regular verbs

*Last Saturday, Sam's team **played** against Devonport.*
*Their fans **watched** the match.*
*Later Sam **talked** to Justin about his day.*

Regelmäßige Verben

Bei **regelmäßigen** Verben hängst du ***ed*** an den Infinitiv, um das *simple past* zu bilden:

play → ***played*** [pleɪd] ***film*** → ***filmed*** [fɪlmd]
talk → ***talked*** [tɔːkt] ***watch*** → ***watched*** [wɒtʃt]

*I/you/he/she/it/we/you/they **played, talked, …***

◄ Es gibt für alle Personen nur eine Form.

! Beachte folgende Besonderheiten:

1 *Their fans were there when they **arrived**.*

1 Ein stummes ***e*** fällt weg: ***arrive*** → ***arrived***

2 *They **stopped** Devonport's best player.*

2 Nach einem einzelnen, betonten Vokal wird der Konsonant verdoppelt: ***stop*** → ***stopped***

3 *In the second half, they **tried** to play better.*

3 Ein ***y*** nach Konsonant wird zu ***ied***: ***try*** → ***tried***

4 *Their fans **shouted** and **shouted**.*

4 Nach ***t*** und ***d*** wird die ***ed***-Endung [ɪd] ausgesprochen: ***shouted*** ['ʃaʊtɪd], ***needed*** ['niːdɪd]

→ *p. 100, exercises 1–2*

b) Irregular verbs

	Infinitiv:
*Last Saturday, Sam's team **went** to Devonport.*	***go***
*Their fans **came** too.*	***come***
*They **had** a great time.*	***have***
*Sam's team **won** the match.*	***win***
*When Sam **saw** his dad, he showed him his medal.*	***see***

→ *p. 100, exercises 1–4*

Unregelmäßige Verben

Wie im Deutschen gibt es auch im Englischen eine Reihe von **unregelmäßigen** Verben.
Jedes unregelmäßige Verb hat eine eigene Form für das *simple past*, die du einzeln lernen musst.

◄ Links findest du einige Beispiele.

→ *Liste der unregelmäßigen Verben, S. 269–270*

GF 23 The simple past (II): negative statements

Die einfache Form der Vergangenheit (II): verneinte Aussagesätze

*Sam **didn't run**. He walked. And he **didn't look** happy.*
*Sam **didn't like** the ride on the Big Wheel.*
*And he **didn't see** any sights.*

Eine Aussage im *simple past* **verneinst** du mit ***didn't*** + **Infinitiv** (Langform: *did not*).

Vergleiche: *Lucy **looked** happy.*
*Sam **didn't look** happy.*
(nicht: *Sam didn't look~~ed~~ happy.*)

*I/you/he/she/it/we/you/they **didn't play, go, …***

◄ Dies gilt für alle Personen und für regelmäßige und unregelmäßige Verben.

Verneinte Aussagen

Vergleiche:	Simple present	Simple past
	I **don't like** the Big Wheel.	I **didn't like** the Big Wheel.
	Sam **doesn't like** the Big Wheel.	Sam **didn't like** the Big Wheel.

→ *p. 103, exercises 1–3*

Sieh dir die Bilder an und vervollständige die Sätze in deinem Übungsheft.

1  *I …n't watch TV last night.*

2  *Justin … film his friends last Friday.*

3  *Emily … make … this morning.*

4  *Sam … basketball yesterday.*

GF 24 The simple past (III): questions and short answers

Die einfache Form der Vergangenheit (III): Fragen und Kurzantworten

Did *Sam* ***like*** *the ride on the Big Wheel?*
– No, he ***didn't****.*

Did *you* ***have*** *a good Sunday?*
– Yes, I ***did****. / No, I* ***didn't****.*

What did *you* ***do****?* ***Where did*** *you* ***go****?*

Fragen im *simple past* bildest du mit ***did***.

Vergleiche: *Lucy* ***looked*** *happy.*
Did *Sam* ***look*** *happy?*
(nicht: *Did Sam looked happy?*)

◄ Das Fragewort steht wie immer am Satzanfang.

Fragen und Kurzantworten im simple present und im simple past

Simple present	Simple past
Do you **like** the Big Wheel? – Yes, I **do**. / No I, **don't**.	**Did** you **like** the Big Wheel? – Yes, I **did**. / No I, **didn't**.
Does Sam **like** the Big Wheel? – Yes, he **does**. / No, he **doesn't**.	**Did** Sam **like** the Big Wheel? – Yes, he **did**. / No, he **didn't**.
Why do you **like** the Big Wheel?	**Why did** you **like** the Big Wheel?

➔ *p. 108, exercises 1–2*

Frage nach den Personen in Klammern.
Beispiel: *Abby missed the bus. (Maya?)* Did Maya miss the bus?

1 *Abby saw a group of seals on the beach. (Lucy?)*
2 *Justin made a video for his dad. (Sam?)*
3 *Abby and her brothers sailed to a beach near Ivy Island. (Sam and Lily?)*
4 *Devonport scored 24 points in the first half. (Plymstock?)*
5 *Morph walked around the library on Saturday. (Silky?)*

GF 25 *must, needn't, mustn't*

1 *I* ***must*** *take the dog for a walk now.*
Ich **muss** jetzt mit dem Hund rausgehen.

2 *I* ***needn't*** *do my homework now.*
Ich **muss** jetzt **nicht** meine Hausaufgaben machen.

3 *But I* ***mustn't*** *forget to do it later.*
Aber ich **darf nicht** vergessen, sie später zu erledigen.

➔ *p. 109, exercise 3*

! 1 Mit ***must*** drückt man aus, dass jemand etwas **tun muss**.

2 Mit ***needn't*** sagt man, dass jemand etwas **nicht tun muss/nicht zu tun braucht**.

3 Mit ***mustn't*** drückt man aus, dass jemand etwas **nicht tun darf**.

Unit 5

GF 26 The present progressive Die Verlaufsform der Gegenwart

a) Simple present und present progressive

Simple present *I* ***get up*** *at 6:30 every morning. My sister* ***plays*** *hockey. She* ***goes*** *to training two afternoons every week.*

Present progressive

Einfache Form und Verlaufsform der Gegenwart

Du kennst bereits das *simple present* und weißt, dass man mit dem *simple present* über die **Gegenwart** spricht.

Auch das *present progressive* bezieht sich auf die **Gegenwart**. Man verwendet es, wenn man sagen will, was **gerade passiert** oder was **man gerade tut**. (Daher der Name „**Verlaufs**form der Gegenwart": Man spricht damit über etwas, das **gerade im Verlauf** ist.)

Eine Verlaufsform gibt es im Deutschen nicht. Aber manchmal sagen wir „Ich bin gerade dabei, mein Rad zu putzen."

b) Positive and negative statements

It's 8 o'clock. Olivia ***is watching*** *TV.*
Es ist 8 Uhr. Olivia sieht (gerade) fern.

Her brother ***isn't watching*** *TV,* ***he's cleaning*** *his bike.*
Ihr Bruder sieht nicht fern, er putzt (gerade) sein Rad.

Their parents ***are working*** *in the garden.*
Ihre Eltern arbeiten (gerade) im Garten.

1 *Look, the ferry* ***is arriving*** *now.*

2 *Lucy* ***is running****. She doesn't want to miss the ferry.*

➜ *pp. 124–125, exercises 1–6*

Bejahte und verneinte Aussagesätze

Das *present progressive* wird mit ***am/are/is*** + ***-ing*-Form** des Verbs gebildet:
*He****'s cleaning*** *his bike. He* ***isn't watching*** *TV.*

Die *-ing*-Form besteht aus **Infinitiv +** ***ing***:
clean + ing ⟶ ***cleaning*** · ***watch + ing*** ⟶ ***watching***

! Beachte folgende Besonderheiten:

1 Ein stummes **e** fällt weg: ***arrive*** ⟶ ***arriving***

2 Nach einem einzelnen, betonten Vokal wird der Konsonant verdoppelt: ***run*** ⟶ ***running***

c) Questions and short answers

Fragen und Kurzantworten

In Fragen sind Subjekt *(you, he)* und *am/are/is* vertauscht.

Die Kurzantworten kennst du bereits vom Verb ***be*** (vgl. GF 2c auf S. 185).

Fragewörter stehen wie immer am Satzanfang.

Vergleiche:

	He ***is working****.*
Entscheidungsfrage:	***Is*** *he* ***working****?*
Frage mit Fragewort:	***Why is*** *he* ***working****?*

Present progressive

+	–	?
I'm working	I'm not working	Am I working?
You're working	You aren't working	Are you working?
He's/She's/It's working	He/She/It isn't working	Is he/she/it working?
We're/You're/They're working	We/You/They aren't working	Are we/you/they working?

➜ *p. 128, exercises 1–2*

GF 27 Word order (III): Subordinate clauses Wortstellung (III): Nebensätze

Maya likes Plymouth because she ***likes the sea****.*

Maya mag Plymouth, weil sie **das Meer** mag.

➜ *p. 133, exercise 2*

Im Gegensatz zum Deutschen ist in englischen Nebensätzen die Wortstellung genauso wie im Hauptsatz:
S–V–O: ***subject – verb – object***
(Subjekt – Prädikat – Objekt)

GF 28 *some* and *any* and their compounds *some* und *any* und ihre Zusammensetzungen

a) *some/any*

\+ *I've made* ***some biscuits****. And there's* ***some milk*** *too.*
… ein paar Kekse … … etwas Milch …

◀ ***some*** steht vor allem in **bejahten** Aussagesätzen (+). Es bedeutet „einige, ein paar" *(some scones/CDs/boys/…)* oder „etwas" *(some milk/money/music/…)*.

– *I can't see* ***any dogs****. And there aren't* ***any cats****.*
… keine Hunde … … keine Katzen …

◀ ***any*** steht vor allem in **verneinten** Aussagesätzen (–) und in **Fragen** (?).

? *Do you have* ***any questions****?*
Habt ihr (irgendwelche) Fragen?

! Im Deutschen kann man fragen „Gibt es noch Fragen?" oder „Habt ihr (irgendwelche) Fragen?", aber im Englischen steht meist *any*: *Do you have any questions?*

➜ *p. 134, exercise 4*

b) *somebody/anybody – something/anything*

+	*I think there's* ***someone*** *at the door.*	jemand
–	*No, there isn't* ***anybody*** *there.*	niemand
?	*Can you see* ***anyone****?*	(irgend)jemand
+	*Let's go and get* ***something*** *to eat.*	etwas
–	*I'm too nervous. I can't eat* ***anything****.*	nichts
?	*Is there* ***anything*** *I can do for you?*	(irgend)etwas

◀ Für die **Zusammensetzungen** mit ***some*** *(somebody/someone, something)* und ***any*** *(anybody/anyone, anything)* gelten dieselben Regeln.

➜ *p. 135, exercise 5*

Grammatical terms (Grammatische Fachbegriffe)

adjective [ˈædʒɪktɪv]	Adjektiv (Eigenschaftswort)	*good, new, green, interesting, …*
adverb [ˈædvɜːb]	Adverb	*today, there, outside, very, …*
adverb of frequency [ˈfriːkwənsi]	Häufigkeitsadverb	*always, usually, often, sometimes, never*
article [ˈɑːtɪkl]	Artikel	*the, a, an*
conjunction [kənˈdʒʌŋkʃn]	Konjunktion	*and, but, …; because, when, …*
imperative [ɪmˈperətɪv]	Imperativ (Befehlsform)	*Open your books. Don't talk.*
infinitive [ɪnˈfɪnətɪv]	Infinitiv (Grundform des Verbs)	*(to) open, (to) go, …*
irregular verb [ɪˈregjələ]	unregelmäßiges Verb	*(to) go – went, (to) see – saw, …*
negative statement [ˈnegətɪv]	verneinter Aussagesatz	*I don't like oranges.*
noun [naʊn]	Nomen, Substantiv	*Justin, girl, man, time, name, …*
object [ˈɒbdʒɪkt]	Objekt	*Justin has* ***a new camera****.*
past [pɑːst]	Vergangenheit	
personal pronoun [ˌpɜːsənl ˈprəʊnaʊn]	Personalpronomen (persönliches Fürwort)	*I, you, he, she, it, we, they; me, you, him, her, it, us, them*
plural [ˈplʊərəl]	Plural, Mehrzahl	
positive statement [ˈpɒzətɪv]	bejahter Aussagesatz	*I like oranges.*
possessive determiner [pəˌzesɪv dɪˈtɜːmɪnə]	Possessivbegleiter (besitzanzeigender Begleiter)	*my, your, his, her, its, our, their*
possessive form [pəˌzesɪv ˈfɔːm]	s-Genitiv, of-Fügung	*Sam's sister, the Blackwells' house, …*

Grammatical terms (Grammatische Fachbegriffe)

preposition [ˌprepə'zɪʃn]	Präposition	*after, at, in, into, near, …*
present progressive [ˌpreznt prə'gresɪv]	Verlaufsform der Gegenwart	*Olivia **is playing** cards.*
pronoun ['prəʊnaʊn]	Pronomen (Fürwort)	
pronunciation [prəˌnʌnsi'eɪʃn]	Aussprache	
question ['kwestʃən]	Frage(satz)	
question word ['kwestʃn wɜːd]	Fragewort	*who?, what?, when?, where?, how?, …*
regular verb ['regjələ]	regelmäßiges Verb	*(to) help – helped, (to) look – looked, …*
short answer [ˌʃɔːt_'ɑːnsə]	Kurzantwort	*Yes, I am. / No, we don't. / …*
simple past [ˌsɪmpl 'pɑːst]	einfache Form der Vergangenheit	*Olivia **played** cards last Friday.*
simple present [ˌsɪmpl 'preznt]	einfache Form der Gegenwart	*Olivia **plays** cards every Friday evening.*
singular ['sɪŋgjələ]	Singular, Einzahl	
spelling ['spelɪŋ]	Schreibweise, Rechtschreibung	
statement ['steɪtmənt]	Aussage(satz)	
sub-clause ['sʌbklɔːz]	Nebensatz	*I like Plymouth **because I like the sea**.*
subject ['sʌbdʒɪkt]	Subjekt	***Justin/He** has a new camera.*
verb [vɜːb]	**1.** Verb; **2.** Prädikat	*go, help, look, see, …* *Reading **can be** fun.*
word order ['wɜːd_ˌɔːdə]	Wortstellung	
yes/no question	Entscheidungsfrage	*Are you 14? Do you like oranges?*

Lösungen der Grammar-File-Aufgaben

p. 183 a) *it, she, they, you, we* (5)

p. 183 b)
1 *Look, a snake. – **It**'s big.*
2 *This is my cat Susie. – How old is **she**?*
3 *And this is my dog Victor. – **He**'s nice.*
4 *Where are your rabbits? – **They**'re in my room.*

p. 185/1 **3, 5**

p. 185/2
1 Singular (ein Bruder)
2 Plural (mehrere Brüder)
3 Plural (mehrere Mädchen)
4 Plural (mehrere Schüler/innen)
5 Singular (ein Schüler oder eine Schülerin)
6 Singular (ein Mädchen)

p. 186
1 ***There's** a computer on the desk.*
2 ***There aren't any** books on the desk.*
3 ***Are there any** pencils on the desk?*
*– Yes, **there are**.*
4 ***Is there a** ball on the desk?*
*– No, **there isn't**.*
5 ***Are there any** CDs on the desk?*
***– No, there aren't**.*
6 ***Is there a** ruler on the desk?*
***– Yes, there is**.*

p. 188/1
1 *I like card games.*
2 *My sister **likes** football.*
3 *My dog always **sleeps** in his basket.*
4 *Susie can sleep on my bed.*
5 *Seals eat fish.*
6 *Silky **eats** crabs too.*

p. 188/2a *watch**es**, touch**es**, go**es**, catch**es**, do**es***

p. 188/2b **1A, 2C, 3B, 4B, 5B, 6C, 7A, 8B, 9A, 10B**

p. 189
1 *Dilip and Sanjay **don't live** in South Africa.*
2 *Uncle Dasan **doesn't live** in Britain.*
3 *He goes to a sports school, but he **doesn't do** sport.*
4 *Maya **doesn't go** to Plymstock School.*
5 *My cats **don't sleep** at night – they play.*
6 *I **don't have** a cat, I have a rabbit.*

p. 190
1 ***We can play cards when you come home.***
2 ***Today you can do your homework in the dining room.***
3 ***My room is too small so we usually meet at Emily's house.***
4 ***Justin doesn't live with his dad because his dad has a job in Boston.***
5 ***After breakfast I always feed my cat.***

p. 191/1a
1 ***Does Lucy play basketball too?***
2 ***Does Maya play games at weekends too?***
3 ***Do Sam and Lily live in a nice house too?***
4 ***Does Lucy visit Abby at weekends too?***
5 ***Does Sam make video films too?***
6 ***Do Abby's brothers go sailing too?***

p. 191/1b **1A, 2B, 3C**

p. 191/2
1 ***When does Maya visit Abby?***
2 ***Where does Abby live?***
3 ***Why do Abby's brothers go sailing?***
4 ***What do you do in your free time?***

p. 193
1 ***much** meat* — **2** ***many** hamburgers*
3 ***many** friends* — **4** ***much** tea*

p. 194
1 *Kids **usually** like ice cream.*
2 *It is **often** very cold in Germany in January.*
3 *Sam **always** goes to basketball on Thursdays.*
4 *I **never** eat scones for breakfast.*
5 *Morph **sometimes** plays cards in the evenings.*

p. 197/1
1 *I **didn't** watch TV last night.*
2 *Justin **didn't** film his friends last Friday.*
3 *Emily **didn't** make **her bed** this morning.*
4 *Sam **didn't play** basketball yesterday.*

p. 197/2
1 ***Did Lucy see a group of seals on the beach?***
2 ***Did Sam make a video for his dad?***
3 ***Did Sam and Lily sail to a beach near Ivy Island?***
4 ***Did Plymstock score 24 points in the first half?***
5 ***Did Silky walk around the library on Saturday?***

Das **Vocabulary** (S. 201 – 242) enthält alle Wörter und Wendungen deines Englischbuches, die du lernen musst. Sie stehen in der Reihenfolge, in der sie im Buch zum ersten Mal vorkommen.

Hier siehst du, wie das **Vocabulary** aufgebaut ist:

Diese Zahl gibt die **Seite** an, auf der die Wörter zum ersten Mal vorkommen. p. 16 = Seite 16

Die **Lautschrift** zeigt dir, wie ein Wort ausgesprochen wird. Eine Übersicht über alle **Lautschriftzeichen** findest du auf S. 272. Die Lautschriftzeichen stehen auch unten auf den **Vocabulary**-Seiten.

Eingerückte Wörter lernst du am besten zusammen mit dem vorausgehenden Wort, weil die beiden zusammengehören.

p. 16	**board** [bɔːd]	Tafel	
	chair [tʃeə]	Stuhl	
	clock [klɒk]	(Wand-, Stand-, Turm-)Uhr	
	watch [wɒtʃ]	Armbanduhr	
	door [dɔː]	Tür	
	window ['wɪndəʊ]	Fenster	

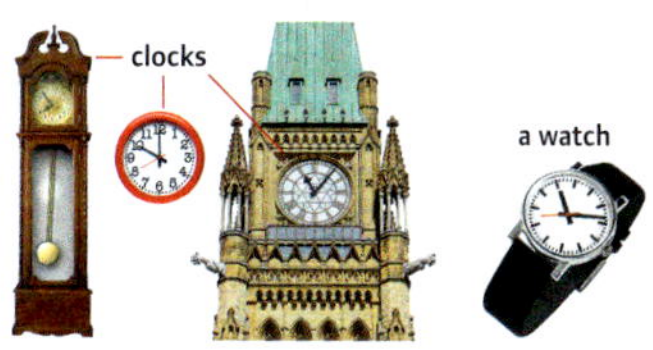

p. 17

Numbers

15 **fifteen** [ˌfɪf'tiːn]	20 **twenty** ['twenti]	40 **forty** ['fɔːti]
16 **sixteen** [ˌsɪks'tiːn]	21 **twenty-one** [ˌtwenti'wʌn]	50 **fifty** ['fɪfti]
17 **seventeen** [ˌsevn'tiːn]	22 **twenty-two** [ˌtwenti'tuː]	60 **sixty** ['sɪksti]
18 **eighteen** [ˌeɪ'tiːn]	…	70 **seventy** ['sevnti]
19 **nineteen** [ˌnaɪn'tiːn]	30 **thirty** ['θɜːti]	80 **eighty** ['eɪti]
	31 **thirty-one** [ˌθɜːti'wʌn]	90 **ninety** ['naɪnti]
	32 **thirty-two** [ˌθɜːti'tuː]	100 **a hundred / one hundred** [ə'hʌndrəd], [ˌwʌn'hʌndrəd]
➜ *Numbers*, p. 272	…	

Das **rote Ausrufezeichen** bedeutet: Vorsicht, hier macht man leicht Fehler!

	(to) **count** [kaʊnt]	zählen	
p. 20	**new** [njuː]	neu	new ◄► old
	uniform ['juːnɪfɔːm]	(Schul-)Uniform	
	nice [naɪs]	nett, schön	
	too [tuː]	auch	❗ Jack is from Berlin. – I'm from Berlin **too**. – Ich bin **auch** aus Berlin.
p. 21	**profile** ['prəʊfaɪl]	Profil; Beschreibung, Porträt	❗ Betonung: **pro**file ['prəʊfaɪl]
	(to) come [kʌm]	kommen	
	home [həʊm]	Heim, Zuhause	

Dies ist das „Gegenteil"-Zeichen: „**new** ist das Gegenteil von **old**".

home

Maya is **at home**.	daheim, zu Hause
Let's **go home**.	nach Hause gehen
Sam, **come home**.	nach Hause kommen

Diese **Kästen** solltest du dir immer besonders gut ansehen: Hier sind Vokabeln zu einem bestimmten Thema zusammengestellt. Oder du erfährst mehr über ein Wort und wie es verwendet wird.

Tipps zum Wörterlernen findest du im **Skills File** auf den Seiten 174 und 175.

Im **Vocabulary** werden folgende **Abkürzungen** verwendet:

p. = page (Seite)	pp. = pages (Seiten)
sth. = something (etwas)	sb. = somebody (jemand)
jn. = jemanden	jm. = jemandem
pl = *plural* (Mehrzahl)	
infml = *informal* (umgangssprachlich)	

Wenn du **nachschlagen** möchtest, was ein englisches Wort bedeutet oder wie man es ausspricht, dann verwende das **English – German Dictionary** auf den Seiten 243 – 257. Und wenn du vergessen hast, wie etwas auf Englisch heißt, dann kann dir das **German – English Dictionary** auf den Seiten 258 – 269 eine erste Hilfe sein.

Eine Übersicht über **Classroom English** und **Arbeitsanweisungen** findest du am Ende des Buches ab Seite 275.

Auf den folgenden zwei Seiten findest du eine Liste von blau gedruckten **Wörtern und Wendungen**. Bei diesen Vokabeln handelt es sich um Wortschatz, den du schon aus der Grundschule kennst.

Auch auf den **Vocabulary**-Seiten 204 – 242 sind Wörter und Wendungen, die dir in der Grundschule begegnet sind, blau gedruckt.

Grundschulwortschatz

Wörter

$ (dollar) ['dɒlə], € (euro) ['jʊərəʊ], £ (pound) [paʊnd]	Dollar, Euro, Pfund	
It's € 8.	Es kostet 8 Euro.	How much is it? – **It's € 10.**
a hot dog / an apple [ən‿'æpl]	ein Hot Dog / ein Apfel	Wenn das Folgewort am Anfang mit einem Vokal gesprochen wird, lautet der unbestimmte Artikel an: an **apple**, aber a **hot dog**.
black/green tea [tiː]	Schwarzer/Grüner Tee	
butter ['bʌtə]	Butter	
chicken ['tʃɪkɪn]	Huhn, Hühnchen	
chips [tʃɪps]	Pommes Frites	
ham [hæm]	Schinken	
hot chocolate ['tʃɒklət]	Heiße Schokolade	
plum [plʌm]	Pflaume	
strawberry ['strɔːbəri]	Erdbeere	
Dear … [dɪə]	Liebe(r) …	**Dear** Paula, … / Thank you, my **dear**.
Halloween [ˌhæləʊ'iːn]	Halloween	**Halloween** is on October 31.
hamster ['hæmstə]	Hamster	**Hamsters** are my favourite animals.
His/Her/Its name is …	Er/Sie/Es heißt …; Sein/Ihr Name ist …	
OK	OK, okay; in Ordnung	She's **OK**.
pullover ['pʊləʊvə]	Pullover	Her **pullover** is blue.
(to) ride (a horse) [ˌraɪd‿ə 'hɔːs]	reiten	He **rides** his horse.
(to) ride a bike [ˌraɪd‿ə 'baɪk]	Fahrrad fahren	She **rides** her bike.
skateboard ['skeɪtbɔːd]	Skateboard	Do you like your new **skateboard**?
snowboard ['snəʊbɔːd]	Snowboard	Do you like your new **snowboard**?
sweet [swiːt]	süß	Hot chocolate is **sweet**.
sweets [swiːts]	Süßigkeiten	I love **sweets**!

Grundschulwortschatz

Wendungen

at my house	bei mir zu Hause	
at … o'clock	um … Uhr	
Can you come to my party?	Kannst du zu meiner Party kommen?	
Please come to my party!	Bitte komm zu meiner Party!	
Can you play …? / Can you ride a bike?	Kannst du … spielen? / Kannst du Rad fahren?	
Do you like …? – Yes, I do./No, I don't.	Magst du …? – Ja./Nein.	
English is on …	Englisch ist am …	
Happy Birthday!	Herzlichen Glückwunsch zum Geburtstag!	
Happy Thanksgiving!	Fröhliches Thanksgiving!	
Have you got any pets?	Hast du Haustiere?	
How much is it?	Was kostet das? / Wie teuer ist das?	
I go to school in the morning. / I go to school at … o'clock.	Ich gehe morgens in die Schule. / Ich gehe um … Uhr in die Schule.	
I'm (very) happy/sad.	Ich bin (sehr) glücklich/traurig.	
I'm fine, thanks.	Mir geht es gut, danke.	
No, I'm sorry.	Nein, tut mir leid.	
Not quite.	Nicht ganz.	
My classroom / My teacher / My school / My hobby is …	Mein Klassenzimmer / Mein/e Lehrer/in / Meine Schule / Mein Hobby ist …	
They are here / there / under / in front of / in / behind / next to …	Sie sind hier / dort / unter / vor / in / hinter / neben …	
This is my family / my pet / my room.	Dies ist meine Familie / mein Haustier / mein Zimmer.	
We have a big/… house.	Wir haben ein großes/… Haus.	
What's your hobby?	Was ist dein Hobby?	
When is …? When are …?	Wann ist …? Wann sind …?	*Kurzform:* When's …?
Where is …? Where are …?	Wo ist …? Wo sind …?	*Kurzform:* Where's …?
Who is …? Who are …?	Wer ist …? Wer sind …?	*Kurzform:* Who's …?
Why (not)?	Warum (nicht)?	
You're welcome.	Gern geschehen.	

Here we go

pp. 8/9	**Here we go.** [ˌhɪə wi ˈɡəʊ]	Los geht's. / Jetzt geht's los.	
	Hello. [həˈləʊ]	Hallo. / Grüß Gott.	
	My name is Silky. [maɪ ˈneɪm‿ɪz]	Ich heiße Silky. (*wörtlich:* Mein Name ist Silky.)	[z] ist ein weiches „s" wie in „**s**" in „lesen".
	I'm a seal. [aɪm] (= **I am** a seal.)	Ich bin eine Robbe.	❗ Das englische Wort **I** (= „ich") wird immer großgeschrieben – auch wenn es nicht am Satzanfang steht.
	a seal [ə ˈsiːl]	eine Robbe	[iː] ist ein langes „i" wie in „Wien".
	I'm **two years old**. [ˌtuː jɪəz‿ˈəʊld]	Ich bin zwei Jahre alt.	[ɪə] klingt wie das „ier" in „**hier**".

Numbers

1 **one** [wʌn]	5 **five** [faɪv]	9 **nine** [naɪn]	13 **thirteen** [ˌθɜːˈtiːn]
2 **two** [tuː]	6 **six** [sɪks]	10 **ten** [ten]	14 **fourteen** [ˌfɔːˈtiːn]
3 **three** [θriː]	7 **seven** [ˈsevn]	11 **eleven** [ɪˈlevn]	
4 **four** [fɔː]	8 **eight** [eɪt]	12 **twelve** [twelv]	➔ *Numbers*, p. 272

I'm from Plymouth. [frɒm], [frəm]	Ich bin aus Plymouth. / Ich komme aus Plymouth.	
in England [ɪn‿ˈɪŋɡlənd]	in England	❗ Ländernamen werden großgeschrieben: in England
What about you? [əˈbaʊt]	Und du? / Und was ist mit dir? Und ihr? / Und was ist mit euch?	*Englisch:* **you** *Deutsch:* **du – dich – dir** **ihr – euch – euch** **Sie – Sie – Ihnen**
what? [wɒt]	was?	Der Laut [ɒ] klingt wie das „o" in „**doch**".
Silky's questions [ˈkwestʃənz]	Silkys Fragen	
What's your name?	Wie heißt du? / Wie heißt ihr?	

your [jɔː], [jə]	dein/e; euer/eure; Ihr/e	
Are you ...? [ˈɑː ju]	Bist du ...?	**Are you** a boy or a girl?
boy [bɔɪ]	Junge	[ɔɪ] klingt ähnlich wie das „eu" in „**Heu**".
or [ɔː]	oder	
girl [ɡɜːl]	Mädchen	[ɜː] klingt etwa so wie der Laut in „T-Shirt".
How old are you? [haʊ]	Wie alt bist du?	
Where are you from? [weə]	Woher kommst du?	
where? [weə]	wo? / wohin?	[eə] kennst du aus dem Wort „**fair**".
Meet your classmates. [miːt]	Triff deine Mitschüler/innen. / Lerne deine Mitschüler/innen kennen.	

[b] **boat** · [p] **pool** · [d] **dad** · [t] **ten** · [g] **good** · [k] **cat** · [m] **mum** · [n] **no** · [ŋ] **song** · [l] **hello** · [r] **red** · [w] **we** · [j] **you**

classmate ['klɑːsmeɪt]	Mitschüler/in, Klassenkamerad/in	[ɑː] ist ein langes „a" wie in „Kram".
card (to) [kɑːd]	Karte (an)	
and [ænd], [ənd]	und	[æ] kennst du aus „(Rock-, Pop-)Band"
I like … [laɪk]	Ich mag …	
the [ðə]	der, die, das; die	
colour ['kʌlə]	Farbe	
blue [bluː]	blau	
red [red]	rot	
yellow ['jeləʊ]	gelb	

tip [tɪp]	Tipp	
(to)* **find** [faɪnd]	finden	
word [wɜːd]	Wort	

Let's go to England. [lets]	Lass(t) uns nach England gehen / fahren.	
(to) go [gəʊ]	gehen; fahren	[əʊ] kennst du aus dem Wort „Show".
to [tu], [tə]	zu, nach	
(to) come [kʌm]	kommen	
(to) **see** [siː]	sehen; besuchen	[s] ist ein hartes, scharfes „s" wie in „lassen".
hometown [ˌhəʊm'taʊn]	Heimatstadt	
town [taʊn]	Stadt	

Welcome to Plymouth

p. 10 Welcome **to** Plymouth. ['welkəm]	Willkommen in Plymouth.	Der Laut [ə] ist ein schwaches „e" wie am Ende von „bitte".
Silky's **tour of** Plymouth ['tʊər‿əv]	Silkys Rundgang / Rundfahrt / Reise durch Plymouth	[ʊə] klingt ähnlich wie das „ur" in „Kur".
river ['rɪvə]	Fluss	[v] klingt wie „Vampir" – nicht wie „Vater"!
castle ['kɑːsl]	Burg, Schloss	
(swimming) pool [puːl]	Schwimmbad, Schwimmbecken	
tower ['taʊə]	Turm	
hill [hɪl]	Hügel	
boat [bəʊt]	Boot	
sea [siː]	Meer	

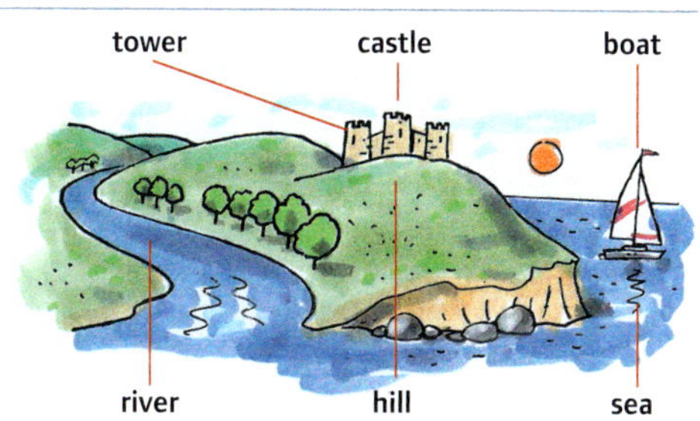

big wheel [bɪg 'wiːl]	Riesenrad	
big [bɪg]	groß	
can [kæn], [kən]	können	

* Mit dem vorangestellten **(to)** ist der Infinitiv (die Grundform des Verbs) gekennzeichnet.

[f] **f**ather · [v] ri**v**er · [s] **s**ister · [z] plea**s**e · [ʃ] **sh**op · [ʒ] televi**s**ion · [tʃ] **t**ea**ch**er · [dʒ] **G**ermany · [θ] **th**anks · [ð] **th**is · [h] **h**ere

	on **the map** [ɒn ðə 'mæp]	auf der Landkarte; auf dem Stadtplan	
p. 11	**zoo** [zuː]	Zoo	! Aussprache: **zoo** [zuː] – Der Anfangslaut ist wie im deutschen Namen „Susie".
	house [haʊs]	Haus	
	tree [triː]	Baum	
	Silky's **song** [sɒŋ]	Silkys Lied, Silkys Song	[ŋ] ist wie „ng" in „Di**ng**".
	who? [huː]	wer?	*Englisch:* **who?** – *Deutsch:* **wer?** *Englisch:* **where?** – *Deutsch:* **wo? / wohin?**
	Is it Monday? ['ɪz‿ɪt]	Ist es Montag?	

The days of the week

Monday ['mʌndeɪ], ['mʌndi]	Montag	**Saturday** ['sætədeɪ], ['sætədi]	Samstag
Tuesday ['tjuːzdeɪ], ['tjuːzdi]	Dienstag	**Sunday** ['sʌndeɪ], ['sʌndi]	Sonntag
Wednesday ['wenzdeɪ], ['wenzdi]	Mittwoch		
Thursday ['θɜːzdeɪ], ['θɜːzdi]	Donnerstag	! Die Wochentage werden immer großgeschrieben.	
Friday ['fraɪdeɪ], ['fraɪdi]	Freitag		

every day / colour / boat ['evri]	jeder Tag / jede Farbe / jedes Boot	
great [greɪt]	großartig	

A week in Plymouth

p. 12	at [æt], [ət]	*(in Ortsangaben)* an, bei, in; *(in Zeitangaben)* um, an	
	near [nɪə]	in der Nähe von, nahe (bei)	Silky is **near** the boat. ! *Nicht:* … ~~in the near of~~ …
	on Monday/Tuesday/…	am Montag/Dienstag/…	
	she's … [ʃiːz] **(= she is)**	sie ist …	[ʃ] klingt wie das „sch" in „**sch**ön".
p. 13	**photo** ['fəʊtəʊ]	Foto	*Englisch:* **in the photo** *Deutsch:* **auf dem Foto**
	Look, … [lʊk]	Sieh mal, … / Schau mal, …	
	it's … [ɪts] **(= it is)**	er/sie/es ist …	*Englisch:* **it** – *Deutsch:* **er/sie/es** the **river** … **it's** big – **er** ist groß the **town** … **it's** old – **sie** ist alt the **photo** … **it's** great – **es** ist großartig
	here [hɪə]	hier; hierher	

[iː] green · [i] happy · [ɪ] big · [e] red · [æ] cat · [ɑː] class · [ɒ] song · [ɔː] door · [uː] blue · [ʊ] book · [ʌ] mum · [ɜː] girl · [ə] a partner

Yes, that's right. [ˌjes ðæts ˈraɪt]	Ja, das ist richtig. / Ja, das stimmt.	[ð] klingt etwa wie ein gelispeltes „Wiese".
No, **that's wrong.** [ˌnəʊ ðæts ˈrɒŋ]	Nein, das ist falsch. / Nein, das stimmt nicht.	! Aussprache – das "w" wird nicht gesprochen: **wrong** [rɒŋ]
my **favourite** day [ˈfeɪvərɪt]	mein Lieblingstag	
rhyme [raɪm]	Reim; Vers	
There are … [ˈðeər‿ɑː]	Es sind … / Es gibt …	**There are** two boys and two girls in the boat.
There's … [ðeəz] **(= There is …)**	Es ist … / Es gibt …	**There's** a girl on the tower.
lots of … [ˈlɒts‿əv] / **a lot of …**	viel …, viele …	**lots of** books/ **a lot of** books
animal [ˈænɪml]	Tier	
Follow me. [ˈfɒləʊ miː]	Folge mir. / Folgt mir.	
me [miː]	mich; mir	*Englisch:* **me** / Come and see **me**. / Follow **me**. — *Deutsch:* **mich – mir** / Besuche **mich**. / Folge **mir**.

My favourite animal

14/15	**ant** [ænt]	Ameise
	bear [beə]	Bär
	bird [bɜːd]	Vogel
	butterfly [ˈbʌtəflaɪ], *pl* **butterflies** [ˈbʌtəflaɪz]	Schmetterling
	cat [kæt]	Katze
	dog [dɒg]	Hund
	elephant [ˈelɪfənt]	Elefant
	frog [frɒg]	Frosch
	giraffe [dʒəˈrɑːf]	Giraffe
	guinea pig [ˈgɪni pɪg]	Meerschweinchen
	horse [hɔːs]	Pferd
	lion [ˈlaɪən]	Löwe
	monkey [ˈmʌŋki]	Affe
	pig [pɪg]	Schwein
	rabbit [ˈræbɪt]	Kaninchen
	rat [ræt]	Ratte
	snake [sneɪk]	Schlange
	whale [weɪl]	Wal

an elephant [æn], [ən]	ein Elefant	! **an** **e**lephant, **an** **a**nt, **an** **a**nimal – **a** **b**ear, **a** **h**orse, **a** **m**onkey

[eɪ] name · [aɪ] time · [ɔɪ] boy · [əʊ] old · [aʊ] town · [ɪə] here · [eə] where · [ʊə] tour

picture ['pɪktʃə]	Bild	*Englisch:* **in the picture** *Deutsch:* **auf dem Bild**
strange [streɪndʒ]	seltsam, komisch	[dʒ] kennst du aus „Jeans" und „**J**ob".

Colours

red [red]	rot	**brown** [braʊn]	braun	**purple** ['pɜːpl]	violett, lila
yellow ['jeləʊ]	gelb	**orange** ['ɒrɪndʒ]	orange	**white** [waɪt]	weiß
blue [bluː]	blau	**grey** [greɪ]	grau	**black** [blæk]	schwarz
green [griːn]	grün	**pink** [pɪŋk]	pink, rosa		

ruler ['ruːlə]	Lineal	
game [geɪm]	Spiel	
with [wɪð]	mit	
leg [leg]	Bein	
without [wɪ'ðaʊt]	ohne	**with ◄► without**
too [tuː]	auch	! Jack is from Berlin. – I'm from Berlin **too**. – Ich bin **auch** aus Berlin.
(to) have [hæv], [həv]	haben	I **have** a cat and two rabbits.
pet [pet]	Haustier	
now [naʊ]	nun, jetzt	[aʊ] klingt wie das „au" wie in „bl**au**".
time [taɪm]	Zeit; Uhrzeit	
for [fɔː], [fə]	für	
English ['ɪŋglɪʃ]	Englisch; englisch	! Das englische Wort **English** wird immer großgeschrieben.
lesson ['lesn]	(Unterrichts-)Stunde	

Our English class

p. 16 **our** ['aʊə]	unser/e	
class [klɑːs]	(Schul-)Klasse	
Mr Schwarz ['mɪstə]	Herr Schwarz	
Mrs Schwarz ['mɪsɪz]	Frau Schwarz	
teacher ['tiːtʃə]	Lehrer/in	[tʃ] klingt wie „tsch" in „**tsch**üs".
school [skuːl]	Schule	
classroom ['klɑːsruːm]	Klassenzimmer	
cupboard ['kʌbəd]	Schrank	[ʌ] klingt wie das kurze „a" in „K**a**mm".
desk [desk]	Schreibtisch	
thing [θɪŋ]	Sache, Ding	
rubber ['rʌbə]	Radiergummi	
pen [pen]	Kugelschreiber, Stift, Füller	
board [bɔːd]	Tafel	
chair [tʃeə]	Stuhl	

[b] **boat** · [p] **pool** · [d] **dad** · [t] **ten** · [g] **good** · [k] **cat** ·
[m] **mum** · [n] **no** · [ŋ] **song** · [l] **hello** · [r] **red** · [w] **we** · [j] **you**

clock [klɒk]	(Wand-, Stand-, Turm-)Uhr	
watch [wɒtʃ]	Armbanduhr	
door [dɔː]	Tür	
window ['wɪndəʊ]	Fenster	
This is … ['ðɪs‿ɪz]	Dies ist … / Das ist …	
school bag ['skuːl bæg]	Schultasche	
book [bʊk]	Buch	
exercise book ['eksəsaɪz bʊk]	Schulheft, Übungsheft	
pencil ['pensl]	Bleistift	
pencil case ['pensl keɪs]	Federmäppchen	
glue stick ['gluː stɪk]	Klebestift	
glue [gluː]	Klebstoff	
sharpener ['ʃɑːpnə]	(An-)Spitzer	
Let me show you …	Lass mich dir … zeigen.	
(to) **show** [ʃəʊ]	zeigen	**Show** me your hometown, Silky.
Simon **says …** [sez]	Simon sagt …	
(to) put [pʊt]	legen, stellen, *(etwas wohin)* tun	**Put** the photos in the box.
(to) **talk (to)** [tɔːk]	reden (mit), sich unterhalten (mit)	
(to) open ['əʊpən]	öffnen, aufmachen	
(to) **touch** [tʌtʃ]	berühren, anfassen	
(to) give [gɪv]	geben	Can you **give** me your rubber?

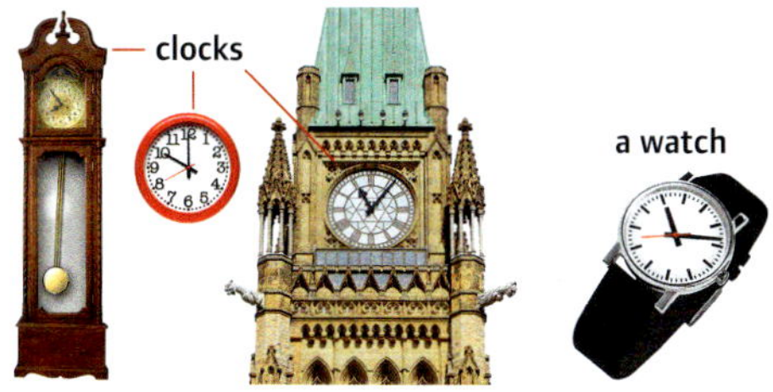

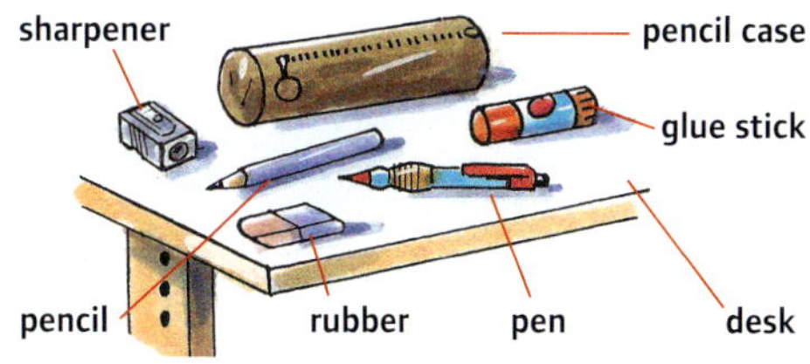

p. 17

Numbers

15 **fifteen** [ˌfɪf'tiːn]	20 **twenty** ['twenti]	40 **forty** ['fɔːti]
16 **sixteen** [ˌsɪks'tiːn]	21 **twenty-one** [ˌtwenti'wʌn]	50 **fifty** ['fɪfti]
17 **seventeen** [ˌsevn'tiːn]	22 **twenty-two** [ˌtwenti'tuː]	60 **sixty** ['sɪksti]
18 **eighteen** [ˌeɪ'tiːn]	…	70 **seventy** ['sevnti]
19 **nineteen** [ˌnaɪn'tiːn]	30 **thirty** ['θɜːti]	80 **eighty** ['eɪti]
	31 **thirty-one** [ˌθɜːti'wʌn]	90 **ninety** ['naɪnti]
	32 **thirty-two** [ˌθɜːti'tuː]	100 **a hundred / one hundred** [ə'hʌndrəd], [ˌwʌn'hʌndrəd]
➜ *Numbers*, p. 272	…	

Die Betonungszeichen

Die **Betonungszeichen** ['] und [ˌ] stehen immer vor der betonten Silbe. ['] zeigt die Hauptbetonung, [ˌ] zeigt die Nebenbetonung.
Im Deutschen sagt man **neunzehn** (Hauptbetonung auf der ersten Silbe). Die englische Zahl **nineteen** hat die Hauptbetonung auf **-teen**: [ˌnaɪn'tiːn].
Also Vorsicht bei der Aussprache:
19 **nineteen** [ˌnaɪn'tiːn] – 90 **ninety** ['naɪnti]

Der Bindebogen

Der **Bindebogen** [‿] in der Lautschrift zeigt an, dass zwei Wörter beim Sprechen aneinandergebunden und wie ein Wort gesprochen werden. Beispiele:

seven‿ants	[sevn‿'ænts]
boys‿and girls	[ˌbɔɪz‿ənd 'gɜːlz]
in‿our class	[ɪn‿aʊə 'klɑːs]
12 years‿old	[twelv jɪəz‿'əʊld]

telephone ['telɪfəʊn]	Telefon	
o [əʊ]	Null *(in Telefonnummern)*	**!** Du schreibst: 0166 204 … Du sagst: **o** one **double** six two **o** four …
double ['dʌbl]	Doppel-	

[f] father · [v] river · [s] sister · [z] please · [ʃ] shop · [ʒ] television · [tʃ] teacher · [dʒ] Germany · [θ] thanks · [ð] this · [h] here

What time is it?	Wie spät ist es?	
Thank you. ['θæŋk juː]	Danke.	
ten o'clock [ə'klɒk]	10 Uhr / 22 Uhr	It's 1 **o'clock** now.
half past ten ['hɑːf pɑːst]	halb elf (10.30 / 22.30)	
quarter to eleven ['kwɔːtə tʊ]	Viertel vor elf (10.45 / 22.45)	
quarter past ten ['kwɔːtə pɑːst]	Viertel nach zehn (10.15 / 22.15)	
See you later.	Bis bald. / Bis nachher.	
later ['leɪtə]	später	

Unit 1 The first day at school

p. 20 **the first day** [fɜːst]	der erste Tag	
at school	in der Schule	*English:* **at school** – *German:* **in der Schule**
kid [kɪd] *(infml)*	Kind; Jugendliche(r)	
her **best** friend [hɜː ˌbest 'frend]	ihr bester Freund / ihre beste Freundin	
they're **…** [ðeə] (= **they are** [ðeɪ‿ɑː])	sie sind …	
flat [flæt]	Wohnung	
their first day [ðeə]	ihr erster Tag	
new [njuː]	neu	**new** ◄► **old**
uniform ['juːnɪfɔːm]	(Schul-)Uniform	
nice [naɪs]	nett, schön	
(to) know [nəʊ]	wissen; kennen	
brother ['brʌðə]	Bruder	
sister ['sɪstə]	Schwester	
student ['stjuːdənt]	Schüler/in; Student/in	! Betonung: **student** ['stjuːdənt]
but [bʌt], [bət]	aber	Luca is ten, **but** Jack is fourteen.
he/she/it isn't … ['ɪznt] (= **he/she/it is not** [nɒt])	er/sie/es ist nicht …; er/sie/es ist kein/e …	Maya **isn't** at Plymstock School. And **she isn't** a teacher – she's a student.
his mum [hɪz]	seine Mama	**I** – **my** name; **you** – **your** name; **he** – **his** name; **she** – **her** name; **it** – **its** name; **we** – **our** names; **you** – **your** names; **they** – **their** names
mum [mʌm]	Mama, Mutti	
mother ['mʌðə]	Mutter	
dad [dæd]	Papa, Vati	
father ['fɑːðə]	Vater	
navy ['neɪvi]	Marine	
(to) **look at** [lʊk]	anschauen, ansehen	
dark [dɑːk]	dunkel	

[iː] green · [i] happy · [ɪ] big · [e] red · [æ] cat · [ɑː] class · [ɒ] song · [ɔː] door · [uː] blue · [ʊ] book · [ʌ] mum · [ɜː] girl · [ə] a partner

	please [pli:z]	bitte	Can you open the window, **please**?
	You're late. [leɪt]	Du bist spät dran. / Du bist zu spät.	
	(to) **wait (for)** [weɪt]	warten (auf)	
	minute ['mɪnɪt]	Minute	! Betonung: **minute** ['mɪnɪt]
p. 21	**profile** ['prəʊfaɪl]	Profil; Beschreibung, Porträt	! Betonung: **profile** ['prəʊfaɪl]
	library ['laɪbrəri]	Bibliothek, Bücherei	
	home [həʊm]	Heim, Zuhause	**home** Maya is **at home**. – daheim, zu Hause Let's **go home**. – nach Hause gehen Sam, **come home**. – nach Hause kommen

Part A

p. 22	**before** school/lessons [bɪ'fɔ:]	vor der Schule *(vor Schulbeginn)* / vorm Unterricht	
	you aren't ... [ɑ:nt] **(= you are not)**	du bist nicht ...; du bist kein/e ...; ihr seid nicht ...; ihr seid kein/e ...	**You aren't** at my school. And **you aren't** a student.
	there [ðeə]	da, dort; dahin, dorthin	Let's go to the park. Let's meet our friends **there**. **here ◄► there**
	sad [sæd]	traurig	
	Don't go. [dəʊnt]	Gehe nicht.	
	Bye. [baɪ] *(auch:* Bye-bye.)	Servus. / Pfiati. / Auf Wiedersehen.	**Hello. ◄► Bye. / Bye-bye.**
	Watch out! [ˌwɒtʃ‿'aʊt]	Pass auf! / Vorsicht!	
	(I'm) sorry. ['sɒri]	Tut mir leid. / Entschuldigung.	
	So? [səʊ]	Und? / Na und?	
	Nice **to** meet you.	Freut mich, dich/euch/Sie kennenzulernen.	**English "to" – German "zu"** Nice **to** meet you. – kennen**zu**lernen It's time **to** go now. – **zu** gehen It's nice **to** see you. – **zu** sehen
	(to) **hurry up** [ˌhʌri‿'ʌp]	sich beeilen	
	friendly ['frendli]	freundlich	
p. 23	shoe [ʃu:]	Schuh	
	trainer ['treɪnə]	Turnschuh	
	(to) **forget** [fə'get]	vergessen	
	(to) **wear** [weə]	tragen *(Kleidung)*	**Wear** black shoes. Don't **wear** trainers.
	British ['brɪtɪʃ]	britisch	
	different ['dɪfrənt]	verschieden; anders	The Coombe Dean uniform is **different**.

[eɪ] name · [aɪ] time · [ɔɪ] boy · [əʊ] old ·
[aʊ] town · [ɪə] here · [eə] where · [ʊə] tour

	I don't like green. [dəʊnt]	Ich mag Grün nicht. / Ich mag kein Grün.	**I like … ◄► I don't like …**
	Have a go. [ˌhæv‿ə 'gəʊ]	Versuch's mal.	
p. 24	**language** ['læŋgwɪdʒ]	Sprache	
	form (of) [fɔːm]	Form (von)	"am", "is" and "are" are **forms of** "be".
	of [ɒv], [əv]	von	a map **of** Britain
	long [lɒŋ]	lang	At German schools, a lesson is 45 minutes **long**.
	short [ʃɔːt]	kurz	**long ◄► short**
	people ['piːpl]	Leute, Menschen	The **people** in Plymouth are nice.
p. 25	**silly** ['sɪli]	albern; blöd	
	sentence ['sentəns]	Satz	
p. 26	**apostrophe** [ə'pɒstrəfi]	Apostroph, Auslassungszeichen	! Betonung: **apostrophe** [ə'pɒstrəfi]
	ball [bɔːl]	Ball	a **football**
	help [help]	Hilfe	
	(to) help [help]	helfen	Can you **help** me, please?
	after the s ['ɑːftə]	nach dem s	**after** the s ◄► **before** the s
	speaker ['spiːkə]	Sprecher/in	
	(to) **speak** [spiːk]	sprechen	Can you **speak** English?

Part B

p. 28	**Miss** Bell [mɪs]	Frau Bell *(übliche Anrede von Lehrerinnen)*	Can I open the window, **Miss**?
	(to) play [pleɪ]	spielen	Let's **play** football.
	Good morning. [gʊd 'mɔːnɪŋ]	Guten Morgen.	
	so [səʊ]	also; deshalb, daher	It's your first day at school, **so** let me show you the school.
	(to) **come in**	hereinkommen	
	(to) **start** [stɑːt]	anfangen, beginnen	
	(to) **throw** [θrəʊ]	werfen	
	(to) **ask** [ɑːsk]	fragen	Can I start? – **Ask** Miss Bell. *English:* Can I **ask** you a **question**? *German:* Kann ich dir eine **Frage stellen**?
	(to) **catch** [kætʃ]	fangen	(to) **throw a ball ◄►** (to) **catch a ball**
	(to) **answer** ['ɑːnsə]	antworten; beantworten	(to) **ask ◄►** (to) **answer**
	answer ['ɑːnsə]	Antwort	
	about **yourself** [əˌbaʊt jɔː'self]	über dich selbst	*English:* **about** me/you/yourself/Miss Bell *German:* **über** mich/dich/dich selbst/Frau Bell
	birthday ['bɜːθdeɪ]	Geburtstag	

[b] **boat** · [p] **pool** · [d] **dad** · [t] **ten** · [g] **good** · [k] **cat** · [m] **mum** · [n] **no** · [ŋ] **song** · [l] **hello** · [r] **red** · [w] **we** · [j] **you**

	September [sep'tembə]	September	❗ Monatsnamen werden großgeschrieben: in September
	(to) **do** [duː]	machen, tun	
	(to) **live** [lɪv]	leben; wohnen	Justin and his mum **live** in Plymouth.
	at 14 Dean Street [striːt]	in der Deanstraße 14	*English:* They live **at 14 Dean Street**. *German:* Sie wohnen **in der Deanstraße 14**.
	then [ðen]	dann	Throw the ball. **Then** ask a question.
	again [ə'gen]	wieder; noch einmal	Can you say that **again**, please?
	timetable ['taɪmteɪbl]	Stundenplan	
p. 29	(to) **think (about)** [θɪŋk]	nachdenken (über)	**Think about** the questions.
	(school) subject ['sʌbdʒɪkt]	Schulfach	❗ Betonung: **subject** ['sʌbdʒɪkt]

School subjects

art [ɑːt]	Kunst	**ICT**[1] [ˌaɪ siː 'tiː]	Informations- und Kommunikationstechnologie
design and technology [dɪˌzaɪn‿ənd tek'nɒlədʒi]	Design und Technik	**maths** [mæθs]	Mathematik
French [frentʃ]	Französisch	**music** ['mjuːzɪk]	Musik
geography [dʒi'ɒgrəfi]	Geografie	**PE**[2] [ˌpiː‿'iː]	Sportunterricht, Turnen
history ['hɪstri]	Geschichte	**religion** [rɪ'lɪdʒən]	Religion
		science ['saɪəns]	Naturwissenschaft

[1] *Information and Communication Technology*
[2] *Physical Education*

p. 30	**hour** ['aʊə]	Stunde	❗ Das „h" wird nicht gesprochen: **hour** ['aʊə]
	lunch [lʌntʃ]	Mittagessen	
	break [breɪk]	Pause	
	(to) **learn** [lɜːn]	lernen	
p. 31	**month** [mʌnθ]	Monat	

The months

1 **January** ['dʒænjuəri] Januar
2 **February** ['februəri] Februar
3 **March** [mɑːtʃ] März
4 **April** ['eɪprəl] April
5 **May** [meɪ] Mai
6 **June** [dʒuːn] Juni
7 **July** [dʒu'laɪ] Juli
8 **August** ['ɔːgəst] August
9 **September** [sep'tembə] September
10 **October** [ɒk'təʊbə] Oktober
11 **November** [nəʊ'vembə] November
12 **December** [dɪ'sembə] Dezember

❗ Monatsnamen werden immer großgeschrieben.

[f] **f**ather · [v] ri**v**er · [s] **s**ister · [z] plea**s**e · [ʃ] **sh**op · [ʒ] televi**s**ion · [tʃ] tea**ch**er · [dʒ] **G**ermany · [θ] **th**anks · [ð] **th**is · [h] **h**ere

second ['sekənd]	zweite(r, s)	
third [θɜːd]	dritte(r, s)	
when? [wen]	wann?	

1	**one**	eins	1st	**first**	erste(r, s)
2	**two**	zwei	2nd	**second**	zweite(r, s)
3	**three**	drei	3rd	**third**	dritte(r, s)
4	**four**	vier	4th	**fourth**	vierte(r, s)
5	**five**	fünf	5th	**fifth**	fünfte(r, s)

➔ *Numbers*, p. 272

Birthdays

My birthday **is** in May. **When's** your birthday?	Ich **habe** im Mai Geburtstag. **Wann hast** du Geburtstag?
– My birthday is in August. **On** 5th August.	– Ich habe im August Geburtstag. **Am** 5. August.

! Du schreibst: **on 5th August** – du sagst: **on the fifth of August**

(to) write [raɪt]	schreiben	! Das „w" wird nicht gesprochen: **write** ['raɪt]

Part C

p. 32 (to) **count** [kaʊnt]	zählen	
Are there any …? ['eni]	Gibt es (irgendwelche) …?	**Are there any** English students at your school?
(to) **spell** [spel]	buchstabieren	
(to) **work** [wɜːk]	arbeiten	
(to) read [riːd]	lesen	
(to) **watch** [wɒtʃ]	*sich etwas* anschauen; beobachten	
(to) **fall asleep** [ˌfɔːl‿ə'sliːp]	einschlafen	
place [pleɪs]	Ort, Platz, Stelle	Plymouth is a great **place**.
this place/break/subject	dieser Ort / diese Pause / dieses Fach	
these places/breaks/subjects [ðiːz]	diese Orte/Pausen/Fächer	*Singular:* **this place** – *Plural:* **these places**
I don't know.	Ich weiß (es) nicht.	
them [ðem], [ðəm]	sie; ihnen	Look, there are the boys. Can you see **them**? Let's talk to **them**.
(to) eat [iːt]	essen	
What colour …?	Welche Farbe …?	
canteen [kæn'tiːn]	Kantine, (Schul-)Mensa	
gym [dʒɪm]	Turnhalle	
We're finished. ['fɪnɪʃt]	Wir sind fertig.	**We're finished.** What can we do now?
back [bæk]	zurück	
we can't … [kɑːnt]	wir können nicht …	I can speak English, but I **can't** speak French.
(to) **win** [wɪn]	gewinnen	
him [hɪm]	ihn; ihm	Look, there's Sam. Can you see **him**? Let's help **him**.
winner ['wɪnə]	Gewinner/in, Sieger/in	
p. 33 **everyday** ['evrideɪ]	Alltags-	

look • see • watch

• **Look** at the picture.	(hin)schauen
• Can you **see** the cat?	sehen
• Can I **watch** a DVD?	anschauen
Let's **watch** the seals.	beobachten

[iː] green · [i] happy · [ɪ] big · [e] red · [æ] cat · [ɑː] class · [ɒ] song · [ɔː] door · [uː] blue · [ʊ] book · [ʌ] mum · [ɜː] girl · [ə] a partner

	workbook ['wɜːkbʊk]	Arbeitsheft	
	page [peɪdʒ]	Seite	*English:* What **page** are we **on**? *German:* **Auf** welcher **Seite** sind wir?
	toilet ['tɔɪlət]	Toilette	! Betonung: **toilet** ['tɔɪlət]
	What's for homework? ['həʊmwɜːk]	Was haben wir als Hausaufgabe auf?	*English:* **Do your homework now.** *German:* **Mach jetzt deine Hausaufgaben.**
	homework ['həʊmwɜːk]	Hausaufgabe(n)	! **homework** hat keinen Plural: *English:* Where **is** your **homework**? *German:* Wo **sind** deine **Hausaufgaben**?
p. 34	**There aren't any …** ['eni]	Es gibt/sind keine …	**There are** two cats in my photo. **Are there any** cats in your photo? – No, **there aren't any** cats in my photo.
	in German/English	auf Deutsch/Englisch	
p. 35	**pronunciation** [prəˌnʌnsi'eɪʃn]	Aussprache	
	sound [saʊnd]	Laut	
	how to do sth.	wie man etwas macht / machen kann / machen soll	I don't know **how to do** this exercise. Can you help me?
	(to) **link** [lɪŋk]	verbinden, verknüpfen	You can **link** two sentences with "and".
	group (of) [gruːp]	Gruppe	*English:* a **group of** boys/girls *German:* eine **Gruppe** Jungen/Mädchen

Text: Chaos at the corner shop

p. 36	**chaos** ['keɪɒs]	Chaos	
	corner shop ['kɔːnə ʃɒp]	Laden an der Ecke; Tante-Emma-Laden	
	master ['mɑːstə]	Meister/in	
	yoghurt ['jɒgət]	Joghurt	*English:* **yoghurt** – *German:* **Joghurt**
	little ['lɪtl]	klein	This is Lily, my **little** sister.
p. 37	**always** ['ɔːlweɪz]	immer	
	that group [ðæt], [ðət]	die Gruppe (dort), jene Gruppe	
	those groups [ðəʊz]	die Gruppen (dort); jene Gruppen	*Singular:* **that group** – *Plural:* **those groups**
	(to) swim [swɪm]	schwimmen	
	like boys [laɪk]	wie Jungen	
	swimmer ['swɪmə]	Schwimmer/in	
	(to) **be good at** kung fu	gut sein in Kung-Fu	Are you **good at** football?
	feeling ['fiːlɪŋ]	Gefühl	
	angry ['æŋgri]	wütend	She's **happy**. He isn't **happy**.
	happy ['hæpi]	glücklich, froh	
	surprised [sə'praɪzd]	überrascht	
	(to) **act out** [ˌækt‿'aʊt]	vorspielen	
	the **next** picture [nekst]	das nächste Bild	
	man, *pl* **men** [mæn], [men]	Mann	! one **man** – two, three, four **men**

[eɪ] name · [aɪ] time · [ɔɪ] boy · [əʊ] old ·
[aʊ] town · [ɪə] here · [eə] where · [ʊə] tour

	woman, *pl* **women** ['wʊmən], ['wɪmɪn]	Frau	! one **woman** – two, three, four **women**

Your task

p. 38	**task** [tɑːsk]	Aufgabe	

Let's prepare for a test

p. 39	(to) **prepare (for)** [prɪ'peə]	sich vorbereiten (auf)	
	test [test]	Test	
	Which words ...? [wɪtʃ]	Welche Wörter ...?	**Which** words and **which** book?
	a pair (of) [peə]	ein Paar	*English:* **a pair of** trainers *German:* **ein Paar** Turnschuhe 
	like this	so	Play the game **like this**: ...
p. 40	**mixed bag** [ˌmɪkst 'bæg]	*etwa:* bunte Mischung	
	warm [wɔːm]	warm	

Access to cultures: GB and the UK

p. 42	**access (to)** ['ækses]	Zugang, Zutritt (zu)	
	culture ['kʌltʃə]	Kultur	! Betonung: **culture** ['kʌltʃə]
	GB (Great Britain) ['brɪtn]	Großbritannien	= England, Scotland, Wales
	the UK (the United Kingdom) [ˌjuː 'keɪ], [juˌnaɪtɪd 'kɪŋdəm]	das Vereinigte Königreich	= England, Scotland, Wales and Northern Ireland
	It says here: ...	Hier steht: ... / Es heißt hier: ...	
	million ['mɪljən]	Million	*English:* **two million** – *German:* **zwei Millionen**
	country ['kʌntri], *pl* **countries**	Land	Germany is a big **country**.
	capital ['kæpɪtl]	Hauptstadt	Berlin is the **capital** of Germany.
	summer ['sʌmə]	Sommer	 **spring** **summer** **autumn** **winter**
	port [pɔːt]	Hafenstadt	
	ship [ʃɪp]	Schiff	
	famous (for) ['feɪməs]	berühmt (für, wegen)	Plymouth is **famous for** the Hoe.
	museum [mju'ziːəm]	Museum	
	Welsh [welʃ]	Walisisch; walisisch	

Unit 2 Homes and families

pp. 44/45	**family** ['fæməli], *pl* **families**	Familie	*English:* the Blackwell **family** *German:* **Familie** Blackwell

[b] **boat** · [p] **pool** · [d] **dad** · [t] **ten** · [g] **good** · [k] **cat** ·
[m] **mum** · [n] **no** · [ŋ] **song** · [l] **hello** · [r] **red** · [w] **we** · [j] **you**

road [rəʊd]	Straße *(Landstraße zwischen Orten; Straße in Orten)*	• **ohne Hausnummer:** **in Dean Street / in Beach Road** in der Dean Street / in der Beach Road • **mit Hausnummer:** **at 14 Dean Street / at 8 Beach Road** in der Dean Street 14 / in der Beach Road 8
garden ['gɑ:dn]	Garten	
upstairs [ˌʌp'steəz]	oben; nach oben	
downstairs [ˌdaʊn'steəz]	unten; nach unten	

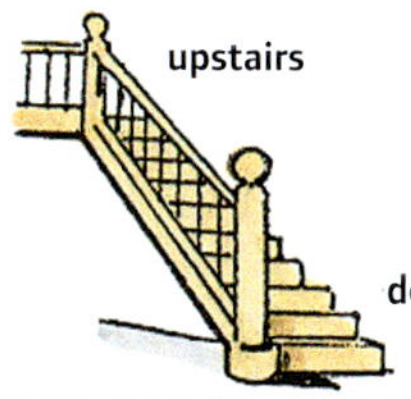

bedroom ['bedru:m]	Schlafzimmer	
bathroom ['bɑ:θru:m]	Badezimmer, Bad	
dining room ['daɪnɪŋ ru:m]	Esszimmer	
kitchen ['kɪtʃɪn]	Küche	
living room ['lɪvɪŋ ru:m]	Wohnzimmer	
armchair ['ɑ:mtʃeə]	Sessel	
bed [bed]	Bett	
lamp [læmp]	Lampe	
shelf [ʃelf], *pl* **shelves** [ʃelvz]	Regal	! one **shelf** – two, three, four **shelves**

sofa ['səʊfə]	Sofa	
table ['teɪbl]	Tisch	
toy [tɔɪ]	Spielzeug	
TV [ˌti:'vi:]	Fernsehen, Fernsehgerät	
(to) **watch TV**	fernsehen	

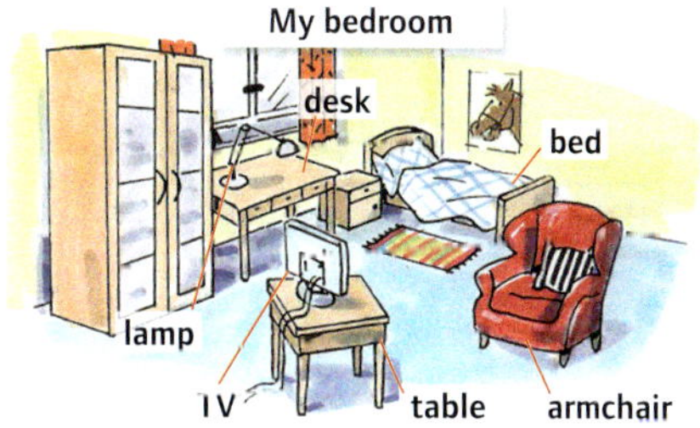

small [smɔ:l]	klein	**big** ◄► **small**

Part A

p. 46	(to) **wake up** [ˌweɪk_'ʌp]	aufwachen	**Wake up**! It's time for school! (to) **fall asleep** ◄► (to) **wake up**
	(to) **have breakfast** ['brekfəst]	frühstücken	
	a plate of … [pleɪt]	ein Teller …	
	crab [kræb]	Krebs	

in the afternoon [ˌɑ:ftə'nu:n]	nachmittags, am Nachmittag
in the evening ['i:vnɪŋ]	abends, am Abend

[f] **f**ather · [v] ri**v**er · [s] **s**ister · [z] plea**s**e · [ʃ] **sh**op · [ʒ] televi**s**ion · [tʃ] tea**ch**er · [dʒ] **G**ermany · [θ] **th**anks · [ð] **th**is · [h] **h**ere

• **in** the morning	morgens, am Morgen	• **on** Monday	am Montag
in the afternoon	nachmittags, am Nachmittag	**on** Mondays	montags, an Montagen
in the evening	abends, am Abend		

fish [fɪʃ], *pl* **fish**	Fisch	! one **fish** – two, three, four **fish**
dinner ['dɪnə]	Abendessen, Abendbrot	(to) **have breakfast** – frühstücken (to) **have lunch** – zu Mittag essen (to) **have dinner** – zu Abend essen
(to) **sit** [sɪt]	sitzen; sich setzen	
rock [rɒk]	Fels, Felsen	
(to) **text** a friend [tekst]	einem Freund / einer Freundin eine SMS schicken	I wake up, I have breakfast, and then I **text** my friends.
after that	danach	In the morning, I have breakfast. **After that** I go to school.
p. 47 **her** [hɜː]	sie; ihr	Look, there's Abby. Can you see **her**? Let's help **her**.
(to) **go sailing** ['seɪlɪŋ]	segeln; segeln gehen	Abby and Maya **go sailing** at Wembury Sailing Club.
into the kitchen ['ɪntʊ]	in die Küche (hinein)	
(to) **make** [meɪk]	machen; herstellen	
a cup of … [kʌp]	eine Tasse …	**a cup of tea** 
tea [tiː]	Tee	
paper ['peɪpə]	Papier; Zeitung	
at the weekend [ˌwiːk'end]	am Wochenende	
at night [ət 'naɪt]	nachts, in der Nacht	! **in the morning/afternoon/evening** **at night, at the weekend**
(to) **sleep** [sliːp]	schlafen	Our cat always **sleeps** on the sofa.
(to) **feed** [fiːd]	füttern	Can I **feed** the rabbits?
no … [nəʊ]	kein …, keine …	There's **no** school at weekends.
us [ʌs], [əs]	uns	We're here. Can you see **us**? Please help **us**.
of course [əv 'kɔːs]	natürlich, selbstverständlich	
basket ['bɑːskɪt]	Korb	My dog Ben always sleeps in his **basket** on the floor. 
floor [flɔː]	Fußboden	
trophy ['trəʊfi], *pl* **trophies**	Pokal; Trophäe	**trophies** 
away [ə'weɪ]	weg, fort	
mad [mæd]	verrückt	
(to) **think** [θɪŋk]	denken, glauben	I **think** Silky is nice.
so cool/nice/… [səʊ]	so cool/nett/…	
(to) **go for a walk** [wɔːk]	einen Spaziergang machen, spazieren gehen	
p. 48 **person** ['pɜːsn]	Person	! Betonung: **person** ['pɜːsn] one **person** – two, three, four **people**
p. 49 (to) **run** [rʌn]	rennen, laufen	
(to) **go shopping** ['ʃɒpɪŋ]	einkaufen gehen	On Saturday mornings I **go shopping** with Mum.
phrase [freɪz]	Ausdruck, (Rede-)Wendung	

[iː] green · [i] happy · [ɪ] big · [e] red · [æ] cat · [ɑː] class · [ɒ] song · [ɔː] door · [uː] blue · [ʊ] book · [ʌ] mum · [ɜː] girl · [ə] a partner

	usually ['ju:ʒuəli]	meistens, normalerweise, gewöhnlich	
	sometimes ['sʌmtaɪmz]	manchmal	Mum **sometimes** comes home very late.
p. 51	(to) **have fun** [fʌn]	Spaß haben, sich amüsieren	

Part B

p. 52	**uncle** ['ʌŋkl]	Onkel	your father's or your mother's brother
	aunt [ɑ:nt]	Tante	your father's or your mother's sister
	sport [spɔ:t]	Sport; Sportart	Plymstock is a **sports** school.
	(to) **do sport**	Sport treiben	On Saturdays, I always **do sport**.
	near here	(hier) in der Nähe	Is there a sports shop **near here**?
	he doesn't have time	er hat keine Zeit	
	only ['əʊnli]	nur, bloß	
	often ['ɒfn], ['ɒftən]	oft	We **often** do sport on Saturdays.
	(to) **tell (about)** [tel]	erzählen (von); berichten (über)	**Tell me about** your family.
	all [ɔ:l]	alles; alle	Can you tell me **all** about Plymstock School? I have five friends, and they **all** live near here.
	…, you know. [nəʊ]	…, weißt du. / …, wissen Sie.	We're a big family, **you know**.
	cousin ['kʌzn]	Cousin, Cousine	! Betonung: **cousin** ['kʌzn]
p. 53	**grandma** ['grænmɑ:]	Oma	
	farm [fɑ:m]	Bauernhof, Farm	
	Well, … [wel]	Nun, … / Also, … / Na ja, …	
	till 12 o'clock [tɪl]	bis 12 Uhr	On Sundays I often sleep **till** 10 o'clock.
p. 54	**They've got a house …** [gɒt] **(= They have got a house …)**	Sie haben ein Haus …	

grand-	**Groß-**
grandfather, grandpa	Großvater, Opa
grandmother, grandma	Großmutter, Oma

German "haben"

Im *simple present* wird oft **have got** für das deutsche „haben" verwendet:

Kurzformen: **I've got**, you**'ve got**, we**'ve got**, they**'ve got**
he**'s got**, she**'s got**, it**'s got**

The Blackwells **have got** a house near the sea.
They **haven't got** a boat.
My aunt **has got** a dog. **Have** you **got** a dog?
– Yes, I **have**. / No, I **haven't**.

p. 55	**family tree**	(Familien-)Stammbaum	a **family tree** 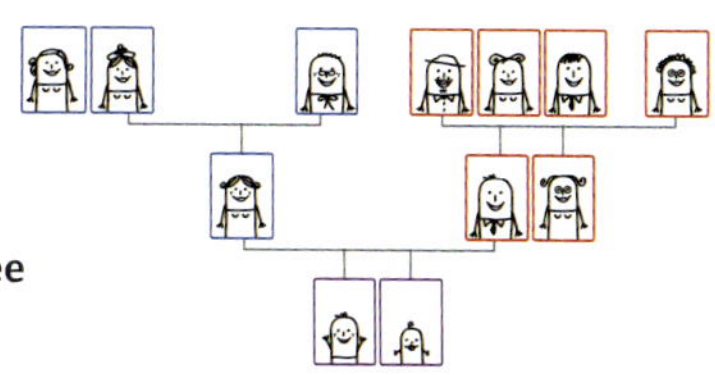
	dead [ded]	tot	
	divorced [dɪ'vɔ:st]	geschieden	
	married (to) ['mærɪd]	verheiratet (mit)	*English:* **married to** *German:* **verheiratet mit** 
	single ['sɪŋgl]	ledig, alleinstehend	
	twins *(pl)* [twɪnz]	Zwillinge	

[eɪ] name · [aɪ] time · [ɔɪ] boy · [əʊ] old ·
[aʊ] town · [ɪə] here · [eə] where · [ʊə] tour

Part C

p. 56 **What's for** lunch?	Was gibt es zum Mittagessen?	
roast beef [ˌrəʊst ˈbiːf]	Rinderbraten	
potato [pəˈteɪtəʊ], *pl* **potatoes**	Kartoffel	
yummy [ˈjʌmi] *(infml)*	lecker	
vegetables *(pl)* [ˈvedʒtəblz]	Gemüse	*English:* **Vegetables are** good for you. *German:* **Gemüse ist** gut für dich.
soup [suːp]	Suppe	vegetables  soup 
dessert [dɪˈzɜːt]	Nachtisch, Nachspeise	
fruit salad [ˌfruːt ˈsæləd]	Obstsalat	fruit salad  scones 
ice cream [ˌaɪs ˈkriːm]	(Speise-)Eis	
scone [skɒn]	*kleines rundes Milchbrötchen, leicht süß, oft mit Rosinen*	
What would you like? [wʊd]	Was hättest du gern? / Was möchtest du?	
I'd like … [ˌaɪd ˈlaɪk] (= **I would like …**)	Ich hätte gern … / Ich möchte …	
What would you like to eat?	Was möchtest du essen?	
hot [hɒt]	heiß	hot  cold 
cold [kəʊld]	kalt	
(to) drink [drɪŋk]	trinken	
drink [drɪŋk]	Getränk	
sandwich [ˈsænwɪtʃ], [ˈsænwɪdʒ]	Sandwich, *(zusammengeklapptes)* belegtes Brot	    
cake [keɪk]	Kuchen	
cream [kriːm]	Sahne	
jam [dʒæm]	Marmelade	! Das englische Wort **marmalade** [ˈmɑːməleɪd] wird nur für Marmelade aus Zitrusfrüchten verwendet.
p. 57 **food** [fuːd]	Essen; Lebensmittel; Futter	
biscuit [ˈbɪskɪt]	Plätzchen, Keks	*German* **Keks** – *English* **biscuit** *German* **Kuchen** – *English* **cake**

[b] **b**oat · [p] **p**ool · [d] **d**ad · [t] **t**en · [g] **g**ood · [k] **c**at · [m] **m**um · [n] **n**o · [ŋ] so**ng** · [l] he**ll**o · [r] **r**ed · [w] **w**e · [j] **y**ou

bread [bred]	Brot	
cheese [tʃi:z]	Käse	
meat [mi:t]	Fleisch	
milk [mɪlk]	Milch	
water ['wɔ:tə]	Wasser	

other ['ʌðə]	andere(r, s)	The cheese is on the table. Where is the **other** food?

Text: Saturday in Plymouth

p. 60	(to) **remember** [rɪ'membə]	sich erinnern (an)	*English:* Can you **remember** the name? *German:* Kannst du dich **an** den Namen **erinnern**?
	present ['preznt]	Geschenk	a **present**
	café ['kæfeɪ]	Café	
	(to) **film** [fɪlm]	filmen	
	harbour ['hɑ:bə]	Hafen	
	seagull ['si:gʌl]	Möwe	
	(to) **shout** [ʃaʊt]	schreien, rufen	
	suddenly ['sʌdnli]	plötzlich, auf einmal	
	down [daʊn]	hinunter, herunter; nach unten	
	(to) take [teɪk]	nehmen, mitnehmen; (weg-, hin)bringen	Thanks for the book. Can I **take** it with me? **Take** the chairs into the dining room, please.
	maybe ['meɪbi]	vielleicht	
	(to) **jump** [dʒʌmp]	springen	Can you **jump** **onto** your desk?
	onto the boat ['ɒntʊ]	auf das Boot (hinauf)	
	police officer [pə'li:s‿ˌɒfɪsə]	Polizist/in	
	(to) **look** happy/angry/…	glücklich/wütend/… aussehen	
	worried ['wʌrid]	besorgt, beunruhigt	

look
- **Look**, Sam. There's a seagull.
  Schau mal, Sam. Da ist eine Möwe.
- **Look at** the pictures.
  Sieh dir die Bilder an.
- Your school uniform **looks** great.
  Deine Schuluniform sieht toll aus.

	hair [heə]	Haar, Haare	*English:* Your **hair is** too long. *German:* Deine **Haare sind** zu lang.
	clothes *(pl)* [kləʊðz]	Kleidung, Kleidungsstücke	
	jeans *(pl)* [dʒi:nz]	Jeans	

clothes und **jeans** sind Plural-Wörter:
- All her **clothes are** red.
  Ihre gesamte **Kleidung ist** rot.
- My **jeans are** blue. **They're** new.
  Meine **Jeans ist** blau. **Sie ist** neu.

p. 61	why? [waɪ]	warum?	Lucy is sad. – **Why**? – Maya goes to a different school.

[f] **f**ather · [v] ri**v**er · [s] si**s**ter · [z] plea**s**e · [ʃ] **sh**op · [ʒ] televi**s**ion ·
[tʃ] tea**ch**er · [dʒ] **G**ermany · [θ] **th**anks · [ð] **th**is · [h] **h**ere

	never ['nevə]	nie, niemals	My brother **never** feeds our dog. I always feed it. 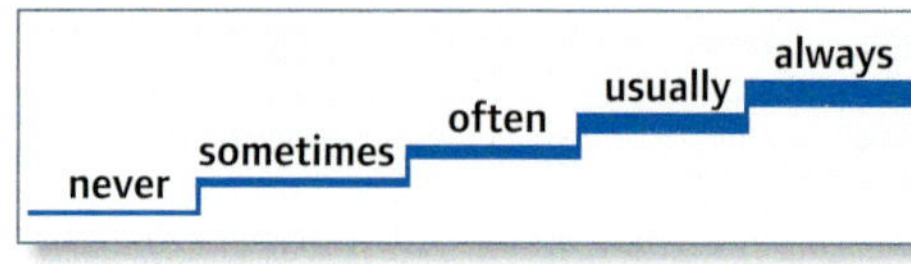
	(to) **be in trouble** ['trʌbl]	in Schwierigkeiten sein; Ärger kriegen	
	story ['stɔːri], *pl* **stories**	Geschichte, Erzählung	! one **story** – two, three, four **stories**
	it shows **that …** [ðæt], [ðət]	es zeigt, dass …	

Let's prepare for a test

p. 64	**curry** ['kʌri]	Curry(gericht)	

Access to cultures: Special days

p. 66	**special** ['speʃl]	besondere(r, s)	! Betonung: **special** ['speʃl]
	Christmas ['krɪsməs]	Weihnachten	

Christmas

- **Merry Christmas!** [ˌmeri 'krɪsməs] – Frohe Weihnachten!
- **Christmas Eve** [ˌkrɪsməs_'iːv] – Heiligabend
- **Christmas Day** – 1. Weihnachtstag (25. Dezember)
- **Boxing Day** ['bɒksɪŋ deɪ] – 2. Weihnachtstag (26. Dezember)
- **Christmas pudding** [ˌkrɪsməs 'pʊdɪŋ] – *kein Pudding im deutschen Sinn, sondern ein Nachtisch aus Butter, Zucker, Mehl, Rosinen, Nüssen, Eiern, Gewürzen, der traditionell zu Weihnachten gegessen wird*

	light [laɪt]	Licht	
	candle ['kændl]	Kerze	a **candle** 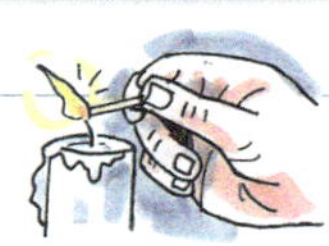
	turkey ['tɜːkɪ]	Pute, Truthahn	 a **turkey**
	cracker ['krækə]	Knallbonbon	
	That's fun.	Das macht Spaß.	
	paper hat ['peɪpə hæt]	Papierhut	
p. 67	**invitation (to)** [ˌɪnvɪ'teɪʃn]	Einladung (zu, nach)	
	everybody ['evribɒdi] (or: **everyone** ['evriwʌn])	jeder; alle	**Everybody** knows that London is in England. (*or:* **Everyone** knows …)
	wish [wɪʃ]	Wunsch	

[iː] green · [i] happy · [ɪ] big · [e] red · [æ] cat · [ɑː] class · [ɒ] song · [ɔː] door · [uː] blue · [ʊ] book · [ʌ] mum · [ɜː] girl · [ə] a partner

Unit 3 Clubs and hobbies

p. 68/69	**hobby** ['hɒbi], *pl* **hobbies**	Hobby	
	some [sʌm], [səm]	einige, ein paar; etwas	There are **some** sandwiches for you on the table. And there's **some** milk too.
	(to) **join a club** [dʒɔɪn]	in einen Klub eintreten; sich einem Klub anschließen	You like basketball? **Join** our basketball club!
	more [mɔː]	mehr	For **more** help, go to page 68. Can you tell me **more** about the clubs at your school?
	information (about) *(no pl)* [ˌɪnfə'meɪʃn]	Information(en) (über)	! Das englische Wort **information** hat keinen Plural: *English:* Here**'s** the **information** about our club. *German:* Hier **sind** die **Information**en …
	4 **pm** [ˌpiː_'em]	4 Uhr nachmittags / 16 Uhr	! • Bei Uhrzeiten wird **pm** verwendet, wenn der Nachmittag oder Abend gemeint ist. • **am** wird verwendet, wenn der Morgen oder Vormittag gemeint ist. • **am** und **pm** stehen nie mit **o'clock** – also nur: **at 4 am / at 4 pm** (nicht: at 4 ~~o'clock pm~~)
	4 **am** [ˌeɪ_'em]	4 Uhr morgens	
	(to) **edit** ['edɪt]	bearbeiten; schneiden *(Film, Video)*	
	gardening ['gɑːdnɪŋ]	Gärtnern, Gartenarbeit	
	(to) **grow** [grəʊ]	anbauen, anpflanzen	
	(to) **sell** [sel]	verkaufen	
	kit [kɪt]	Ausrüstung	
	quiet ['kwaɪət]	ruhig, still, leise	Be **quiet**, please. I have lots of homework.
	young [jʌŋ]	jung	**young** ◄► **old**
	(to) **choose** [tʃuːz]	aussuchen, (aus)wählen; sich aussuchen	Look at the information on our school website. Then **choose** one or two clubs.
	area ['eəriə]	Bereich; Gebiet, Gegend	The Samba Club meets in the Music **area**. I live in an **area** with lots of shops.
	lunchtime ['lʌntʃtaɪm]	Mittagszeit	We can meet in the canteen **at lunchtime**. (*German:* … **mittags** …)
	instrument ['ɪnstrəmənt]	Instrument	! Betonung: **instrument** ['ɪnstrəmənt]
	(to) **sing** [sɪŋ]	singen	
	(to) **dance** [dɑːns]	tanzen	
	from … to …	von … bis …	The Film-Making Club meets **from** 3 **to** 4 pm.

Part A

p. 70	(to) **get** angry/cold/… [get]	wütend/kalt/… werden	My dad is great. He never **gets** angry.
	wet [wet]	nass	
	umbrella [ʌm'brelə]	Schirm, Regenschirm	With an **umbrella**, you can't get wet.
	funny ['fʌni]	witzig, komisch	
	very funny/wet/… ['veri]	sehr witzig/nass/…	
	joke [dʒəʊk]	Witz	

[eɪ] name · [aɪ] time · [ɔɪ] boy · [əʊ] old · [aʊ] town · [ɪə] here · [eə] where · [ʊə] tour

	because [bɪˈkɒz]	weil	Why are you angry? – **Because** you're late.
	really [ˈrɪəli]	wirklich	Our Maths teacher is **really** nice. I know some very good jokes. – **Really**?
	(to) **have to** go/work/… [ˈhæv tə]	gehen/arbeiten/… müssen	Look, it's late. We **have to** go now.
	What's the matter? [ˈmætə]	Was ist denn? / Was ist los?	You look so sad. **What's the matter?**
p. 71	**What's she like?**	Wie ist sie? / Wie ist sie so?	You know Kristen Stewart? Really? **What's she like?**
	(to) **visit** [ˈvɪzɪt]	besuchen	Can we **visit** Grandma on Sunday?
	(to) **love** [lʌv]	lieben, sehr mögen	
	nothing [ˈnʌθɪŋ]	(gar) nichts	
	list [lɪst]	Liste	
	(to) **want** [wɒnt]	(haben) wollen	
	work [wɜːk]	Arbeit	
	(to) **want to do**	tun wollen	*English:* I **want to** dance. *German:* Ich **möchte** tanzen.
	(to) **sound** [saʊnd]	klingen, sich *(gut usw.)* anhören	A garden party? That **sounds** great.
	(to) **make friends**	Freunde finden	Join the Samba Club and **make** new **friends**.
p. 72	**activity** [ækˈtɪvəti], *pl* **activities**	Aktivität	! Betonung: **ac<u>ti</u>vity** [ækˈtɪvəti]
	chess [tʃes]	Schach	
	drum [drʌm]	Trommel	*English:* (to) play **the drums** / **the piano** *German:* **Schlagzeug** spielen / **Klavier** spielen
	piano [piˈænəʊ]	Klavier, Piano	
	gymnastics [dʒɪmˈnæstɪks]	Gymnastik, Turnen	
	skating [ˈskeɪtɪŋ]	Inlineskaten, Rollschuhlaufen	**skates**
	riding [ˈraɪdɪŋ]	Reiten	
	judo [ˈdʒuːdəʊ]	Judo	

Sports and other activities

You **<u>do</u>** …
judo, yoga, gymnastics, kung fu, sport, …

You **<u>play</u>** …
basketball, football, tennis, games, chess, cards, the drums, the piano, …

You **<u>go</u>** …
sailing, skating, swimming, riding, dancing, …

p. 73	(to) **guess** [ges]	raten, erraten	Can you **guess** how old I am?
	(to) **clean** [kliːn]	sauber machen, putzen	I can't go swimming now. I have to **clean** my room.
p. 74	(to) **collect** [kəˈlekt]	sammeln	My friend Jamie **collects** comics.
	free [friː]	frei	Can we meet at 1 o'clock? Are you **free**? *English:* **free time** • **free-time activities** *German:* **Freizeit** • **Freizeitaktivitäten**
	(to) **ask** sb. **to do** sth.	jemanden bitten, etwas zu tun	You can always **ask** your teacher **to** help you.
	(to) **try** [traɪ]	(aus)probieren; versuchen	**Try** a scone. They're really yummy. Sam always **tries** to help his sister Lily. ! I/you/we/they **try** • he/she/it **tries**

[b] **boat** · [p] **pool** · [d] **dad** · [t] **ten** · [g] **good** · [k] **cat** ·
[m] **mum** · [n] **no** · [ŋ] **song** · [l] **hello** · [r] **red** · [w] **we** · [j] **you**

	table ['teɪbl]	Tabelle	
	(to) **need** [niːd]	brauchen, benötigen	

	guitar [gɪ'tɑː]	Gitarre	*English:* (to) play **the guitar** *German:* **Gitarre** spielen
	beach [biːtʃ]	Strand	

p. 75	**outside** [ˌaʊt'saɪd]	draußen; nach draußen	Where's the dog? – **Outside**, in the garden. It's hot in here. Let's go **outside**.
	inside [ˌɪn'saɪd]	drinnen; nach drinnen	**inside** ◄► **outside**
	jump [dʒʌmp]	Sprung	
	letter ['letə]	Brief	

Part B

p. 76	many ['meni]	viele	I have lots of questions, but I don't have **many** answers.
	much [mʌtʃ]	viel	Dad works so **much**. He doesn't have **much** time.

much („viel") – many („viele")

viel	**How much** tea do we need? **Wie viel** Tee …?	– We don't need **much** tea, but we need **lots of** milk. – … nicht **viel** Tee … **viel** Milch
viele	**How many** scones do we need? **Wie viele** Scones …?	– We don't need **many** scones, but we need **lots of** sandwiches. – … nicht **viele** Scones … **viele** Sandwiches

(to) **finish** sth. ['fɪnɪʃ]	etwas beenden; mit etwas fertig werden/sein	**Finish** your homework, then you can go skating. Do you always **finish** school at 2 o'clock?
Come on, Dad.	Na los, Dad! / Komm, Dad!	
How are you? [haʊ‿'ɑː ju]	Wie geht's? / Wie geht es dir/euch?	

Listen, Justin. ['lɪsn]	Hör zu, Justin.	**Listen**, please. – Hör(t) zu, bitte. **Listen to** me. – Hör(t) mir zu, bitte. **Listen to** the song. – Hör dir/Hört euch den Song an.
(to) **listen** ['lɪsn]	zuhören, horchen	
job [dʒɒb]	Job, (Arbeits-)Stelle	
studio ['stjuːdiəʊ]	Studio	
programme ['prəʊgræm]	Programm, (Radio-, Fernseh-)Sendung	! Betonung: **programme** ['prəʊgræm]
What programmes …?	Welche Programme …? / Welche Art von Programmen …?	**What TV programmes** do you watch and **what books** do you read?
midnight ['mɪdnaɪt]	Mitternacht	

[f] **f**ather · [v] **r**i**v**er · [s] **s**ister · [z] plea**s**e · [ʃ] **sh**op · [ʒ] televi**s**ion ·
[tʃ] tea**ch**er · [dʒ] **G**ermany · [θ] **th**anks · [ð] **th**is · [h] **h**ere

	too late/cold/big/… [tuː]	zu spät/kalt/groß/…	We can't go swimming. It's much **too** cold.
	(to) **get up** [ˌget‿ˈʌp]	aufstehen	My mother **gets up** at 6 o'clock every morning.
	How do you like it?	Wie findest du es (sie/ihn)? / Wie gefällt es (sie/er) dir?	
	It's about a seagull.	Es geht um eine Möwe. / Es handelt von einer Möwe.	I can't go skating, I want to watch a video. **It's about** a kung fu master.
	(to) **send** sth. **to** sb. [send]	jm. etwas schicken, senden	
	idea [aɪˈdɪə]	Idee; Vorstellung	I have a great **idea** for a video about Plymouth. Justin has no **idea** about his dad's work.
p. 77	(to) **hear** [hɪə]	hören	**listen • hear** **Listen.** Can you **hear** the dogs in the street? • (to) **listen (to)** zuhören, horchen • (to) **hear** hören (können)
	I like swimming/sailing/…	Ich schwimme/segele/… gern.	I **like dancing** and my sister **likes singing**.
p. 78	**partner** [ˈpɑːtnə]	Partner/in	
	today [təˈdeɪ]	heute	
	(to) **phone** sb. [fəʊn]	jn. anrufen	
	phone call [ˈfəʊn kɔːl] (*kurz auch:* **call**)	Anruf; Telefongespräch	
p. 79	(to) **happen (to)** [ˈhæpən]	geschehen, passieren (mit)	What **happens** in Plymouth?
	when [wen]	wenn	Can we play cards **when** you come home?
	no one [ˈnəʊ wʌn] (or: **nobody** [ˈnəʊbədi])	niemand	**everyone, everybody ◄► no one, nobody**

Part C

p. 80	**on Saturday afternoon**	am Samstagnachmittag	! **in the morning/afternoon/evening** *aber:* **on Saturday afternoon / on Monday morning** *usw.*
	(to) **ride a bike** [ˌraɪd‿ə ˈbaɪk]	Rad fahren	
	bike [baɪk]	Fahrrad	
	(to) **stop** [stɒp]	anhalten, stoppen	
	tired [ˈtaɪəd]	müde	She's **tired**.
	(to) **be thirsty** [ˈθɜːsti]	durstig sein, Durst haben	
	chocolate [ˈtʃɒklət]	Schokolade	! Betonung: **chocolate** [ˈtʃɒklət]
	(to) **turn** sth. **on** [ˌtɜːn‿ˈɒn]	etwas einschalten	
	all of Plymouth	ganz Plymouth, das ganze Plymouth	
	someone [ˈsʌmwʌn] (or: **somebody** [ˈsʌmbədi])	jemand	There's **someone/ somebody** at the door, I think.
	something [ˈsʌmθɪŋ]	etwas	Can I ask you **something**?

[iː] green · [i] happy · [ɪ] big · [e] red · [æ] cat · [ɑː] class · [ɒ] song · [ɔː] door · [uː] blue · [ʊ] book · [ʌ] mum · [ɜː] girl · [ə] a partner

	behind [bɪ'haɪnd]	hinter	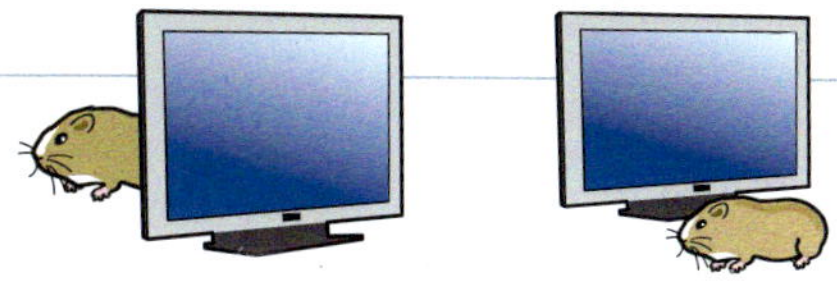
	in front of [ɪn 'frʌnt‿əv]	vor	**behind** the TV ◄► **in front of** the TV
	(to) **turn around** [ˌtɜːn‿ə'raʊnd]	sich umdrehen	
	ghost [gəʊst]	Geist, Gespenst	
	ready ['redi]	bereit, fertig	Are you **ready**? Can we go?
	loud [laʊd]	laut	**loud** ◄► **quiet**
p. 81	**scary** ['skeəri]	unheimlich, gruselig	I can tell you a **scary** story.
	traveller ['trævələ]	Reisende(r)	
	(to) **travel** ['trævl]	reisen	We always **travel** to Spain in June.
	part [pɑːt]	Teil	
	(to) **be called** [kɔːld]	heißen, genannt werden	Asterix has a very big friend. He**'s called** Obelix. (= His name is Obelix.)
	restaurant ['restrɒnt]	Restaurant	! Betonung: **restaurant** ['restrɒnt]
	visitor ['vɪzɪtə]	Besucher/in, Gast	
	former ['fɔːmə]	ehemalige(r, s), frühere(r, s)	Our music studio is in a **former** school house.
	floor [flɔː]	Stock(werk)	You can find men's clothes on the second **floor**.
	(to) **imagine** sth. [ɪ'mædʒɪn]	sich etwas vorstellen	**Imagine** you're Silky. Tell your partner about Plymouth Sound.
	life [laɪf], *pl* **lives** [laɪvz]	Leben	*English:* **Life** in Plymouth is fun. *German:* **Das Leben** in Plymouth …
	in 1580	im Jahr 1580	
	child [tʃaɪld], *pl* **children** ['tʃɪldrən]	Kind	! one **child** – two, three, four **children**
	ticket ['tɪkɪt]	Eintrittskarte	
	pound (£) [paʊnd]	Pfund *(britische Währung)*	£1.50 = one pound fifty
	(to) **come along** [ˌkʌm‿ə'lɒŋ]	mitkommen, herkommen	
p. 82	**end** [end]	Ende, Schluss	
p. 83	**letter** ['letə]	Buchstabe	
	capital letter [ˌkæpɪtl 'letə]	Großbuchstabe	
	(to) **use** [juːz]	benutzen, verwenden	Can I **use** your mobile, please?
	etc. (et cetera) [et'setərə]	usw. (und so weiter)	
	the same	der-/die-/dasselbe	In English, you use capital letters for names. That's **the same** in German.
	city ['sɪti], *pl* **cities**	Stadt, Großstadt	
	church [tʃɜːtʃ]	Kirche	
	word order ['wɜːd‿ɔːdə]	Wortstellung	
p. 84	**box** [bɒks]	Kasten, Kiste, Kästchen	
	address [ə'dres]	Adresse, Anschrift	What's your **address**? – 14 New Street. *English:* **address** – *German:* **Adresse**

[eɪ] name · [aɪ] time · [ɔɪ] boy · [əʊ] old ·
[aʊ] town · [ɪə] here · [eə] where · [ʊə] tour

	bus [bʌs]	Bus	
	(to) **add** [æd]	hinzufügen, addieren	What happens when you **add** blue to yellow?
	consonant ['kɒnsənənt]	Konsonant, Mitlaut	
	ending ['endɪŋ]	Endung	
	vowel ['vaʊəl]	Vokal, Selbstlaut	
	(to) **call** [kɔːl]	anrufen; rufen; nennen	Can you **call** me at 6? Here's my phone number. Please **call** your dog. It's in our garden. Her name is Jessica, but we **call** her Jess.
p. 85	**stress** [stres]	Betonung	

Text: The captain's ghost

p. 86	(to) **take place** [teɪk 'pleɪs]	stattfinden; spielen, sich abspielen *(Geschichte, Handlung)*	The story **takes place** in Plymouth.
	sound [saʊnd]	Geräusch; Klang	
	attic ['ætɪk]	Dachboden	*English:* **in the attic** *German:* **auf dem Dachboden**
	boring ['bɔːrɪŋ]	langweilig	
	mouth [maʊθ]	Mund; Maul	
	diary ['daɪəri], *pl* **diaries**	Tagebuch; Kalender	
	sick [sɪk]	krank	
	money ['mʌni]	Geld	
	(to) **hope** [həʊp]	hoffen	I **hope** you like my school uniform.
	bottle ['bɒtl]	Flasche	
	(to) **smell** [smel]	riechen	Can you **smell** the cake? It **smells** great!
	Me too.	Ich auch.	*English:* I'm from Plymouth. – **Me too**. *German:* Ich bin aus Plymouth. – **Ich auch**.
	out of ... ['aʊt‿əv]	aus ... (heraus/hinaus)	 **into** the house ◄► **out of** the house
	moon [muːn]	Mond	
	(to) **walk** [wɔːk]	(zu Fuß) gehen	
	along the street/the river/... [ə'lɒŋ]	die Straße/den Fluss/... entlang	*English:* Go **along the street**. *German:* Gehe **die Straße entlang**.
	Oh, it's you.	Ach, du bist es.	

[b] **boat** · [p] **pool** · [d] **dad** · [t] **ten** · [g] **good** · [k] **cat** · [m] **mum** · [n] **no** · [ŋ] **song** · [l] **hello** · [r] **red** · [w] **we** · [j] **you**

	(to) **bark** [bɑːk]	bellen	
	step [step]	Schritt	
	voice [vɔɪs]	Stimme	
p. 87	**thief** [θiːf], *pl* **thieves** [θiːvz]	Dieb/in	
	hand [hænd]	Hand	
	(to) **fight** [faɪt]	kämpfen	
	coin [kɔɪn]	Münze	 some **coins**
	(to) **taste** [teɪst]	schmecken	This soup smells nice, but it **tastes** funny.
	dream [driːm]	Traum	
	perfect [ˈpɜːfɪkt]	perfekt, ideal	! stress: **perfect** [ˈpɜːfɪkt]
	(to) **understand** [ˌʌndəˈstænd]	verstehen	Can you speak English, please? I don't **understand** German.

Let's prepare for a test

p. 89	**junior team** [ˈdʒuːniə tiːm]	Jugendmannschaft, Juniorenmannschaft	
	trumpet [ˈtrʌmpɪt]	Trompete	
	tomato [təˈmɑːtəʊ], *pl* **tomatoes**	Tomate	**tomatoes** 
p. 91	**age** [eɪdʒ]	Alter	

Access to cultures: Shopping

p. 92	**pence (p)** [pens]	Pence *(Plural von „penny")*	

British money – pounds and pence

You say:	You write:		
one p [piː] (= penny)	**1p**	**How much is** the watch?	**Was kostet** die Uhr?
fifty p [piː] / **fifty pence** [pens]	**50p**	**How much are** the DVDs?	**Was kosten** die DVDs?
one pound / a pound	**£1**		
five pounds	**£5**	The watch **is** £35.	Die Uhr **kostet** …
two pounds fifty	**£2.50**	The DVDs **are** £12.95.	Die DVDs **kosten** …

	felt pen [ˌfelt ˈpen]	Filzstift	
p. 93	**shopping centre** [ˈʃɒpɪŋ sentə]	Einkaufszentrum	
	supermarket [ˈsuːpəmɑːkɪt]	Supermarkt	
	closed [kləʊzd]	geschlossen	
	Easter [ˈiːstə]	Ostern	
	They're £2.75 **each**. [iːtʃ]	Sie kosten je 2 Pfund 75. *(2,75 pro Stück)*	
	size [saɪz]	Größe	It's a nice T-shirt, but it's not the right **size**. It's too small.

Unit 4 Weekends

p. 94	**garage** ['gærɑːʒ], ['gærɪdʒ]	Garage	
	life jacket ['laɪf dʒækɪt]	Schwimmweste	a **life jacket** 
	magazine [ˌmægə'ziːn]	Zeitschrift	
	mobile phone [ˌməʊbaɪl 'fəʊn] (*kurz auch:* **mobile**)	Mobiltelefon, Handy	**!** **„Handy"** klingt zwar englisch, ist es aber nicht. Auf Englisch heißt es immer **mobile** oder **mobile phone**.
	note [nəʊt]	Notiz, Mitteilung	
	sand [sænd]	Sand	
	shorts *(pl)* [ʃɔːts]	Shorts, kurze Hose	
	plan [plæn]	Plan	
	match [mætʃ]	Spiel, Wettkampf, Match	
	(to) **break** [breɪk]	zerbrechen, kaputt machen; brechen, kaputt gehen	Don't play football here. You don't want to **break** a window!
	island ['aɪlənd]	Insel	
p. 95	**cinema** ['sɪnəmə]	Kino	
	lake [leɪk]	(Binnen-)See	**!** the **lake** – der See • the **sea** – das Meer, die See
	grandparents ['grænpeərənts]	Großeltern	
	parents ['peərənts]	Eltern	
	shopping mall ['ʃɒpɪŋ mɔːl] (*kurz auch:* **mall**)	*(großes)* Einkaufszentrum	

Part A

p. 96	(we/you/they) **were** [wɜː], [wə]	*Vergangenheitsform von „be"*	
	(I/he/she/it) **was** [wɒz], [wəz]	*Vergangenheitsform von „be"*	
	yesterday ['jestədeɪ], ['jestədi]	gestern	**Yesterday** I was late for school. My teacher wasn't happy.
	last weekend/Friday/... [lɑːst]	letztes Wochenende / letzten Freitag / ...	**last** weekend – **this** weekend – **next** weekend
	I'm **sorry about ...**	Es tut mir leid wegen ...	I'm **sorry about** your grandpa. He was a very nice man.
	(to) **be busy** ['bɪzi]	beschäftigt sein; viel zu tun haben	I can't help you. **I'm busy**.
	fantastic [fæn'tæstɪk]	fantastisch	
	actor ['æktə]	Schauspieler/in	
	exciting [ɪk'saɪtɪŋ]	aufregend, spannend	**exciting** ◄► **boring**
	Guess what, Dad ...	Stell dir vor, Dad ... / Weißt du was, Dad ...	
	still [stɪl]	(immer) noch	My sister is seven, and she **still** can't read.
	chain [tʃeɪn]	Kette	a **chain** 

[iː] **green** · [i] **happy** · [ɪ] **big** · [e] **red** · [æ] **cat** · [ɑː] **class** · [ɒ] **song** · [ɔː] **door** · [uː] **blue** · [ʊ] **book** · [ʌ] **mum** · [ɜː] **girl** · [ə] **a partner**

p. 97	**not … either** ['aɪðə], ['iːðə]	auch nicht	Maya was at Lucy's house, and her brother wasn't at home **either**.
	Was it fun?	Hat es Spaß gemacht?	! Swimming **is fun**. – Schwimmen **macht Spaß**. That joke **was funny**. – Der Witz **war lustig**.
	whose? [huːz]	wessen?	**Whose** shoe is this? – It's Sam's.

Part B

p. 98/99	**against** [ə'genst]	gegen	Sam's team played **against** Devonport.
	final ['faɪnl]	Finale, Endspiel	! stress: **final** ['faɪnl]
	excited [ɪk'saɪtɪd]	aufgeregt, gespannt	! Sam was **excited** about the final. – **aufgeregt** It was an **exciting** day for Sam. – **aufregend**
	on the way to … [weɪ]	auf dem Weg zu/nach …	
	went [went]	*Vergangenheitsform von „go"*	Yesterday we **went** to Devonport.
	(to) go **by minibus** [baɪ 'mɪnibʌs]	mit dem Kleinbus fahren	 We went **by minibus** **by bus** **by car**.
	came [keɪm]	*Vergangenheitsform von „come"*	Uncle Amar **came** to dinner again last night.
	had [hæd]	*Vergangenheitsform von „have" und von „have got"*	Yesterday we **had** breakfast at 6 o'clock. My grandparents **had** a dog. We've got two cats.

had

had ist die Vergangenheitsform von **(to) have** und von **have got**.

Vergleiche: My parents often **have** parties. They **had** a party last Friday.
We**'ve got** a dog now. When I was little, I **had** a rabbit. ! Vorsicht! Nicht *I ~~had got~~ a rabbit.*

	half, *pl* **halves** [hɑːf], [hɑːvz]	Hälfte; Halbzeit	
	(to) **score** [skɔː]	ein Tor schießen, einen Treffer erzielen	
	point [pɔɪnt]	Punkt	Three **points** for the right answer!
	That helped us **a lot**. [ə 'lɒt]	Das hat uns sehr geholfen.	He likes her **a lot**.
	won [wʌn]	*Vergangenheitsform von „win"*	Sam and his friends **won** the match last Saturday.
	up and down [ˌʌp_ən 'daʊn]	auf und ab; rauf und runter	
	up [ʌp]	hinauf, herauf; (nach) oben	
	when [wen]	als	**when** 1. **When**'s your birthday? – **wann** 2. Call me **when** you're back, please. – **wenn** 3. He called me **when** he was back. – **als**
	(to) **arrive** [ə'raɪv]	ankommen, eintreffen	The bus **arrived** at 6:20 pm.
	saw [sɔː]	*Vergangenheitsform von „see"*	I **saw** John yesterday. He looked sick.
	medal ['medl]	Medaille	! stress: **medal** ['medl]
	better ['betə]	besser	Devonport was good, but Plymstock was **better**.
p. 100	**past** [pɑːst]	Vergangenheit	

[eɪ] **name** · [aɪ] **time** · [ɔɪ] **boy** · [əʊ] **old** ·
[aʊ] **town** · [ɪə] **here** · [eə] **where** · [ʊə] **tour**

	around the library / the beach [ə'raʊnd]	in der Bücherei / auf dem Strand umher	We walked **around** the town for two hours and saw lots of nice things.
	between [bɪ'twiːn]	zwischen	**between** the rabbits
p. 101	**visit** ['vɪzɪt]	Besuch	

Part C

p. 102	(to) **miss** [mɪs]	verpassen	Sorry I'm late – I **missed** the bus.
	ride [raɪd]	Fahrt	

Unregelmäßige Vergangenheitsformen (Irregular simple past forms)

(to) **do**	**did** [dɪd]	tun, machen	(to) **ride** a bike	**rode** a bike [rəʊd]	Rad fahren
(to) **eat**	**ate** [et], [eɪt]	essen	(to) **run**	**ran** [ræn]	laufen, rennen
(to) **fall** asleep	**fell** asleep [fel]	einschlafen	(to) **sing**	**sang** [sæŋ]	singen
(to) **forget**	**forgot** [fə'gɒt]	vergessen	(to) **write**	**wrote** [rəʊt]	schreiben

➜ *List of irregular verbs*, pp. 269–270

	over to … ['əʊvə]	hinüber zu/nach …	
	picnic ['pɪknɪk]	Picknick	
	Sam **didn't run**. ['dɪdnt]	Sam rannte nicht.	he **ran/watched** ◄► he **didn't run** / **didn't watch**
	(to) **sit down** [ˌsɪt 'daʊn], *simple past:* **sat down** [sæt]	sich hinsetzen	After the football match, the players **sat down** and had something to drink.
	far [fɑː]	weit (entfernt)	
	all right [ɔːl 'raɪt]	okay; in Ordnung	
	problem ['prɒbləm]	Problem	**!** stress: **<u>pro</u>blem** ['prɒbləm]
	high [haɪ]	hoch	
	sights *(pl)* [saɪts]	Sehenswürdigkeiten	
	(to) **make a wish** [wɪʃ]	sich etwas wünschen	
	the **missing** words ['mɪsɪŋ]	die fehlenden Wörter	
	early ['ɜːli]	früh	I have to get up very **early** on school days.

Unregelmäßige Vergangenheitsformen (Irregular simple past forms)

(to) **feed**	**fed** [fed]	füttern	(to) **say**	**said** [sed]	sagen
(to) **hear**	**heard** [hɜːd]	hören	(to) **swim**	**swam** [swæm]	schwimmen
(to) **make**	**made** [meɪd]	machen; herstellen	(to) **take**	**took** [tʊk]	nehmen; bringen
(to) **meet**	**met** [met]	(sich) treffen	(to) **think**	**thought** [θɔːt]	denken, glauben

➜ *List of irregular verbs*, pp. 269–270

p. 103	**true** [truː]	wahr	
p. 104	(to) **save** [seɪv]	retten	
	hurt [hɜːt]	verletzt	
	the dog **couldn't** swim ['kʊdnt]	der Hund konnte nicht schwimmen	We **could** hear the cat, but we **couldn't** see it.
	police *(pl)* [pə'liːs]	Polizei	**!** *English:* The **police are** here. *German:* Die **Polizei ist** hier.
	county ['kaʊnti]	Grafschaft *(in Großbritannien)*	
p. 105	(to) **clap** [klæp]	(Beifall) klatschen	*English:* **Clap your hands**. *German:* **Klatscht in die Hände**.
	intonation [ˌɪntə'neɪʃn]	Intonation, Satzmelodie	

Part D

p. 106 (to) **smile** [smaɪl]	lächeln	
(to) **bite** [baɪt], *simple past:* **bit** [bɪt]	beißen	Don't feed the horses – they **bite**.
just [dʒʌst]	(einfach) nur, bloß	Don't **just** sit there. Come and help me.
bell [bel]	Klingel, Glocke	
birth [bɜːθ]	Geburt	*English:* **at birth** – *German:* **bei der Geburt**
soon [suːn]	bald	It's my birthday **soon**. Can I have a party?
(to) **become** [bɪˈkʌm], *simple past:* **became** [bɪˈkeɪm]	werden	Suddenly it **became** dark. ! (to) **become** heißt **werden** (nicht ~~bekommen~~) – zu „bekommen" siehe weiter unten (to) **get**
spot [spɒt]	Fleck, Punkt	There's a **spot** on your T-shirt. – I know. It's ketchup.
(to) **weigh** [weɪ]	wiegen	How much do you **weigh**?
over 20 people/years/...	über/mehr als 20 Leute/Jahre/...	
kilogram [ˈkɪləgræm], **kilo** [ˈkiːləʊ] **(kg)**	Kilogramm, Kilo	
wild [waɪld]	wild	! pronunciation: **wild** [waɪld]
watcher [ˈwɒtʃə]	Beobachter/in	verb: (to) **watch** – noun: **watcher**
you **mustn't** do it [ˈmʌsnt]	du darfst es nicht tun	You **mustn't** touch the plates. They're hot.
close (to) [kləʊs]	nah, dicht (bei, an)	You mustn't go too **close to** wild animals.
metre [ˈmiːtə]	Meter	
about [əˈbaʊt]	ungefähr	There were **about** 300 people in the park.
... **a day/week/year**	... pro Tag/Woche/Jahr	Grey seals eat about 5 kilos of fish **a day**.
you **needn't** do it [ˈniːdnt]	du musst es nicht tun, du brauchst es nicht zu tun	I can do the exercise. You **needn't** help me.
(to) **get** [get], *simple past:* **got** [gɒt]	bekommen	
enough [ɪˈnʌf]	genug	

get, *simple past:* **got**

Did you **get** nice presents?	**bekommen**
Mum **gets** angry when I'm late.	**werden**
I always **get up** at 7 o'clock.	**aufstehen**

hard [hɑːd]	schwer, schwierig; hart	This exercise isn't **hard**. You can do it. It's **hard** work to learn a language.
baby seal	Robbenjunges; Heuler	
(to) **grow** [grəʊ], *simple past:* **grew** [gruː]	wachsen	Bananas don't **grow** in cold countries. ! (to) **grow** = **1.** wachsen; **2.** anbauen, anpflanzen
(to) **leave** [liːv], *simple past:* **left** [left]	verlassen; zurücklassen	Dad **leaves** the house at 8 am and starts work at 9. Don't **leave** your dog in the car when it's hot.
must [mʌst]	müssen	Young seals **must** learn to catch fish.

must – needn't – mustn't

Mit **must** drückt man aus, dass jemand etwas **tun muss**:

I **must** feed the cats.
Ich muss die Katzen füttern.

Mit **needn't** drückt man aus, dass jemand etwas **nicht zu tun braucht**:

I **needn't** feed the cats. Mum fed them this morning.
Ich muss die Katzen nicht füttern. ...

Mit **mustn't** drückt man aus, dass jemand etwas **nicht tun darf**:

You **mustn't** feed the seals in the zoo.
Du darfst die Robben im Zoo nicht füttern.

(to) **practise** [ˈpræktɪs]	üben, trainieren	

[f] **f**ather · [v] **r**i**v**er · [s] **s**i**s**ter · [z] plea**s**e · [ʃ] **sh**op · [ʒ] televi**s**ion · [tʃ] **t**ea**ch**er · [dʒ] **G**ermany · [θ] **th**anks · [ð] **th**is · [h] **h**ere

p. 107	(to) **stay** [steɪ]	bleiben	Can we **stay** at home this summer?
p. 108	**holidays** *(pl)* ['hɒlədeɪz]	Ferien	
p. 109	(to) **hurt,** *simple past:* **hurt** [hɜːt]	verletzen; schmerzen, wehtun	**hurt** **1. verletzen** Horses can **hurt** you. They can bite. **2. schmerzen** My legs/These shoes **hurt**. I need a break. **3. verletzt** Look, that man is **hurt**. We have to help him.
	noise [nɔɪz]	Geräusch, Lärm	
	if [ɪf]	wenn, falls	! **if** you see them – **wenn/falls** du sie siehst **when** you see them – **wenn/sobald** du sie siehst
	(to) **bring** [brɪŋ], *simple past:* **brought** [brɔːt]	(mit-, her)bringen	

German "bringen"

(to) **bring** = **mitbringen, herbringen**

Bring me the paper, Max.

(to) **take** = **wegbringen, hinbringen**

And now **take** it to Dad.

	anything ['eniθɪŋ]	(irgend)etwas	Is there **anything** to eat here? („Gibt es hier (irgend)etwas zu essen?")
	snack [snæk]	Snack, Imbiss	
p. 110	**together** [tə'geðə]	zusammen	We have breakfast **together** on Sunday mornings.
	news *(no pl)* [njuːz]	Nachrichten	! Das englische Wort **news** ist Singular: *English:* **That's good news.** *German:* **Das sind gute Nachrichten.**
	paragraph ['pærəgrɑːf]	Absatz *(in einem Text)*	! stress: **paragraph** ['pærəgrɑːf]
	title ['taɪtl]	Titel, Überschrift	
	drawing ['drɔːɪŋ]	Zeichnung	
	caption ['kæpʃn]	Bildunterschrift	
	order ['ɔːdə]	Reihenfolge	
	(to) **think of** sth.	sich etwas ausdenken; an etwas denken	Read the story and **think of** a good title. I often **think of** our holidays in France last summer.
	another [ə'nʌðə]	ein(e) andere(r, s); noch ein(e)	I don't like red. Can I use **another** colour? (= a different colour) Can I have **another** biscuit? They're yummy.
	(to) **arrange** [ə'reɪndʒ]	anordnen	
	What is the story about?	Wovon handelt die Geschichte? / Worum geht es in der Geschichte?	
	(to) **go with** sth.	zu etwas passen; zu etwas gehören	Lot's of people say brown doesn't **go with** blue. The first text **goes with** the third picture.
p. 111	**also** ['ɔːlsəʊ]	auch	I play football, and I **also** play basketball.
	(to) **buy** [baɪ], *simple past:* **bought** [bɔːt]	kaufen	(to) **buy** ◄► (to) **sell**

[iː] green · [i] happy · [ɪ] big · [e] red · [æ] cat · [ɑː] class · [ɒ] song · [ɔː] door · [uː] blue · [ʊ] book · [ʌ] mum · [ɜː] girl · [ə] a partner

Text: A baby seal

p. 112 **bright** [braɪt]	strahlend, leuchtend, hell	**bright** ◄► **dark**
eye [aɪ]	Auge	
(to) **move** [muːv]	bewegen; sich bewegen	
over ['əʊvə]	über	She has a poster of a pop group **over** her desk. Can you jump **over** your chair?
(to) **be hungry** ['hʌŋgri]	hungrig sein, Hunger haben	
(to) **push** [pʊʃ]	drücken, schieben, stoßen	
head [hed]	Kopf	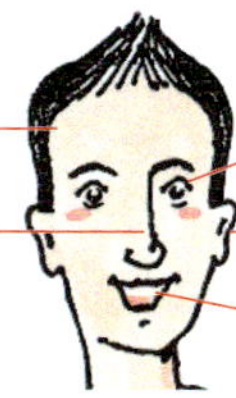
body ['bɒdi]	Körper	

Unregelmäßige Vergangenheitsformen (Irregular simple past forms)

(to) **drink**	**drank** [dræŋk]	trinken	(to) **sit**	**sat** [sæt]	sitzen; sich setzen
(to) **find**	**found** [faʊnd]	finden	(to) **throw**	**threw** [θruː]	werfen
(to) **put**	**put** [pʊt]	legen, stellen, *(wohin)* tun	(to) **wake up**	**woke up** [wəʊk]	aufwachen

➜ *List of irregular verbs*, pp. 269–270

sun [sʌn]	Sonne	
(to) **go down** [ˌgəʊ 'daʊn]	untergehen *(Sonne)*	
(to) **steer** [stɪə]	steuern, lenken	
only ['əʊnli]	erst	My sister can't read – she's **only** four.
someone **is right**	jemand hat Recht	Jonathan says Aberdeen is in England. I think he'**s right**. – No, he'**s wrong**. Aberdeen is in Scotland!
someone **is wrong**	jemand irrt sich; jemand hat Unrecht	*English:* **You're right/wrong.** *German:* **Du hast Recht/Unrecht.**
front [frʌnt]	Vorderseite	
Did you get it? *(infml)*	Hast du es verstanden? / Hast du es mitbekommen?	
p. 113 **slow** [sləʊ]	langsam	
(to) **hit** sth. [hɪt], *simple past:* **hit**	gegen etwas prallen, stoßen	John is hurt – his car **hit** a bus in Dean Street this morning.
(to) **pull** [pʊl]	ziehen	 (to) **push** ◄► (to) **pull**
careful ['keəfl]	vorsichtig	Be **careful** – seals can bite.
rescue ['reskjuː]	Rettung; Rettungs-	
(to) **be cold**	frieren	*English:* **I'm cold.** *German:* **Mir ist kalt. / Ich friere.**
(to) **die** [daɪ]	sterben	

	cage [keɪdʒ]	Käfig	a **cage** 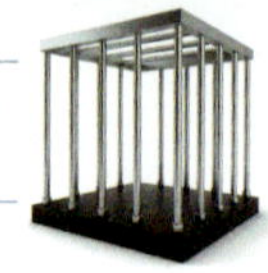
	poor [pɔː], [pʊə]	arm	
	before [bɪˈfɔː]	bevor	Do your homework **before** you go out.
	soft [sɒft]	weich	
	silky [ˈsɪlki]	seidig	I love to touch my dog's ears – they are so **silky**.

Let's prepare for a test

p. 115	**opposite** [ˈɒpəzɪt]	Gegenteil	What's the ~ of "dark"? – "Bright."
	egg [eg]	Ei	
	large [lɑːdʒ]	groß	
	surprise [səˈpraɪz]	Überraschung	A present? For me? That's a nice **surprise**!
p. 116	**noisy** [ˈnɔɪzi]	laut, lärmend, voller Lärm	noun: **noise** – adjective: **noisy**
p. 117	**sure** [ʃʊə], [ʃɔː]	sicher	Ask Mum. I'm **sure** she knows the answer. Can I have your pen? – Yes, **sure**.
	all day	den ganzen Tag (lang)	
	once [wʌns]	einmal	
	unfriendly [ʌnˈfrendli]	unfreundlich	**friendly** ◄► **unfriendly**
	(to) **go on a boat trip** [trɪp]	einen Bootsausflug machen	
	unhappy [ʌnˈhæpi]	unglücklich	**happy** ◄► **unhappy**
	that's why	deshalb, darum	Oliver was sick. **That's why** he didn't come to school.
	train [treɪn]	Zug	I met two boys from Italy **on the train** to Berlin. (… **im** Zug nach Berlin)
	first [fɜːst]	zuerst, als Erstes	You can watch TV later, but do your homework **first**.

Access to cultures: London

p. 118	**I'd love to …**	Ich würde sehr gern …	**I'd love to** go to London.
	queen [kwiːn]	Königin	
	tradition [trəˈdɪʃn]	Tradition	! stress: **tra<u>di</u>tion** [trəˈdɪʃn]
	parliament [ˈpɑːləmənt]	Parlament	! Schreibung: **par<u>lia</u>ment**
	natural history [ˌnætʃrəl ˈhɪstri]	Naturkunde	
	dinosaur [ˈdaɪnəsɔː]	Dinosaurier	
	time	Mal	Is this your first **time** in England? ! **time** = **1.** Zeit; Uhrzeit; **2.** Mal
	for miles [maɪlz]	meilenweit	1 **mile** = 1.6 kilometres
	top [tɒp]	Spitze, oberes Ende	You can see for miles from the **top** of the tower.
	concert [ˈkɒnsət]	Konzert	! stress: **<u>con</u>cert** [ˈkɒnsət]
	grass [grɑːs]	Gras; Rasen	

[b] boat · [p] pool · [d] dad · [t] ten · [g] good · [k] cat ·
[m] mum · [n] no · [ŋ] song · [l] hello · [r] red · [w] we · [j] you

world [wɜːld]	Welt	*English:* the best beach **in the world** *German:* der beste Strand **der Welt** / **auf der Welt**
tourist ['tʊərɪst]	Tourist/in	! stress: **tourist** ['tʊərɪst]
through [θruː]	durch	I can't see **through** the window – it's too dark.
market ['mɑːkɪt]	Markt	
theatre ['θɪətə]	Theater	! stress: **theatre** ['θɪətə]

p. 119 **left – right**

Do you write with your **left** hand or your **right** hand?	Schreibst du mit der **linken** oder mit der **rechten** Hand?
I looked **left** and **right** but I couldn't see my friends.	Ich sah **nach links** und **nach rechts**, aber …
On the left, you can see Morris, my cat.	**Links/Auf der linken Seite** …
My dog Alice is **on the right**.	**Rechts/Auf der rechten Seite** …

in the middle ['mɪdl]	in der Mitte	
background ['bækgraʊnd]	Hintergrund	There are two boys in the **foreground**. In the **background**, you can see a lake.
foreground ['fɔːgraʊnd]	Vordergrund	
next to ['nekst tʊ]	neben	The hotel is **next to** the church.

Unit 5 By the sea

p. 120 **by** the sea [baɪ]	am Meer	
p. 121 (to) **feel** [fiːl], *simple past:* **felt** [felt]	fühlen; sich fühlen	Take my hand. Can you **feel** how cold it is? I always **feel** happy when I'm by the sea.
face [feɪs]	Gesicht	
(to) **look for** sth. ['lʊk fɔː]	etwas suchen	

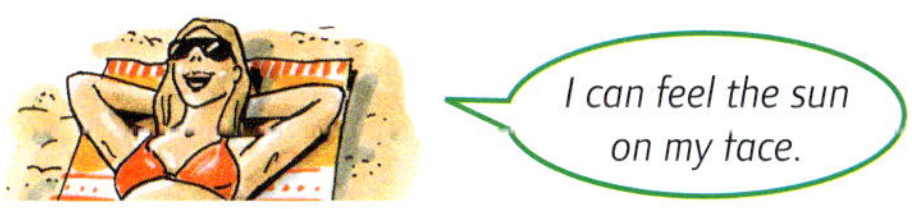

Unregelmäßige Vergangenheitsformen (Irregular simple past forms)

(to) **break**	**broke** [brəʊk]	(zer)brechen	(to) **send**	**sent** [sent]	schicken, senden
(to) **catch**	**caught** [kɔːt]	fangen	(to) **sleep**	**slept** [slept]	schlafen
(to) **fight**	**fought** [fɔːt]	kämpfen	(to) **understand**	**understood** [ˌʌndə'stʊd]	verstehen
(to) **grow**	**grew** [gruː]	anbauen, anpflanzen			
(to) **read**	**read** [red]	lesen	(to) **wear**	**wore** [wɔː]	tragen *(Kleidung)*

➔ *List of irregular verbs*, pp. 269–270

Part A

p. 122 **ferry** ['feri]	Fähre	
(to) run **after** sb. [ˌrʌn‿'ɑːftə]	hinter jm. herrennen	"Come back," he shouted when he ran **after** his dog.
fast [fɑːst]	schnell	

fast ◄► slow

at the moment ['məʊmənt]	gerade, im Moment	! Betonung: **moment** ['məʊmənt]
a kind of … [kaɪnd]	eine Art (von) …	I like all **kinds of** music, but I never listen to jazz.

[f] **f**ather · [v] ri**v**er · [s] **s**ister · [z] plea**s**e · [ʃ] **sh**op · [ʒ] televi**s**ion ·
[tʃ] tea**ch**er · [dʒ] **G**ermany · [θ] **th**anks · [ð] **th**is · [h] **h**ere

	rucksack ['rʌksæk]	Rucksack	
	(to) **be over** ['əʊvə]	vorbei sein, zu Ende sein	They looked sad. The holidays **were over**.
	(to) **laugh** [lɑːf]	lachen	
	almost ['ɔːlməʊst]	fast, beinahe	It's **almost** six. 
	(It's) my turn. [tɜːn]	Ich bin dran / an der Reihe.	I'm finished. Now it's **your turn**.
p. 124	(to) **smell** sth. [smel]	an etwas riechen	Look, the dog is **smelling** the school bag. 
p. 125	**routine** [ruː'tiːn]	Routine	
	It's me.	Ich bin's.	

Part B

p. 126	**talk** [tɔːk]	Vortrag, Referat, Rede	*English:* (to) **give a talk (about)** *German:* **einen Vortrag/eine Rede halten (über)**
	sleepover ['sliːpəʊvə]	Pyjama-Party, Schlafparty	
	bad [bæd]	schlecht, schlimm	**good ◄► bad**
	shark [ʃɑːk]	Hai	
	at last [ət 'lɑːst]	endlich, schließlich	We waited for a long time. **At last**, the bus arrived.
	blond (*bei Frauen oft:* **blonde)** [blɒnd]	blond	
	(to) **take photos**	fotografieren, Fotos machen	
	interesting ['ɪntrəstɪŋ]	interessant	
p. 127	**line** [laɪn]	Zeile	! Abkürzungen: **l.** 15 = **line** 15 (Zeile 15) **ll.** 15–18 = **lines** 15–18 (Zeilen 15–18)
	the biggest … ['bɪgɪst]	der/die/das größte …	
	coast [kəʊst]	Küste	
	planet ['plænɪt]	Planet	! Betonung: **planet** ['plænɪt]
	ocean ['əʊʃn]	Ozean	
	centre ['sentə]	Zentrum; Mitte	
	price [praɪs]	(Kauf-)Preis	
p. 128	**important** [ɪm'pɔːtnt]	wichtig	
p. 129	**postcard** ['pəʊstkɑːd]	Postkarte	

[iː] green · [i] happy · [ɪ] big · [e] red · [æ] cat · [ɑː] class · [ɒ] song · [ɔː] door · [uː] blue · [ʊ] book · [ʌ] mum · [ɜː] girl · [ə] a partner

Part C

p. 130

Unregelmäßige Vergangenheitsformen (Irregular simple past forms)

(to) **choose**	**chose** [tʃəʊz]	aussuchen, auswählen	(to) **sell**	**sold** [səʊld]	verkaufen
(to) **give**	**gave** [geɪv]	geben	(to) **speak**	**spoke** [spəʊk]	sprechen
(to) **know**	**knew** [njuː]	wissen; kennen	(to) **tell**	**told** [təʊld]	erzählen, berichten

➡ *List of irregular verbs*, pp. 269–270

not … yet [jet]	noch nicht	Are you ready? – No, I'm **not** ready **yet**. I can't find my mobile. (*oder kurz:* No, **not yet**. I can't find my mobile.)
(to) **agree with** sb. [ə'griː]	jm. zustimmen	*English:* I **agree with you**. *German:* Ich **stimme dir zu**.
(to) **agree on** sth.	sich auf etwas einigen	We have to **agree on** a day for our party.
(to) **smuggle** ['smʌgl]	schmuggeln	(to) **smuggle** · **smuggler** (Schmuggler/in) · **smuggling** (der Schmuggel, das Schmuggeln)
sign [saɪn]	Schild; Zeichen	The **sign** says it's only ten minutes to the zoo. 
village ['vɪlɪdʒ]	Dorf	
(to) **point to** sth. [pɔɪnt]	auf etwas zeigen, deuten	He **pointed to** the clock. "We're late," he said.
fat [fæt]	dick, fett	
under ['ʌndə]	unter	Where are my shoes? – **Under** your desk. 
(to) **explain** sth. **to** sb. [ɪk'spleɪn]	jm. etwas erklären, erläutern	*English:* Can you **explain** that **to me**? *German:* Kannst du **mir** das **erklären**?
clever ['klevə]	klug, schlau	
(to) **draw** [drɔː], *simple past:* **drew** [druː]	zeichnen	He's **drawing** a picture of his mum.
(to) **go on** [ˌgəʊ_'ɒn], *simple past:* **went on**	weiterreden, fortfahren; weitermachen	She stopped in the middle of her sentence, smiled, then **went on**. That's enough for now. Let's **go on** after lunch.
p. 131 **century** ['sentʃəri]	Jahrhundert	
lonely ['ləʊnli]	einsam	
pepper ['pepə]	Pfeffer	
expensive [ɪk'spensɪv]	teuer	£60 for a T-shirt? That's too **expensive**.
cheap [tʃiːp]	billig, preiswert	**cheap ◄► expensive**
goods *(pl)* [gʊdz]	Waren, Güter	
(to) **hide** [haɪd], *simple past:* **hid** [hɪd]	(sich) verstecken	Can you **hide** this box for me? It's a present for my mother. My little sister often **hides** under her bed.
check [tʃek]	Überprüfung, Kontrolle	
(to) **check** [tʃek]	(über)prüfen, kontrollieren	
subtitle ['sʌbtaɪtl]	Untertitel	

[eɪ] **name** · [aɪ] **time** · [ɔɪ] **boy** · [əʊ] **old** ·
[aʊ] **town** · [ɪə] **here** · [eə] **where** · [ʊə] **tour**

	author ['ɔːθə]	Autor/in	
p. 132	(to) **prepare** sth. [prɪ'peə]	etwas vorbereiten	
	character ['kærəktə]	Figur, Person *(in Roman, Film, Theaterstück usw.)*	
	likes and dislikes *(pl)* [dɪs'laɪks]	Vorlieben und Abneigungen	Tell me about your **likes and dislikes**. – Well, I like football and hip hop, but I don't like tennis.
	keyword ['kiːwɜːd]	Schlüsselwort	
	(to) **copy** ['kɒpi]	kopieren, abschreiben	
	easy ['iːzi]	leicht, einfach	Her talk was **easy** to understand.
p. 133	**sub-clause** ['sʌbklɔːz]	Nebensatz	
	nervous ['nɜːvəs]	nervös, aufgeregt	! Betonung: **nervous** ['nɜːvəs]
p. 134	**reason** ['riːzn]	Grund, Begründung	
	holiday ['hɒlədeɪ]	Urlaub	*English:* (to) be **on holiday** / (to) go **on holiday** *German:* **in Urlaub** sein / **in Urlaub** fahren
	First, … [fɜːst]	Erstens, …	**First, …** Erstens, … **Second, …** Zweitens, … **Third, …** Drittens, … **Fourth, …** Viertens, …
	beautiful ['bjuːtɪfl]	schön	Their garden isn't just nice – it's **beautiful**.
	view (of) [vjuː]	Aussicht, Blick (auf)	We had a great **view of** the sea from our hotel.
	(to) **drive** [draɪv], *simple past:* **drove** [drəʊv]	*(mit dem Auto)* fahren	Does your mother **drive** to work? – No, she usually goes by bus.
	north [nɔːθ]	Norden; Nord-	
	(to) **climb** [klaɪm]	klettern; hinaufklettern (auf)	! Aussprache – das „b" wird nicht gesprochen: **climb** [klaɪm] *English:* (to) **climb** a tree / a tower *German:* **auf** einen Baum / einen Turm **klettern**
	mountain ['maʊntən]	Berg	
	national ['næʃnəl]	national, National-	! stress: **national** ['næʃnəl]
	popular (with) ['pɒpjələ]	populär, beliebt (bei)	*English:* Beatles songs are still very **popular with** a lot of people. *German:* … beliebt **bei** …
	dangerous ['deɪndʒərəs]	gefährlich	
	everything ['evriθɪŋ]	alles	**everything** ◄► **nothing**
	full (of) [fʊl]	voll (von, mit)	Parts of Devon are **full of** tourists in the summer.
	fun park ['fʌn pɑːk]	Vergnügungspark	
	excellent ['eksələnt]	ausgezeichnet, hervorragend	
p. 135	(to) **know about** sth.	sich mit etwas auskennen; über etwas Bescheid wissen	
	(to) **be lucky**	Glück haben	! Sie **hatte Glück**. = She was **lucky**. Sie **war glücklich**. = She was **happy**.

[b] **boat** · [p] **pool** · [d] **dad** · [t] **ten** · [g] **good** · [k] **cat** ·
[m] **mum** · [n] **no** · [ŋ] **song** · [l] **hello** · [r] **red** · [w] **we** · [j] **you**

	(to) stand up [ˌstænd_ˈʌp], *simple past:* **stood up** [stʊd]	aufstehen	(to) **sit down** ◄► (to) **stand up**
p. 136	(to) **get off (the bus/boat)** [ˌget_ˈɒf], *simple past:* **got off**	(aus dem Bus/Boot) aussteigen	**Get off the bus** at Green Road. I live in the white house.
	(to) **get** [get], *simple past:* **got**	gelangen, (hin)kommen	Excuse me, how do I **get** to the zoo, please?
p. 137	**symbol** [ˈsɪmbl]	Symbol	! Betonung: **symbol** [ˈsɪmbl]
	(to) **decide** [dɪˈsaɪd]	beschließen, sich entscheiden	We **decided** to do a project about Dartmoor.

Text: The pepper smugglers

p. 138	**play** [pleɪ]	Theaterstück	
	scene [siːn]	Szene	! Aussprache – das "c" wird nicht gesprochen: **scene** [siːn]
	farmer [ˈfɑːmə]	Bauer/Bäuerin, Landwirt/in	
	rich [rɪtʃ]	reich	**rich** ◄► **poor**
	dress [dres]	Kleid	
	Good luck! [lʌk]	Viel Glück!	
	(to) **hold** [həʊld], *simple past:* **held** [held]	halten	Can you **hold** my bag, please? I can't open the door.
	cart [kɑːt]	Karren	
	like that	so *(auf diese Weise)*	Don't do it **like that**. Look, do it like I'm doing.
p. 139	**sword** [sɔːd]	Schwert	! Aussprache – das "w" wird nicht gesprochen: **sword** [sɔːd]
	Goodbye. [ˌgʊdˈbaɪ]	Auf Wiedersehen.	
	(to) **point** sth. **at** sb. [pɔɪnt]	etwas auf Jn. richten	She **pointed** her camera **at** him.
	prison [ˈprɪzn]	Gefängnis	
	(to) **fall** [fɔːl], *simple past:* **fell** [fel]	fallen, stürzen; hinfallen	Yesterday my brother **fell** into our swimming pool.
	(to) **sneeze** [sniːz]	niesen	

Your task

p. 140	**Bavaria** [bəˈveəriə]	Bayern	
	(to) **organize** [ˈɔːgənaɪz]	organisieren; ordnen	! stress: **organize** [ˈɔːgənaɪz]

Let's prepare for a test

p. 142	**race** [reɪs]	Rennen	 **a bike race**
	smile [smaɪl]	Lächeln	verb: (to) **smile** – noun: **smile**
p. 143	(to) **leave** [liv], *simple past:* **left** [left]	(ab)fahren; (weg)gehen	When does the last bus to Plymouth **leave**? Get your jacket. We're **leaving**.

[f] father · [v] river · [s] sister · [z] please · [ʃ] shop · [ʒ] television · [tʃ] teacher · [dʒ] Germany · [θ] thanks · [ð] this · [h] here

Access to cultures: The USA and Canada

p. 144	**state** [steɪt]	Staat	
	He **is going to** visit his dad.	Er hat vor, seinen Vater zu besuchen. / Er wird seinen Vater besuchen.	

Access to cultures: English as a world language

p. 146	**official** [ə'fɪʃl] *(adj)*	amtlich, Amts-	! stress: **official** [ə'fɪʃl]
p. 147	**Spanish** ['spænɪʃ]	Spanisch; spanisch	
	a bit [ə 'bɪt]	ein bisschen, etwas	Australian English is **a bit** different from British English.
	per cent (%) [pə'sent]	Prozent	
	international [ˌɪntə'næʃnəl]	international	**national ◄► international**
	Polish ['pəʊlɪʃ]	Polnisch; polnisch	

Partner A

1 Part A Practice

5 Who's in the photo? *(be)*

← *p.25*

Partner A:

a) Say as much as you can about *one* of these boys.
Don't say his name. Can your partner guess who it is?
You can use these ideas to make sentences.
The boy in my photo is/isn't from Plymouth.
He's …
His dad …

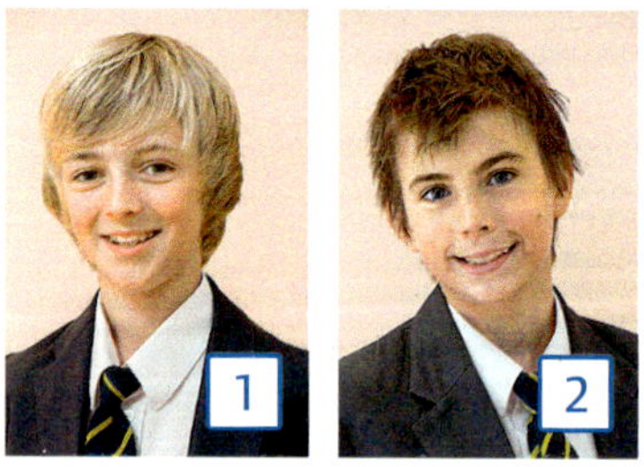

b) Listen to your partner. Who is the girl in his/her photo?

5 Part B Practice

1 Is he drinking? (Present progressive: questions)

← *p.128*

Partner A: Answer Partner B's questions about pictures 4–6.
Use short answers (*Yes, he is.* / *No, he isn't.*, etc.).

[iː] green · [i] happy · [ɪ] big · [e] red · [æ] cat · [ɑː] class · [ɒ] song · [ɔː] door · [uː] blue · [ʊ] book · [ʌ] mum · [ɜː] girl · [ə] a partner

Das **Dictionary** besteht aus **zwei alphabetischen Wörterlisten**:
English – German (S. 243 – 257) und **German – English** (S. 258 – 269)

Im **English – German Dictionary** kannst du nachschlagen, wenn du wissen möchtest, was ein englisches Wort bedeutet, wie man es ausspricht oder wie es geschrieben wird.

Im **Dictionary** werden folgende **Abkürzungen und Symbole** verwendet:

sth. = something (etwas) sb. = somebody (jemand) jn. = jemanden jm. = jemandem
pl = *plural* (Mehrzahl) *infml* = *informal* (umgangssprachlich)
° Mit diesem Kringel sind Wörter markiert, die nicht zum Lernwortschatz gehören.

Die **Fundstellenangaben** zeigen, wo ein Wort zum ersten Mal in *Access Bayern 5* vorkommt.
Die Ziffern in Klammern bezeichnen Seitenzahlen: (3) = S. 3 HWG (8/9) = Here we go, S. 8 – 9 1 (21) = Unit 1, S. 21

Tipps zur Arbeit mit einem Wörterbuch findest du im Skills File auf Seite 178.

A

a [ə] ein, eine HWG (8/9) **... a day/week/year** ... pro Tag/Woche/Jahr 4 (106) **a bit** ein bisschen, etwas 5 (147)

°**Aboriginal Australians** [æbəˌrɪdʒənl ɒ'streɪliənz] Ureinwohner/innen Australiens

about [ə'baʊt]:
1. about me/you/yourself/Miss Bell über mich/dich/dich selbst/Frau Bell 1 (28) **It's about a seagull.** Es geht um eine Möwe. / Es handelt von einer Möwe. 3 (76) **What about you?** Und du/ihr? / Und was ist mit dir/euch? HWG (8/9) **What is the story about?** Wovon handelt die Geschichte? / Worum geht es in der Geschichte? 4 (110)
2. about 300 people ungefähr 300 Leute 4 (106)

access ['ækses] Zugang, Zutritt 1 (42)

act out [ˌækt‿'aʊt] vorspielen 1 (37)

action ['ækʃn] Action; Handlung, Tat 3 (80)

°**active** ['æktɪv] aktiv

activity [æk'tɪvəti] Aktivität 3 (72) **free-time activities** Freizeitaktivitäten 3 (74)

actor ['æktə] Schauspieler/in 4 (96)

add (to) [æd] hinzufügen, ergänzen, addieren (zu) 3 (84)

address [ə'dres] Adresse, Anschrift 3 (84)

after ['ɑːftə]:
1. after the s nach dem s 1 (26) **after that** danach 2 (46)
2. run after sb. hinter jm. herrennen 5 (122)

afternoon [ˌɑːftə'nuːn] Nachmittag 2 (46) **in the afternoon** nachmittags, am Nachmittag 2 (46) **on Saturday afternoon** am Samstagnachmittag 3 (80)

again [ə'gen] wieder; noch einmal 1 (28)

against [ə'genst] gegen 4 (98/99)

age [eɪdʒ] Alter 3 (91)

agree [ə'griː]: **agree with sb.** jm. zustimmen 5 (130) **agree on sth.** sich auf etwas einigen 5 (130)

°**alive** [ə'laɪv] lebend; lebendig

all [ɔːl] alles; alle 2 (52) **all day** den ganzen Tag (lang) 4 (117) **all of Plymouth** ganz Plymouth, das ganze Plymouth 3 (80)

all right [ɔːl 'raɪt] okay; in Ordnung 4 (88)

almost ['ɔːlməʊst] fast, beinahe 5 (122)

°**alone** [ə'ləʊn] allein

along [ə'lɒŋ]
1. along the street / the river / ... die Straße / den Fluss / ... entlang 3 (86)
2. come along mitkommen, herkommen 3 (81) °**sing along** mitsingen

°**aloud** [ə'laʊd] laut

°**alphabet** ['ælfəbet] Alphabet

°**already** [ɔːl'redi] schon

also ['ɔːlsəʊ] auch 4 (111)

always ['ɔːlweɪz] immer 1 (37)

am: 4 am [ˌeɪ‿'em] 4 Uhr morgens 3 (68/69)

an [æn, ən] ein, eine HWG (14)

and [ænd, ənd] und HWG (8/9)

angry ['æŋgri] wütend 1 (37)

animal ['ænɪml] Tier HWG (13)

another [ə'nʌðə]:
1. ein(e) andere(r, s) 4 (110)
2. noch ein(e) 4 (110)

answer ['ɑːnsə]:
1. antworten; beantworten 1 (28)
2. Antwort 1 (28)

ant [ænt] Ameise HWG (14)

any ['eni]: **Are there any ...?** Gibt es (irgendwelche) ...? 1 (32) **There aren't any ...** Es gibt keine / Es sind keine ... 1 (34)

anybody ['enibɒdi]: **anybody?** (irgend)jemand? 5 (135) **not ... anybody** niemand 5 (135)

anyone ['eniwʌn]: **anyone?** (irgend) jemand? 5 (135) **not ... anyone** niemand 5 (135)

anything ['eniθɪŋ]: **anything?** (irgend)etwas? 4 (109) **not ... anything** nichts 5 (135)

apostrophe [ə'pɒstrəfi] Apostroph, Auslassungszeichen 1 (26)

April ['eɪprəl] April 1 (31)

aquarium [ə'kweəriəm] Aquarium; Aquarienhaus 5 (126)

are ['ɑː] bist; sind; seid HWG (8/9) **Are you ...?** Bist du ...? HWG (8/9) **The DVDs are ...** Die DVDs kosten ... 3 (92)

area ['eəriə] Bereich; Gebiet, Gegend 3 (68/69)

aren't [ɑːnt]: **you aren't** du bist nicht ...; du bist kein/e ...; ihr seid nicht ...; ihr seid kein/e ... 1 (22)

armchair ['ɑːmtʃeə] Sessel 2 (44)

around [ə'raʊnd]:
1. around the library in der Bücherei umher 4 (100)
°**2.** um ... herum **run around** herumrennen

arrange [ə'reɪndʒ] anordnen 4 (110)

arrive [əˈraɪv] ankommen, eintreffen 4 (98/99)
art [ɑːt] Kunst 1 (29)
°**as** [æz, əz]:
1. während
2. **as much as** so viel wie
3. **as one word** als ein Wort
ask [ɑːsk] fragen 1 (28) **ask a question** eine Frage stellen 1 (28) **ask sb. to do sth.** jemanden bitten, etwas zu tun 3 (74) °**ask sb. for sth.** jn. um etwas bitten
at [æt, ət] *(in Ortsangaben)* an, bei, in; *(in Zeitangaben)* um, an HWG (12) **at 14 Dean Street** in der Deanstraße 14 1 (28) **at home** daheim, zu Hause 1 (21) **at last** endlich, schließlich 5 (126) °**at least** zumindest, wenigstens **at lunchtime** mittags 3 (68/69) **at the moment** gerade, im Moment 5 (122) **at night** nachts, in der Nacht 2 (47) **at school** in der Schule 1 (20) **at the weekend** am Wochenende 2 (47)
ate [et, eɪt] *simple past of* **eat**
attic [ˈætɪk] Dachboden 3 (86) **in the attic** auf dem Dachboden 3 (86)
August [ˈɔːgəst] August 1 (31)
aunt [ɑːnt] Tante 2 (52)
author [ˈɔːθə] Autor/in 5 (131)
autumn [ˈɔːtəm] Herbst 1 (42)
away [əˈweɪ] weg, fort 2 (47)

B

baby seal [ˈbeɪbi siːl] Robbenjunges; Heuler 4 (106)
back [bæk]
1. zurück 1 (32)
°2. Rücken
background [ˈbækgraʊnd] Hintergrund 4 (119) **background file** Hintergrundinformation(en) (3)
bad [bæd] schlecht, schlimm 5 (126)
bag [bæg] Tasche, Beutel, Tüte HWG (16) **school bag** Schultasche HWG (16)
ball [bɔːl] Ball 1 (26)
band [bænd] Band, (Musik-)Gruppe 4 (118)
bark [bɑːk] bellen 3 (86)
basket [ˈbɑːskɪt] Korb 2 (47)
basketball [ˈbɑːskɪtbɔːl] Basketball 2 (48)
bathroom [ˈbɑːθruːm] Badezimmer 2 (45)
Bavaria [bəˈveəriə] Bayern 5 (140)
be [bi], *simple past:* **was, were:**
1. sein 1 (24)
°2. werden
beach [biːtʃ] Strand 3 (74)
bear [beə] Bär HWG (14)
beautiful [ˈbjuːtɪfl] schön 5 (134)
became [bɪˈkeɪm] *simple past of* **become**
because [bɪˈkɒz] weil 3 (70)
become [bɪˈkʌm], *simple past:* **became** werden 4 (106)
bed [bed] Bett 2 (44)
bedroom [ˈbedruːm] Schlafzimmer 2 (45)
beef [biːf]: **roast beef** Rinderbraten 2 (56)
°**been** [biːn]: **where we've been** wo wir gewesen sind
before [bɪˈfɔː]:
1. bevor 4 (113)
2. vor 1 (22) **before school/lessons** vor der Schule *(vor Schulbeginn)* / vorm Unterricht 1 (22)
behind [bɪˈhaɪnd] hinter 3 (80)
bell [bel] Klingel, Glocke 4 (106)
°**below** [bɪˈləʊ] unterhalb (von)
best [best]: **the best …** der/die/das beste …; die besten … 1 (20)
better [ˈbetə] besser 4 (98/99)
between [bɪˈtwiːn] zwischen 4 (100)
big [bɪg] groß HWG (10) **big wheel** Riesenrad HWG (10) **the biggest …** der/die/das größte … 5 (127)
bike [baɪk] Fahrrad 3 (80) **ride a bike** Fahrrad fahren 3 (80)
°**binoculars** *(pl)* [bɪˈnɒkjələz] Fernglas
bird [bɜːd] Vogel HWG (14)
birth [bɜːθ] Geburt 4 (106)
birthday [ˈbɜːθdeɪ] Geburtstag 1 (28) **My birthday is in May.** Ich habe im Mai Geburtstag. 1 (31) **My birthday is on 5th August.** Ich habe am 5. August Geburtstag. 1 (31) **When's your birthday?** Wann hast du Geburtstag? 1 (31)
biscuit [ˈbɪskɪt] Plätzchen, Keks 2 (57)
bit [bɪt]: **a bit** ein bisschen, etwas 5 (147)
bite [baɪt]:
1. *(simple past:* **bit***)* beißen 4 (106)
°2. **in one bite** mit einem Bissen
black [blæk] schwarz HWG (15)
blond *(bei Frauen oft:* **blonde***)* [blɒnd] blond 5 (126)
blue [bluː] blau HWG (15)
°**boa constrictor** [ˈbəʊə kənstrɪktə] Abgottschlange, *Boa constrictor*
board [bɔːd] (Wand-)Tafel HWG (16)
boat [bəʊt] Boot, Schiff HWG (10)
body [ˈbɒdi] Körper 4 (112)
book [bʊk] Buch HWG (16)
bookshop [ˈbʊkʃɒp] Buchladen, Buchhandlung 4 (101)
boring [ˈbɔːrɪŋ] langweilig 3 (86)
bottle [ˈbɒtl] Flasche 3 (86)
bought [bɔːt] *simple past of* **buy**
box [bɒks] Kasten, Kiste, Kästchen 3 (84)
Boxing Day [ˈbɒksɪŋ deɪ] 2. Weihnachtstag (26. Dezember) 2 (66)
boy [bɔɪ] Junge HWG (8/9)
°**bracket** [ˈbrækɪt] Klammer *(in Texten)*
bread [bred] Brot 2 (57)
break [breɪk] Pause 1 (30)
break [breɪk], *simple past:* **broke:**
1. zerbrechen, kaputt machen 4 (94)
2. brechen, kaputt gehen 4 (94)
breakfast [ˈbrekfəst] Frühstück 2 (46) **have breakfast** frühstücken 2 (46)
bright [braɪt] strahlend, leuchtend, hell 4 (112)
bring [brɪŋ], *simple past:* **brought** (mit-, her)bringen 4 (109)
British [ˈbrɪtɪʃ] britisch 1 (23)
broke [brəʊk] *simple past of* **break**
brother [ˈbrʌðə] Bruder 1 (20)
brought [brɔːt] *simple past of* **bring**
brown [braʊn] braun HWG (15)
°**bubble** [ˈbʌbl]: **speech bubble** Sprechblase
bus [bʌs] Bus 3 (84) **go by bus** mit dem Bus fahren 4 (98/99)
busy [ˈbɪzi]: **be busy** beschäftigt sein; viel zu tun haben 4 (96)
but [bʌt, bət] aber 1 (20)
°**butter** [ˈbʌtə] Butter
butterfly [ˈbʌtəflaɪ] Schmetterling HWG (14)
buy [baɪ], *simple past:* **bought** kaufen 4 (111)
by [baɪ]:
1. **by the sea** am Meer 5 (102)
2. **go by car/minibus/…** mit dem Auto/Kleinbus/… fahren 4 (98/99)
Bye. [baɪ] *(auch:* **Bye-bye.***)* Servus. / Auf Wiedersehen. 1 (22)

C

café [ˈkæfeɪ] Café 2 (60)
cage [keɪdʒ] Käfig 4 (113)
cake [keɪk] Kuchen 2 (56)

call [kɔːl]:
1. rufen; anrufen; nennen 3 (84)
2. Anruf; Telefongespräch 5 (125)

called [kɔːld]: **be called** heißen, genannt werden 3 (81)

came [keɪm] *simple past of* **come**

camera ['kæmərə] Kamera, Fotoapparat 2 (60)

cameraman ['kæmrəmæn], *pl* **cameramen** ['kæmrəmen] Kameramann 4 (96)

can [kæn, kən] können HWG (10) **we cannot** ['kænɒt], **we can't** [kɑːnt] ... wir können nicht ... 1 (32)

candle ['kændl] Kerze 2 (66)

canteen [kæn'tiːn] Kantine, (Schul-)Mensa 1 (32)

°**cap** [kæp] Mütze, Kappe

capital ['kæpɪtl] Hauptstadt 1 (42)

capital letter [ˌkæpɪtl 'letə] Großbuchstabe 3 (83)

captain ['kæptɪn] Kapitän/in 3 (81)

caption ['kæpʃn] Bildunterschrift 4 (110)

car [kɑː] Auto 4 (98/99) **go by car** mit dem Auto fahren 4 (98/99)

card (to) [kɑːd] Karte (an) HWG (8/9)

°**care** [keə]: **take care of sb./sth.** sich um etwas/jn. kümmern

careful ['keəfl] vorsichtig 4 (113)

cart [kɑːt] Karren 5 (138)

castle ['kɑːsl] Burg, Schloss HWG (10)

cat [kæt] Katze HWG (14) °**big cat** Großkatze

catch [kætʃ], *simple past:* **caught** fangen 1 (28)

caught [kɔːt] *simple past of* **catch**

°**celebrity** [sə'lebrəti] berühmte Persönlichkeit

centre ['sentə] Zentrum; Mitte 3 (93)

century ['sentʃəri] Jahrhundert 5 (131)

chain [tʃeɪn] Kette 4 (96)

chair [tʃeə] Stuhl HWG (16)

°**chance** [tʃɑːns] Chance

°**change** [tʃeɪndʒ] (sich) (ver-)ändern

°**change** [tʃeɪndʒ] wechseln

chaos ['keɪɒs] Chaos 1 (36)

character ['kærəktə] Figur, Person *(in Roman, Film, Theaterstück)* 5 (132)

cheap [tʃiːp] billig, preiswert 5 (131)

check [tʃek]:
1. Überprüfung, Kontrolle 5 (131)
2. (über)prüfen, kontrollieren 5 (131)

°**checklist** [tʃek] Checkliste, Prüfliste

cheese [tʃiːz] Käse 2 (57)

chess [tʃes] Schach 3 (72)

°**chick** [tʃɪk] Küken

child [tʃaɪld], *pl* **children** ['tʃɪldrən] Kind 3 (81)

chocolate ['tʃɒklət] Schokolade 3 (80)

choose [tʃuːz], *simple past:* **chose** aussuchen, (aus)wählen; sich aussuchen 3 (68/69)

°**chorus** ['kɔːrəs] Refrain

chose [tʃəʊz] *simple past of* **choose**

Christmas ['krɪsməs] Weihnachten 2 (66) **Christmas Day** 1. Weihnachtstag (25. Dezember) 2 (66) **Christmas Eve** Heiligabend 2 (66) **Christmas pudding** *kein Pudding, sondern ein Nachtisch aus Butter, Zucker, Mehl, Rosinen, Nüssen, Eiern, Gewürzen, der traditionell zu Weihnachten gegessen wird* 2 (66) **Merry Christmas!** Frohe Weihnachten! 2 (66)

church [tʃɜːtʃ] Kirche 3 (83)

cinema ['sɪnəmə] Kino 4 (95)

°**circle** ['sɜːkl] Kreis

city ['sɪti] Stadt, Großstadt 3 (83)

clap [klæp] (Beifall) klatschen 4 (105) **Clap your hands.** Klatscht in die Hände. 4 (105)

class [klɑːs] (Schul-)Klasse HWG (16) °**in class** im Unterricht

classmate ['klɑːsmeɪt] Mitschüler/in, Klassenkamerad/in HWG (8/9)

classroom ['klɑːsruːm] Klassenzimmer HWG (16)

clean [kliːn] sauber machen, putzen 3 (73)

clever ['klevə] klug, schlau 5 (130)

climb [klaɪm] klettern; hinaufklettern (auf) 5 (134) **climb a tree/a tower** auf einen Baum/einen Turm klettern 5 (134)

clock [klɒk] (Wand-, Stand-, Turm-)Uhr HWG (16)

close (to) [kləʊs] nah, dicht (bei, an) 4 (106)

°**close** [kləʊz] schließen, zumachen

closed [kləʊzd] geschlossen 3 (93)

°**cloth** [klɒθ] Tuch

clothes *(pl)* [kləʊðz] Kleidung, Kleidungsstücke 2 (60)

club [klʌb] Klub 2 (47) **join a club** [dʒɔɪn] in einen Klub eintreten; sich einem Klub anschließen 3 (68/69)

coast [kəʊst] Küste 5 (127)

coin [kɔɪn] Münze 3 (87)

cold [kəʊld] kalt 2 (56) **be cold** frieren 4 (113)

collect [kə'lekt] sammeln 3 (74)

colour ['kʌlə] Farbe HWG (8/9)

°**column** ['kɒləm] Spalte

come [kʌm], *simple past:* **came** kommen HWG (8/9) **come along** mitkommen, herkommen 3 (81) **come home** nach Hause kommen 1 (21) **come in** hereinkommen 1 (28) **Come on, Dad.** Na los, Dad! / Komm, Dad! 3 (76)

°**comic strip** ['kɒmɪk ˌstrɪp] Comicstrip

°**communication** [kəˌmjuːnɪ'keɪʃn] Kommunikation **Information and Communications Technology** Informations- und Kommunikationstechnologie 1 (29)

°**compare** [kəm'peə] vergleichen

°**complete** [kəm'pliːt] vervollständigen

computer [kəm'pjuːtə] Computer 1 (32)

concert ['kɒnsət] Konzert 4 (118)

consonant ['kɒnsənənt] Konsonant, Mitlaut 3 (84)

°**conversation** [ˌkɒnvə'seɪʃn] Gespräch, Unterhaltung

cool [kuːl] cool 1 (22)

copy ['kɒpi] kopieren, abschreiben 5 (132)

corner ['kɔːnə] Ecke 1 (36) **corner shop** Laden an der Ecke; Tante-Emma-Laden 1 (36)

cornflakes ['kɔːnfleɪks] Cornflakes 2 (57)

°**correct** [kə'rekt] korrigieren, verbessern

°**correction** [kə'rekʃn] Korrektur, Berichtigung

could [kʊd]: **he could ...** er konnte ... 4 (104) **we couldn't ...** ['kʊdnt] wir konnten nicht ... 4 (104)

count [kaʊnt] zählen 1 (32)

country ['kʌntri] Land 1 (42)

county ['kaʊnti] Grafschaft *(in Großbritannien)* 4 (104)

course [kɔːs] Kurs, Lehrgang (3)

cousin ['kʌzn] Cousin, Cousine 2 (52)

crab [kræb] Krebs 2 (46)

cracker ['krækə] Knallbonbon 2 (66)

cream [kriːm] Sahne 2 (56) °**cream tea** [ˌkriːm 'tiː] *Mahlzeit mit Tee, Scones, Marmelade und Sahne*

cricket ['krɪkɪt] Cricket 2 (52)

culture ['kʌltʃə] Kultur 1 (42)

cup [kʌp]: **a cup of tea** eine Tasse Tee 2 (47)

cupboard ['kʌbəd] Schrank HWG (16)

curry ['kʌri] Curry(gericht) 2 (64)

D

dad [dæd] Papa, Vati 1 (20)
dance [dɑːns] tanzen 3 (68/69)
dangerous ['deɪndʒərəs] gefährlich 5 (134)
dark [dɑːk] dunkel 1 (20)
°**date** [deɪt] Verabredung, Date
day [deɪ] Tag HWG (11) **all day** den ganzen Tag (lang) 4 (117) **day of the week** Wochentag HWG (11) **my favourite day** mein Lieblingstag HWG (13) °**one day** eines Tages
dead [ded] tot 2 (55)
December [dɪ'sembə] Dezember 1 (31)
decide [dɪ'saɪd] beschließen, sich entscheiden 5 (137)
deck [dek] Deck *(eines Schiffes)* 5 (139)
°**describe** [dɪ'skraɪb] beschreiben
design and technology [dɪˌzaɪn‿ənd tek'nɒlədʒi] Design und Technik 1 (29)
desk [desk] Schreibtisch HWG (16)
dessert [dɪ'zɜːt] Nachtisch, Nachspeise 2 (56)
°**detective** [dɪ'tektɪv] Detektiv/in
°**dialogue** ['daɪəlɒg] Dialog
diary ['daɪəri] Tagebuch; Kalender 3 (86)
dictionary ['dɪkʃənri] alphabetisches Wörterverzeichnis, Wörterbuch (3)
did [dɪd] *simple past of* **do** **he didn't run** ['dɪdnt] Er rannte nicht. 4 (102)
die [daɪ] sterben 4 (113)
different ['dɪfrənt] verschieden; anders 1 (23) °**different from** anders als °**in different ways** auf verschiedene Weise
dining room ['daɪnɪŋ ruːm] Esszimmer 2 (45)
dinner ['dɪnə] Abendessen, Abendbrot 2 (46) **have dinner** zu Abend essen 2 (46)
dinosaur ['daɪnəsɔː] Dinosaurier 4 (118)
°**director** [də'rektə] Direktor/in
°**dirt** [dɜːt] Dreck
disco ['dɪskəʊ] Disko 4 (118)
°**discovery** [dɪ'skʌvəri] Entdeckung
dislikes [dɪs'laɪks]: **likes and dislikes** *(pl)* Vorlieben und Abneigungen 5 (132)
°**diver** ['daɪvə] Taucher/in
divorced [dɪ'vɔːst] geschieden 2 (55)
do [duː], *simple past:* **did** machen, tun 1 (28) **do sport** Sport treiben 2 (52) **Don't go.** Gehe nicht. 1 (22) **he doesn't have time** er hat keine Zeit 2 (52)
dog [dɒg] Hund HWG (14)
door [dɔː] Tür HWG (16)
°**dot** [dɒt] Punkt, Pünktchen
double ['dʌbl] Doppel- HWG (17)
down [daʊn] hinunter, herunter; nach unten 2 (60) °**down to the ground** nach unten auf den Boden **up and down** auf und ab; rauf und runter 4 (98/99)
downstairs [ˌdaʊn'steəz] unten; nach unten *(im Haus)* 2 (45)
drank [dræŋk] *simple past of* **drink**
draw [drɔː], *simple past:* **drew** zeichnen 5 (130)
drawing ['drɔːɪŋ] Zeichnung 4 (110)
dream [driːm] Traum 3 (87)
dress [dres] Kleid 5 (138)
drew [druː] *simple past of* **draw**
drink [drɪŋk]:
1. *(simple past:* **drank***)* trinken 2 (56)
2. Getränk 2 (56)
drive [draɪv], *simple past:* **drove** *(mit dem Auto)* fahren 5 (134)
drove [drəʊv] *simple past of* **drive**
drum [drʌm] Trommel 3 (72) **drums** *(pl)* Schlagzeug 3 (72) **play the drums** Schlagzeug spielen 3 (72)
DVD [ˌdiːviː'diː] DVD 1 (31)

E

each [iːtʃ]: **They're £ 2.75 each.** Sie kosten je 2 Pfund 75. *(2,75 pro Stück)* 3 (93) °**each team/speaker** jedes Team/jede/r Sprecher/in
ear [ɪə] Ohr 4 (112)
early ['ɜːli] früh 4 (102)
°**easier** ['iːziə] leichter, einfacher
Easter ['iːstə] Ostern 3 (93)
easy ['iːzi] leicht, einfach 5 (132)
eat [iːt], *simple past:* **ate** essen 1 (32)
edit ['edɪt] bearbeiten; schneiden *(Film, Video)* 3 (68/69)
egg [eg] Ei 4 (115)
eight [eɪt] acht HWG (8/9)
either ['aɪðə, 'iːðə]: **not … either** auch nicht 4 (97)
elephant ['elɪfənt] Elefant HWG (14)
eleven [ɪ'levn] elf HWG (8/9)
°**Elizabethan** [ɪˌlɪzə'biːθn] elisabethanisch *(aus dem Zeitalter der Königin Elisabeth I., 1558–1603)*
email ['iːmeɪl] E-Mail 2 (49)
end [end] Ende, Schluss 3 (82) °**in the end** schließlich, am Ende, zum Schluss
ending ['endɪŋ] Endung 3 (84)
English ['ɪŋglɪʃ] Englisch; englisch HWG (15) **in English** auf Englisch 1 (34)
enough [ɪ'nʌf] genug 4 (106)
etc. (et cetera) [et'setərə] usw. (und so weiter) 3 (83)
evening ['iːvnɪŋ] Abend 2 (46) **in the evening** abends, am Abend 2 (46)
every day/colour/boat ['evri] jeder Tag / jede Farbe / jedes Boot HWG (11)
everybody ['evribɒdi] jeder; alle 2 (67)
everyday ['evrideɪ] Alltags- 1 (33)
everyone ['evriwʌn] jeder; alle 2 (67)
everything ['evriθɪŋ] alles 5 (134)
°**example** [ɪg'zɑːmpl] Beispiel **for example** zum Beispiel
excellent ['eksələnt] ausgezeichnet, hervorragend 5 (134)
excited [ɪk'saɪtɪd] aufgeregt, gespannt 4 (98/99)
exciting [ɪk'saɪtɪŋ] aufregend, spannend 4 (96)
exercise ['eksəsaɪz] Aufgabe, Übung HWG (16)
exercise book ['eksəsaɪz bʊk] Schulheft, Übungsheft HWG (16)
expensive [ɪk'spensɪv] teuer 5 (131)
°**expert** ['ekspɜːt] Experte, Expertin, Fachmann, Fachfrau
explain sth. to sb. [ɪk'spleɪn] jm. etwas erklären, erläutern 5 (130)
eye [aɪ] Auge 4 (112)

F

face [feɪs] Gesicht 5 (121)
fair [feə] fair, gerecht 4 (112)
fall [fɔːl], *simple past:* **fell** fallen, stürzen; hinfallen 5 (139) **fall asleep** einschlafen 1 (32)
family ['fæməli] Familie 2 (44) **the Blackwell family** (die) Familie Blackwell 2 (44) °**family name** Familienname, Nachname **family tree** (Familien-)Stammbaum 2 (55)
famous (for) ['feɪməs] berühmt (für, wegen) 3 (90)
fan [fæn] Fan, Anhänger/in 4 (98/99)
fantastic [fæn'tæstɪk] fantastisch 4 (96)
far [fɑː] weit (entfernt) 4 (102)
farm [fɑːm] Bauernhof, Farm 2 (53)

farmer ['fɑːmə] Bauer/Bäuerin, Landwirt/in 5 (138)
fast [fɑːst] schnell 5 (122)
fat [fæt] dick, fett 5 (130)
father ['fɑːðə] Vater 1 (20)
favourite ['feɪvərɪt]: **my favourite day** mein Lieblingstag HWG (13)
February ['februəri] Februar 1 (31)
feed [fiːd], *simple past:* **fed** füttern 2 (47) **feeding time** Fütterungszeit 5 (126)
°**feedback** *(no pl)* ['fiːdbæk] Rückmeldung, Feedback
feel [fiːl], *simple past:* **felt** fühlen; sich fühlen 5 (121)
feeling ['fiːlɪŋ] Gefühl 1 (37)
fell [fel] *simple past of* **fall**
felt [felt] *simple past of* **feel**
felt pen [ˌfelt 'pen] Filzstift 3 (92)
°**fence** [fens] Zaun
ferry ['feri] Fähre 5 (122)
fight [faɪt], *simple past:* **fought** kämpfen 3 (87) °**fight for sth.** um etwas kämpfen
file [faɪl]: **background file** Hintergrundinformation(en) (3) **grammar file** Zusammenfassung der Grammatik jeder Unit (3) **skills file** Übersicht über Lern- und Arbeitstechniken (3)
°**fill** [fɪl] füllen °**fill sth. in 1.** etwas einsetzen; **2.** etwas ausfüllen
film [fɪlm]:
1. filmen 2 (60)
2. Film 3 (68/69)
final ['faɪnl] Finale, Endspiel 4 (98/99)
find [faɪnd], *simple past:* **found** finden HWG (8/9) **Find someone who ...** Finde jemanden, der ... 3 (73)
fine [faɪn]: **Fine, thanks.** Gut, danke. 3 (76)
°**finger** ['fɪŋgə] Finger
finish ['fɪnɪʃ]:
1. enden 5 (127)
2. finish sth. etwas beenden; mit etwas fertig werden/sein 3 (76)
°**3.** vervollständigen; abschließen
finished ['fɪnɪʃt]: **We're finished.** Wir sind fertig. 1 (32)
first [fɜːst] zuerst, als Erstes 4 (117) **the first day** der erste Tag 1 (20) **First, ...** Erstens, ... 5 (134)
fish [fɪʃ], *pl* **fish** Fisch 2 (46)
°**fishing** ['fɪʃɪŋ] Angeln, Fischen
°**fishing village** ['fɪʃɪŋ ˌvɪlɪdʒ] Fischerdorf
five [faɪv] fünf HWG (8/9)
flat [flæt] Wohnung 1 (20)
floor [flɔː]:
1. Fußboden 2 (47)
2. Stock(werk) 3 (81)
°**flyer** ['flaɪə] Flyer, Flugblatt
follow ['fɒləʊ] folgen HWG (13) **Follow me.** Folg(t) mir. HWG (13)
food [fuːd] Essen; Lebensmittel; Futter 2 (57)
football ['fʊtbɔːl] Fußball 1 (26)
for [fɔː, fə] für HWG (15) **for miles** meilenweit 4 (118) **What's for lunch?** Was gibt es zum Mittagessen? 2 (56) **What's for homework?** Was haben wir als Hausaufgabe auf? 1 (33)
foreground ['fɔːgraʊnd] Vordergrund 4 (119)
forget [fə'get], *simple past:* **forgot** vergessen 1 (23)
form (of) [fɔːm] Form (von) 1 (24)
former ['fɔːmə] ehemalige(r, s), frühere(r, s) 3 (81)
fought [fɔːt] *simple past of* **fight**
found [faʊnd] *simple past of* **find**
four [fɔː] vier HWG (8/9)
free [friː] frei 3 (74) **free time** Freizeit, freie Zeit 3 (74) **free-time activities** Freizeitaktivitäten 3 (74)
French [frentʃ] Französisch 1 (29)
Friday ['fraɪdeɪ, 'fraɪdi] Freitag HWG (11)
friend ['frend] Freund/in 1 (20)
friendly ['frendli] freundlich 1 (22)
frog [frɒg] Frosch HWG (14)
from [frɒm, frəm] aus, von HWG (8/9) **from ... to ...** von ... bis ... 3 (68/69)
front [frʌnt] Vorderseite 4 (112) **in front of** vor *(räumlich)* 3 (80) °**at the front** vorn °**to the front** nach vorn
fruit [fruːt] Obst, Früchte; Frucht 2 (56) **fruit salad** Obstsalat 2 (56)
full (of) [fʊl] voll (von/mit) 5 (134) °**full sentences** ganze Sätze
fun [fʌn] Spaß 2 (51) **have fun** Spaß haben, sich amüsieren 2 (51) °**a fun place** ein Ort, an dem man Spaß haben kann **That sounds fun.** Das klingt nach Spaß. 3 (71) **That's fun.** Das macht Spaß. 2 (66) **Was it fun?** Hat es Spaß gemacht? 4 (97)
funny ['fʌni] witzig, komisch 3 (70)
fun park ['fʌn pɑːk] Vergnügungspark 5 (134)

G

game [geɪm] Spiel HWG (15)
°**game plan** ['geɪm plæn] Strategie, Schlachtplan
°**gang** [gæŋ] Gruppe
°**gap** [gæp] Lücke
garage ['gærɑːʒ, 'gærɪdʒ] Garage 4 (94)
garden ['gɑːdn] Garten 2 (45)
gardening ['gɑːdnɪŋ] Gärtnern, Gartenarbeit 3 (68/69)
°**gate** [geɪt] Tor
gave [geɪv] *simple past of* **give**
geography [dʒi'ɒgrəfi] Geografie 1 (29)
German ['dʒɜːmən] Deutsch; deutsch 1 (25) **in German** auf Deutsch 1 (34)
get [get], *simple past:* **got:**
1. bekommen 4 (106) **Did you get it?** *(infml)* Hast du es verstanden? / Hast du es mitbekommen? 4 (112)
2. gelangen, (hin)kommen 5 (136)
3. get off (the bus/boat) (aus dem Bus/Boot) aussteigen 5 (136)
4. get angry/cold/... wütend/kalt/... werden 3 (70) °**get ready (for)** sich fertig machen (für), sich vorbereiten (auf)
5. get up aufstehen 3 (76)
°**6.** holen **Get more words if you need them.** Hol dir mehr Wörter, wenn du sie brauchst.
ghost [gəʊst] Geist, Gespenst 3 (80)
giraffe [dʒə'rɑːf] Giraffe HWG (14)
girl [gɜːl] Mädchen HWG (8/9)
give [gɪv], *simple past:* **gave:**
1. geben HWG (16) °**Give me a hug.** Umarme mich. °**give sb. a squeeze** jn. drücken
2. give a talk (about) einen Vortrag / eine Rede halten (über) 5 (126)
glue [gluː] Klebstoff HWG (16)
glue stick ['gluː stɪk] Klebestift HWG (16)
go [gəʊ], *simple past:* **went:**
1. gehen; fahren HWG (8/9) **go by car/minibus/...** mit dem Auto/Kleinbus/... fahren 4 (98/99) **go down** untergehen *(Sonne)* 4 (112) **go for a walk** spazieren gehen, einen Spaziergang machen 2 (47) **go home** nach Hause gehen 1 (21) °**go marching** marschieren **go on** weiterreden, fortfahren; weitermachen 5 (130) **go on a boat trip** einen Bootsausflug machen 4 (117) **go sailing** segeln; segeln gehen 2 (47) **go shopping** einkaufen gehen 2 (49) °**go together** zusammenpassen, zusammengehören **go with sth.** zu etwas gehören, zu etwas passen

4 (110) **Here we go.** Los geht's. / Jetzt geht's los. HWG (8/9)
2. Have a go. Versuch's mal. 1 (23)
°**goat** [gəʊt] Ziege
going to ['gəʊɪŋ tʊ]**: He is going to visit his dad.** Er hat vor, seinen Vater zu besuchen. / Er wird seinen Vater besuchen. 5 (144)
gold [gəʊld] Gold 3 (86)
good [gʊd] gut 1 (28) **be good at kung fu** gut sein in Kung-Fu; gut Kung-Fu können 1 (37) **Good luck!** Viel Glück! 5 (138) **Good morning.** Guten Morgen. 1 (28)
Goodbye. [ˌgʊd'baɪ] Auf Wiedersehen. 5 (139)
goods *(pl)* [gʊdz] Waren, Güter 5 (131)
got [gɒt] *simple past of* **get**
°**grab** [græb] greifen
grammar file ['græmə ˌfaɪl] Zusammenfassung der Grammatik (3)
grandfather ['grænfɑːðə] Großvater 2 (53)
grandma ['grænmɑː] Oma 2 (53)
grandmother ['grænmʌðə] Großmutter 2 (53)
grandpa ['grænpɑː] Opa 2 (53)
grandparents *(pl)* ['grænpeərənts] Großeltern 4 (95)
grass [grɑːs] Gras; Rasen 4 (118)
great [greɪt] großartig HWG (11)
Great Britain (GB) Großbritannien 1 (42)
green [griːn] grün HWG (15)
°**greeting** ['griːtɪŋ] Gruß
grew [gruː] *simple past of* **grow**
grey [greɪ] grau HWG (15)
°**grey seal** [ˌgreɪ 'siːl] Kegelrobbe *(Halichoerus grypus)*
°**ground** [graʊnd] Boden **down to the ground** nach unten auf den Boden
group (of) [gruːp] Gruppe 1 (35)
°**group word** Oberbegriff
grow [grəʊ], *simple past:* **grew:**
1. anbauen, anpflanzen 3 (68/69)
2. wachsen 4 (106)
guess [ges] raten, erraten 3 (73)
Guess what, Dad ... Stell dir vor, Papa ... / Weißt du was, Papa ... 4 (96)
guinea pig ['gɪni pɪg] Meerschweinchen HWG (14)
guitar [gɪ'tɑː] Gitarre 3 (74) **play the guitar** Gitarre spielen 3 (74)
gym [dʒɪm] Turnhalle 1 (32)
gymnastics [dʒɪm'næstɪks] Gymnastik, Turnen 3 (72)

H

had [hæd] *simple past of* **have** *and* **have got**
hair [heə] Haar, Haare 2 (60)
half [hɑːf], *pl* **halves** [hɑːvz] Hälfte; Halbzeit 4 (98/99) **half past ten** halb elf (10.30 / 22.30) HWG (17)
hand [hænd] Hand 3 (87)
°**handmade** [ˌhænd'meɪd] von Hand gefertigt
happen (to) ['hæpən] passieren, geschehen (mit) 3 (79)
happy ['hæpi] glücklich, froh 1 (37)
harbour ['hɑːbə] Hafen 2 (60)
hard [hɑːd] schwer, schwierig; hart 4 (106)
has [hæz]**: he/she has** er/sie hat 2 (47)
hat [hæt] Hut 2 (66)
have [hæv, həv], *simple past:* **had** haben HWG (15) **Have a go.** Versuch's mal. 1 (23) **have breakfast** frühstücken 2 (46) **have dinner** zu Abend essen 2 (46) **have fun** Spaß haben, sich amüsieren 2 (51) **have lunch** zu Mittag essen 2 (46) **have to do** tun müssen 3 (70) °**Just have a look.** Schau einfach mal.
have got [hæv 'gɒt, həv 'gɒt], *simple past:* **had** haben 2 (54)
he [hiː] er 1 (20)
head [hed] Kopf 4 (112)
hear [hɪə], *simple past:* **heard** hören 3 (77)
heard [hɜːd] *simple past of* **hear**
held [held] *simple past of* **hold**
Hello. [hə'ləʊ] Hallo. / Grüß Gott. HWG (8/9)
help [help]**:**
1. Hilfe 1 (26)
2. helfen 1 (26)
her [hɜː, hə]**:**
1. ihr, ihre 1 (20) **her best friend** ihr bester Freund / ihre beste Freundin 1 (20)
2. sie; ihr 2 (47)
here [hɪə] hier; hierher HWG (13)
Here we go. Los geht's. / Jetzt geht's los. HWG (8/9) **near here** (hier) in der Nähe 2 (52)
°**hero** ['hɪərəʊ] Held/in
hid [hɪd] *simple past of* **hide**
hide [haɪd], *simple past:* **hid** sich verstecken, etwas verstecken 5 (131)
high [haɪ] hoch 4 (102) °**High School** ['haɪ skuːl] *Schule für 11- bis 18-Jährige*
hill [hɪl] Hügel HWG (10)
°**hillwalking** ['hɪlwɔːkɪŋ] Bergwandern
him [hɪm] ihn; ihm 1 (32)
his [hɪz]**: his friend** sein Freund / seine Freundin 1 (20)
history ['hɪstri] Geschichte 1 (29)
natural history [ˌnætʃrəl 'hɪstri] Naturkunde 4 (118)
hit [hɪt], *simple past:* **hit** prallen, stoßen gegen 4 (113)
hobby ['hɒbi] Hobby 3 (68/69)
hold [həʊld], *simple past:* **held** halten 5 (138) °**hold onto sth.** sich an etwas festhalten °**hold sth. up** **1.** etwas aufhalten; **2.** etwas hochhalten
holiday ['hɒlədeɪ] Urlaub 5 (134)
be/go on holiday in Urlaub sein/fahren 5 (134)
°**holidaymaker** ['hɒlədeɪˌmeɪkə] Urlauber/in
holidays *(pl)* ['hɒlədeɪz] Ferien 4 (108)
home [həʊm] Heim, Zuhause 1 (21)
at home daheim, zu Hause 1 (21)
come/go home nach Hause kommen/gehen 1 (21)
hometown [ˌhəʊm'taʊn] Heimatstadt HWG (8/9)
homework ['həʊmwɜːk] Hausaufgabe(n) 1 (33) **Do your homework.** Mach deine Hausaufgaben. 1 (33) **What's for homework?** Was haben wir als Hausaufgabe auf? 1 (33)
hope [həʊp] hoffen 3 (86)
horse [hɔːs] Pferd HWG (14)
hot [hɒt] heiß 2 (56)
hour ['aʊə] Stunde 1 (30)
house [haʊs] Haus HWG (11)
how [haʊ] wie HWG (8/9) **How are you?** Wie geht's? / Wie geht es dir/euch? 3 (76) **How do you like it?** Wie findest du es (sie/ihn)? / Wie gefällt es (sie/er) dir? 3 (76) **How many?** Wie viele? 3 (76) **How much?** Wie viel? 3 (76) **How much are ...?** Was kosten ...? 3 (92) **How much is ...?** Was kostet ...? 3 (92) **How old are you?** Wie alt bist du? HWG (8/9) **how to do sth.** wie man etwas macht / machen kann / machen soll 1 (35)
°**hug** [hʌg]**: give sb. a hug** jn. umarmen
hundred: a/one hundred [ə'hʌndrəd, ˌwʌn'hʌndrəd] einhundert HWG (17)

hungry ['hʌŋgri]: **be hungry** hungrig sein, Hunger haben 4 (112)
°**hurrah** [hə'rɑː] hurra
hurry up [ˌhʌri‿'ʌp] sich beeilen 1 (22)
hurt, *simple past:* **hurt** [hɜːt] schmerzen, wehtun; verletzen 4 (109)

I

I [aɪ] ich HWG (8/9) **I'm a seal. (= I am ...)** Ich bin eine Robbe. HWG (8/9) **I'm from Plymouth.** Ich bin/komme aus Plymouth. HWG (8/9) **I'm two years old.** Ich bin zwei Jahre alt. HWG (8/9) °**I spy with my little eye** *entspricht dem Spiel* "Ich sehe was, was du nicht siehst"
ice cream [ˌaɪs 'kriːm] (Speise-)Eis 2 (56)
ICT [ˌaɪ siː 'tiː] Informations- und Kommunikationstechnologie 1 (29)
idea [aɪ'dɪə] Idee; Vorstellung 3 (76)
if [ɪf] wenn, falls 4 (109)
imagine sth. [ɪ'mædʒɪn] sich etwas vorstellen 3 (81)
important [ɪm'pɔːtnt] wichtig 5 (128)
in [ɪn] in HWG (8/9) **come in** hereinkommen 1 (28) **in 1580** im Jahr 1580 3 (81) °**in class** im Unterricht °**in different ways** auf verschiedene Weise **in England** in England HWG (8/9) **in front of** vor *(räumlich)* 3 (80) **in German/English** auf Deutsch/Englisch 1 (34) **in the afternoon** nachmittags, am Nachmittag 2 (46) **in the attic** auf dem Dachboden 3 (86) °**in the end** schließlich, am Ende, zum Schluss **in the evening** abends, am Abend 2 (46) **in the middle** in der Mitte 4 (119) **in the morning** morgens, vormittags, am Morgen/Vormittag 2 (46) **in the photo** auf dem Foto HWG (13) **in the picture** auf dem Bild HWG (14) **in the world** auf der Welt 4 (118)
°**Indian** ['ɪndiən] indisch; Inder/in
information (about/on) *(no pl)* [ˌɪnfə'meɪʃn] Information(en) (über) 3 (68/69) **Information and Communications Technology** Informations- und Kommunikationstechnologie 1 (29)
°**insect** ['ɪnsekt] Insekt
inside [ˌɪn'saɪd] drinnen; nach drinnen 3 (75)
instrument ['ɪnstrəmənt] Instrument 3 (68/69)
interesting ['ɪntrəstɪŋ] interessant 5 (126)
international [ˌɪntə'næʃnəl] international 5 (147)
internet ['ɪntənet] Internet 4 (109) **on the internet** im Internet 4 (109)
into ['ɪntʊ]: **into the kitchen** in die Küche (hinein) 2 (47)
intonation [ˌɪntə'neɪʃn] Intonation, Satzmelodie 2 (67)
invitation (to) [ˌɪnvɪ'teɪʃn] Einladung (zu, nach) 4 (105)
is [ɪz]: **Is it Monday?** Ist es Montag? HWG (11) **Is that you?** Bist du's? / Bist du das? 3 (86) **The camera is ...** Die Kamera kostet ... 3 (92)
island ['aɪlənd] Insel 4 (94)
isn't ['ɪznt]: **he/she/it isn't (= is not)** er/sie/es ist nicht ... 1 (20)
it [ɪt] er, sie, es HWG (13) °**Sam is it** Sam ist Fänger *(beim Fangenspielen)*
it's ... (= it is) [ɪts] er/sie/es ist ... HWG (13)
its name [ɪts] sein Name / ihr Name 1 (20)

J

°**jacket** ['dʒækɪt] Jacke
jam [dʒæm] Marmelade 2 (56)
January ['dʒænjuəri] Januar 1 (31)
jeans *(pl)* [dʒiːnz] Jeans 2 (60)
job [dʒɒb] Job, (Arbeits-)Stelle 3 (76)
join a club [dʒɔɪn] in einen Klub eintreten; sich einem Klub anschließen 3 (68/69) °**join sth.** etwas verbinden
joke [dʒəʊk] Witz 3 (70)
judo ['dʒuːdəʊ] Judo 3 (72)
July [dʒu'laɪ] Juli 1 (31)
jump [dʒʌmp]:
1. springen 2 (60)
2. Sprung 3 (75)
June [dʒuːn] Juni 1 (31)
°**jungle** ['dʒʌŋgl] Dschungel
junior team ['dʒuːniə tiːm] Jugendmannschaft, Juniorenmannschaft 3 (89)
just [dʒʌst] (einfach) nur, bloß 4 (106) °**Just have a look.** Schau einfach mal.

K

°**karate** [kə'rɑːti] Karate
keyword ['kiːwɜːd] Schlüsselwort 5 (132)
kid [kɪd] Kind 1 (20)
kilogram, kilo (kg) ['kiːləʊ, 'kɪləgræm] Kilogramm, Kilo 4 (106)
kind [kaɪnd]: **a kind of ...** eine Art (von) ... 5 (122)
°**king** [kɪŋ] König
°**kiss** [kɪs] küssen
kit [kɪt] Ausrüstung 3 (68/69)
kitchen ['kɪtʃɪn] Küche 2 (45)
°**knee** [niː] Knie
knew [njuː] *simple past of* **know**
know [nəʊ], *simple past:* **knew** wissen; kennen 1 (20) **know about sth.** sich mit etwas auskennen; über etwas Bescheid wissen 5 (135) **I don't know.** Ich weiß (es) nicht. 1 (32) **..., you know.** ..., weißt du. / ..., wissen Sie. 2 (52)
kung fu [ˌkʌŋ 'fuː] Kung Fu 1 (37)

L

°**label** ['leɪbl] beschriften, beschildern
°**ladder** ['lædə] (die) Leiter
lake [leɪk] (Binnen-)See 4 (95)
lamp [læmp] Lampe 2 (44)
language ['læŋgwɪdʒ] Sprache 1 (24)
large [lɑːdʒ] groß 4 (115)
last [lɑːst]:
1. **last weekend/Friday** letztes Wochenende / letzten Freitag 4 (96)
2. **at last** endlich, schließlich 5 (126)
late [leɪt] spät 1 (20) **You're late.** Du bist spät dran. / Du bist zu spät. 1 (20)
later ['leɪtə] später HWG (17) **See you later.** Bis bald. / Bis nachher. HWG (17)
laugh [lɑːf] lachen 5 (122)
learn [lɜːn] lernen 1 (30)
leave [liːv], *simple past:* **left:**
1. (ab)fahren; (weg)gehen 5 (143)
2. verlassen; zurücklassen 4 (106)
°**leave room** Platz lassen
left [left]:
1. *siehe* **leave**
2. linke(r, s); (nach) links 4 (119) **on the left** links/auf der linken Seite 4 (119)
leg [leg] Bein HWG (15)
lesson ['lesn] (Unterrichts-)Stunde HWG (15) **before lessons** vorm Unterricht 1 (22)
let [let], *simple past:* **let:** lassen HWG (16) **Let me show you ...** Lass mich dir ... zeigen. HWG (16) **Let's ...** Lass(t) uns ... HWG (8/9) **Let's**

go to England. Lass(t) uns nach England gehen/fahren. HWG (8/9)
letter ['letə]:
1. Brief 3 (75)
2. Buchstabe 3 (83)
library ['laɪbrəri] Bibliothek, Bücherei 1 (21)
life [laɪf], *pl* **lives** [laɪvz] Leben 3 (81)
life jacket ['laɪf dʒækɪt] Schwimmweste 4 (94)
light [laɪt] Licht 2 (66)
like [laɪk]:
1. mögen, gernhaben HWG (8/9) **I like ...** Ich mag ... HWG (8/9) **I like swimming/sailing/...** Ich schwimme/segele/... gern. 3 (77) **I don't like ...** Ich mag ... nicht. / Ich mag kein ... 1 (23) **I'd like ...** Ich hätte gern ... / Ich möchte ... 2 (56) **I'd like to go** Ich möchte gehen / Ich würde gern gehen 5 (121) °**like sth. about sth.** etwas an etwas mögen
2. like boys wie Jungen 1 (37) **like this** so *(auf diese Weise)* 1 (39) **like that** so *(auf diese Weise)* 5 (138) **What's she like?** Wie ist sie? / Wie ist sie so? 3 (71)
likes and dislikes *(pl)* [ˌlaɪks‿ən 'dɪslaɪks] Vorlieben und Abneigungen 5 (132)
line [laɪn]:
1. Zeile 5 (127)
°**2.** Reihe
°**3.** Linie
link [lɪŋk] verbinden, -knüpfen 1 (35)
lion ['laɪən] Löwe HWG (14)
list [lɪst] Liste 3 (71)
listen ['lɪsn] zuhören, horchen 3 (76)
listen to sb. jm. zuhören 3 (76)
listen to sth. sich etwas anhören 3 (76) **Listen, Justin.** Hör zu, Justin. 3 (76)
°**litre** ['liːtə] Liter
little ['lɪtl] klein 1 (36) °**the little one** der/die/das Kleine
live [lɪv] leben; wohnen 1 (28)
°**live** [laɪv] lebend, lebendig
living room ['lɪvɪŋ ruːm] Wohnzimmer 2 (45)
lonely ['ləʊnli] einsam 5 (131)
long [lɒŋ] lang 1 (24)
look [lʊk]:
1. schauen 1 (20): **Look, ...** [lʊk] Sieh mal, ... / Schau mal, ... HWG (13) **look at** anschauen, ansehen 1 (20) **look happy/angry/...** glücklich/wütend/... aussehen 2 (60) **look for sth.** etwas suchen 5 (121)
°**2. Just have a look.** Schau einfach mal.
lot [lɒt]: **a lot** viel 5 (130) **That helped us a lot.** Das hat uns sehr geholfen. 4 (98/99) **lots of .../a lot of ...** viel ..., viele ... HWG (13)
loud [laʊd] laut 3 (80) °**read sth. out loud** etwas vorlesen
love [lʌv] lieben, sehr mögen 3 (71)
I'd love to ... Ich würde sehr gern ... 4 (118)
luck [lʌk]: **Good luck!** Viel Glück! 5 (138)
lucky ['lʌki]: **be lucky** Glück haben 5 (135)
lunch [lʌntʃ] Mittagessen 1 (30)
have lunch zu Mittag essen 2 (46)
What's for lunch? Was gibt es zum Mittagessen? 2 (56)
lunchtime ['lʌntʃtaɪm] Mittagszeit 3 (68/69) **at lunchtime** mittags 3 (68/69)

M

mad [mæd] verrückt 2 (47)
made [meɪd] *simple past of* **make**
°**madman** ['mædmən] Irrer, Verrückter
magazine [ˌmægə'ziːn] Zeitschrift 4 (94)
make [meɪk], *simple past:* **made:**
1. machen; herstellen 2 (47) **make a wish** sich etwas wünschen 4 (102)
make friends Freunde finden 3 (71)
°**make sth. better** etwas verbessern
°**2.** bilden
mall [mɔːl] (großes) Einkaufszentrum 4 (95)
man [mæn], *pl* **men** [men] Mann 1 (37)
many ['meni] viele 3 (76) **How many?** Wie viele? 3 (76)
map [mæp] Landkarte; Stadtplan HWG (10) **on the map** auf der Landkarte; auf dem Stadtplan HWG (10)
March [mɑːtʃ] März 1 (31)
°**marching** ['mɑːtʃɪŋ]: **go marching** marschieren
°**mark** [mɑːk] markieren
market ['mɑːkɪt] Markt 4 (118)
marmalade ['mɑːməleɪd] Marmelade *(aus Zitrusfrüchten)* 2 (56)
married (to) ['mærɪd] verheiratet (mit) 2 (55)
°**mascot** ['mæskət] Maskottchen
master ['mɑːstə] Meister/in 1 (36)
match [mætʃ]:
1. Spiel, Wettkampf, Match 4 (94)
°**2. match sth. (to sth.)** etwas (zu etwas) zuordnen
maths [mæθs] Mathematik 1 (29)
matter: What's the matter? ['mætə] Was ist denn? / Was ist los? 3 (70)
May [meɪ] Mai 1 (31)
maybe ['meɪbi] vielleicht 2 (60)
me [miː] mich; mir HWG (13) **It's me.** Ich bin's. 5 (125) **Me too.** Ich auch. 3 (86)
°**mean** [miːn] bedeuten
°**meaning** ['miːnɪŋ] Bedeutung
meat [miːt] Fleisch 2 (57)
medal ['medl] Medaille 4 (98/99)
mediation [ˌmiːdi'eɪʃn] Sprachmittlung, Mediation (3)
meet [miːt], *simple past:* **met:**
1. treffen; kennenlernen HWG (8/9)
Meet your classmates. Triff deine Mitschüler/innen. / Lerne deine Mitschüler/innen kennen. HWG (8/9)
Nice to meet you. Freut mich, dich/euch/Sie kennenzulernen. 1 (22)
2. sich treffen 1 (32)
°**memory** ['meməri] Erinnerung, Gedächtnis
men [men] *plural of* **man** 1 (37)
Merry Christmas! [ˌmeri 'krɪsməs] Frohe Weihnachten! 2 (66)
met [met] *simple past of* **meet**
metre ['miːtə] Meter 4 (106)
°**square metre** Quadratmeter
°**mice** [maɪs] *plural of* **mouse**
middle ['mɪdl] Mitte 4 (119)
midnight ['mɪdnaɪt] Mitternacht 3 (76)
mile [maɪl] Meile *(ca. 1,6 km)* 4 (118)
for miles meilenweit 4 (118)
milk [mɪlk] Milch 2 (57)
million ['mɪljən] Million 1 (42)
°**mime** [maɪm] vorspielen, pantomimisch darstellen
mind map ['maɪnd mæp] Mindmap 2 (50)
minibus ['mɪnibʌs] Kleinbus 4 (98/99)
go by minibus mit dem Kleinbus fahren
minute ['mɪnɪt] Minute 1 (20) **wait a minute** Warte einen Moment. / Moment mal. 1 (20)
miss [mɪs] verpassen 4 (102)
Miss [mɪs]: **Miss Bell** Frau Bell *(übliche Anrede von Lehrerinnen)* 1 (28)
missing ['mɪsɪŋ]: **the missing words** die fehlenden Wörter 4 (102)
°**mistake** [mɪ'steɪk] Fehler
mixed [mɪkst] gemischt 1 (40)
mixed bag *etwa:* bunte Mischung 1 (40)

mobile (phone) [ˌməʊbaɪl 'fəʊn] Mobiltelefon, Handy 4 (94)
moment ['məʊmənt] Moment 5 (122) **at the moment** gerade, im Moment 5 (122)
Monday ['mʌndeɪ, 'mʌndi] Montag HWG (11) **on Monday** am Montag HWG (12)
money ['mʌni] Geld 3 (86)
monkey ['mʌŋki] Affe HWG (14)
monster ['mɒnstə] Monster 1 (42)
month [mʌnθ] Monat 1 (31)
moon [mu:n] Mond 3 (86)
more [mɔ:] mehr 3 (68/69) °**more than once** mehr als einmal °**three more words** drei weitere Wörter
morning ['mɔ:nɪŋ] Morgen, Vormittag 1 (28) **Good morning.** Guten Morgen. 1 (28) **in the morning** morgens, vormittags, am Morgen/Vormittag 2 (46)
°**most** [məʊst]**: the most** die meisten
mother ['mʌðə] Mutter 1 (20)
mountain ['maʊntən] Berg 5 (134)
°**mouse** [maʊs], *pl* **mice** [maɪs] Maus
mouth [maʊθ] Mund; Maul 3 (86)
move [mu:v]**:**
1. bewegen; sich bewegen 4 (112)
°**2.** Bewegung
MP3 player [ˌem pi: 'θri: ˌpleɪə] MP3-Spieler 1 (31)
Mr Schwarz ['mɪstə] Herr Schwarz HWG (16)
Mrs Schwarz ['mɪsɪz] Frau Schwarz HWG (16)
much [mʌtʃ] viel 3 (76) **How much …?** Wie viel …? 3 (76) **How much are …?** Was kosten …? 3 (92) **How much is …?** Was kostet …? 3 (92)
mum [mʌm] Mama, Mutti 1 (20)
museum [mju'zi:əm] Museum 1 (42)
music ['mju:zɪk] Musik 1 (29)
must [mʌst] müssen 4 (106) **you mustn't do it** ['mʌsnt] du darfst es nicht tun 4 (106)
my [maɪ] mein/e HWG (8/9) **My birthday is in May.** Ich habe im Mai Geburtstag. 1 (31) **My birthday is on 5th August.** Ich habe am 5. August Geburtstag. 1 (31) **my favourite day** mein Lieblingstag HWG (13) **My name is Silky.** Ich heiße Silky. HWG (8/9)
°**myself** [maɪ'self] selbst

N

name [neɪm]**:**
1. Name HWG (8/9) **My name is Silky.** Ich heiße Silky. HWG (8/9) **What's your name?** Wie heißt du? / Wie heißt ihr? HWG (8/9)
°**2.** nennen
national ['næʃnəl] national, National- 5 (134)
natural history [ˌnætʃrəl 'hɪstri] Naturkunde 4 (118)
navy ['neɪvi] Marine 1 (20)
near [nɪə] in der Nähe von, nahe (bei) HWG (12) **near here** (hier) in der Nähe 2 (52)
°**neck** [nek] Hals, Nacken
need [ni:d] brauchen, benötigen 3 (74) **you needn't do it** ['ni:dnt] du musst es nicht tun 4 (106)
°**negative** ['negətɪv] negativ
nervous ['nɜ:vəs] nervös, aufgeregt 5 (133)
never ['nevə] nie, niemals 2 (61)
new [nju:] neu 1 (20)
news *(no pl)* [nju:z] Nachrichten 4 (110)
next [nekst]**: the next picture/question** das nächste Bild / die nächste Frage 1 (37) °**What's next?** Was kommt als Nächstes?
next to ['nekst tʊ] neben 4 (119)
nice [naɪs] nett, schön 1 (20) **Nice to meet you.** Freut mich, dich/euch/Sie kennenzulernen. 1 (22)
night [naɪt] Nacht 2 (47) **at night** nachts, in der Nacht 2 (47)
nine [naɪn] neun HWG (8/9)
no [nəʊ]**:**
1. nein HWG (13) **No, that's wrong.** Nein, das ist falsch. / Nein, das stimmt nicht. HWG (13)
2. kein, keine 2 (47)
nobody ['nəʊbədi] niemand 3 (79)
noise [nɔɪz] Geräusch, Lärm 4 (109)
noisy ['nɔɪzi] laut, lärmend, voller Lärm 4 (116)
no one ['nəʊ wʌn] niemand 3 (79)
north [nɔ:θ] Norden; Nord- 5 (134)
nose [nəʊz] Nase 4 (112)
not [nɒt] nicht 1 (20) **he/she/it is not** [nɒt] er/sie/es ist nicht … 1 (20) **not … yet** noch nicht 5 (130)
note [nəʊt] Notiz, Mitteilung 4 (94) °**take notes** sich Notizen machen
nothing ['nʌθɪŋ] (gar) nichts 3 (71)
November [nəʊ'vembə] November 1 (31)
now [naʊ] nun, jetzt HWG (15)
number ['nʌmbə] Zahl, Nummer, Ziffer HWG (8/9)

O

o [əʊ] Null *(in Telefonnummern)* HWG (17)
ocean ['əʊʃn] Ozean 5 (127)
o'clock: ten o'clock [ə'klɒk] 10/22 Uhr HWG (17)
October [ɒk'təʊbə] Oktober 1 (31)
°**octopus** ['ɒktəpəs] Krake
of [ɒv, əv] von 1 (24)
of course [əv 'kɔ:s] natürlich, selbstverständlich 2 (47)
°**off sth.** [ɒf] von etwas herunter
official [ə'fɪʃl] amtlich, Amts- 5 (146)
often ['ɒfn, 'ɒftən] oft 2 (52)
oh [əʊ]**: Oh, it's you.** Ach, du bist es. 3 (86)
old [əʊld] alt HWG (8/9) **How old are you?** Wie alt bist du? HWG (8/9)
on [ɒn] auf HWG (10) **on Monday** am Montag HWG (12) **on Monday afternoon** am Montagnachmittag 3 (80) **on the map** auf der Landkarte; auf dem Stadtplan HWG (10) **on the left** links/auf der linken Seite 4 (119) **on the right** rechts/auf der rechten Seite 4 (119) °**on the road to** auf der Straße nach
once [wʌns] einmal 4 (117)
one [wʌn] eins HWG (8/9) °**one by one** einzeln; einer nach dem anderen °**one day** eines Tages °**the little one** der/die/das Kleine
only ['əʊnli]**:**
1. nur, bloß 2 (52)
2. erst 4 (112)
onto ['ɒntʊ] auf (… hinauf) 2 (60)
open ['əʊpən]**:**
1. öffnen, aufmachen HWG (16); sich öffnen 3 (86)
2. geöffnet, offen 1 (32)
opposite ['ɒpəzɪt] Gegenteil 4 (115)
or [ɔ:] oder HWG (8/9)
orange ['ɒrɪndʒ] orange HWG (15)
order ['ɔ:də] Reihenfolge 4 (110)
°**ordinal number** [ˌɔ:dɪnl 'nʌmbə] Ordinalzahl, Ordnungszahl
organize ['ɔ:gənaɪz] organisieren; ordnen 5 (140)
other ['ʌðə] andere(r, s) 2 (57)
°**otter** ['ɒtə] Otter
our ['aʊə] unser/e HWG (16)
out ['aʊt]**: out of …** ['aʊt‿əv] aus … (heraus/hinaus) 3 (86) °**read sth. out loud** etwas vorlesen

outside [ˌaʊt'saɪd] draußen; nach draußen 3 (75)
over ['əʊvə]:
1. über 4 (112) **over to ...** hinüber zu/nach ... 4 (102)
2. over 20 people/years/... über 20 Leute/Jahre/... 4 (106)
3. be over vorbei sein, zu Ende sein 5 (122)
°**own** [əʊn] eigene(r, s)

P

p [piː] *Abkürzung für „pence", „penny"* 3 (92)
page [peɪdʒ] Seite 1 (33) **What page are we on?** Auf welcher Seite sind wir? 1 (33)
°**paint** [peɪnt] Farbe
pair [peə] Paar 1 (39) **a pair of ...** ein Paar ... 1 (39)
°**palm tree** ['pɑːm triː] Palme
paper ['peɪpə]:
1. Zeitung 2 (47)
2. Papier 2 (47) °**a piece of paper** ein Stück Papier
paragraph ['pærəgrɑːf] Absatz *(in einem Text)* 4 (110)
parents *(pl)* ['peərənts] Eltern 4 (95)
park [pɑːk] Park 2 (48)
parliament ['pɑːləmənt] Parlament 4 (118)
part [pɑːt] Teil 3 (81)
partner ['pɑːtnə] Partner/in 3 (78)
party ['pɑːti] Party 1 (31)
past [pɑːst]:
1. Vergangenheit 4 (100)
2. half past ten halb elf (10.30 / 22.30) HWG (17) **quarter past ten** Viertel nach zehn (10.15 / 22.15) HWG (17)
PE [ˌpiː‿'iː] Sportunterricht, Turnen 1 (29)
pen [pen] Kugelschreiber, Stift, Füller HWG (16)
pence [pens] Pence *(plural of* **penny***)* 3 (92)
pencil ['pensl] Bleistift HWG (16)
pencil case ['pensl keɪs] Federmäppchen HWG (16)
people ['piːpl] Leute, Menschen 1 (24)
pepper ['pepə] Pfeffer 5 (131)
per cent (%) [pə'sent] Prozent 5 (147)
perfect ['pɜːfɪkt] perfekt, ideal 3 (87)
person ['pɜːsn] Person 2 (48)
pet [pet] Haustier HWG (15)
phone [fəʊn]:
1. Telefon 4 (94)
2. phone sb. jn. anrufen 3 (78)
phone call ['fəʊn kɔːl] Anruf; Telefongespräch 3 (78)
photo ['fəʊtəʊ] Foto HWG (13) **in the photo** auf dem Foto HWG (13) **take photos** fotografieren 5 (126)
phrase [freɪz] Ausdruck, (Rede-)Wendung 2 (49)
Physical Education [ˌfɪzɪkl‿ˌedʒu'keɪʃn] Sportunterricht, Turnen 1 (29)
piano [pi'ænəʊ] Klavier, Piano 3 (72)
play the piano Klavier spielen 3 (72)
°**pick up** [ˌpɪk‿'ʌp] aufheben
picnic ['pɪknɪk] Picknick 4 (102)
picture ['pɪktʃə] Bild HWG (14) **in the picture** auf dem Bild HWG (14)
°**piece** [piːs]: **a piece of paper** ein Stück Papier
pig [pɪg] Schwein HWG (14)
pink [pɪŋk] pink, rosa HWG (15)
pizza ['piːtsə] Pizza 2 (57)
place [pleɪs] Ort, Platz, Stelle 1 (32) **take place** stattfinden; spielen, sich abspielen *(Geschichte, Handlung)* 3 (86)
plan [plæn] Plan 4 (94)
planet ['plænɪt] Planet 5 (127)
plate [pleɪt]: **a plate of ...** ein Teller ... 2 (46)
play [pleɪ]:
1. spielen 1 (28) °**play ball** mit dem Ball spielen **play the drums** Schlagzeug spielen 3 (72) **play the guitar** Gitarre spielen 3 (74) **play the piano** Klavier spielen 3 (72)
2. abspielen *(CD, DVD)* 2 (48)
3. Theaterstück 5 (138)
player ['pleɪə] Spieler/in 4 (98/99)
°**playground** ['pleɪgraʊnd] Spielplatz
please [pliːz] bitte 1 (20)
pm: 4 pm [ˌpiː‿'em] 4 Uhr nachmittags / 16 Uhr 3 (68/69)
°**poem** ['pəʊɪm] Gedicht
point [pɔɪnt]:
1. Punkt 4 (98/99)
2. point to sth. auf etwas zeigen, deuten 5 (130)
3. point sth. at sb. etwas auf jn. richten 5 (130)
police *(pl)* [pə'liːs] Polizei 4 (104)
police officer [pə'liːs‿ˌɒfɪsə] Polizist/in 2 (60)
policeman [pə'liːsmən] Polizist 5 (128)
Polish ['pəʊlɪʃ] Polnisch; polnisch 5 (147)
°**pony** ['pəʊni] Pony
pool [puːl]:
1. Schwimmbad, -becken HWG (10)
°**2.** Gezeitentümpel
poor [pɔː, pʊə] arm 4 (113)
popular (with) ['pɒpjələ] populär, beliebt (bei) 5 (134)
port [pɔːt] Hafenstadt 1 (42)
°**positive** ['pɒzətɪv] positiv
postcard ['pəʊstkɑːd] Postkarte 5 (129)
poster ['pəʊstə] Poster HWG (16)
potato [pə'teɪtəʊ], *pl* **potatoes** Kartoffel 2 (56) **roast potatoes** *(pl) im Backofen in Fett gebackene Kartoffeln* 2 (56)
pound [paʊnd] Pfund *(britische Währung)* 3 (81)
practice ['præktɪs] Übung (3)
practise ['præktɪs] üben, trainieren 4 (106)
prepare (for) [prɪ'peə] sich vorbereiten (auf) 1 (39) **prepare sth.** etwas vorbereiten 5 (132)
°**preposition** [ˌprepə'zɪʃn] Präposition
present ['preznt] Geschenk 2 (60)
price [praɪs] (Kauf-)Preis 5 (127)
prison ['prɪzn] Gefängnis 5 (139)
problem ['prɒbləm] Problem 4 (102)
profile ['prəʊfaɪl] Profil; Beschreibung, Porträt 1 (21)
programme ['prəʊgræm] Programm *(auch im Theater usw.)*; (Radio-, Fernseh-)Sendung 3 (76) **What programmes ...?** Welche Programme ...? / Welche Art von Programmen ...? 3 (76)
project ['prɒdʒekt] Projekt 4 (109)
pronunciation [prəˌnʌnsi'eɪʃn] Aussprache 1 (35)
°**propeller** [prə'pelə] Propeller
pull [pʊl] ziehen 4 (113) °**pull up** herausreißen
purple ['pɜːpl] violett, lila HWG (15)
push [pʊʃ] drücken, schieben, stoßen 4 (112)
put [pʊt], *simple past:* **put** legen, stellen, *(etwas wohin)* tun HWG (16) °**put sth. in** etwas einsetzen °**Put up your hand.** Melde dich. / Heb deine Hand.

Q

quarter ['kwɔːtə]: **quarter past ten** Viertel nach zehn (10.15 / 22.15) HWG (17) **quarter to eleven** Viertel vor elf (10.45 / 22.45) HWG (17)

queen [kwiːn] Königin 4 (118)
question ['kwestʃən] Frage HWG (8/9)
°**questionnaire** [ˌkwestʃə'neə] Fragebogen
quiet ['kwaɪət] ruhig, still, leise 3 (68/69)
quiz [kwɪz] Quiz, Ratespiel 1 (32)

R

rabbit ['ræbɪt] Kaninchen HWG (14)
race [reɪs] Rennen 5 (142)
°**rain** [reɪn] Regen
°**rally** ['ræli] Rallye
ran [ræn] *simple past of* **run**
rat [ræt] Ratte HWG (14)
°**rattle** ['rætl] klappern
read [riːd], *simple past:* **read** [red] lesen 1 (32) °**read sth. out loud** etwas vorlesen
ready ['redi] bereit, fertig 3 (80)
really ['rɪəli] echt, wirklich 3 (70)
reason ['riːzn] Grund 5 (134)
red [red] rot HWG (8/9)
religion [rɪ'lɪdʒən] Religion 1 (29)
remember [rɪ'membə] sich erinnern (an) 2 (60) °**remember to do sth.** daran denken, etwas zu tun
°**rattle** ['rætl] klappern
°**repeat** [rɪ'piːt] wiederholen
rescue ['reskjuː] Rettung; Rettungs- 4 (113)
°**rest** [rest] Rest
restaurant ['restrɒnt] Restaurant 3 (81)
°**rewrite** [ˌriː'raɪt] neu schreiben, umarbeiten
°**Rhesus monkey** ['riːsəs ˌmʌŋki] Rhesusaffe
rhyme [raɪm] Reim; Vers HWG (13)
rich [rɪtʃ] reich 5 (138)
ride [raɪd]:
1. Fahrt 4 (102)
°**2.** *(simple past:* **rode***)* reiten
ride a bike [ˌraɪd‿ə 'baɪk], *simple past:* **rode** Fahrrad fahren 3 (80)
riding ['raɪdɪŋ] Reiten 3 (72)
right [raɪt]:
1. richtig HWG (13) **sb. is right** jemand hat Recht 4 (112)
2. rechte(r, s); (nach) rechts 4 (119) **on the right** rechts/auf der rechten Seite 4 (119)
°**3. right away** sofort
river ['rɪvə] Fluss HWG (10)
road [rəʊd] Straße 2 (44) **at 8 Beach Road** in der Beach Road (Nummer) 8 2 (44) **in Beach Road** in der Beach Road 2 (44) °**on the road to** auf der Straße nach
°**roar** [rɔː] brüllen
roast beef [ˌrəʊst 'biːf] Rinderbraten 2 (56)
roast potatoes *(pl)* [ˌrəʊst pə'teɪtəʊz] *im Backofen in Fett gebackene Kartoffeln* 2 (56)
°**rock** [rɒk]]: **London rocks.** London rockt.
rock [rɒk] Fels, Felsen 2 (46)
°**rock pool** ['rɒk puːl] Gezeitentümpel
rode [rəʊd] *simple past of* **ride**
°**role** [rəʊl] Rolle
room [ruːm] Zimmer, Raum HWG (16)
routine [ruː'tiːn] Routine 5 (125)
rubber ['rʌbə] Radiergummi HWG (16)
rucksack ['rʌksæk] Rucksack 5 (122)
ruler ['ruːlə] Lineal HWG (15)
run [rʌn], *simple past:* **ran** rennen, laufen 2 (49) **run after sb.** hinter jm. herrennen 5 (122) °**run around** herumrennen

S

sad [sæd] traurig 1 (22)
°**safari path** [sə'fɑːri pɑːθ] Safaripfad
said [sed] *simple past of* **say**
sailing ['seɪlɪŋ]: **go sailing** segeln; segeln gehen 2 (47) **sailing boat** Segelboot 2 (60)
salad ['sæləd] Salat *(als Gericht oder Beilage)* 2 (56) **fruit salad** Obstsalat 2 (56)
°**salt** [sɔːlt] Salz
samba ['sæmbə] Samba 3 (68/69)
same [seɪm]: **the same** der-/die-/dasselbe; dieselben 3 (83)
sand [sænd] Sand 4 (94)
sandwich ['sænwɪtʃ, 'sænwɪdʒ] Sandwich, (zusammengeklapptes) belegtes Brot 2 (56)
°**sandy** ['sændi] sandig
sang [sæŋ] *simple past of* **sing**
sat [sæt] *simple past of* **sit**
Saturday ['sætədeɪ, 'sætədi] Samstag HWG (11) **on Saturday afternoon** am Samstagnachmittag 3 (80)
save [seɪv] retten 4 (104)
saw [sɔː] *simple past of* **see**
say [seɪ], *simple past:* **said** sagen 1 (28) **It says here: …** [sez] Hier steht: … / Es heißt hier: … 1 (42)
°**scarf** [skɑːf] Schal
scary ['skeəri] unheimlich, gruselig 3 (81)
scene [siːn] Szene 5 (138)
school [skuːl] Schule HWG (16) **at school** in der Schule 1 (20) **before school** vor der Schule *(vor Schulbeginn)* 1 (22) **in front of the school** vor der Schule *(vor dem Gebäude)* 1 (22) **school bag** Schultasche HWG (16)
science ['saɪəns] Naturwissenschaft 1 (29)
scone [skɒn] *kleines rundes Milchbrötchen, leicht süß* 2 (56)
score [skɔː] ein Tor schießen, einen Treffer erzielen 4 (98/99)
°**scorpion** ['skɔːpiən] Skorpion
sea [siː] Meer HWG (10) °**sea life** Meeresleben
°**seafood** ['siːfuːd] Meeresfrüchte
seagull ['siːgʌl] Möwe 2 (60)
seal [siːl] Robbe HWG (8/9)
second ['sekənd] zweite(r, s) 1 (31) **Second, …** Zweitens, … 5 (134)
°**secret** ['siːkrət] Geheimnis
see [siː], *simple past:* **saw** sehen; besuchen HWG (8/9) **See you later.** Bis bald. / Bis nachher. HWG (17)
sell [sel], *simple past:* **sold** verkaufen 3 (68/69)
send [send], *simple past:* **sent**: **send sth. to sb.** jm. etwas schicken, senden 3 (76)
sent [sent] *simple past of* **send**
sentence ['sentəns] Satz 1 (25)
September [sep'tembə] September 1 (28)
°**set** [set] Satz *(Karten)*
°**setting** ['setɪŋ] Schauplatz
seven ['sevn] sieben HWG (8/9)
°**shape** [ʃeɪp] Form, Gestalt
shark [ʃɑːk] Hai 5 (126)
sharpener ['ʃɑːpnə] (An-)Spitzer HWG (16)
she [ʃiː] sie HWG (12)
shelf [ʃelf], *pl* **shelves** [ʃelvz] Regal 2 (44)
ship [ʃɪp] Schiff 1 (42)
shoe [ʃuː] Schuh 1 (23)
shop [ʃɒp] Laden 1 (36) **corner shop** Laden an der Ecke; Tante-Emma-Laden 1 (36)
°**shop assistant** ['ʃɒp‿əˌsɪstənt] Verkäufer/in
shopping ['ʃɒpɪŋ]: **go shopping** einkaufen gehen 2 (49) **shopping centre** Einkaufszentrum 3 (93) **shopping mall** (großes) Einkaufszentrum 4 (95)
short [ʃɔːt] kurz 1 (24) °**short form** Kurzform

shorts *(pl)* [ʃɔːts] Shorts, kurze Hose 4 (94)
shout [ʃaʊt] schreien, rufen 2 (60)
show [ʃəʊ] zeigen HWG (16)
sick [sɪk] krank 3 (86)
°**side** [saɪd] Seite
sights *(pl)* [saɪts] Sehenswürdigkeiten 4 (102)
sign [saɪn] Schild; Zeichen 5 (130)
°**signal** ['sɪgnəl] Signal
silky ['sɪlki] seidig 4 (113)
silly ['sɪli]:
1. albern; blöd 1 (25)
2. Dummerchen 5 (126)
°**similar** ['sɪmələ] ähnlich
sing [sɪŋ], *simple past:* **sang** singen 3 (68/69)
°**singer** ['sɪŋə] Sänger/in
single ['sɪŋgl] ledig, alleinstehend 2 (55)
sister ['sɪstə] Schwester 1 (20)
sit [sɪt], *simple past:* **sat** sitzen; sich setzen 2 (46) **sit down** sich hinsetzen 4 (102)
six [sɪks] sechs HWG (8/9)
size [saɪz] Größe 3 (93)
skates [skeɪts] Inlineskates 3 (72)
skating ['skeɪtɪŋ] Inlineskaten, Rollschuhlaufen 3 (72)
skills *(pl)* [skɪlz]: **skills file** Übersicht über Lern- und Arbeitstechniken (3) **study skills** Lern- und Arbeitstechniken (3)
°**skype** [skaɪp] per Skype telefonieren
sleep [sliːp]:
1. *(simple past:* **slept***)* schlafen 2 (47)
°**2.** Schlaf
sleepover ['sliːpəʊvə] Pyjama-Party, Schlafparty 5 (126)
slept [slept] *simple past of* **sleep**
slow [sləʊ] langsam 4 (113)
small [smɔːl] klein 2 (44)
smell [smel] riechen 3 (86) **smell sth.** an etwas riechen 5 (124)
smile [smaɪl]:
1. lächeln 4 (106) **smile at sb.** jn. anlächeln 5 (122)
2. Lächeln 5 (142)
smiley ['smaɪli] Smiley 1 (37)
smuggle ['smʌgl] schmuggeln 5 (130)
smuggler ['smʌglə] Schmuggler/in 5 (130)
smuggling ['smʌglɪŋ] der Schmuggel, das Schmuggeln 5 (130)
snack [snæk] Snack, Imbiss 4 (109)
snake [sneɪk] Schlange HWG (14)
sneeze [sniːz] niesen 5 (139)
so [səʊ]:
1. also; deshalb, daher 1 (28)
2. so cool/nice so cool/nett 2 (47)
3. So? Und? / Na und? 1 (22)
sofa ['səʊfə] Sofa 2 (44)
soft [sɒft] weich 4 (113)
sold [səʊld] *simple past of* **sell**
some [sʌm] einige, ein paar; etwas 3 (68/69)
somebody ['sʌmbədi] jemand 3 (80)
someone ['sʌmwʌn] jemand 3 (80)
something ['sʌmθɪŋ] etwas 3 (80)
sometimes ['sʌmtaɪmz] manchmal 2 (49)
song [sɒŋ] Lied, Song HWG (11)
soon [suːn] bald 4 (106)
sorry ['sɒri]: **(I'm) sorry.** Tut mir leid. / Entschuldigung. 1 (22) **I'm sorry about …** Es tut mir leid wegen … 4 (96)
sound [saʊnd]:
1. klingen, sich anhören 3 (71)
2. Geräusch; Klang 3 (86)
3. Laut 1 (35) °**sound group** Lautgruppe
°**sound** [saʊnd] Meerenge, Sund
soup [suːp] Suppe 2 (56)
°**south** [saʊθ] Süden, südlich, Süd-
°**south-west** [ˌsaʊθ'west] Südwesten
spaghetti [spə'geti] Spagetti 2 (57)
Spanish ['spænɪʃ] Spanisch; spanisch 5 (147)
speak [spiːk], *simple past:* **spoke** sprechen 1 (27)
speaker ['spiːkə] Sprecher/in 1 (27)
special ['speʃl] besondere(r, s) 2 (66)
°**speech bubble** ['spiːtʃ bʌbl] Sprechblase
spell [spel] buchstabieren 1 (32)
spoke [spəʊk] *simple past of* **speak**
sport [spɔːt] Sport; Sportart 2 (52) **do sport** Sport treiben 2 (52)
spot [spɒt] Fleck, Punkt 4 (106)
°**spray** [spreɪ] sprühen
spring [sprɪŋ] Frühling 1 (42)
°**spy** [spaɪ]: **I spy with my little eye** *entspricht dem Spiel* „Ich sehe was, was du nicht siehst"
°**square metre** [ˌskweə 'miːtə] Quadratmeter
°**squeeze** [skwiːz]: **give sb. a squeeze** jn. drücken
stand up [ˌstænd‿'ʌp], *simple past:* **stood up** aufstehen 5 (135)
star [stɑː]:
1. (Film-, Pop-)Star 2 (47)
°**2.** Stern
start [stɑːt] anfangen, beginnen 1 (28)
state [steɪt] Staat 5 (144)
°**statement** ['steɪtmənt] Aussage
stay [steɪ] bleiben 4 (107)
steer [stɪə] steuern, lenken 4 (112)
step [step] Schritt 3 (86)
°**stick** [stɪk] Stock
still [stɪl] (immer) noch 4 (96)
stood [stʊd] *simple past of* **stand**
stop [stɒp] anhalten, stoppen 3 (80)
story ['stɔːri] Geschichte, Erzählung 2 (61)
strange [streɪndʒ] seltsam, komisch HWG (14)
°**strangle** ['stræŋgl] erdrosseln
street [striːt] Straße 1 (28) **at 14 Dean Street** in der Deanstraße 14 1 (28) **in Dean Street** in der Deanstraße 2 (44)
stress [stres] Betonung 3 (85)
°**stressed syllable** [strest 'sɪləbl] betonte Silbe
°**stripe** [straɪp] Streifen
student ['stjuːdənt] Schüler/in; Student/in 1 (20)
studio ['stjuːdiəʊ] Studio 3 (76)
study skills ['stʌdi ˌskɪlz] Lern- und Arbeitstechniken (3)
sub-clause ['sʌbklɔːz] Nebensatz 5 (133)
subject ['sʌbdʒɪkt] Schulfach 1 (29)
subtitle ['sʌbtaɪtl] Untertitel 5 (131)
°**suck up** [ˌsʌk‿'ʌp] aufsaugen
suddenly ['sʌdnli] plötzlich, auf einmal 2 (60)
°**sugar** ['ʃʊgə] Zucker
summer ['sʌmə] Sommer 1 (42)
sun [sʌn] Sonne 4 (112)
Sunday ['sʌndeɪ, 'sʌndi] Sonntag HWG (11)
°**sunglasses** *(pl)* ['sʌnglɑːsɪz] Sonnenbrille
supermarket ['suːpəmɑːkɪt] Supermarkt 3 (93)
sure [ʃʊə, ʃɔː] sicher 4 (117)
°**surfing** ['sɜːfɪŋ] Wellenreiten, Surfen
surprise [sə'praɪz] Überraschung 4 (115)
surprised [sə'praɪzd] überrascht 1 (37)
swam [swæm] *simple past of* **swim**
°**swap** [swɒp] tauschen
swim [swɪm], *simple past:* **swam** schwimmen 1 (37)
swimmer ['swɪmə] Schwimmer/in 1 (37)
swimming pool ['swɪmɪŋ puːl] Schwimmbad, Schwimmbecken HWG (10)
sword [sɔːd] Schwert 5 (139)
°**syllable** ['sɪləbl]: **stressed syllable** betonte Silbe

symbol ['sɪmbl] Symbol 5 (137)

T

table ['teɪbl]:
1. Tisch 2 (44)
2. Tabelle 3 (74)
°**tag** [tæg] Fangen *(Spiel)*
take [teɪk], *simple past:* **took** nehmen, mitnehmen; (weg-, hin)bringen 2 (60) **take place** stattfinden; spielen, sich abspielen *(Geschichte, Handlung)* 3 (86) **take photos** fotografieren 5 (126) °**take care of sb./sth.** sich um etwas/jn. kümmern °**take notes** sich Notizen machen °**take turns** sich abwechseln
talk [tɔːk]:
1. Vortrag, Referat, Rede 5 (126) **give a talk (about)** einen Vortrag / eine Rede halten (über) 5 (126)
2. talk (to) reden (mit), sich unterhalten (mit) HWG (16)
°**tall** [tɔːl] hoch, groß
task [tɑːsk] Aufgabe 1 (38)
taste [teɪst] schmecken 3 (87)
°**tattoo** [tə'tuː] Tätowierung
tea [tiː] Tee 2 (47)
teacher ['tiːtʃə] Lehrer/in HWG (16)
team [tiːm] Team, Mannschaft 1 (25)
°**tease sb.** [tiːz] sich über jn. lustig machen
°**technology** [tek'nɒlədʒi] Technologie **Information and Communications Technology** Informations- und Kommunikationstechnologie 1 (29)
°**teeth** [tiːθ] *plural of* **tooth**
telephone ['telɪfəʊn] Telefon HWG (17)
tell [tel], *simple past:* **told**: **tell sb. about sth.** jm. von etwas erzählen; jm. über etwas berichten 2 (52)
ten [ten] zehn HWG (8/9)
tennis ['tenɪs] Tennis 3 (70)
test [test] Test 1 (39)
text [tekst]:
1. text sb. jm. eine SMS schicken 2 (46)
2. Text (3)
°**than** [ðən]: **more than once** mehr als einmal
Thank you. ['θæŋk juː] Danke. HWG (17)
Thanks. ['θæŋks] Danke. 2 (47)
that [ðæt, ðət]:
1. it shows that … es zeigt, dass … 2 (61)
2. that group die Gruppe (dort), jene Gruppe 1 (37)
3. that's das ist HWG (13) **that's why** deshalb, darum 4 (117) **after that** danach 2 (46)
the [ðə] der, die, das; die HWG (8/9)
theatre ['θɪətə] Theater 4 (118)
their [ðeə] ihr 1 (20) **their first day** ihr erster Tag 1 (20)
them [ðem, ðəm] sie; ihnen 1 (32)
then [ðen] dann 1 (28)
there [ðeə] da, dort; dahin, dorthin 1 (22) **There are …** ['ðeər‿ɑː] Es sind … / Es gibt … HWG (13) **There's …** [ðeəz] Es ist/gibt … HWG (13)
these [ðiːz] diese (hier) 1 (32)
they [ðeɪ] sie *(Plural)* 1 (20) **they're (= they are)** sie sind … 1 (20)
thief [θiːf], *pl* **thieves** [θiːvz] Dieb/in 3 (87)
thing [θɪŋ] Sache, Ding, Gegenstand HWG (16)
think [θɪŋk], *simple past:* **thought** denken, glauben 2 (47) **think (about)** nachdenken (über) 1 (29) **think of sth.** sich etwas ausdenken; an etwas denken 4 (110)
third [θɜːd] dritte(r, s) 1 (31) **Third, …** Drittens, … 5 (134)
thirsty ['θɜːsti]: **be thirsty** durstig sein, Durst haben 3 (80)
this [ðɪs]:
1. This is … Dies ist … / Das ist … HWG (16)
2. this place/break/subject dieser Ort / diese Pause / dieses Fach 1 (32) °**this time** diesmal
those [ðəʊz] die … dort; jene … 1 (37)
thought [θɔːt] *simple past of* **think**
three [θriː] drei HWG (8/9)
threw [θruː] *simple past of* **throw**
through [θruː] durch 4 (118)
throw [θrəʊ], *simple past:* **threw** werfen 1 (28)
Thursday ['θɜːzdeɪ, 'θɜːzdi] Donnerstag HWG (11)
°**tick** [tɪk] ankreuzen, abhaken
ticket ['tɪkɪt]:
1. Eintrittskarte 3 (81)
2. Fahrkarte 5 (136)
°**tickle** ['tɪkl] kitzeln
°**tiger** ['taɪgə] Tiger
till [tɪl]: **till 1 o'clock** bis 1 Uhr 2 (53)
time [taɪm]:
1. Zeit; Uhrzeit HWG (15) **feeding time** Fütterungszeit 5 (126) **free time** Freizeit, freie Zeit 3 (74) **free-time activities** Freizeitaktivitäten 3 (74) °**time traveller** Zeitreisende(r) **What time is it?** Wie spät ist es? HWG (17)
2. Mal 4 (118)
timetable ['taɪmteɪbl] Stundenplan 1 (28)
tip [tɪp] Tipp HWG (8/9)
tired ['taɪəd] müde 3 (80)
title ['taɪtl] Titel, Überschrift 4 (110)
to [tu, tə]:
1. zu, nach HWG (8/9) **from … to …** von … bis … 3 (68/69)
2. Nice to meet you. Freut mich, dich/euch/Sie kennenzulernen. 1 (22)
3. quarter to eleven Viertel vor elf (10.45 / 22.45) HWG (17)
today [tə'deɪ] heute 3 (78)
together [tə'geðə] zusammen 4 (110)
toilet ['tɔɪlət] Toilette 1 (33)
told [təʊld] *simple past of* **tell**
tomato [tə'mɑːtəʊ], *pl* **tomatoes** Tomate 3 (89)
°**tongue-twister** ['tʌŋ twɪstə] Zungenbrecher
too [tuː]:
1. auch HWG (15)
2. too late/cold/big/… zu spät/kalt/groß/… 3 (76)
took [tʊk] *simple past of* **take**
°**tooth** [tuːθ], *pl* **teeth** [tiːθ] Zahn
top [tɒp]:
1. Spitze, oberes Ende 4 (118)
2. Spitzen- 4 (111)
3. Top, Oberteil 5 (122)
touch [tʌtʃ] berühren, anfassen HWG (16)
tour (of) ['tʊər‿əv] Rundgang, Rundfahrt, Reise (durch) HWG (10)
tourist ['tʊərɪst] Tourist/in 4 (118)
°**towards sb.** [tə'wɔːdz] jm. entgegen
tower ['taʊə] Turm HWG (10)
town [taʊn] Stadt HWG (8/9)
toy [tɔɪ] Spielzeug 2 (44)
tradition [trə'dɪʃn] Tradition 4 (118)
train [treɪn] Zug 4 (117)
trainer ['treɪnə] Turnschuh 1 (23)
training ['treɪnɪŋ] Training(sstunde) 3 (91)
°**trampoline** ['træmpəliːn] Trampolin
°**translate** [træns'leɪt] übersetzen
travel ['trævl] reisen 3 (81)
traveller ['trævələ] Reisende(r) 3 (81) °**time traveller** Zeitreisende(r)
tree [triː] Baum HWG (11)
trip [trɪp] Ausflug; Reise 4 (117) **go on a boat trip** einen Bootsausflug machen 4 (117)
trophy ['trəʊfi] Pokal; Trophäe 2 (47)
trouble ['trʌbl]: **be in trouble** in Schwierigkeiten sein; Ärger kriegen 2 (61)

true [truː] wahr 4 (103)
trumpet ['trʌmpɪt] Trompete 3 (89)
°**trunk** [trʌŋk] Rüssel
try [traɪ] (aus)probieren; versuchen 3 (74)
T-shirt ['tiːʃɜːt] T-Shirt 2 (60)
Tuesday ['tjuːzdeɪ, 'tjuːzdi] Dienstag HWG (11) **on Tuesday** am Dienstag HWG (12)
turkey ['tɜːki] Pute, Truthahn 2 (66)
turn around [ˌtɜːn‿ə'raʊnd]:
1. sich umdrehen 3 (80)
2. wenden, umdrehen 4 (112)
turn sth. on [ˌtɜːn‿'ɒn] etwas einschalten 3 (80)
turn [tɜːn]: **(It's) my turn.** Ich bin dran / an der Reihe. 5 (122) °**take turns** sich abwechseln *(etwas zu tun)* °**Whose turn is it?** Wer ist dran / Wer ist an der Reihe?
TV [ˌtiː'viː] Fernsehen, Fernsehgerät 2 (44)
twelve [twelv] zwölf HWG (8/9)
°**twice** [twaɪs] zweimal
twins *(pl)* [twɪnz] Zwillinge 2 (55)
two [tuː] zwei HWG (8/9) °**two by two** zu zweit; in Zweiergruppen
°**typical** ['tɪpɪkl] typisch

U

umbrella [ʌm'brelə] Schirm, Regenschirm 3 (70)
uncle ['ʌŋkl] Onkel 2 (52)
under ['ʌndə] unter 5 (130)
°**underlined** [ˌʌndə'laɪnd] unterstrichen
understand [ˌʌndə'stænd], *simple past:* **understood** verstehen 3 (87)
unfriendly [ʌn'frendli] unfreundlich 4 (117)
unhappy [ʌn'hæpi] unglücklich 4 (117)
uniform ['juːnɪfɔːm] Uniform 1 (20)
unit ['juːnɪt] Kapitel, Lektion (3)
united [ju'naɪtɪd] vereinigt 1 (42) **the United Kingdom UK)** [juˌnaɪtɪd 'kɪŋdəm] das Vereinigte Königreich 1 (42)
up [ʌp] hinauf, herauf; (nach) oben 4 (98/99) **up and down** auf und ab; rauf und runter 4 (98/99)
upstairs [ˌʌp'steəz] oben; nach oben *(im Haus)* 2 (45)
us [ʌs, əs] uns 2 (47)
use [juːz] benutzen, verwenden 3 (83)
°**useful** ['juːsfl] nützlich
usually ['juːʒuəli] meistens, normalerweise, gewöhnlich 2 (49)

V

vegetables *(pl)* ['vedʒtəblz] Gemüse 2 (56)
very ['veri] sehr 3 (70)
video ['vɪdiəʊ] Video 3 (68/69)
video camera ['vɪdiəʊ ˌkæmərə] Videokamera 2 (60)
view (of) [vjuː] Aussicht, Blick (auf) 5 (134)
village ['vɪlɪdʒ] Dorf 5 (130)
visit ['vɪzɪt]:
1. besuchen 3 (71)
2. Besuch 4 (101)
visitor ['vɪzɪtə] Besucher/in, Gast 3 (81)
vocabulary [və'kæbjələri] Vokabelverzeichnis, Wörterverzeichnis (3)
voice [vɔɪs] Stimme 3 (86)
vowel ['vaʊəl] Vokal, Selbstlaut 3 (84)

W

wait (for) [weɪt] warten (auf) 1 (20) **wait a minute** Warte einen Moment. / Moment mal. 1 (20)
wake up [ˌweɪk‿'ʌp], *simple past:* **woke up**:
1. aufwachen 2 (46)
°2. **wake sb. up** jn. wecken
walk [wɔːk]:
1. Spaziergang 2 (47) **go for a walk** spazieren gehen, einen Spaziergang machen 2 (47)
2. (zu Fuß) gehen 3 (86) °**walk around** herumlaufen
want [wɒnt]: **want sth.** etwas (haben) wollen 3 (71) **want to do sth.** etwas tun wollen 3 (71)
warm [wɔːm] warm 1 (40) °**warmest** ['wɔːmɪst] wärmste(r, s)
was [wɒz, wəz] *simple past of* **be**
°**wasp** [wɒsp] Wespe
watch [wɒtʃ]:
1. Armbanduhr HWG (16)
2. sich etwas anschauen; beobachten 1 (32) **watch TV** fernsehen 2 (44) **Watch out!** Pass auf! / Vorsicht! 1 (22)
watcher ['wɒtʃə] Beobachter/in 4 (106)
water ['wɔːtə] Wasser 2 (57)
way [weɪ]:
1. Weg 4 (98/99) **on the way to …** auf dem Weg zu/nach … 4 (98/99)
°2. Art, Weise **in different ways** auf verschiedene Weise
we [wiː] wir 1 (20)
wear [weə], *simple past:* **wore** tragen *(Kleidung)* 1 (23)
website ['websaɪt] Website 3 (68/69)
Wednesday ['wenzdeɪ, 'wenzdi] Mittwoch HWG (11)
week [wiːk] Woche HWG (11)
weekend [ˌwiːk'end] Wochenende 2 (47) **at the weekend** am Wochenende 2 (47)
weigh [weɪ] wiegen 4 (106)
Welcome to Plymouth. ['welkəm] Willkommen in Plymouth. HWG (10)
Welsh [welʃ] Walisisch; walisisch 1 (42)
Well, … [wel] Nun, … / Also, … / Na ja, … 2 (53)
went [went] *simple past of* **go**
were [wɜː, wə] *simple past of* **be**
wet [wet] nass 3 (70)
whale [weɪl] Wal HWG (14)
what? [wɒt] was? HWG (8/9) **What about you?** Und du/ihr? / Und was ist mit dir/euch? HWG (8/9) **What colour …?** Welche Farbe …? 1 (32) **What is the story about?** Wovon handelt die Geschichte? Worum geht es in der Geschichte? 4 (110) **What page are we on?** Auf welcher Seite sind wir? 1 (33) **What programmes …?** Welche Programme …? / Welche Art von Programmen …? 3 (76) **What time is it?** Wie spät ist es? HWG (17) **What would you like?** Was hättest du gern? / Was möchtest du? 2 (56) **What would you like to eat?** Was möchtest du essen? 2 (56) **What's your name?** Wie heißt du? / Wie heißt ihr? HWG (8/9) **What's for lunch?** Was gibt es zum Mittagessen? 2 (56) **What's for homework?** Was haben wir als Hausaufgabe auf? 1 (33) °**What's next?** Was kommt als Nächstes? **What's she like?** Wie ist sie (so)? 3 (71)
wheel [wiːl]: **big wheel** Riesenrad HWG (10)
when [wen]:
1. wenn 3 (79)
2. als 4 (98/99)
3. **when?** wann? 1 (31) **When's your birthday?** Wann hast du Geburtstag? 1 (31)
where? [weə] wo? / wohin? HWG (8/9) **Where are you from?** Woher kommst du? HWG (8/9)

which? [wɪtʃ] welche(r, s)? 1 (39) **Which words ...?** Welche Wörter ...? 1 (39)
white [waɪt] weiß HWG (15)
who? [huː] wer? HWG (11)
°**whole** [həʊl] ganze(r, s), gesamte(r, s)
whose? [huːz] wessen? 4 (97)
why? [waɪ] warum? 2 (61) **that's why** deshalb, darum 4 (117)
wild [waɪld] wild 4 (106)
win [wɪn], *simple past:* **won** gewinnen 1 (32)
window ['wɪndəʊ] Fenster HWG (16)
winner ['wɪnə] Gewinner/in, Sieger/in 1 (32)
winter ['wɪntə] Winter 1 (42)
wish [wɪʃ] Wunsch 2 (67) **make a wish** sich etwas wünschen 4 (102)
with [wɪð]
1. mit HWG (15)
2. bei 2 (61)
without [wɪ'ðaʊt] ohne HWG (15)
woke [wəʊk] *simple past of* **wake**
woman ['wʊmən], *pl* **women** ['wɪmɪn] Frau 1 (37)
won [wʌn] *simple past of* **win**
°**woof** [wʊf] wau, wau
word [wɜːd] Wort HWG (8/9) °**group word** Obergriff **word order** Wortstellung 3 (83)
wordbank ['wɜːdˌbæŋk] „Wortspeicher" (3)
wore [wɔː] *simple past of* **wear**
work [wɜːk]
1. arbeiten 1 (32)
2. Arbeit 3 (71)
workbook ['wɜːkbʊk] Arbeitsheft 1 (33)
world [wɜːld] Welt 4 (118) **in the world** auf der Welt 4 (118)
worried ['wʌrid] besorgt, beunruhigt 2 (60)
would [wʊd]: **What would you like?** Was hättest du gern? / Was möchtest du? 2 (56) **What would you like to eat?** Was möchtest du essen? 2 (56) °**he'd (= he would) let us in** er würde uns hereinlassen **I'd (= I would) like ...** Ich möchte ... 2 (56)
°**wrap** [ræp] wickeln
write [raɪt], *simple past:* **wrote** schreiben 1 (31) °**write down** aufschreiben
wrong [rɒŋ]:
1. falsch, verkehrt HWG (13)
2. sb. is wrong jemand irrt sich; jemand hat Unrecht 4 (112)
wrote [rəʊt] *simple past of* **write**

Y

year [jɪə]:
1. Jahr HWG (8/9)
2. Jahrgang(sstufe) 1 (20)
yellow ['jeləʊ] gelb HWG (15)
yes [jes] ja HWG (13)
yesterday ['jestədeɪ, 'jestədi] gestern 4 (96)
yet [jet]: **not ... yet** noch nicht 5 (130)
yoga ['jəʊgə] Yoga 3 (72)
yoghurt ['jɒgət] Joghurt 1 (36)
you [juː] du; Sie; ihr; dir; dich; euch; Ihnen HWG (8/9)
young [jʌŋ] jung 3 (68/69)

Early finisher – answers

1 ***Coombe Dean School***

2 Photo B.
0 ball • 3 books • 5 cards • 2 CD • 1 clock • 0 computer • 1 DVD • 1 glue stick • 1 lamp • 1 map • 4 pens • 2 pencils • 0 pencil case • 2 photos • 2 rubbers • 1 ruler • 0 sharpener • 1 telephone

3 a) *There is no "**k**" in Ann's activity, so she doesn't go **skating**.*
b) *There is no "**g**" at the end of Leo's activity, so he plays **football** or does **judo**.*
c) *Henry's activity has eight letters in it, so he plays **football** or goes **swimming**.*
d) *Leo's activity does not have four letters (**judo**), so he plays **football**.*
*Henry doesn't play **football**, so he goes **swimming**.*
*So Ann does **judo**.*
*And Maria goes **skating**.*
Leo plays football, Henry goes swimming, Maria goes skating and Ann does judo.

4 a) *Not October but **Mary**. ("Mary's mum ...")*
b) *It's **your** name: "You're the driver ..."*
c) *Tuesday, Thursday and **today**.*
d) *No boat is nearer, because the two boats **meet**.*
e) *The letter **S**: Plym**S**tock.*
f) *You are the most intelligent animal.*

5 1 *Silky, page 8: Are you a boy or a girl?*
2 *Morph, page 21: I'm Morph, I'm Morph from Plymstock School.*
3 *Silky, page 11: Hey, hey Hoe, here we go!*
4 *Sam, page 36: Go and find the yoghurt, little sister!*
5 *Sam, page 56: Roast beef with roast potatoes? Yummy!*
6 *Sam, page 70: What's grey and never gets wet?*
7 *A man near the harbour, page 60: Boat tours! See all the navy ships!*
8 *Abby, page 113: She looks so soft. Call her Silky.*
9 *The captain's ghost, page 87: Stop! Thieves! Give me back my book!*
10 *Tim Blackwell, page 47: Help! A mad sister and a mad dog!*

Das **German – English Dictionary** enthält den **Lernwortschatz** von *Access Bayern 5*.
Es kann dir eine erste Hilfe sein, wenn du vergessen hast, wie etwas auf Englisch heißt.

Wenn du wissen möchtest, wo das entsprechende englische Wort zum ersten Mal in deinem Schülerbuch vorkommt, dann kannst du im **English – German Dictionary** (S. 243–257) nachschlagen.

Im **German – English Dictionary** werden folgende **Abkürzungen** verwendet:

sth. = something (etwas) sb. = somebody (jemand) jn. = jemanden jm. = jemandem
pl = *plural* (Mehrzahl) *infml* = *informal* (umgangssprachlich)

A

ab: auf und ab up and down [ˌʌp‿ən ˈdaʊn]
Abend evening [ˈiːvnɪŋ] **am Abend** in the evening **zu Abend essen** have dinner [ˈdɪnə]
Abendbrot, Abendessen dinner [ˈdɪnə]
abends in the evening [ˈiːvnɪŋ]
aber but [bʌt], [bət]
abfahren leave [liːv]
Abneigungen: Vorlieben und Abneigungen likes and dislikes *(pl)* [ˌlaɪks‿ən ˈdɪslaɪks]
Absatz *(in einem Text)* paragraph [ˈpærəgrɑːf]
abschreiben copy [ˈkɒpi]
abspielen *(CD usw.)* play [pleɪ] **sich abspielen** *(Geschichte, Handlung)* take place
acht eight [eɪt]
addieren (zu) add (to) [æd]
Adresse address [əˈdres]
Affe monkey [ˈmʌŋki]
Aktivität activity [ækˈtɪvəti]
albern silly [ˈsɪli]
alle all [ɔːl]; *(jeder)* everyone [ˈevriwʌn], everybody [ˈevribɒdi]
alleinstehend *(ledig)* single [ˈsɪŋgl]
alles all [ɔːl]; everything [ˈevriθɪŋ]
Alltags- everyday [ˈevrideɪ]
als **1.** *(zeitlich)* when [wen] **2. als Erstes** first [fɜːst]
also **1.** *(deshalb, daher)* so [səʊ] **2. Also, …** Well, … [wel]
alt old [əʊld] **Ich bin zwei Jahre alt.** I'm two years old. **Wie alt bist du?** How old are you?
Alter age [eɪdʒ]
am **1.** *(in Ortsangaben)* at [æ], [ət] **am Meer** by the sea [baɪ] **2.** *(in Zeitangaben)* **am Abend** in the evening **am Montag/Dienstag/…** on Monday/Tuesday/… **am Morgen** in the morning **am Nachmittag** in the afternoon **am Samstagmorgen** on Saturday afternoon **am Wochenende** at the weekend
Ameise ant [ænt]
amtlich, Amts- official [əˈfɪʃl]
amüsieren: sich amüsieren have fun [fʌn]
an *(in Ortsangaben)* at [æ], [ət] **an britischen Schulen** at British schools
anbauen *(anpflanzen)* grow [grəʊ]
andere(r, s) other [ˈʌðə] **ein anderer …/eine andere …/ein anderes …** another … [əˈnʌðə]
anders *(verschieden)* different [ˈdɪfrənt]
anfangen start [stɑːt]
anfassen touch [tʌtʃ]
anhalten stop [stɒp]
anhören **1. sich etwas anhören** listen to sth. [ˈlɪsn] **Hör dir/Hört euch den Song an.** Listen to the song. **2. sich gut anhören** *(gut klingen)* sound good [saʊnd]
ankommen arrive [əˈraɪv]
anlächeln: jn. anlächeln smile at sb. [smaɪl]
anordnen *(in eine bestimmte Ordnung bringen)* arrange [əˈreɪndʒ]
anpflanzen grow [grəʊ]
Anruf phone call [ˈfəʊn kɔːl], *(kurz auch:)* call
anrufen call [kɔːl]; phone [fəʊn]
anschauen: sich etwas anschauen watch sth. [wɒtʃ]; look at sth. [lʊk]
anschließen: sich einem Klub anschließen join a club [dʒɔɪn]
Anschrift address [əˈdres]
ansehen: sich etwas ansehen watch sth. [wɒtʃ]; look at sth. [lʊk]
Anspitzer sharpener [ˈʃɑːpnə]
Antwort answer [ˈɑːnsə]
antworten answer [ˈɑːnsə]
Apostroph apostrophe [əˈpɒstrəfi]
April April [ˈeɪprəl]
Aquarienhaus aquarium [əˈkweəriəm]
Aquarium aquarium [əˈkweəriəm]
Arbeit work [wɜːk]; *(Job, Stelle)* job [dʒɒb]
arbeiten work [wɜːk]
Arbeitsheft workbook [ˈwɜːkbʊk]
Ärger kriegen/haben be in trouble [ˈtrʌbl]
arm poor [pɔː], [pʊə]
Armbanduhr watch [wɒtʃ]
Art: eine Art (von) … a kind of … [kaɪnd]
auch: auch aus Berlin from Berlin too [tuː]; also from Berlin [ˈɔːlsəʊ] **Ich auch.** Me too. **auch nicht** not … either [ˈaɪðə, ˈiːðə]
auf on [ɒn] **auf das Boot (hinauf)** onto the boat [ˈɒntʊ] **auf dem Bild/Foto** in the picture/photo **auf dem Dachboden** in the attic **auf der Welt** in the world **auf einmal** suddenly **auf dem Weg zu/nach …** on the way to … **auf der Landkarte/dem Stadtplan** on the map **auf Deutsch/Englisch** in German/English **auf und ab** up and down **Auf welcher Seite sind wir?** What page are we on? **Auf Wiedersehen.** Goodbye.; Bye-bye.; Bye.
Aufgabe task; exercise [ˈeksəsaɪz]
aufgeregt *(gespannt)* excited [ɪkˈsaɪtɪd]; *(nervös)* nervous [ˈnɜːvəs]
aufmachen open [ˈəʊpən]
aufregend exciting [ɪkˈsaɪtɪŋ]
aufstehen stand up [ˌstænd‿ˈʌp]; get up [ˌget‿ˈʌp]; *(aus dem Bett)* get up
aufwachen wake up [ˌweɪk‿ˈʌp]
Auge eye [aɪ]
Augenblick moment [ˈməʊmənt]
August August [ˈɔːgəst]
aus from [frɒm], [frəm] **aus … heraus/hinaus** out of … [ˈaʊt‿əv] **Ich bin aus/komme aus Plymouth.** I'm from Plymouth.
ausdenken: sich etwas ausdenken think of sth. [θɪŋk]

Ausdruck *(Redewendung)* phrase [freɪz]
Ausflug trip [trɪp]
ausgezeichnet excellent ['eksələnt]
auskennen: sich mit etwas auskennen know about sth.
Auslassungszeichen *(Apostroph)* apostrophe [ə'pɒstrəfi]
ausprobieren try [traɪ]
Ausrüstung kit [kɪt]
aussehen: glücklich/wütend/... aussehen look happy/angry/...
Aussicht (auf) view (of) [vjuː]
Aussprache pronunciation [prəˌnʌnsi'eɪʃn]
aussteigen get off [ˌget‿'ɒf] **aus dem Bus/Boot aussteigen** get off the bus/boat
aussuchen: (sich) etwas aussuchen choose sth. [tʃuːz]
auswählen: etwas auswählen choose sth. [tʃuːz]
Auto car [kɑː] **mit dem Auto fahren** go by car
Autor/in author ['ɔːθə]

B

Bad, Badezimmer bathroom ['bɑːθruːm]
bald soon [suːn] **Bis bald.** See you (later).
Ball ball [bɔːl]
Band *(Musikgruppe)* band [bænd]
Bär bear [beə]
Basketball basketball ['bɑːskɪtbɔːl]
Bauer/Bäuerin farmer ['fɑːmə]
Bauernhof farm [fɑːm]
Baum tree [triː]
Bayern Bavaria [bə'veəriə]
beantworten answer ['ɑːnsə]
bearbeiten *(Texte, Videos)* edit ['edɪt]
beeilen: sich beeilen hurry up [ˌhʌri‿'ʌp]
beenden: etwas beenden finish sth. ['fɪnɪʃ]
befragen: jn. befragen interview sb. ['ɪntəvjuː]
beginnen start [stɑːt]
bei *(in Ortsangaben)* at [æt], [ət] **bei den Blackwells zu Hause** at the Blackwells' house **bei jm. sein** be with sb. [wɪð]
Beifall klatschen clap [klæp]
Bein leg [leg]
beinahe almost ['ɔːlməʊst]
beißen bite [baɪt]
bekommen get [get]
beliebt (bei) popular (with) ['pɒpjələ]
bellen bark [bɑːk]
benötigen need [niːd]
benutzen use [juːz]
beobachten watch [wɒtʃ]
Beobachter/in watcher ['wɒtʃə]
Bereich area ['eəriə]
bereit ready ['redi]
Berg mountain ['maʊntən]
berichten: jm. etwas berichten tell sb. about sth. [tel]
berühmt (für, wegen) famous (for ['feɪməs]
berühren touch [tʌtʃ]
beschäftigt sein *(viel zu tun haben)* be busy ['bɪzi]
Bescheid: über etwas Bescheid wissen know about sth.
beschließen decide [dɪ'saɪd]
besondere(r, s) special ['speʃl]
besorgt worried ['wʌrid]
besser better ['betə]
beste(r, s) best [best] **ihr bester Freund / ihre beste Freundin** her best friend
Besuch visit ['vɪzɪt]
besuchen: jn. besuchen visit sb. ['vɪzɪt]; see sb. [siː]
Besucher/in visitor ['vɪzɪtə]
Betonung stress [stres]
Bett bed [bed]
beunruhigt worried ['wʌrid]
Beutel bag [bæg]
bevor before [bɪ'fɔː]
bewegen; sich bewegen move [muːv]
Bibliothek library ['laɪbrəri]
Bild picture ['pɪktʃə] **auf dem Bild** in the picture
Bildunterschrift caption ['kæpʃn]
billig cheap [tʃiːp]
bis *(zeitlich)* till [tɪl] **bis zwölf Uhr** till twelve o'clock **Bis bald. / Bis nachher.** See you later. **von ... bis ...** from ... to ...
bisschen: ein bisschen traurig a bit sad [bɪt]
bitte please [pliːz]
bitten: jemanden bitten, etwas zu tun ask sb. to do sth. [ɑːsk]
blau blue [bluː]
bleiben stay [steɪ]
Bleistift pencil ['pensl]
Blick (auf) *(Aussicht)* view (of) [vjuː]
blöd *(albern)* silly ['sɪli]
blond blond *(bei Frauen oft:* blonde) [blɒnd]
bloß only ['əʊnli]; *(einfach nur)* just [dʒʌst]
Boot boat [bəʊt] **einen Bootsausflug machen** go on a boat trip
brauchen need [niːd]
braun brown [braʊn]
brechen *(kaputt gehen)* break [breɪk]
Brief letter ['letə]
bringen *(weg-, hinbringen)* take [teɪk]; *(mit-, herbringen)* bring [brɪŋ]
britisch British ['brɪtɪʃ]
Brot bread [bred]
Bruder brother ['brʌðə]
Buch book [bʊk]
Bücherei library ['laɪbrəri]
Buchhandlung bookshop ['bʊkʃɒp]
Buchstabe letter ['letə]
buchstabieren spell [spel]
Burg castle ['kɑːsl]
Bus bus **mit dem Bus fahren** go by bus

C

Café café ['kæfeɪ]
Chaos chaos ['keɪɒs]
Computer computer [kəm'pjuːtə]
cool cool [kuːl]
Cornflakes cornflakes ['kɔːnfleɪks]
Cousin, Cousine cousin ['kʌzn]

D

da, dahin *(dort, dorthin)* there [ðeə]
Dachboden attic ['ætɪk] **auf dem Dachboden** in the attic
daheim at home [ət 'həʊm]
daher *(deshalb)* so [səʊ]
danach after that
Danke. Thank you. ['θæŋk juː]; Thanks. **Danke, gut.** Fine, thanks.
dann then [ðen]
darum that's why
das *(Artikel)* the [ðə]
das (dort) that [ðæt] **das (dort) ist ...** that's ... **das (dort) sind ...** those are ...
dass that [ðæt], [ðət] **es zeigt, dass ...** it shows that ...
dasselbe the same [seɪm]
Deck deck [dek]
dein(e) ... your ... [jɔː], [jə]
denken think [θɪŋk] **an etwas denken** think of sth.
denn: Was ist denn? What's the matter? ['mætə]
der *(Artikel)* the [ðə]
der ... (dort) that ... [ðæt] **der ... (hier)** this ... [ðɪs]

der *(Relativpronomen)*: **Finde jemanden, der ...** Find someone who ...
derselbe the same [seɪm]
deshalb so [səʊ]; that's why
Design design [dɪ'zaɪn]
deuten: auf etwas deuten *(zeigen)* point to sth. [pɔɪnt]
Deutsch; deutsch German ['dʒɜːmən]
Dezember December [dɪ'sembə]
dich you [juː]
dicht (bei, an) close (to) [kləʊs]
dick fat [fæt]
die *(Artikel)* the [ðə]
die ... (dort) *(Singular)* that ... [ðæt]; *(Plural)* those ... [ðəʊz] **die ... (hier)** *(Singular)* this ... [ðɪs]; *(Plural)* these ... [ðiːz]
dieselbe(n) wie the same [seɪm]
Dieb/in thief [θiːf], *pl* thieves [θiːvz]
Dienstag Tuesday ['tjuːzdeɪ, 'tjuːzdi]
dies (hier) this [ðɪs] **dies (hier) ist ...** this is ... **dies (hier) sind ...** these are ...
diese(r, s): dieser Ort / diese Pause / dieses Fach this place/ break/subject **diese Orte/Pausen/Fächer** these places/breaks/ subjects
Ding thing [θɪŋ]
Dinosaurier dinosaur ['daɪnəsɔː]
dir you [juː]
Disko disco ['dɪskəʊ]
Donnerstag Thursday ['θɜːzdeɪ, 'θɜːzdi]
Doppel- double ['dʌbl]
Dorf village ['vɪlɪdʒ]
dort, dorthin there [ðeə]
dran: Ich bin dran. (It's) my turn. [tɜːn]
draußen outside [,aʊt'saɪd] **nach draußen** outside
drei three [θriː]
drinnen inside [,ɪn'saɪd] **nach drinnen** inside
dritte(r, s) third [θɜːd] **Drittens, ...** Third, ...
drücken *(schieben, stoßen)* push [pʊʃ]
du you [juː]
Dummerchen silly ['sɪli]
dunkel dark [dɑːk]
durch through [θruː]
dürfen: du darfst es nicht tun you mustn't do it ['mʌsnt]
Durst haben be thirsty ['θɜːsti]
durstig sein be thirsty ['θɜːsti]
DVD DVD [,diːviː'diː]

E

Ecke corner ['kɔːnə] **Laden an der Ecke** *(„Tante-Emma-Laden")* corner shop ['kɔːnə ʃɒp]
ehemalige(r, s) former ['fɔːmə]
Ei egg [eg]
ein(e) *(Artikel)* a, an [ə], [ən] **ein anderer .../eine andere .../ein anderes ...** another ... [ə'nʌðə] **ein paar** *(einige)* some [sʌm], [səm]
einfach 1. *(nicht schwierig)* easy ['iːzi] **2. einfach nur** just [dʒʌst]
einhundert a hundred, one hundred ['hʌndrəd]
einige some [sʌm], [səm]
einigen: sich auf etwas einigen agree on sth. [ə'griː]
einkaufen gehen go shopping ['ʃɒpɪŋ]
Einkaufszentrum shopping centre; shopping mall ['ʃɒpɪŋ mɔːl], *(kurz auch:)* mall
Einladung (zu, nach) invitation (to) [,ɪnvɪ'teɪʃn]
einmal once [wʌns] **auf einmal** *(plötzlich)* suddenly ['sʌdnli] **noch einmal** again [ə'gen]
eins one [wʌn]
einsam lonely ['ləʊnli]
einschalten: etwas einschalten turn sth. on [,tɜːn_'ɒn]
einschlafen fall asleep [,fɔːl_ə'sliːp]
eintreffen arrive [ə'raɪv]
eintreten: in einen Klub eintreten join a club [dʒɔɪn]
Eintrittskarte ticket ['tɪkɪt]
Eis *(Speiseeis)* ice cream [,aɪs 'kriːm]
Elefant elephant ['elɪfənt]
elf eleven [ɪ'levn]
Eltern parents ['peərənts]
E-Mail email ['iːmeɪl]
Ende end [end] **zu Ende sein** be over ['əʊvə]
enden finish ['fɪnɪʃ]
endlich *(schließlich)* at last [ət 'lɑːst]
Endspiel final ['faɪnl]
Endung ending ['endɪŋ]
Englisch; englisch English ['ɪŋglɪʃ]
entlang: die Straße/den Fluss/... entlang along the street/the river/ ... [ə'lɒŋ]
entscheiden: sich entscheiden decide [dɪ'saɪd]
Entschuldigung. *(Tut mir leid.)* (I'm) sorry. ['sɒri]
er 1. *(männliche Person)* he [hiː] **2.** *(Ding; Tier)* it [ɪt]
ergänzen (zu) add (to) [æd]
erinnern: sich an etwas erinnern remember sth. [rɪ'membə]
erklären: jm. etwas erklären explain sth. to sb. [ɪk'spleɪn]
erläutern: jm. etwas erläutern explain sth. to sb. [ɪk'spleɪn]
erraten guess [ges]
erst only ['əʊnli]
erste(r, s) first [fɜːst] **als Erstes** first **der erste Tag** the first day **Erstens, ...** First, ...
erzählen (von) tell (about) [tel]
Erzählung story ['stɔːri]
erzielen: einen Treffer erzielen score [skɔː]
es it [ɪt] **es ist ... / es gibt ...** there's ... **es sind ... / es gibt ...** there are ... **Ach, du bist es.** Oh, it's you. **Bist du es?** Is that you?
essen eat [iːt] **zu Abend / zu Mittag essen** have dinner / have lunch
Essen *(Lebensmittel)* food [fuːd]
Esszimmer dining room ['daɪnɪŋ ruːm]
etwas 1. something ['sʌmθɪŋ]; *(in Fragen)* anything ['eniθɪŋ] **2.** *(ein bisschen)* some [sʌm], [səm] **etwas traurig** a bit sad
euch you [juː]
euer .../eure ... your ... [jɔː], [jə]

F

Fähre ferry ['feri]
fahren go [gəʊ]; *(ein Auto)* drive [draɪv]; *(abfahren)* leave [liːv] **mit dem Bus/Auto fahren** go by bus/ car **Rad fahren** ride a bike [,raɪd_ə 'baɪk]
Fahrkarte ticket ['tɪkɪt]
Fahrrad bike [baɪk]
Fahrt ride [raɪd]
fair fair [feə]
fallen *(stürzen)* fall [fɔːl]
falls if [ɪf]
falsch wrong [rɒŋ] **Nein, das ist falsch.** No, that's wrong.
Familie family ['fæməli] **Familie Blackwell** the Blackwell family
Fan fan [fæn]
fangen catch [kætʃ]
fantastisch fantastic [fæn'tæstɪk]
Farbe colour ['kʌlə]
Farm farm [fɑːm]
fast almost ['ɔːlməʊst]
Februar February ['februəri]
Federmäppchen pencil case ['pensl keɪs]

fehlen: die fehlenden Wörter the missing words ['mɪsɪŋ]
Fels, Felsen rock [rɒk]
Fenster window ['wɪndəʊ]
Ferien holidays *(pl)* ['hɒlədeɪz]
fernsehen watch TV [ˌwɒtʃ tiː'viː]
Fernsehen, Fernsehgerät TV [ˌtiː'viː]
fertig **1. mit etwas fertig werden/sein** finish sth. ['fɪnɪʃ] **Wir sind fertig.** *(Wir haben es erledigt.)* We're finished. ['fɪnɪʃt]
2. *(bereit)* ready ['redi] **Wir sind fertig.** *(Wir sind bereit.)* We're ready.
fett fat [fæt]
Figur *(in Roman, Film, Theaterstück usw.)* character ['kærəktə]
Film film [fɪlm]
filmen film [fɪlm]
Filzstift felt pen [ˌfelt 'pen]
Finale final ['faɪnl]
finden find [faɪnd] **Freunde finden** make friends **Wie findest du ...?** How do you like ...?
Fisch fish [fɪʃ], *pl* fish
Flasche bottle ['bɒtl]
Fleck spot [spɒt]
Fleisch meat [miːt]
Fluss river ['rɪvə]
folgen follow ['fɒləʊ]
Form (von) form (of) [fɔːm]
fort away [ə'weɪ]
fortfahren *(weiterreden)* go on [ˌgəʊ_'ɒn]
Foto photo ['fəʊtəʊ] **auf dem Foto** in the photo **Fotos machen** take photos
Fotoapparat camera ['kæmərə]
fotografieren take photos [ˌteɪk 'fəʊtəʊz]
Frage question ['kwestʃn] **eine Frage stellen** ask a question
fragen ask [ɑːsk]
Französisch; französisch French [frentʃ]
Frau **1.** woman ['wʊmən], *pl* women ['wɪmɪn]
2. Frau Schwarz Mrs Schwarz ['mɪsɪz]
3. *(übliche Anrede von Lehrerinnen)* **Frau Bell** Miss Bell [mɪs]
frei free [friː]
Freitag Friday ['fraɪdeɪ], ['fraɪdi]
Freizeit free time [ˌfriː 'taɪm]
Freizeitaktivitäten free-time activities [ˌfriːtaɪm_æk'tɪvətiz]
freuen: Freut mich, dich/euch/Sie kennenzulernen. Nice to meet you.
Freund/in friend [frend] **Freunde finden** make friends
freundlich friendly ['frendli]
Freut mich, dich/euch/Sie kennenzulernen. Nice to meet you.
frieren be cold [kəʊld]
froh *(glücklich)* happy ['hæpi] **Frohe Weinachten!** Merry Christmas!
Frosch frog [frɒg]
Frucht fruit [fruːt]
früh early ['ɜːli]
frühere(r, s) former ['fɔːmə]
Frühling spring [sprɪŋ]
Frühstück breakfast ['brekfəst]
frühstücken have breakfast
fühlen; sich fühlen feel [fiːl]
Füller pen [pen]
fünf five [faɪv]
für for [fɔː], [fə]
Fuß: zu Fuß gehen walk [wɔːk]
Fußball football ['fʊtbɔːl]
Fußboden floor [flɔː]
Futter food [fuːd]
füttern feed [fiːd]
Fütterungszeit feeding time ['fiːdɪŋ taɪm]

G

ganz: das ganze Plymouth, ganz Plymouth all of Plymouth **den ganzen Tag (lang)** all day
gar nichts nothing ['nʌθɪŋ]
Garage garage ['gærɑːʒ], ['gærɪdʒ]
Garten garden ['gɑːdn]
Gartenarbeit gardening ['gɑːdnɪŋ]
Gärtnern gardening ['gɑːdnɪŋ]
Gast *(Besucher/in)* visitor ['vɪzɪtə]
gebackene Kartoffeln *(im Backofen in Fett gebacken)* roast potatoes [rəʊst pə'teɪtəʊz]
geben give [gɪv] **Es gibt ...** *(Singular)* There's ...; *(Plural)* There are ... **Gibt es (irgendwelche) ...?** Are there any ...? ['eni] **Was gibt es zum Mittagessen?** What's for lunch?
Gebiet area ['eəriə]
Geburt birth [bɜːθ]
Geburtstag birthday ['bɜːθdeɪ] **Ich habe am 5. Mai Geburtstag.** My birthday is on 5th May. **Ich habe im Mai Geburtstag.** My birthday is in May. **Wann hast du Geburtstag?** When's your birthday?
gefährlich dangerous ['deɪndʒərəs]
gefallen: Wie gefällt dir ...? How do you like ...?
Gefängnis prison ['prɪzn]
Gefühl feeling ['fiːlɪŋ]
gegen against [ə'genst]
Gegend area ['eəriə]
Gegenteil opposite ['ɒpəzɪt]
gehen go [gəʊ]; *(zu Fuß gehen)* walk [wɔːk] **einkaufen gehen** go shopping ['ʃɒpɪŋ] **Los geht's. / Jetzt geht's los.** Here we go. **nach Hause gehen** go home **segeln gehen** go sailing ['seɪlɪŋ] **spazieren gehen** go for a walk [wɔːk] **Wie geht's? / Wie geht es dir/euch/Ihnen?** How are you? **Worum geht es in der Geschichte?** What is the story about? **Es geht um eine Möwe.** It's about a seagull.
gehören: zu etwas gehören *(zu etwas passen)* go with sth.
Geist ghost [gəʊst]
gelangen *(hinkommen)* get [get]
gelb yellow ['jeləʊ]
Geld money ['mʌni]
gemischt mixed [mɪkst]
Gemüse vegetables *(pl)* ['vedʒtəblz]
genannt werden *(heißen)* be called [kɔːld]
genug enough [ɪ'nʌf]
geöffnet open ['əʊpən]
Geografie geography [dʒi'ɒgrəfi]
gerade *(im Moment)* at the moment ['məʊmənt]
Geräusch sound [saʊnd]; *(Lärm)* noise [nɔɪz]
gern: Ich tanze/singe/... gern. I like dancing/singing/... **Ich hätte gern ...** I'd like ... [ˌaɪd 'laɪk] (= I would like ...) **Ich würde gern gehen.** I'd like to go. **Ich würde sehr gern ...** I'd love to ... **Was hättest du gern?** What would you like? [wʊd]
gernhaben like [laɪk]
Geschäft *(Laden)* shop [ʃɒp]
geschehen (mit) happen (to) ['hæpən]
Geschenk present ['preznt]
Geschichte **1.** *(vergangene Zeiten)* history ['hɪstri]
2. *(Erzählung)* story ['stɔːri]
geschieden divorced [dɪ'vɔːst]
geschlossen closed [kləʊzd]
Gesicht face [feɪs]
gespannt *(aufgeregt)* excited [ɪk'saɪtɪd]
Gespenst ghost [gəʊst]
gestern yesterday ['jestədeɪ], ['jestədi]
Getränk drink [drɪŋk]
gewinnen win [wɪn]
Gewinner/in winner ['wɪnə]

gewöhnlich *(normalerweise)* usually ['ju:ʒuəli]
Giraffe giraffe [dʒə'rɑ:f]
Gitarre guitar [gɪ'tɑ:] **Gitarre spielen** play the guitar
glauben *(denken)* think [θɪŋk]
Glocke bell [bel]
Glück: Viel Glück! Good luck! [lʌk] **Glück haben** be lucky ['lʌki]
glücklich happy ['hæpi]
Gold gold [gəʊld]
Grafschaft *(in Großbritannien)* county ['kaʊnti]
Gras grass [grɑ:s]
grau grey [greɪ]
groß big [bɪg]; large [lɑ:dʒ] **der/die/das größte ...; die größten ...** the biggest ... ['bɪgɪst]
großartig great [greɪt]
Großbuchstabe capital letter [ˌkæpɪtl 'letə]
Größe size [saɪz]
Großeltern grandparents ['grænpeərənts]
Großmutter grandmother ['grænmʌðə]
Großstadt city ['sɪti]
Großvater grandfather ['grænfɑ:ðə]
grün green [gri:n]
Grund *(Begründung)* reason ['ri:zn]
Gruppe group (of) [gru:p]
gruselig scary ['skeəri]
Grüß Gott. Hello. [hə'ləʊ]
gut good [gʊd] **gut sein in Kung-Fu / gut Kung-Fu können** be good at kung fu **Danke, gut.** Fine, thanks. **Guten Morgen.** Good morning. [gʊd 'mɔ:nɪŋ]
Güter goods *(pl)* [gʊdz]
Gymnastik gymnastics [dʒɪm'næstɪks]

H

Haar, Haare hair [heə]
haben have [hæv], [həv]; have got [hæv 'gɒt], [həv 'gɒt] **Durst haben** be thirsty ['θɜ:sti] **Glück haben** be lucky **Hunger haben** be hungry ['hʌŋgri] **Ich habe im Mai Geburtstag.** My birthday is in May. **jemand hat Recht** someone is right **jemand hat Unrecht** someone is wrong **viel zu tun haben** *(beschäftigt sein)* be busy ['bɪzi] **Wann hast du Geburtstag?** When's your birthday?
Hafen harbour ['hɑ:bə]
Hafenstadt port [pɔ:t]
Hai shark [ʃɑ:k]
halb elf (10.30 / 22.30) half past ten ['hɑ:f pɑ:st]
Halbzeit half [hɑ:f], *pl* halves [hɑ:vz]
Hälfte half [hɑ:f], *pl* halves [hɑ:vz]
Hallo. Hello. [hə'ləʊ]
halten hold [həʊld] **einen Vortrag/eine Rede halten (über)** give a talk (about)
Hand hand [hænd]
handeln: Es handelt von einer Möwe. It's about a seagull. **Wovon handelt die Geschichte?** What is the story about?
Handy mobile phone [ˌməʊbaɪl 'fəʊn], *(kurz auch:)* mobile
hart hard [hɑ:d]
Hauptstadt capital ['kæpɪtl]
Haus house [haʊs] **nach Hause gehen** go home **nach Hause kommen** come home **zu Hause** at home
Hausaufgabe(n) homework ['həʊmwɜ:k] **Hausaufgaben machen** do my / your / ... homework **Was haben wir als Hausaufgabe auf?** What's for homework?
Haustier pet [pet]
Heiligabend Christmas Eve [ˌkrɪsməs‿'i:v]
Heim *(Zuhause)* home [həʊm]
Heimatstadt hometown [ˌhəʊm'taʊn]
heiß hot [hɒt]
heißen *(genannt werden)* be called [kɔ:ld] **Es heißt hier: ...** It says here: ... **Ich heiße ...** My name is ... **Wie heißt du?** What's your name?
helfen help [help]
hell bright [braɪt]
herauf up [ʌp]
heraus: aus ... heraus out of ... ['aʊt‿əv]
herbringen bring [brɪŋ]
Herbst autumn ['ɔ:təm]
hereinkommen come in [ˌkʌm‿'ɪn]
Herr Schwarz Mr Schwarz ['mɪstə]
herrennen: hinter jm. herrennen run after sb. [ˌrʌn‿'ɑ:ftə]
herunter down [daʊn]
Heuler *(Robbenjunges)* baby seal ['beɪbi si:l]
heute today [tə'deɪ]
hervorragend excellent ['eksələnt]
hier here [hɪə] **hier in der Nähe** near here
hierher here [hɪə]
Hilfe help [help]
hinauf up [ʌp] **auf das Boot hinauf** onto the boat ['ɒntʊ]
hinaufklettern (auf) climb [klaɪm]
hinaus: aus ... hinaus out of ... ['aʊt‿əv]
hinbringen take [teɪk]
hinein: in die Küche hinein into the kitchen ['ɪntʊ]
hinfallen fall [fɔ:l]
hinkommen *(gelangen)* get [get]
hinsetzen: sich hinsetzen sit down [ˌsɪt 'daʊn]
hinter behind [bɪ'haɪnd] **hinter jm. herrennen** run after sb. [ˌrʌn‿'ɑ:ftə]
Hintergrund background ['bækgraʊnd]
hinüber zu/nach ... over to ... ['əʊvə]
hinunter down [daʊn]
hinzufügen (zu) add (to) [æd]
Hobby hobby ['hɒbi]
hoch high [haɪ]
hoffen hope [həʊp]
horchen listen ['lɪsn]
hören hear [hɪə]
Hügel hill [hɪl]
Hund dog [dɒg]
Hunger haben be hungry ['hʌŋgri]
hungrig sein be hungry ['hʌŋgri]
Hut hat [hæt]

I

ich I [aɪ] **Ich auch.** Me too. **Ich bin's.** It's me.
ideal *(perfekt)* perfect ['pɜ:fɪkt]
Idee idea [aɪ'dɪə]
ihm him [hɪm]; *(bei Dingen, Tieren)* it
ihn him [hɪm]; *(bei Dingen, Tieren)* it
ihnen them [ðem], [ðəm]
Ihnen *(höfliche Anrede)* you [ju:]
ihr *(Plural von „du")* you [ju:]
ihr: Hilf ihr. Help her. [hɜ:]
ihr(e) ... *(vor Nomen; besitzanzeigend)*
1. *(zu „she")* her ... [hɜ:, hə]
2. *(zu „it")* its ... [ɪts]
3. *(zu „they")* their ... [ðeə]
Ihr(e) ... *(vor Nomen; besitzanzeigend)* *(zur höflichen Anrede „you")* your ... [jɔ:, jə]
im: im Jahr 1580 in 1580
Imbiss snack [snæk]
immer always ['ɔ:lweɪz] **immer noch** still [stɪl]
in in [ɪn]; *(in Ortsangaben auch oft:)* at [æt], [ət] **in der Beach Road** in Beach Road **in der Beach Road 8**

at 8 Beach Road **in der Dean Street** in Dean Street **in der Dean Street 14** at 14 Dean Street **in der Nacht** at night **in der Nähe von** near **in der Schule** at school **in die Küche (hinein)** into the kitchen **in England** in England **in Ordnung** all right **in Schwierigkeiten sein** be in trouble ['trʌbl]
Information(en) (über) information (about) *(no pl)* [ˌɪnfə'meɪʃn]
Informations- und Kommunikationstechnologie ICT [ˌaɪ siː 'tiː] (Information and Communication Technology)
Inlineskaten skating ['skeɪtɪŋ]
Inlineskates skates [skeɪts]
Insel island ['aɪlənd]
Instrument instrument ['ɪnstrəmənt]
interessant interesting ['ɪntrəstɪŋ]
international international [ˌɪntə'næʃnəl]
Internet internet ['ɪntənet] **im Internet** on the internet
Intonation intonation [ˌɪntə'neɪʃn]
irgendetwas? anything? ['eniθɪŋ]
irgendjemand? anybody? / anyone? ['enibɒdi, 'eniwʌn]
irgendwelche: Gibt es irgendwelche ...? Are there any ...? ['eni]
irren: jemand irrt sich *(jemand hat Unrecht)* someone is wrong [rɒŋ]

J

ja yes [jes] **Ja, das ist richtig. / Ja, das stimmt.** Yes, that's right.
Jahr year [jɪə]
Jahrgang, Jahrgangsstufe year [jɪə]
Jahrhundert century ['sentʃəri]
Januar January ['dʒænjuəri]
je: Sie kosten je 2 Pfund 75. *(2,75 pro Stück)* They're £ 2.75 each. [iːtʃ]
Jeans jeans *(pl)* [dʒiːnz]
jede(r, s): jeder Tag / jede Farbe / jedes Boot every day/colour/boat ['evri]
jeder *(alle)* everyone ['evriwʌn], everybody ['evribɒdi]
jemand someone ['sʌmwʌn], somebody ['sʌmbədi]; *(in Fragen)* anybody? / anyone? ['enibɒdi, 'eniwʌn] **Finde jemanden, der ...** Find someone who ...
jene(r, s): jene Gruppe that group **jene Gruppen** those groups
jetzt now [naʊ]
Job job [dʒɒb]
Joghurt yoghurt ['jɒgət]
Judo judo ['dʒuːdəʊ]
Jugendliche(r) kid [kɪd] *(infml)*
Jugendmannschaft junior team ['dʒuːniə tiːm]
Juli July [dʒu'laɪ]
jung young [jʌŋ]
Junge boy [bɔɪ]
Juni June [dʒuːn]
Juniorenmannschaft junior team ['dʒuːniə tiːm]

K

Käfig cage [keɪdʒ]
Kalender diary ['daɪəri]
kalt cold [kəʊld]
Kamera camera ['kæmərə]
Kameramann cameraman, *pl* -men ['kæmrəmən]
kämpfen fight [faɪt]
Kaninchen rabbit ['ræbɪt]
Kantine canteen [kæn'tiːn]
Kapitän/in captain ['kæptɪn]
kaputt gehen break [breɪk] **etwas kaputt machen** break sth.
Karren cart [kɑːt]
Karte (an) card (to) [kɑːd]
Kartoffel potato [pə'teɪtəʊ], *pl* potatoes
Käse cheese [tʃiːz]
Kästchen box [bɒks]
Kasten box [bɒks]
Katze cat [kæt]
kaufen buy [baɪ]
kein(e) no [nəʊ] **Es gibt/sind keine ...** There aren't any ... ['eni] **Ich bin kein Junge.** I'm not a boy. **Ich mag kein Grün.** I don't like green. **er hat keine Zeit** he doesn't have time
Keks biscuit ['bɪskɪt]
kennen know [nəʊ]
kennenlernen meet [miːt] **Freut mich, dich/euch/Sie kennenzulernen.** Nice to meet you.
Kerze candle ['kændl]
Kette chain [tʃeɪn]
Kilogramm, Kilo (kg) kilogram ['kɪləgræm], kilo ['kiːləʊ] (kg)
Kind child [tʃaɪld], *pl* children ['tʃɪldrən]; *(infml auch:)* kid [kɪd]
Kino cinema ['sɪnəmə]
Kirche church [tʃɜːtʃ]
Kiste box [bɒks]
Klang sound [saʊnd]
Klasse class [klɑːs]
Klassenkamerad/in classmate ['klɑːsmeɪt]
Klassenzimmer classroom ['klɑːsruːm]
klatschen *(Beifall)* clap [klæp]
Klavier piano [pi'ænəʊ] **Klavier spielen** play the piano
Klebestift glue stick ['gluː stɪk]
Klebstoff glue [gluː]
Kleid dress [dres]
Kleidung, Kleidungsstücke clothes *(pl)* [kləʊðz]
klein little ['lɪtl]; small [smɔːl]
klettern climb [klaɪm] **auf einen Baum/einen Turm klettern** climb a tree/a tower
Klingel bell [bel]
klingen sound [saʊnd]
Klub club [klʌb] **in einen Klub eintreten / sich einem Klub anschließen** join a club [dʒɔɪn]
klug clever ['klevə]
Knallbonbon cracker ['krækə]
komisch **1.** *(lustig)* funny ['fʌni] **2.** *(seltsam, merkwürdig)* funny; strange [streɪndʒ]
kommen come [kʌm]; *(gelangen, hinkommen)* get [get] **Ich komme aus Plymouth.** I'm from Plymouth. **Komm, Dad!** *(Na los, Dad!)* Come on, Dad. **nach Hause kommen** come home
Königin queen [kwiːn]
Königreich: das Vereinigte Königreich the United Kingdom (UK) [juˌnaɪtɪd 'kɪŋdəm]
können can [kæn], [kən] **Ich kann nicht ... / du kannst nicht ...** *usw.* I can't ... / you can't ... *etc.* [kɑːnt] **gut Kung-Fu können** be good at kung fu
konnte(n): ich konnte ... / du konntest ... *usw.* I could ... / you could ... *etc.* [kʊd] **ich konnte nicht ... / du konntest nicht ...** *usw.* I couldn't ... / you couldn't ... *etc.* [kʊdnt]
Konsonant consonant ['kɒnsənənt]
Kontrolle *(Überprüfung)* check [tʃek]
kontrollieren *(überprüfen)* check [tʃek]
Konzert concert ['kɒnsət]
Kopf head [hed]
kopieren copy ['kɒpi]
Korb basket ['bɑːskɪt]
Körper body ['bɒdi]
kosten: Die Kamera kostet ... The camera is ... **Die DVDs kosten ...** The DVDs are ... **Was/Wie viel**

kostet …? How much is …? **Was/ Wie viel kosten …?** How much are …?
krank sick [sɪk]
Krebs *(Tier)* crab [kræb]
Kricket cricket ['krɪkɪt]
Küche kitchen ['kɪtʃɪn]
Kuchen cake [keɪk]
Kugelschreiber pen [pen]
Kultur culture ['kʌltʃə]
Kunst art [ɑːt]
kurz short [ʃɔːt]
Küste coast [kəʊst]

L

lächeln smile [smaɪl]
Lächeln smile [smaɪl]
lachen laugh [lɑːf]
Laden shop [ʃɒp] **Laden an der Ecke** *(„Tante-Emma-Laden")* corner shop ['kɔːnə ʃɒp]
Lampe lamp [læmp]
Land country ['kʌntri]
Landkarte map ['mæp] **auf der Landkarte** on the map
Landwirt/in farmer ['fɑːmə]
lang long [lɒŋ]
langsam slow [sləʊ]
langweilig boring ['bɔːrɪŋ]
Lärm noise [nɔɪz] **voller Lärm** noisy ['nɔɪzi]
lärmend noisy ['nɔɪzi]
lassen: Lass mich dir … zeigen. Let me show you … **Lass(t) uns …** Let's … **Lass(t) uns nach England gehen/fahren.** Let's go to England.
laufen run [rʌn]
laut loud [laʊd]; *(voller Lärm)* noisy ['nɔɪzi]
Laut sound [saʊnd]
Leben life [laɪf], *pl* lives [laɪvz]
leben *(wohnen)* live [lɪv]
lecker yummy ['jʌmi] *(infml)*
ledig *(alleinstehend)* single ['sɪŋgl]
legen *(hinlegen, ablegen)* put [pʊt]
Lehrer/in teacher ['tiːtʃə]
leicht *(einfach)* easy ['iːzi]
leid: Es tut mir leid (wegen …) I'm sorry (about …)
leise quiet ['kwaɪət]
lenken steer [stɪə]
lernen learn [lɜːn]
lesen read [riːd]
letzte(r, s) last [lɑːst] **letztes Wochenende / letzten Freitag** last weekend/Friday
leuchtend bright [braɪt]
Leute people ['piːpl]
Licht light [laɪt]
lieben love [lʌv]
Lieblings-: mein Lieblingstag my favourite day ['feɪvərɪt]
Lied song [sɒŋ]
lila purple ['pɜːpl]
Lineal ruler ['ruːlə]
linke(r, s) left [left] **auf der linken Seite** on the left **nach links** left
Liste list [lɪst]
los: Los geht's. / Jetzt geht's los. Here we go. **Was ist los?** What's the matter? ['mætə]
Löwe lion ['laɪən]

M

machen *(tun)* do [duː]; *(herstellen)* make [meɪk] **einen Bootsausflug machen** go on a boat trip **einen Spaziergang machen** go for a walk [wɔːk] **Fotos machen** take photos **Hat es Spaß gemacht?** Was it fun?
Mädchen girl [gɜːl]
Mai May [meɪ]
Mal time [taɪm]
Mama mum [mʌm]
manchmal sometimes ['sʌmtaɪmz]
Mann man [mæn], *pl* men [men]
Mannschaft team [tiːm]
Marine navy ['neɪvi]
Markt market ['mɑːkɪt]
Marmelade jam [dʒæm]; *(aus Zitrusfrüchten)* marmalade ['mɑːməleɪd]
März March [mɑːtʃ]
Mathematik maths [mæθs]
Maul mouth [maʊθ]
Medaille medal ['medl]
Meer sea [siː] **am Meer** by the sea
Meerschweinchen guinea pig ['gɪni pɪg]
mehr more [mɔː]
Meile mile [maɪl]
meilenweit for miles
mein(e) … my … [maɪ]
meistens usually ['juːʒuəli]
Meister/in master ['mɑːstə]
Mensa *(Kantine)* canteen [kæn'tiːn]
Menschen people ['piːpl]
Meter metre ['miːtə]
mich me [miː]
Milch milk [mɪlk]
Million million ['mɪljən]
Minute minute ['mɪnɪt]
mir me [miː]
mit with [wɪð] **mit dem Bus/Auto fahren** go by bus/car
mitkommen come along [ə'lɒŋ]
Mitlaut consonant ['kɒnsənənt]
Mitschüler/in classmate ['klɑːsmeɪt]
Mittag: zu Mittag essen have lunch [lʌntʃ]
Mittagessen lunch [lʌntʃ]
mittags at lunchtime ['lʌntʃtaɪm]
Mittagszeit lunchtime ['lʌntʃtaɪm]
Mitte middle ['mɪdl]; *(Zentrum)* centre ['sentə]
Mitternacht midnight ['mɪdnaɪt]
Mittwoch Wednesday ['wenzdeɪ, -di]
Mobiltelefon mobile phone [ˌməʊbaɪl 'fəʊn], *(kurz auch:)* mobile
möchte: Ich möchte … (haben) I'd like … [ˌaɪd 'laɪk] (= I would like …) **Ich möchte gehen.** I'd like to go. **Was möchtest du (haben)?** What would you like? [wʊd] **Was möchtest du essen?** What would you like to eat?
mögen like [laɪk] **Ich mag …** I like … **Ich mag Grün nicht. / Ich mag kein Grün.** I don't like green.
Moment moment ['məʊmənt] **im Moment** at the moment **Warte einen Moment. / Moment mal.** Wait a minute.
Monat month [mʌnθ]
Mond moon [muːn]
Monster monster ['mɒnstə]
Montag Monday ['mʌndeɪ, 'mʌndi]
Morgen *(Vormittag)* morning ['mɔːnɪŋ] **am Morgen** in the morning
morgens in the morning ['mɔːnɪŋ]
Möwe seagull ['siːgʌl]
MP3-Player, MP3-Spieler MP3 player [ˌempiː'θriː ˌpleɪə]
müde tired ['taɪəd]
Mund mouth [maʊθ]
Münze coin [kɔɪn]
Museum museum [mju'ziːəm]
Musik music ['mjuːzɪk]
müssen must [mʌst]; have to ['hæv tə] **arbeiten müssen** have to work **du musst es nicht tun** you needn't do it ['niːdnt]
Mutter mother ['mʌðə]
Mutti mum [mʌm]

N

Na: Na ja, … Well, … [wel] **Na los, Dad!** *(Komm, Dad!)* Come on, Dad. **Na und?** So? [səʊ]
nach **1.** *(örtlich)* to [tu], [tə] **nach draußen** outside [ˌaʊt'saɪd] **nach**

drinnen inside [ˌɪn'saɪd] **nach Hause gehen** go home **nach Hause kommen** come home **nach oben** up; *(im Haus)* upstairs [ˌʌp'steəz] **nach unten** down; *(im Haus)* downstairs [ˌdaʊn'steəz] **2.** *(zeitlich)* after ['ɑːftə] **Viertel nach zehn (10.15 / 22.15)** quarter past ten ['kwɔːtə pɑːst]
nachdenken (über) think (about) [θɪŋk]
Nachmittag afternoon [ˌɑːftə'nuːn] **am Nachmittag** in the afternoon
nachmittags in the afternoon [ˌɑːftə'nuːn]
Nachrichten news *(no pl)* [njuːz]
Nachspeise dessert [dɪ'zɜːt]
nächste(r, s) next [nekst] **das nächste Bild / die nächste Frage** the next picture/question
Nacht night [naɪt] **in der Nacht** at night
Nachtisch dessert [dɪ'zɜːt]
nachts at night [ət 'naɪt]
Nähe: in der Nähe von near [nɪə] **hier in der Nähe** near here
nahe (bei) near [nɪə]; close (to) [kləʊs]
Name name [neɪm] **Mein Name ist Silky.** My name is Silky.
Nase nose [nəʊz]
nass wet [wet]
national, National- national ['næʃnəl]
Naturkunde natural history [ˌnætʃrəl 'hɪstri]
natürlich *(selbstverständlich)* of course [əv 'kɔːs]
Naturwissenschaft science ['saɪəns]
neben next to ['nekst tʊ]
Nebensatz sub-clause ['sʌbklɔːz]
nehmen take [teɪk]
nein no [nəʊ] **Nein, das ist falsch. / Nein, das stimmt nicht.** No, that's wrong.
nennen *(rufen, bezeichnen)* call [kɔːl]
nervös nervous ['nɜːvəs]
nett nice [naɪs]
neu new [njuː]
neun nine [naɪn]
nicht not [nɒt] **Gehe nicht.** Don't go. [dəʊnt] **Ich mag Grün nicht.** I don't like green. **Ich weiß (es) nicht.** I don't know. **auch nicht** not … either ['aɪðə, 'iːðə] **noch nicht** not … yet [jet]
nichts not … anything ['eniθɪŋ]
nie never ['nevə]
niemals never ['nevə]
niemand no one ['nəʊ wʌn], nobody ['nəʊbədi]; not … anybody/anyone ['enibɒdi, 'eniwʌn]
niesen sneeze [sniːz]
noch: noch einmal again [ə'gen] **noch nicht** not … yet [jet] **immer noch** still [stɪl] **noch ein(e) …** another … [ə'nʌðə]
Norden; Nord- north [nɔːθ]
normalerweise usually ['juːʒuəli]
Notiz note [nəʊt]
November November [nəʊ'vembə]
Null *(in Telefonnummern)* o [əʊ]
Nummer number
nun now [naʊ] **Nun, …** Well, …
nur only ['əʊnli]; *(einfach nur)* just [dʒʌst]

O

oben *(im Haus)* upstairs [ˌʌp'steəz] **nach oben** up; *(im Haus)* upstairs
Obst fruit [fruːt]
Obstsalat fruit salad [ˌfruːt 'sæləd]
oder or [ɔː]
offen open ['əʊpən]
öffnen; sich öffnen open ['əʊpən]
oft often ['ɒfn], ['ɒftən]
ohne without [wɪ'ðaʊt]
Ohr ear [ɪə]
okay OK [ˌəʊ'keɪ]; all right [ɔːl 'raɪt]
Oktober October [ɒk'təʊbə]
Oma grandma ['grænmɑː]
Onkel uncle ['ʌŋkl]
Opa grandpa ['grænpɑː]
orange(farben) orange ['ɒrɪndʒ]
ordnen *(anordnen, organisieren)* organize ['ɔːgənaɪz]
Ordnung: in Ordnung *(okay)* all right [ɔːl 'raɪt]; OK [ˌəʊ'keɪ]
organisieren organize ['ɔːgənaɪz]
Ort place [pleɪs]
Ostern Easter ['iːstə]
Ozean ocean ['əʊʃn]

P

paar: ein paar *(einige)* some [sʌm], [səm]
Paar pair [peə] **ein Paar …** a pair of …
Papa dad [dæd]
Papier paper ['peɪpə]
Papierhut paper hat ['peɪpə hæt]
Park park [pɑːk]
Parlament parliament ['pɑːləmənt]
Partner/in partner ['pɑːtnə]
Party party ['pɑːti]
Pass auf! *(Vorsicht!)* Watch out! [ˌwɒtʃ_'aʊt]
passen: zu etwas passen *(zu etwas gehören)* go with sth.
passieren (mit) happen (to) ['hæpən]
Pause break [breɪk]
Pence pence [pens]
perfekt perfect ['pɜːfɪkt]
Person person ['pɜːsn]; *(in Roman, Film, Theaterstück usw.)* character ['kærəktə]
Pfeffer pepper ['pepə]
Pferd horse [hɔːs]
Pfund *(britische Währung)* pound (£) [paʊnd]
Piano piano [pi'ænəʊ]
Picknick picnic ['pɪknɪk]
pink pink [pɪŋk]
Pizza pizza ['piːtsə]
Plan plan [plæn]
Planet planet ['plænɪt]
Platz place [pleɪs]
Plätzchen *(Keks)* biscuit ['bɪskɪt]
plötzlich suddenly ['sʌdnli]
Pokal *(Trophäe)* trophy ['trəʊfi]
Polizei police *(pl)* [pə'liːs]
Polizist/in police officer [pə'liːs_ˌɒfɪsə]
Polnisch; polnisch Polish ['pəʊlɪʃ]
populär popular ['pɒpjələ]
Porträt *(Personenbeschreibung)* profile ['prəʊfaɪl]
Poster poster ['pəʊstə]
Postkarte postcard ['pəʊstkɑːd]
prallen: gegen etwas prallen hit sth. [hɪt]
Preis *(Kaufpreis)* price [praɪs]
preiswert *(billig)* cheap [tʃiːp]
pro: … pro Tag/Woche/Jahr … a day/week/year
probieren try [traɪ]
Problem problem ['prɒbləm]
Profil *(Personenbeschreibung, Porträt)* profile ['prəʊfaɪl]
Programm programme ['prəʊgræm]
Projekt project ['prɒdʒekt]
Prozent per cent [pə'sent]
prüfen *(überprüfen)* check [tʃek]
Punkt point [pɔɪnt]; *(Fleck)* spot [spɒt]
Pute turkey ['tɜːki]
putzen clean [kliːn]
Pyjama-Party sleepover ['sliːpəʊvə]

Q

Quiz quiz [kwɪz]

R

Rad *(Fahrrad)* bike [baɪk] **Rad fahren** ride a bike [ˌraɪd‿ə 'baɪk]
Radiergummi rubber ['rʌbə]
raten guess [ges]
Ratte rat [ræt]
rauf und runter up and down [ˌʌp‿ən 'daʊn]
Recht: jemand hat Recht someone is right
rechte(r, s) right [raɪt] **auf der rechten Seite** on the right **nach rechts** right
Rede talk [tɔːk] **eine Rede halten (über)** give a talk (about)
reden (mit) talk (to) [tɔːk]
Referat talk [tɔːk] **ein Referat halten (über)** give a talk (about)
Regal shelf [ʃelf], *pl* shelves [ʃelvz]
Regenschirm umbrella [ʌm'brelə]
reich rich [rɪtʃ]
Reihe: Ich bin an der Reihe. (It's) my turn. [tɜːn]
Reihenfolge order ['ɔːdə]
Reim rhyme [raɪm]
Reise trip [trɪp]
reisen travel ['trævl]
Reisende(r) traveller ['trævələ]
Reiten riding ['raɪdɪŋ]
Religion religion [rɪ'lɪdʒən]
rennen run [rʌn]
Rennen race [reɪs]
Restaurant restaurant ['restrɒnt]
retten save [seɪv]
Rettung rescue ['reskjuː]
richten: etwas auf jn. richten point sth. at sb. [pɔɪnt]
richtig right [raɪt] **Ja, das ist richtig.** Yes, that's right.
riechen smell [smel] **an etwas riechen** smell sth.
Riesenrad big wheel [bɪg 'wiːl]
Rinderbraten roast beef [ˌrəʊst 'biːf]
Robbe seal [siːl]
Robbenjunges baby seal ['beɪbi siːl]
rosa pink [pɪŋk]
rot red [red]
Routine routine [ruː'tiːn]
Rucksack rucksack ['rʌksæk]
rufen call [kɔːl]; shout [ʃaʊt]
ruhig *(leise)* quiet ['kwaɪət]
Rundgang, Rundfahrt (durch) tour (of) ['tʊər‿əv]
runter: rauf und runter up and down [ˌʌp‿ən 'daʊn]

S

Sache thing [θɪŋ]
sagen say [seɪ]
Sahne cream [kriːm]
Salat *(Gericht, Beilage)* salad ['sæləd]
Samba samba ['sæmbə]
sammeln collect [kə'lekt]
Samstag Saturday ['sætədeɪ, 'sætədi]
Sand sand [sænd]
Sandwich sandwich ['sænwɪtʃ], ['sænwɪdʒ]
Satz sentence ['sentəns]
Satzmelodie intonation [ˌɪntə'neɪʃn]
sauber machen clean [kliːn]
Schach chess [tʃes]
schauen look [lʊk]
Schauspieler/in actor ['æktə]
schicken: jm. etwas schicken send sth. to sb. [send] **einem Freund/ einer Freundin eine SMS schicken** text a friend [tekst]
schieben push [pʊʃ]
schießen: ein Tor schießen score [skɔː]
Schiff ship [ʃɪp]
Schild sign [saɪn]
Schirm umbrella [ʌm'brelə]
schlafen sleep [sliːp]
Schlafparty sleepover ['sliːpəʊvə]
Schlafzimmer bedroom ['bedruːm]
Schlagzeug drums *(pl)* [drʌmz] **Schlagzeug spielen** play the drums
Schlange snake [sneɪk]
schlau clever ['klevə]
schlecht bad [bæd]
schließlich at last [ət 'lɑːst]
schlimm bad [bæd]
Schloss castle ['kɑːsl]
Schluss end [end]
Schlüsselwort keyword ['kiːwɜːd]
schmecken taste [teɪst]
schmerzen hurt [hɜːt]
Schmetterling butterfly ['bʌtəflaɪ]
Schmuggel; das Schmuggeln smuggling ['smʌglɪŋ]
schmuggeln smuggle ['smʌgl]
Schmuggler/in smuggler ['smʌglə]
schneiden *(Film, Video bearbeiten)* edit ['edɪt]
schnell fast [fɑːst]
Schokolade chocolate ['tʃɒklət]
schön beautiful ['bjuːtɪfl]; nice [naɪs]
Schrank cupboard ['kʌbəd]
schreiben write [raɪt]
Schreibtisch desk [desk]
schreien shout [ʃaʊt]
Schritt step [step]
Schuh shoe [ʃuː]
Schule school [skuːl] **in der Schule** at school
Schüler/in student ['stjuːdənt]
Schulfach (school) subject ['sʌbdʒɪkt]
Schulheft *(Übungsheft)* exercise book ['eksəsaɪz bʊk]
Schultasche school bag ['skuːl bæg]
schwarz black [blæk]
Schwein pig [pɪg]
schwer *(schwierig)* hard [hɑːd]
Schwert sword [sɔːd]
Schwester sister ['sɪstə]
schwierig hard [hɑːd]
Schwimmbad, Schwimmbecken (swimming) pool [puːl]
schwimmen swim [swɪm]
Schwimmer/in swimmer ['swɪmə]
Schwimmweste life jacket ['laɪf dʒækɪt]
sechs six [sɪks]
See **1.** *(Binnensee)* lake [leɪk] **2.** *(die See, das Meer)* sea [siː]
Segelboot sailing boat ['seɪlɪŋ bəʊt]
segeln sail [seɪl] **segeln gehen** go sailing ['seɪlɪŋ]
sehen see [siː]
Sehenswürdigkeiten sights *(pl)* [saɪts]
sehr very ['veri] **Das hat uns sehr geholfen.** That helped us a lot.
seidig silky ['sɪlki]
sein *(Verb)* be [biː]
sein(e) … *(vor Nomen; besitzanzeigend)*
1. *(zu „he")* his … [hɪz]
2. *(zu „it")* its … [ɪts]
Seite page [peɪdʒ] **Auf welcher Seite sind wir?** What page are we on?
Selbstlaut vowel ['vaʊəl]
selbstverständlich of course [əv 'kɔːs]
seltsam strange [streɪndʒ]
senden: jm. etwas senden send sth. to sb. [send]
Sendung *(im Radio, Fernsehen)* programme ['prəʊgræm]
September September [sep'tembə]
Servus. Bye-bye.; Bye. [baɪ]
Sessel armchair ['ɑːmtʃeə]
setzen: sich setzen sit [sɪt]
Shorts *(kurze Hose)* shorts *(pl)* [ʃɔːts]
sicher *(gewiss)* sure [ʃʊə, ʃɔː]
sie **1.** *(Einzahl; weibliche Person)* she [ʃiː] **Frag sie.** Ask her. [hɜː]
2. *(Einzahl; Ding, Tier)* it [ɪt]
3. *(Mehrzahl)* they [ðeɪ] **Frag sie.** Ask them. [ðem, ðəm]
Sie *(höfliche Anrede)* you [juː, ju]

sieben seven ['sevn]
Sieger/in winner ['wɪnə]
singen sing [sɪŋ]
sitzen sit [sɪt]
SMS text [tekst] **einem Freund/ einer Freundin eine SMS schicken** text a friend
Snack snack [snæk]
so **1.** *(auf diese Weise)* like this / like that
2. so cool/nett/leise/… so cool/ nice/quiet/… [səʊ]
Sofa sofa ['səʊfə]
Sommer summer ['sʌmə]
Sonne sun [sʌn]
Sonntag Sunday ['sʌndeɪ, 'sʌndi]
Spagetti spaghetti [spə'geti]
Spanisch; spanisch Spanish ['spænɪʃ]
spannend *(aufregend)* exciting [ɪk'saɪtɪŋ]
Spaß fun [fʌn] **Spaß haben** have fun [fʌn] **Das macht Spaß.** That's fun. **Hat es Spaß gemacht?** Was it fun?
spät late [leɪt] **Du bist spät dran. / Du bist zu spät.** You're late. **Wie spät ist es?** What time is it?
später later ['leɪtə]
spazieren gehen go for a walk [wɔ:k]
Spaziergang walk [wɔ:k] **einen Spaziergang machen** go for a walk
Spiel game [geɪm]; *(Wettkampf, Match)* match [mætʃ]
spielen play [pleɪ]; *(Geschichte, Handlung)* take place **Gitarre spielen** play the guitar **Klavier spielen** play the piano **Schlagzeug spielen** play the drums
Spieler/in player ['pleɪə]
Spielzeug toy [tɔɪ]
Spitze *(oberes Ende)* top [tɒp]
Spitzer sharpener ['ʃɑ:pnə]
Sport; Sportart sport [spɔ:t] **Sport treiben** do sport
Sportunterricht PE [ˌpi:‿'i:] (Physical Education)
Sprache language ['læŋgwɪdʒ]
sprechen speak [spi:k]
Sprecher/in speaker ['spi:kə]
springen jump [dʒʌmp]
Sprung jump [dʒʌmp]
Staat state [steɪt]
Stadt town [taʊn]; *(Großstadt)* city ['sɪti]
Stadtplan map [mæp] **auf dem Stadtplan** on the map
Stammbaum family tree ['fæməli tri:]
Star star [stɑ:]
stattfinden take place
stehen: Hier steht: … It says here: …
Stelle place [pleɪs]; *(Job, Arbeitsstelle)* job [dʒɒb]
stellen *(hinstellen, abstellen)* put [pʊt] **eine Frage stellen** ask a question
sterben die [daɪ]
steuern steer [stɪə]
Stift *(zum Schreiben)* pen [pen]
still quiet ['kwaɪət]
Stimme voice [vɔɪs]
stimmen: Ja, das stimmt. Yes, that's right. [raɪt] **Nein, das stimmt nicht.** No, that's wrong. [rɒŋ]
Stock(werk) floor [flɔ:]
stoppen stop [stɒp]
stoßen push [pʊʃ] **gegen etwas stoßen** hit sth. [hɪt]
strahlend *(leuchtend hell)* bright [braɪt]
Strand beach [bi:tʃ]
Straße street [stri:t]; road [rəʊd]
Student/in student ['stju:dənt]
Studio studio ['stju:diəʊ]
Stuhl chair [tʃeə]
Stunde hour ['aʊə]; *(Unterrichtsstunde)* lesson ['lesn]
Stundenplan timetable ['taɪmteɪbl]
stürzen fall [fɔ:l]
suchen: etwas suchen look for sth. ['lʊk fɔ:]
Supermarkt supermarket ['su:pəmɑ:kɪt]
Suppe soup [su:p]
Symbol symbol ['sɪmbl]
Szene scene [si:n]

T

Tabelle table ['teɪbl]
Tafel board [bɔ:d]
Tag day [deɪ] **den ganzen Tag (lang)** all day
Tagebuch diary ['daɪəri]
Tante aunt [ɑ:nt]
Tante-Emma-Laden corner shop ['kɔ:nə ʃɒp]
tanzen dance [dɑ:ns]
Tasche bag [bæg]
Tasse: eine Tasse … a cup of … [kʌp]
Team team [ti:m]
Technik, Technologie technology [tek'nɒlədʒi]
Tee tea [ti:]
Teil part [pɑ:t]
Telefon telephone ['telɪfəʊn], *(kurz auch:)* phone
Telefongespräch phone call ['fəʊn kɔ:l], *(kurz auch:)* call
Teller: ein Teller … a plate of … [pleɪt]
Tennis tennis ['tenɪs]
Test test [test]
teuer expensive [ɪk'spensɪv]
Theater theatre ['θɪətə]
Theaterstück play [pleɪ]
Tier animal ['ænɪml]
Tipp tip [tɪp]
Tisch table ['teɪbl]
Titel title ['taɪtl]
Toilette toilet ['tɔɪlət]
Tomate tomato [tə'mɑ:təʊ], *pl* tomatoes
Top *(Oberteil)* top [tɒp]
Tor: ein Tor schießen score [skɔ:]
tot dead [ded]
Tourist/in tourist ['tʊərɪst]
Tradition tradition [trə'dɪʃn]
tragen *(Kleidung)* wear [weə]
trainieren practise ['præktɪs]
Training training ['treɪnɪŋ]
Traum dream [dri:m]
traurig sad [sæd]
treffen; sich treffen meet [mi:t]
Treffer: einen Treffer erzielen score [skɔ:]
trinken drink [drɪŋk]
Trommel drum [drʌm]
Trompete trumpet ['trʌmpɪt]
Trophäe trophy ['trəʊfi]
Truthahn turkey ['tɜ:ki]
T-Shirt T-shirt ['ti:ʃɜ:t]
tun do [du:] **etwas tun müssen** have to do sth. **etwas tun wollen** want to do sth. [wɒnt] **Tut mir leid.** (I'm) sorry. ['sɒri] **viel zu tun haben** be busy ['bɪzi]
Tür door [dɔ:]
Turm tower ['taʊə]
Turnen gymnastics [dʒɪm'næstɪks]; *(Sportunterricht)* PE [ˌpi:‿'i:] (Physical Education)
Turnhalle gym [dʒɪm]
Turnschuh trainer ['treɪnə]

U

üben practise ['præktɪs]
über **1.** *(räumlich)* over ['əʊvə]
2. *(mehr als)* over ['əʊvə] **über 400 Jahre** over 400 years
3. über mich/dich/… about me/ you/… [ə'baʊt] **über dich selbst** about yourself [jɔ:'self]
überprüfen check [tʃek]

Überprüfung check [tʃek]
überrascht surprised [sə'praɪzd]
Überraschung surprise [sə'praɪz]
Überschrift title ['taɪtl]
Übung exercise ['eksəsaɪz]
Übungsheft exercise book ['eksəsaɪz bʊk]
Uhr **1.** *(Armbanduhr)* watch [wɒtʃ]; *(Wand-, Stand-, Turmuhr)* clock [klɒk] **2. 4 Uhr morgens** 4 am [ˌeɪ‿'em] **4 Uhr nachmittags / 16 Uhr** 4 pm [ˌpiː‿'em] **um 1 Uhr / 13 Uhr** at 1 o'clock [ə'klɒk]
Uhrzeit time [taɪm]
um 1 Uhr / 13 Uhr at 1 o'clock [ə'klɒk]
umdrehen *(wenden)* turn around [ˌtɜːn‿ə'raʊnd] **sich umdrehen** turn around
umher: in der Bücherei / auf dem Strand umher around the library/ the beach [ə'raʊnd]
und and [ænd, [ənd] **Und du? / Und was ist mit dir?** What about you? **Und? / Na und?** So? [səʊ]
unfreundlich unfriendly [ʌn'frendli]
ungefähr 30 Leute about 30 people
unglücklich unhappy [ʌn'hæpi]
unheimlich scary ['skeəri]
Uniform uniform ['juːnɪfɔːm]
Unrecht: jemand hat Unrecht someone is wrong [rɒŋ]
uns us [ʌs], [əs]
unser(e) ... our ... ['aʊə]
unten *(im Haus)* downstairs [ˌdaʊn'steəz] **nach unten** down; *(im Haus)* downstairs
unter under ['ʌndə]
untergehen *(Sonne)* go down [daʊn]
unterhalten: sich unterhalten (mit) talk (to) [tɔːk]
Untertitel subtitle ['sʌbtaɪtl]
Urlaub holiday ['hɒlədeɪ] **in Urlaub sein/fahren** be/go on holiday
usw. (und so weiter) etc. (et cetera) [et'setərə]

V

Vater father ['fɑːðə]
Vati dad [dæd]
verbinden link [lɪŋk]
vereinigt united [ju'naɪtɪd] **das Vereinigte Königreich** the United Kingdom (UK) [juˌnaɪtɪd 'kɪŋdəm]
Vergangenheit past [pɑːst]
vergessen forget [fə'get]
Vergnügungspark fun park ['fʌn pɑːk]
verheiratet (mit) married (to) ['mærɪd]
verkaufen sell [sel]
verkehrt wrong [rɒŋ]
verknüpfen link [lɪŋk]
verlassen leave [liːv]
verletzen hurt [hɜːt]
verletzt hurt [hɜːt]
verpassen miss [mɪs]
verrückt mad [mæd]
Vers rhyme [raɪm]
verschieden different ['dɪfrənt]
verstecken; sich verstecken hide [haɪd]
verstehen understand [ˌʌndə'stænd] **Hast du es verstanden?** Did you get it? *(infml)*
versuchen try [traɪ] **Versuch's mal.** Have a go.
verwenden use [juːz]
Video video ['vɪdiəʊ]
Videokamera video camera ['vɪdiəʊ kæmrə]
viel a lot (of); lots (of); much [mʌtʃ] **Viel Glück!** Good luck! [lʌk] **viel zu tun haben** be busy ['bɪzi] **Wie viel kosten ...?** How much are ...? **Wie viel kostet ...?** How much is ...?
viele a lot (of); lots (of); many ['meni]
vielleicht maybe ['meɪbi]
vier four [fɔː]
Viertel: Viertel nach zehn (10.15/ 22.15) quarter past ten ['kwɔːtə pɑːst] **Viertel vor elf (10.45/ 22.45)** quarter to eleven ['kwɔːtə tʊ]
violett purple ['pɜːpl]
Vogel bird [bɜːd]
Vokal vowel ['vaʊəl]
voll (von/mit) full (of) [fʊl]
Volleyball volleyball ['vɒlibɔːl]
von of [ɒv], [əv]; from [frɒm], [frəm] **von ... bis ...** from ... to ...
vor **1.** *(örtlich)* in front of [ɪn 'frʌnt‿əv] **vor der Schule** *(vor dem Schulgebäude)* in front of the school **2.** *(zeitlich)* before [bɪ'fɔː] **vor der Schule** *(vor Schulbeginn)* before school **vorm Unterricht** before lessons **Viertel vor elf (10.45/ 22.45)** quarter to eleven ['kwɔːtə tʊ]
vorbei sein *(zu Ende sein)* be over ['əʊvə]
vorbereiten: etwas vorbereiten prepare sth. [prɪ'peə] **sich vorbereiten (auf)** prepare (for)
Vordergrund foreground ['fɔːgraʊnd]
Vorderseite front [frʌnt]
Vorlieben und Abneigungen likes and dislikes *(pl)* [ˌlaɪks‿ən 'dɪslaɪks]
Vormittag morning ['mɔːnɪŋ]
Vorsicht! *(Pass auf!)* Watch out! [ˌwɒtʃ‿'aʊt]
vorsichtig careful ['keəfl]
vorspielen: etwas vorspielen act sth. out [ˌækt‿'aʊt]
vorstellen: sich etwas vorstellen imagine sth. [ɪ'mædʒɪn] **Stell dir vor, Dad ...** Guess what, Dad ...
Vorstellung *(Idee)* idea [aɪ'dɪə]
Vortrag talk [tɔːk] **einen Vortrag halten (über)** give a talk (about)

W

wachsen grow [grəʊ]
wählen *(aussuchen)* choose [tʃuːz]
wahr true [truː]
Wal whale [weɪl]
Walisisch; walisisch Welsh [welʃ]
wann? when? [wen] **Wann hast du Geburtstag?** When's your birthday.
Waren *(Güter)* goods *(pl)* [gʊdz]
warm warm [wɔːm]
warten (auf) wait (for) [weɪt] **Warte einen Moment.** Wait a minute.
warum? why? [waɪ]
was? what? [wɒt] **Was gibt es zum Mittagessen?** What's for lunch? **Was haben wir als Hausaufgabe auf?** What's for homework? **Was hättest du gern? / Was möchtest du?** What would you like? **Was ist denn? / Was ist los?** What's the matter? **Und was ist mit dir?** What about you?
Wasser water ['wɔːtə]
Website website ['websaɪt]
weg away [ə'weɪ]
Weg way [weɪ] **auf dem Weg zu/ nach ...** on the way to ...
wegen: Es tut mir leid wegen ... I'm sorry about ...
weggehen leave [liːv]
wehtun hurt [hɜːt]
weich soft [sɒft]
Weihnachten Christmas ['krɪsməs] **Frohe Weihnachten!** Merry Christmas! **1. Weihnachtstag (25. Dezember)** Christmas Day **2. Weihnachtstag (26. Dezember)** Boxing Day
weil because [bɪ'kɒz]
weiß white [waɪt]

weit (entfernt) far [fɑː]
weitermachen go on [ˌgəʊ_ˈɒn]
weiterreden go on [ˌgəʊ_ˈɒn]
welche(r, s) **1. Auf welcher Seite sind wir?** What page are we on? **Welche Farbe …?** What colour …? **2.** *(aus einer begrenzten Anzahl)* which [wɪtʃ] **Welche Wörter …?** (= *Welche von diesen Wörtern …?)* Which words …?
Welt world [wɜːld] **auf der Welt** in the world
wenden *(umkehren)* turn around [ˌtɜːn_əˈraʊnd]
wenn when [wen]; *(falls)* if [ɪf]
wer? who? [huː]
werden become [bɪˈkʌm] **wütend/kalt/… werden** get angry/cold/…
werfen throw [θrəʊ]
wessen? whose? [huːz]
Wettkampf *(Match)* match [mætʃ]
wichtig important [ɪmˈpɔːtnt]
wie **1.** *(Fragewort)* how [haʊ] **Wie alt bist du?** How old are you? **Wie findest du …? / Wie gefällt dir …?** How do you like …? **Wie geht's? / Wie geht es dir/euch?** How are you? **Wie heißt du?** What's your name? **Wie ist sie (so)?** What's she like? **Wie spät ist es?** What time is it? **Wie viel kosten …?** How much are …? **Wie viel kostet …?** How much is …? **2. wie Jungen** like boys [laɪk] **3. der-/die-/dasselbe** the same
wieder again [əˈgen]
wiegen weigh [weɪ]
Willkommen in Plymouth. Welcome to Plymouth. [ˈwelkəm]
Winter winter [ˈwɪntə]
wir we [wiː]
wirklich really [ˈrɪəli]
wild wild [waɪld]
wissen know [nəʊ] **über etwas Bescheid wissen** know about sth. **…, weißt du. / …, wissen Sie.** …, you know. [nəʊ] **Weißt du was, Dad …** Guess what, Dad …
Witz joke [dʒəʊk]
witzig funny [ˈfʌni]
wo? where? [weə]
Woche week [wiːk]
Wochenende weekend [ˌwiːkˈend] **am Wochenende** at the weekend
Wochentag day of the week
Woher kommst du? Where are you from?
wohin? where? [weə]
wohnen *(leben)* live [lɪv]
Wohnung flat [flæt]
Wohnzimmer living room [ˈlɪvɪŋ ruːm]
wollen: etwas haben wollen want sth. [wɒnt] **etwas tun wollen** want to do sth.
Wort word [wɜːd]
Wortstellung word order [ˈwɜːd_ɔːdə]
Wovon handelt die Geschichte? What is the story about?
Wunsch wish [wɪʃ]
wünschen: sich etwas wünschen make a wish [wɪʃ]
würde: Ich würde gern … I'd like to … **Ich würde sehr gern …** I'd love to …
wütend angry [ˈæŋgri]

Y

Yoga yoga [ˈjəʊgə]

Z

Zahl number [ˈnʌmbə]
zählen count [kaʊnt]
zehn ten [ten]
Zeichen sign [saɪn]
zeichnen draw [drɔː]
Zeichnung drawing [ˈdrɔːɪŋ]
zeigen show [ʃəʊ] **auf etwas zeigen** point to sth. [pɔɪnt] **es zeigt, dass …** it shows that …
Zeile line [laɪn]
Zeit time [taɪm]
Zeitschrift magazine [ˌmægəˈziːn]
Zeitung paper [ˈpeɪpə]
Zentrum centre [ˈsentə]
zerbrechen break [breɪk]
ziehen pull [pʊl]
Ziffer number [ˈnʌmbə]
Zoo zoo [zuː]
zu **1.** *(örtlich)* to [tu], [tə] **2. zu spät/kalt/groß/…** too late/cold/big/… [tuː] **3. Es ist Zeit zu gehen.** It's time to go. **Nice to meet you.** Freut mich, dich/euch/Sie kennenzulernen.
zuerst first [fɜːst]
Zug train [treɪn]
Zugang (zu) access (to) [ˈækses]
Zuhause home [həʊm]
zuhören listen [ˈlɪsn] **Hör(t) mir zu.** Listen to me.
zurück back [bæk]
zurücklassen leave [liːv]
zusammen together [təˈgeðə]
zustimmen: jm. zustimmen agree with sb. [əˈgriː]
Zutritt (zu) access (to) [ˈækses]
zwei two [tuː]
zweite(r, s) second [ˈsekənd] **Zweitens, …** Second, …
Zwillinge twins *(pl)* [twɪnz]
zwischen between [bɪˈtwiːn]
zwölf twelve [twelv]

Irregular verbs

infinitive	simple past	
(to) **be**	*I/he/she/it* **was**; *you/we/you/they* **were**	sein
(to) **become**	**became**	werden
(to) **bite** [aɪ]	**bit** [ɪ]	beißen
(to) **break** [eɪ]	**broke**	brechen; zerbrechen
(to) **bring**	**brought**	(mit-, her)bringen
(to) **buy**	**bought**	kaufen
(to) **catch**	**caught**	fangen

Irregular verbs

infinitive	simple past	
(to) **choose** [uː]	**chose** [əʊ]	aussuchen, (aus)wählen; sich aussuchen
(to) **come**	**came**	kommen
(to) **do**	**did**	tun, machen
(to) **draw**	**drew**	zeichnen
(to) **drink**	**drank**	trinken
(to) **drive** [aɪ]	**drove** [əʊ]	fahren *(ein Auto/mit dem Auto)*
(to) **eat**	**ate** [et, eɪt]	essen
(to) **fall**	**fell**	fallen, stürzen; hinfallen
(to) **feed**	**fed**	füttern
(to) **feel**	**felt**	fühlen; sich fühlen
(to) **fight**	**fought**	kämpfen
(to) **find**	**found**	finden
(to) **forget**	**forgot**	vergessen
(to) **get**	**got**	bekommen; werden; gelangen, (hin)kommen
(to) **give**	**gave**	geben
(to) **go**	**went**	gehen
(to) **grow**	**grew**	wachsen; anbauen, anpflanzen
(to) **have**	**had**	haben
(to) **hear** [ɪə]	**heard** [ɜː]	hören
(to) **hide** [aɪ]	**hid** [ɪ]	verstecken; sich verstecken
(to) **hit** sth.	**hit**	gegen etwas prallen, stoßen
(to) **hold**	**held**	halten
(to) **hurt**	**hurt**	schmerzen, wehtun; verletzen
(to) **know** [nəʊ]	**knew** [njuː]	wissen; kennen
(to) **leave** [iː]	**left**	(ab)fahren; (weg)gehen; verlassen; zurücklassen
(to) **let**	**let**	lassen
(to) **make**	**made**	machen; herstellen
(to) **meet** [iː]	**met** [e]	treffen; sich treffen; kennenlernen
(to) **put**	**put**	*(etwas wohin)* tun, legen, stellen
(to) **read** [iː]	**read** [e]	lesen
(to) **ride** a bike [aɪ]	**rode** a bike	*(Rad)* fahren
(to) **run**	**ran**	rennen, laufen
(to) **say** [eɪ]	**said** [e]	sagen
(to) **see**	**saw**	sehen
(to) **sell**	**sold**	verkaufen
(to) **send**	**sent**	schicken, senden
(to) **sing**	**sang**	singen
(to) **sit**	**sat**	sitzen; sich setzen
(to) **sleep**	**slept**	schlafen
(to) **speak** [iː]	**spoke**	sprechen
(to) **stand up**	**stood up**	aufstehen
(to) **swim**	**swam**	schwimmen
(to) **take**	**took**	nehmen, mitnehmen; (weg-, hin)bringen
(to) **tell**	**told**	erzählen, berichten
(to) **think**	**thought**	denken, glauben
(to) **throw**	**threw**	werfen
(to) **understand**	**understood**	verstehen
(to) **wake up**	**woke up**	aufwachen
(to) **wear** [eə]	**wore** [ɔː]	tragen *(Kleidung)*
(to) **win**	**won** [ʌ]	gewinnen
(to) **write**	**wrote**	schreiben

Place names (Ortsnamen)

Aquarium [ə'kweəriəm]

Asia ['eɪʒə] *Asien*

the **Atlantic Ocean** [ətˌlæntɪk‿'əʊʃn] *der Atlantik*

Australia [ɒ'streɪliə] *Australien*

Bavaria [bə'veəriə] *Bayern*

the **Barbican** ['bɑ:bɪkən]

Belfast [ˌbel'fɑ:st]

Berlin [bɜ:'lɪn]

Blackawton [ˌblæk'ɔ:tn]

Boston ['bɒstən]

Britain ['brɪtn] *Großbritannien*

Buckingham Palace [ˌbʌkɪŋəm 'pæləs]

Bude [bju:d]

Canada ['kænədə] *Kanada*

Cardiff ['kɑ:dɪf]

the **Caribbean** [ˌkærɪ'bi:ən] *die Karibik*

Cawsand ['kɔ:sænd]

China ['tʃaɪnə]

Church Road [ˌtʃɜ:tʃ 'rəʊd]

Citadel ['sɪtədəl, 'sɪtədel] *Zitadelle*

Clovelly [klə'veli]

Coombe Dean [ˌku:m 'di:n]

Cornwall ['kɔ:nwɔ:l]

Dallas ['dæləs]

Dartmoor ['dɑ:tmɔ:]

Devon ['devn]

Devonport ['devnpɔ:t]

Edinburgh ['edɪnbərə]

Elizabethan House [ɪlɪzəˌbi:θn 'haʊs]

England ['ɪŋglənd] *England*

Exmouth ['eksməθ]

France [frɑ:ns] *Frankreich*

Germany ['dʒɜ:məni] *Deutschland*

Grand Canyon [ˌgrænd 'kænjən]

the **Great Barrier Reef** [ˌgreɪt 'bæriə ri:f]

Great Britain [ˌgreɪt 'brɪtn] *Großbritannien*

High Street ['haɪ stri:t]

the **Hoe** [həʊ]

Hyde Park [ˌhaɪd 'pɑ:k]

India ['ɪndiə] *Indien*

Ireland ['aɪələnd] *Irland*

Ivy Island [ˌaɪvi‿'aɪlənd]

Lido ['laɪdəʊ, 'li:dəʊ]

Loch Ness [ˌlɒx 'nes]

London ['lʌndən]

Los Angeles [lɒs‿'ændʒəli:z, lɔ:s‿'ændʒələs]

Market Square ['mɑ:kɪt skweə]

Mexico ['meksɪkəʊ] *Mexiko*

Miami [maɪ'æmi]

New York [ˌnju: 'jɔ:k]

New Zealand [nju 'zi:lənd] *Neuseeland*

Northern Ireland [ˌnɔ:ðən‿'aɪələnd] *Nordirland*

Pengersick Castle [ˌpeŋgəsɪk 'kɑ:sl]

Plymouth ['plɪməθ]

Plymstock ['plɪmstɒk]

Philadelphia [ˌfɪlə'delfiə]

Poland ['pəʊlənd] *Polen*

Rio ['ri:əʊ]

the **River Plym** [plɪm]

the **River Thames** [temz]

San Francisco [ˌsæn frən'sɪskəʊ]

Scotland ['skɒtlənd] *Schottland*

Smeaton's Tower [ˌsmi:tnz 'taʊə]

South Africa [ˌsaʊθ‿'æfrɪkə] *Südafrika*

Stockbridge ['stɒkbrɪdʒ]

Sutton ['sʌtn]

Sydney ['sɪdni]

Texas ['teksəs]

Torquay [ˌtɔ:'ki:]

Totnes ['tɒtnɪs]

the **UK** [ˌju: 'keɪ] **(Great Britain and Northern Ireland)** *das Vereinigte Königreich*

the **USA** [ˌju:‿es‿'eɪ] *die Vereinigten Staaten von Amerika*

Wales [weɪlz] *Wales*

Washington D.C. [ˌwɒʃɪŋtən di: 'si:]

Wembury ['wembri, 'wembəri]

Woolacombe ['wʊləkəm]

First names (Vornamen)

Abby ['æbi]

Abigail ['æbɪgeɪl]

Albert ['ælbət]

Amar ['æmə, 'ʌmə]

Angelina [ˌændʒə'li:nə]

Angus ['æŋgəs]

Arthur ['ɑ:θə]

Bill [bɪl]

Charles [tʃɑ:lz]

Dasan ['dæsæn, 'dʌsən]

Dave [deɪv]

Dexter ['dekstə]

Dilip ['dɪlɪp]

Ela ['elə]

Elizabeth [i'lɪzəbəθ]

Emily ['eməli]

Emma ['emə]

Flynn [flɪn]

George [dʒɔ:dʒ]

Grace [greɪs]

Harry ['hæri]

Helen ['helən]

Holly ['hɒli]

Jack [dʒæk]

Jake [dʒeɪk]

James [dʒeɪmz]

Jamie ['dʒeɪmi]

Jasper ['dʒæspə]

Jeff [dʒef]

Jenny ['deni]

Jim [dʒɪm]

Josh [dʒɒʃ]

Joshua ['dʒɒʃuə]

Justin ['dʒʌstɪn]

Karen ['kærən]

Katie ['keɪti]

Katy ['keɪti]

Lewis ['lu:ɪs]

Lily ['lɪli]

Lisa ['li:sə]

Lloyd [lɔɪd]

Lucille [lu'si:l]

Lucy ['lu:si]

Luke [lu:k]

Lynn [lɪn]

Maggie ['mægi]

Marc [mɑ:k]

Masood [mə'su:d]

Max [mæks]

May [meɪ]

Maya ['maɪə]

Megan ['megən]

Melissa [mə'lɪsə]

Molly ['mɒli]

Mukesh ['mʊkeʃ]

Oliver ['ɒlɪvə]

Paul [pɔ:l]

Pete [pi:t]

Priya ['pri:jɑ:, 'pri:jə]

Rachel ['reɪtʃl]

Robbie ['rɒbi]

Ruby ['ru:bi]

Ryan ['raɪən]

S'bu [s'bu:]

Sam [sæm]

Samuel ['sæmjuəl]

Sanjay ['sændʒeɪ]

Sarah ['seərə]

Shauna ['ʃɔ:nə]

Simon ['saɪmən]

Sir Francis [sə 'frɑ:nsɪs]

Sophie ['səʊfi]

Steve [sti:v]

Tamwar ['tamwa:]

Thelma ['θelmə]

Tim [tɪm]

Tom [tɒm]

Taylor ['teɪlə]

Val [væl]

Victor ['vɪktə]

Will [wɪl]

Zoe ['zəʊi]

Family names / Surnames (Familiennamen)

Barton ['bɑ:tn]

Bell [bel]

Bennett ['benɪt]

Blackwell ['blækwel]

Charles [tʃɑ:lz]

Collings ['kɒlɪŋz]

Drake [dreɪk]

Einstein ['aɪnstaɪn]

Hacker ['hækə]

Hart [hɑ:t]

Hobbs [hɒbz]

Miller ['mɪlə]

Pascoe ['pæskəʊ]

Sen [sen]

Skinner ['skɪnə]

Smith [smɪθ]

Tyler ['taɪlə]

Tizzard ['tɪzəd]

Willis ['wɪlɪs]

Wood [wʊd]

Wu [wu:]

Other names (Andere Namen)

Mink [mɪŋk]

Morph [mɔ:f]

Omar ['əʊmɑ:]

Raj [rɑ:dʒ]

Sasha ['sæʃə]

Sheba ['ʃi:bə]

Silky ['sɪlki]

Skip [skɪp]

Skype [skaɪp]

Suzie ['su:zi]

Tarzan ['tɑ:zæn, 'tɑ:zn]

Tut [tʌt]

English sounds

[iː]	green, he, sea
[i]	happy, monkey
[ɪ]	big, in, expensive
[e]	red, yes, again, breakfast
[æ]	cat, animal, apple, black
[ɑː]	class, ask, car, park
[ɒ]	song, on, dog, what
[ɔː]	door, or, ball, four, morning
[uː]	blue, ruler, too, two, you
[ʊ]	book, good, pullover
[ʌ]	mum, bus, colour
[ɜː]	girl, early, her, work, T-shirt
[ə]	a partner, again, today
[eɪ]	name, eight, play, great
[aɪ]	time, right, my, I
[ɔɪ]	boy, toilet, noise
[əʊ]	old, no, road, yellow
[aʊ]	town, now, house
[ɪə]	here, year, idea
[eə]	where, pair, share, their
[ʊə]	tour
[b]	boat, table, verb
[p]	pool, paper, shop
[d]	dad, window, good
[t]	ten, letter, at
[g]	good, again, bag
[k]	cat, kitchen, back
[m]	mum, man, remember
[n]	no, one, ten
[ŋ]	song, young, uncle, thanks
[l]	hello, like, old, small
[r]	red, ruler, friend, sorry
[w]	we, where, one
[j]	you, yes, uniform
[f]	family, after, laugh
[v]	river, very, seven, have
[s]	sister, poster, yes
[z]	please, zoo, quiz, his, music
[ʃ]	shop, station, English
[ʒ]	television, usually
[tʃ]	teacher, child, watch
[dʒ]	Germany, job, project, orange
[θ]	thanks, three, bathroom
[ð]	the, this, father, with
[h]	here, who, behind

Am besten kannst du dir die Aussprache der einzelnen Lautzeichen einprägen, wenn du dir zu jedem Zeichen ein einfaches Wort merkst – das [iː] ist der **green**-Laut, das [eɪ] ist der **name**-Laut usw.

English numbers

0	**oh, zero, nil** [əʊ, ˈzɪərəʊ, nɪl]		
1	**one** [wʌn]	1st	**first** [fɜːst]
2	**two** [tuː]	2nd	**second** [ˈsekənd]
3	**three** [θriː]	3rd	**third** [θɜːd]
4	**four** [fɔː]	4th	**fourth** [fɔːθ]
5	**five** [faɪv]	5th	**fifth** [fɪfθ]
6	**six** [sɪks]	6th	**sixth** [sɪksθ]
7	**seven** [ˈsevn]	7th	**seventh** [ˈsevnθ]
8	**eight** [eɪt]	8th	**eighth** [eɪtθ]
9	**nine** [naɪn]	9th	**ninth** [naɪnθ]
10	**ten** [ten]	10th	**tenth** [tenθ]
11	**eleven** [ɪˈlevn]	11th	**eleventh** [ɪˈlevnθ]
12	**twelve** [twelv]	12th	**twelfth** [twelfθ]
13	**thirteen** [ˌθɜːˈtiːn]	13th	**thirteenth** [ˌθɜːˈtiːnθ]
14	**fourteen** [ˌfɔːˈtiːn]	14th	**fourteenth** [ˌfɔːˈtiːnθ]
15	**fifteen** [ˌfɪfˈtiːn]	15th	**fifteenth** [ˌfɪfˈtiːnθ]
16	**sixteen** [ˌsɪksˈtiːn]	16th	**sixteenth** [ˌsɪksˈtiːnθ]
17	**seventeen** [ˌsevnˈtiːn]	17th	**seventeenth** [ˌsevnˈtiːnθ]
18	**eighteen** [ˌeɪˈtiːn]	18th	**eighteenth** [ˌeɪˈtiːnθ]
19	**nineteen** [ˌnaɪnˈtiːn]	19th	**nineteenth** [ˌnaɪnˈtiːnθ]
20	**twenty** [ˈtwenti]	20th	**twentieth** [ˈtwentiəθ]
21	**twenty-one** [ˌtwentiˈwʌn]	21st	**twenty-first** [ˌtwentiˈfɜːst]
22	**twenty-two** [ˌtwentiˈtuː]	22nd	**twenty-second** [ˌtwentiˈsekənd]
23	**twenty-three** [ˌtwentiˈθriː]	23rd	**twenty-third** [ˌtwentiˈθɜːd]
…		…	
30	**thirty** [ˈθɜːti]	30th	**thirtieth** [ˈθɜːtiəθ]
40	**forty** [ˈfɔːti]	40th	**fortieth** [ˈfɔːtiəθ]
50	**fifty** [ˈfɪfti]	50th	**fiftieth** [ˈfɪftiəθ]
60	**sixty** [ˈsɪksti]	60th	**sixtieth** [ˈsɪkstiəθ]
70	**seventy** [ˈsevnti]	70th	**seventieth** [ˈsevntiəθ]
80	**eighty** [ˈeɪti]	80th	**eightieth** [ˈeɪtiəθ]
90	**ninety** [ˈnaɪnti]	90th	**ninetieth** [ˈnaɪntiəθ]
100	**a / one hundred** [əˈhʌndrəd / ˌwʌnˈhʌndrəd]	100th	**hundredth** [ˈhʌndrədθ]
101	**one hundred and one**	101st	**hundred and first**
102	**one hundred and two**	102nd	**hundred and second**
…		…	

Quellenverzeichnis

Titelbild

Schüler (M): Cornelsen/Trevor Burrows Photography, Klassenzimmer (M): Alamy/Flirt

Illustrationen

U2: Karte Cornelsen/Carlos Borrell Eiköter; Burg Irland Cornelsen/Roland Beier; alle anderen Illustrationen Cornelsen/Jeongsook Lee; **S. 4, S. 5:** Cornelsen/Tobias Dahmen, Utrecht/www.tobidahmen.de; **S. 8, S. 9:** Cornelsen/Elke Hanisch; **S. 10, S. 11:** Robbe Cornelsen/Elke Hanisch; alle anderen Illustrationen Cornelsen/Jane Smith; **S. 12–S. 15:** Cornelsen/Elke Hanisch; **S. 16:** Cornelsen/Tobias Dahmen, Utrecht/www.tobidahmen.de; **S. 17:** Robbe, Ameisen (4) Cornelsen/Elke Hanisch; (5), (6) Cornelsen/Tobias Dahmen, Utrecht/www.tobidahmen.de; **S. 18, S. 19, S. 21-S. 23:** Cornelsen/Tobias Dahmen, Utrecht/www.tobidahmen.de; **S. 24:** oben Cornelsen/Tobias Dahmen, Utrecht/www.tobidahmen.de; alle Illustrationen in (1) Cornelsen/M.B. Schulz; **S. 25:** unten Cornelsen/Tobias Dahmen, Utrecht/www.tobidahmen.de; **S. 26:** (A)–(D) Cornelsen/M.B. Schulz; unten 2. von links Cornelsen/Elke Hanisch; **S. 27:** Cornelsen/M.B. Schulz; **S. 29-S. 31:** Cornelsen/Tobias Dahmen, Utrecht/www.tobidahmen.de; **S. 34:** (A), (B) Cornelsen/Christian Bartz; unten Cornelsen/Tobias Dahmen, Utrecht/www.tobidahmen.de; **S. 35:** Cornelsen/Tobias Dahmen, Utrecht/www.tobidahmen.de; **S. 36:** (3)–(4) (M) Cornelsen/M.B. Schulz unter Verwendung von Cornelsen/Trevor Burrows Photography (Fotos); (5)–(8) u. **S. 37:** Cornelsen/M. B. Schulz; **S. 37:** unten Cornelsen/Tobias Dahmen, Utrecht/www.tobidahmen.de; **S. 38–S. 40:** Cornelsen/Tobias Dahmen, Utrecht/www.tobidahmen.de; **S. 42:** links Cornelsen/Tobias Dahmen, Utrecht/www.tobidahmen.de; Karte Cornelsen/Carlos Borrell Eiköter; **S. 44:** Cornelsen/Tobias Dahmen, Utrecht/www.tobidahmen.de; **S. 45:** Cornelsen/Judy Brown; **S. 46:** (1) Cornelsen/Elke Hanisch; (2) Cornelsen/Tobias Dahmen, Utrecht/www.tobidahmen.de; **S. 48:** oben, unten rechts Cornelsen/Tobias Dahmen, Utrecht/www.tobidahmen.de; unten links, unten 2. von rechts Cornelsen/M.B. Schulz; unten 2. von links Cornelsen/Elke Hanisch; **S. 49:** Cornelsen/Tobias Dahmen, Utrecht/www.tobidahmen.de; **S. 50:** unten Cornelsen/Doreen Arnold; **S. 51:** Cornelsen/Tobias Dahmen, Utrecht/www.tobidahmen.de; **S. 52:** Cornelsen/M.B. Schulz; **S. 53-S. 54:** Cornelsen/Tobias Dahmen, Utrecht/www.tobidahmen.de; **S. 55:** (6a) u. unten Cornelsen/Tobias Dahmen, Utrecht/www.tobidahmen.de; **S. 60:** Cornelsen/M.B. Schulz; **S. 61:** (A)-(F) Cornelsen/M.B. Schulz; unten Cornelsen/Tobias Dahmen, Utrecht/www.tobidahmen.de; **S. 63:** Cornelsen/Tobias Dahmen, Utrecht/www.tobidahmen.de; **S. 64:** oben Cornelsen/Tobias Dahmen, Utrecht/www.tobidahmen.de; unten Cornelsen/M.B. Schulz; **S. 66; S. 67:** Morph, **S. 69; S. 72, S. 73, S. 74:** Mindmap Cornelsen/Doreen Arnold; unten rechts Eric Gira/Ungermeyer, Berlin; **S. 77:** oben u. unten **(u. S. 79)** Morph unter Verwendung von Cornelsen/Trevor Burrows Photography (Bücher), **S. 83:** Cornelsen/Tobias Dahmen, Utrecht/www.tobidahmen.de; **S. 84:** Schmetterlinge Cornelsen/Elke Hanisch; alle anderen Illustrationen Cornelsen/Tobias Dahmen, Utrecht/www.tobidahmen.de; **S. 85:** Cornelsen/Tobias Dahmen, Utrecht/www.tobidahmen.de; **S. 86:** Cornelsen/M.B. Schulz**; S. 87**: Cornelsen/M.B. Schulz; **S. 88-S. 90, S. 92-S. 93:** Cornelsen/Tobias Dahmen, Utrecht/www.tobidahmen.de; **S. 94:** Cornelsen/Elke Hanisch; **S. 96:** Cornelsen/Tobias Dahmen, Utrecht/www.tobidahmen.de; **S. 98 / 99:** Illustrationen (1)-(9) Cornelsen/M.B. Schulz; **S. 99:** Illustrationen rechts Cornelsen/Tobias Dahmen, Utrecht/www.tobidahmen.de; **S. 100:** Cornelsen/Tobias Dahmen, Utrecht/www.tobidahmen.de; **S. 101:** Cornelsen/M.B. Schulz; **S. 103 u. S. 105:** Cornelsen/Tobias Dahmen, Utrecht/www.tobidahmen.de; **S. 107:** Cornelsen/M.B. Schulz; **S. 108:** Cornelsen/Tobias Dahmen, Utrecht/www.tobidahmen.de; **S. 110:** Cornelsen/M.B. Schulz; **S. 112 u. S. 113:** Cornelsen/Elke Hanisch; **S. 115-S. 118:** Morph Cornelsen/Tobias Dahmen, Utrecht/www.tobidahmen.de; **S. 120/121:** Illustration Cornelsen/Elke Hanisch; **S. 122:** Cornelsen/Tobias Dahmen, Utrecht/www.tobidahmen.de; **S. 124 u. S. 125:** Cornelsen/M.B. Schulz; **S. 127:** Cornelsen/Tobias Dahmen, Utrecht/www.tobidahmen.de; **S. 128:** oben Cornelsen/Tobias Dahmen, Utrecht/www.tobidahmen.de; (1)-(6) Cornelsen/M.B. Schulz; **S. 131:** Smugglers Cornelsen/M.B. Schulz; **S. 133, S. 135, S. 137:** Cornelsen/Tobias Dahmen, Utrecht/ www.tobidahmen.de; **S. 138-S. 139:** Cornelsen/M.B. Schulz; **S. 141, S. 142, S. 144-S. 146:** Morph Cornelsen/Tobias Dahmen, Utrecht/www.tobidahmen.de; **S. 146** Karte Cornelsen/Carlos Borrell Eiköter; **S. 148-S. 151, S. 153-S. 156, S. 162:** Cornelsen/M.B. Schulz; **S. 166:** Cornelsen/M.B. Schulz; **S. 167:** (1)-(3) Cornelsen/M.B. Schulz; unten Cornelsen/Tobias Dahmen, Utrecht/www.tobidahmen.de; **S. 169:** Cornelsen/Roland Beier; **S. 174:** Cornelsen/Roland Beier; **S. 176:** Mindmaps Cornelsen / Doreen Arnold; **S. 177:** Cornelsen/Roland Beier; **S. 179:** oben Cornelsen/Roland Beier; unten Cornelsen/Tobias Dahmen, Utrecht/www.tobidahmen.de; **S. 180–S. 182:** Cornelsen/Tobias Dahmen, Utrecht/www.tobidahmen.de; **S. 183:** pencil, bag, ruler Cornelsen/Judy Brown; alle anderen Illustrationen Cornelsen/Tobias Dahmen, Utrecht/www.tobidahmen.de; **S. 184, S. 185:** Cornelsen/Tobias Dahmen, Utrecht/www.tobidahmen.de; **S. 186:** oben links, unten rechts Cornelsen/Roland Beier; oben rechts, unten links Cornelsen/Tobias Dahmen, Utrecht/www.tobidahmen.de; **S. 187:** oben, unten Cornelsen/Tobias Dahmen, Utrecht/www.tobidahmen.de; Mitte Cornelsen/Jeongsook Lee; **S. 188-S. 191, S. 193:** Cornelsen/Tobias Dahmen, Utrecht/www.tobidahmen.de; **S. 194:** oben, unten rechts Cornelsen/Tobias Dahmen, Utrecht/www.tobidahmen.de; unten links u. unten Mitte Cornelsen/Roland Beier; **S. 195:** Cornelsen/Tobias Dahmen, Utrecht/www.tobidahmen.de; **S. 197:** oben links, unten Cornelsen/Tobias Dahmen, Utrecht/www.tobidahmen.de; alle anderen Illustrationen Cornelsen/Roland Beier; **S. 198:** Cornelsen/Roland Beier; **S. 201:** unten Cornelsen/Jeongsook Lee; **S. 203:** Cornelsen/Tobias Dahmen, Utrecht/www.tobidahmen.de; **S. 205:** oben Cornelsen/Jeongsook Lee; unten Cornelsen/Roland Beier; **S. 206:** beide Mitte Cornelsen/Elke Hanisch; unten Cornelsen/Jeongsook Lee; **S. 207:** Cornelsen/Roland Beier; **S. 209:** Cornelsen/Roland Beier; **S. 211:** Cornelsen/Roland Beier; **S. 216:** Cornelsen/Roland Beier; **S. 217:** oben, 2. von oben, 2. von unten Cornelsen/Roland Beier; unten Cornelsen/Elke Hanisch; **S. 218:** Cornelsen/Roland Beier; **S. 220:** Illustration Mitte Cornelsen/Roland Beier; hot/cold Cornelsen/Jeongsook Lee; **S. 221, S. 222, S. 224, S. 225:** Cornelsen/Roland Beier; **S. 226:** oben Cornelsen/Roland Beier; unten Cornelsen/Jeongsook Lee; **S. 227:** oben Cornelsen/Jeongsook Lee; unten Cornelsen/Roland Beier; **S. 228, S. 231:** Cornelsen/Roland Beier; **S. 232:** Cornelsen/Jeongsook Lee; **S. 234–S. 241:** Cornelsen/Roland Beier; **S. 242** Cornelsen/M.B. Schulz.

Fotos

S. 4: oben links Okapia/imagebroker/Stefan Huwiler; oben rechts Cornelsen/Trevor Burrows Photography; Mitte Cornelsen/Trevor Burrows Photography; unten rechts Cornelsen/Trevor Burrows Photography; unten links Shutterstock/mubus7; **S. 5:** Cornelsen/Trevor Burrows Photography; **S. 6:** oben Cornelsen/Trevor Burrows Photography; Mitte Photoshot; unten INTERFOTO/Granger, NYC; **S. 7:** Cornelsen/Trevor Burrows Photography; **S. 12/13:** Hintergrund Shutterstock/Melissa King; **S. 12:** (1)-(3) Cornelsen/Trevor Burrows Photography; (4) Alamy/International Photobank; **S. 13:** (5)-(6) Cornelsen/Trevor Burrows Photography; (7) Susanne Bennetreu, Berlin; **S. 16:** Cornelsen/Trevor Burrows Photography; **S. 20:** Cornelsen/Trevor Burrows Photography; **S. 21:** oben links Lucy u. Sam Cornelsen/Trevor Burrows Photography; oben rechts Shutterstock/Matthew Benoit; **S. 22, S. 23:** Cornelsen/Trevor Burrows Photography; **S. 25:** oben Cornelsen/Trevor Burrows Photography; **S. 26:** Cornelsen/Trevor Burrows Photography; **S. 28:** Cornelsen/Trevor Burrows Photography; **S. 30:** Cornelsen/Trevor Burrows Photography; **S. 32:** Cornelsen/Trevor Burrows Photography; **S. 33:** oben u. Mitte Cornelsen/Rockfinch/Claire Cunningham; unten Cornelsen/Sapna Richter**; S. 36** (1)-(2) Cornelsen/Trevor Burrows Photography; **S. 38:** Stefanie Gira, Berlin; **S. 41:** beide Shutterstock/Monkey Business Images; **S. 42:** (1) Shutterstock/v.s.anandhakrishna; (2) Clip Dealer/Monkey Business Images; (3) Shutterstock/Monkey Business Images; (4) Photoshot; **S. 43:** (A) Fotolia/Andrea Todeschini; (B) Photoshot; (C) Shutterstock/JuliusKielaitis; (D) mauritius images/Alamy/Dale O'Dell; **S. 44:** Cornelsen/Trevor Burrows Photography; **S. 45:** oben Shutterstock/mubus7; **S. 47:** Cornelsen/Trevor Burrows Photography; **S. 50:** oben links Shutterstock/Robert Spriggs; oben Mitte Shutterstock/Tatiana Popova; oben rechts Shutterstock/Robert Spriggs; **S. 51:** Pool Shutterstock/Scanrail1; Buch Shutterstock/Andreja Donko; Zwei Shutterstock/Morena Valente, Farbe Shutterstock/monbibi; Lineal Shutterstock/SmileStudio; Schuhe Shutterstock/sommthink; **S. 55:** Bill & Maggie u. Holly u. Lucy Cornelsen/Trevor Burrows Photography; Helen Shutterstock/VICTOR TORRES; George Shutterstock/rl lerich; Lynn Shutterstock/Daxiao Productions, Steve Shutterstock/Nadino; Harry Shutterstock/vgstudio; Karen Shutterstock/Olga Sapeqina; Sam Shutterstock/g-stockstudio; Jim Shutterstock/Jeanette Dietl; Lewis & Lloyd Shutterstock/Richard Upshur; Melissa Shutterstock/Alan Bailey; (1)-(4) Shutterstock/Feliks Kogan; (5) Shutterstock/lalan; **S. 56:** oben Cornelsen/Trevor Burrows Photography; unten Cornelsen/Stefan Höhne, Berlin; **S. 57:** (1) Shutterstock/Sergey Peterman; (2) Shutterstock/marlee; (3) Shutterstock/Kirill Smirnov; (4) Shutterstock/Marc Dietrich; (5) Shutterstock/maxim ibragimov; (6) Shutterstock/aarrows; (7) Shutterstock/monticello; (8) Shutterstock/Seroff; (9) Shutterstock/Nattika; (10) Shutterstock/Subbotina Anna DLL; (11) Shutterstock/Rob Stark; (12) Shutterstock/Africa Studio; (13) Shutterstock/Olga Lyubkina; (14) Shutterstock/Joe Gough; (15) Shutterstock/charles taylor; (16), unten Shutterstock/orinoco-art; **S. 59:** Cornelsen/Rockfinch/Claire Cunningham; **S. 62:** Stefanie Gira, Berlin; **S. 65:** Fotolia/absolutimages; **S. 66:** oben Shutterstock/tchara; Mitte Shutterstock/oliveromg; Weihnachtskarte Shutterstock/Natalia Klenova; Christmas cake Shutterstock/Dulce Rubia; paper hat Shutterstock/Jenny Lilly; candles Shutterstock/Chursina Viktoriia; turkey Shutterstock/Stephen Mcsweeny; cracker Fotolia/Barbara Pheby; Christmas pudding Shutterstock/RTimages; **S. 67:** oben links Shutterstock/Ramona Kaulitzki; oben 2. von links Shutterstock/chispas; oben 2. von rechts Fotolia/Photographee.eu; oben rechts Shutterstock/M. Unal Ozmen; Mitte links Shutterstock/fotohunter; Mitte 2. von links Shutterstock/Mirelle; Mitte rechts Shutterstock/Nitr; unten Fotolia/Larry Rains; **S. 68:** Logo Plymstock School u. Schüler u. Film-Making Cornelsen/Trevor Burrows Photography; Gardening oben Shutterstock/Pavel Lysenko; Gardening unten Shutterstock/viki2win; **S. 69:** Basketball Shutterstock/Yarek Gora; Samba oben links Shutterstock/Pres Panayotov; Samba Club oben rechts Shutterstock/Val Thoermer; Reading Cornelsen/Trevor Burrows Photography; Samba Club unten rechts Fotolia/Brian Scott; Samba Club unten links Fotolia/pixelrobot; **S. 70 u. S. 71:** Cornelsen/Trevor Burrows Photography; **S. 74:** unten links Shutterstock/pakowacz; **S. 75:** Cornelsen/Rockfinch/Claire Cunningham; **S. 76:** Cornelsen/Trevor Burrows Photography; **S. 77 (u. S. 79):** unten Cornelsen/Trevor Burrows Photography

(Bücher) unter Verwendung von Tobias Dahmen, Utrecht/www.tobidahmen.de (Morph); **S. 80:** Cornelsen/Trevor Burrows Photography; **S. 81:** oben Cornelsen/Trevor Burrows Photography; unten links Hintergrund Collage Cornelsen/Susanne Bennetreu unter Verwendung von Fotofinder/images.de/Florilegius (Frau im Vordergrund) und Alamy/The Print Collector (Frau im Hintergrund links sowie Mann im Hintergrund rechts); unten rechts Alamy/Lee Pengelly; **S. 82:** Plymouth City Council (Arts and Heritage) Polly Stock Photography; **S. 85:** Zahl Shutterstock/morenina; Tafel Shutterstock/romvo; Ball Shutterstock/Andresr; Haus Shutterstock/RTimages; Pferd Shutterstock/Abramova Kseniya; Tür Shutterstock/archideaphoto; **S. 89:** oben Shutterstock/Andy Dean Photography; **S. 91:** (1) Shutterstock/Wallenrock; (2) Shutterstock/Lars Hallstrom; (3) Shutterstock/John Wollwerth; (4) Shutterstock/iMarin; unten Shutterstock/2xSamara.com; **S. 92:** oben links Fotolia/asafeliason; oben rechts Shutterstock/vlad.georgescu; (1) Shutterstock/Efetova Anna; (2) Shutterstock/irin-k; (3) Shutterstock/kak2s; (4) Shutterstock/gresei; (5) Shutterstock/AlexMaster; (6) Shutterstock/Tom Wang; (7) Shutterstock/Jaromir Urbanek; (8) Shutterstock/Chiyacat; **S. 94:** (A) Cornelsen/Trevor Burrows Photography; **S. 95:** (C) u. (D) Cornelsen/Trevor Burrows Photography; unten Stefanie Gira, Berlin; **S. 96:** Foto Cornelsen/Trevor Burrows Photography; **S. 98:** Cornelsen/Trevor Burrows Photography; **S. 102:** Cornelsen/Trevor Burrows Photography; **S. 104:** links Shutterstock/merc67; Mitte Photoshot; rechts mauritius images/Alamy / dbphots; **S. 105:** (1) Fotolia/bmf-foto.de; (2) Fotolia/vladvm50; (3) Fotolia/siraphol; (4) Shutterstock/Ethnic Design; (5) Fotolia/quka; (6) Shutterstock/Gordan; **S. 106:** oben Alamy/Gregory Davies; Mitte Shutterstock/Roland IJdema; unten Shutterstock/Nicram Sabod; **S. 109:** Fotolia/aleksandr; **S. 111:** Cornelsen/Rockfinch/Claire Cunningham; **S. 114:** Stefanie Gira, Berlin; **S. 118:** oben rechts Shutterstock/MSSA; (A) Shutterstock/Juergen Faelchle; (B) Shutterstock/PT Images; (C) Shutterstock/Monkey Business Images; (D) Shutterstock/Jess Yu; **S. 119:** (1) Shutterstock/chrisdorney; (2) Interfoto/LatitudeStock/Pawel Libera; (3) Shutterstock/IR Stone; (4) Shutterstock/Keattikorn; (5) Shutterstock/IR Stone; (6) Fotolia/Ljupco Smokovski; (7) Shutterstock/Shaun Jeffers; (8) Shutterstock/Keattikorn; (9) Shutterstock/Elena Rostunova; (10) Shutterstock/Kamira; **S. 120/121:** Hintergrund Cornelsen/Trevor Burrows Photography; **S. 123:** Cornelsen/Trevor Burrows Photography; **S. 126:** Hintergrund Cornelsen/Trevor Burrows Photography; oben rechts Cornelsen/Trevor Burrows Photography; unten links National Marine Aquarium, Plymouth; unten 2. von links National Marine Aquarium, Plymouth; unten 2. von rechts National Marine Aquarium, Plymouth; unten rechts Cornelsen/Trevor Burrows Photography; **S. 127:** unten alle National Marine Aquarium, Plymouth; **S. 129:** (1) Fotolia/pio3; (2) Fotolia/Pavel Losevsky; (3) Shutterstock/S-F; unten Shutterstock/Christine Langer-Pueschel; **S. 130:** Cornelsen/Trevor Burrows Photography; **S. 131:** Cawsand Cornelsen/Trevor Burrows Photography; **S. 132:** Cornelsen/Trevor Burrows Photography; **S. 134:** oben Shutterstock/Undivided; unten Shutterstock/Ron Ellis; **S. 136:** oben, (A) - (F) Cornelsen/Rockfinch/Claire Cunningham; unten Cornelsen/Trevor Burrows Photography; **S. 137:** (1) Shutterstock/NRT; (2) Shutterstock/Umberto Shtanzman; (3) Shutterstock/jocic; (4) Shutterstock/aquariagirl1970; (5) Shutterstock/Africa Studio; (6) Shutterstock/Alina Ku-Ku; **S. 140:** oben Shutterstock/Kletr; 2. von oben akg/Bildarchiv Steffens; 2. von unten Shutterstock/wrangler; unten Andreas Hub/laif; **S. 143:** (A) mauritius images/Alamy/Steve Vidler; (B) Shutterstock/Ian Scott; (C) Fotolia/photology1971; (D) Shutterstock/Tony Brindley; (E) mauritius images/Alamy/James Hughes; (F) Shutterstock/Samot; (1) Shutterstock/Prometheus72; (2) mauritius images/Loop Images; **S. 144:** Karte Shutterstock/Rainer Lesniewski; **S. 145:** (1) Shutterstock/James A. Harris; (2) Shutterstock/Andrew Zarivny; (3) Shutterstock/Vacclav; (4) Shutterstock/Rambleon; (5) Shutterstock/Andrew Zarivny; (6) Shutterstock/upthebanner; unten Shutterstock/Blacqbook; **S. 147:** links oben Shutterstock/Jenkedco; links 2. von oben Shutterstock/v.s.anandhakrishna; links 2. von unten Shutterstock/Lucian Coman; links unten Shutterstock/Juice Team; rechts oben Shutterstock/In Tune; rechts unten Shutterstock/RimDream; **S. 161:** links Shutterstock/merc67; Mitte Photoshot/Photoshot; rechts mauritius images/Alamy/dbphots; **S. 164:** Gareth Evans, Berlin; **S. 166:** Cornelsen/Trevor Burrows Photography; **S. 168:** cow Fotolia/Eric Isselee; goat Shutterstock/Eric Isselee; one sheep Shutterstock/Eric Isselee; three sheep Fotolia/Eric Isselée; one mouse Shutterstock/kontur-vid; three mice Shutterstock/Robert Wroblewski; hamster Shutterstock/Igor Kovalchuk; gerbil Shutterstock/Eric Isselee; tortoise Shutterstock/cynoclub; turtle Shutterstock/DenisNata; budgie Shutterstock/Eric Isselee; canary Shutterstock/Eric Isselee; parrot Shutterstock/prapass; lizard Shutterstock/Angel Simon; biology Shutterstock/TunedIn by Westend61; chemistry Shutterstock/Kiselev Andrey Valerevich; physics Shutterstock/Monkey Business Images; class assembly Shutterstock/Zurijeta; Spanish Shutterstock/alpimages; Italian Shutterstock/alpimages; Latin Shutterstock/stefano carniccio; extracurricular activities oben Shutterstock/oliveromg; ethics Shutterstock/marek Uliasz; social studies Shutterstock/Dawn Hudson; drama Shutterstock/Elnur; extracurricular activities unten Alamy/MBI; **S. 169:** oben links Shutterstock/privilege; unten links Shutterstock/Valentin Mosichev; Mitte Shutterstock/Simon Greig; 2. von links unten Shutterstock/Alexander Raths; 2. von rechts unten Shutterstock/Juriah Mosin; rechts oben Shutterstock/Andresr; rechts unten Shutterstock/Zurijeta; **S. 170:** apples Shutterstock/Valentyn Volkov; pears Shutterstock/Sandra Caldwell; oranges Shutterstock/Valentyn Volkov; strawberries Shutterstock/Picsfive; cherries Shutterstock/Valentyn Volkov; bananas Shutterstock/Tatiana Popova; grapes Shutterstock/Protasov AN; plums Shutterstock/Valentyn Volkov; carrots Shutterstock/mashe; tomatoes Shutterstock/Aleksey Patsyuk; peppers Shutterstock/Ruslan Kuzmenkov; peas Shutterstock/Yasonya; beans Shutterstock/Valentyn Volkov; mushrooms Shutterstock/Yasonya; broccoli Shutterstock/Dionisvera; cauliflower Shutterstock/monticello; cucumber Shutterstock/Anna Sedneva; lettuce Shutterstock/Bakelyt; sweetcorn Shutterstock/Maks Narodenko; grilled steak Shutterstock/Dan Peretz; lamb chops Shutterstock/Robyn Mackenzie; roast chicken Shutterstock/Viktor1; sausages Shutterstock/de2marco; salami Shutterstock/Peter Zijlstra; ham Shutterstock/Michael C. Gray; cold cuts Shutterstock/Zvyagintsev Sergey; fish fingers Shutterstock/Magone; fish filet Shutterstock/Magone; **S. 171:** pasta Shutterstock/windu; pasta salad Shutterstock/Igor Dutina; rice Shutterstock/oriori; boiled eggs Shutterstock/Nattika; scrambled eggs Shutterstock/Nitr; fried eggs Shutterstock/bitt24; omelette Shutterstock/margouillat photo; mashed potatoes Fotolia/Africa Studio; fried potatoes Shutterstock/lorenzo gambaro; chips Shutterstock/Alexandra Lande; potato salad Shutterstock/jreika; coffee Shutterstock/Tiplyashin Anatoly; hot chocolate Shutterstock/Andrey Shtanko; mineral water Shutterstock/monticello; orange juice Shutterstock/victoriaKh; lemonade Shutterstock/GrigoryL; blancmange Shutterstock/Daniel Taeger; fruit flan Shutterstock/Margoe Edwards; jelly with custard Shutterstock/Bildagentur Zoonar GmbH; cupcakes Shutterstock/Everything; butter Shutterstock/Diana Taliun; honey Shutterstock/deniss09; chocolate hazelnut spread Shutterstock/lasha; muesli Shutterstock/Julian Rovagnati; cereals Shutterstock/Kitch Bain; rolls Clip Dealer/Kitch Bain; toast Shutterstock/RusGri; **S. 172:** badminton Shutterstock/andromantic; hockey Alamy/Enigma; ice hockey Shutterstock/Govorov Pavel; table tennis Shutterstock/JJ pixs; volleyball Shutterstock/muzsy; canoeing Shutterstock/Elena Elisseeva; climbing Shutterstock/Frances A. Miller; ice skating Shutterstock/l i g h t p o e t; riding Shutterstock/Fotokostic; rowing Shutterstock/Corepics; skateboarding; Shutterstock/sonya etchison; skating Fotolia/Kathrin39; skiing Shutterstock/gorillaimages; snowboarding Shutterstock/Ipatov; windsurfing Shutterstock/Sean Nel; gymnastics Shutterstock/Denys Kurbatov; judo Alamy Images/Andrzej Gorzkowski; yoga Shutterstock/Malyugin; badminton racket Shutterstock/Alexander Dashewsky; hockey stick Alamy/keith morris; ice hockey stick Shutterstock/Flashon Studio; table tennis bat Shuttertock/JJ pixs; saddle Shutterstock/Oleksiy Rybakov; riding boots Shutterstock/Tim Large; ice skates Shutterstock/Jami Rae; in-line skates Shutterstock/2happy; skateboard Shutterstock/HomeArt; canoe Shutterstock/marekuliasz; paddles Shutterstock/Mega Pixel; rope Fotolia/Václav Mach; climbing gear Fotolia/3dmavr; pads Shutterstock/nito; helmets unten links Shutterstock/Nicholas Piccillo; helmets oben Shutterstock/shutswis; helmets unten rechts Shutterstock/byggarn.se; skis Shutterstock/Denys Kurylow; snowboard Shutterstock/InnerVisionPRO; **S. 173:** ballet Shutterstock/Yuri Arcurs; listening to music Shutterstock/goodluz; playing in a band Alamy/Fancy; playing in the school orchestra Shutterstock/SpeedKingz; rapping Shutterstock/Nejron Photo; singing in a choir Shutterstock/SpeedKingz; clarinet Shutterstock/AVAVA; flute Shutterstock/Fotokostic; recorder Shutterstock/Apollofoto; cello Shutterstock/Fotokostic; saxophone Shutterstock/Anton Albert; trumpet Shutterstock/tobkatrina; violin Shutterstock/Brian Chase; acting Shutterstock/Anneka; drawing Shutterstock/Jeka; making models Alamy/Corbis Super RF; collecting stamps Shutterstock/Phovoir; surfing the internet Shutterstock/LUCARELLI TEMISTOCLE; taking photos Shutterstock/Nina Buday; **S. 176:** Amsterdam Bonnie Glänzer, Berlin; **S. 177:** oben Shutterstock/GJS; **S. 180:** Cornelsen/Trevor Burrows Photography; **S. 201:** links Shutterstock/Olga Mishyna; Mitte Shutterstock/jilawangkun; rechts Shutterstock/Dan Gerber; **S. 204:** Shutterstock/Monkey Business Images; **S. 205:** Shutterstock/Zurijeta; **S. 206:** Clip Dealer/Andy Dean Photography; **S. 207:** Shutterstock/Elnur; **S. 209:** links Shutterstock/Olga Mishyna; Mitte Shutterstock/jilawangkun; rechts Shutterstock/Dan Gerber; **S. 210:** oben Shutterstock/Gemenacom; Mitte alle Shutterstock/wongstock; unten Shutterstock/Vibrant Image Studio; **S. 211:** unten links Shutterstock/Arkady; unten rechts Shutterstock/sommthink; **S. 212:** oben Shutterstock/Volina; unten Shutterstock/R-O-M-A; **S. 213:** unten alle Shutterstock/Alegria; **S. 216:** Shutterstock/Wouter Tolenaars; S. 218 oben Shutterstock/Viktor1; unten Shutterstock/Kuricheva Ekaterina; **S. 219:** oben Shutterstock/NLShop; unten Shutterstock/Oleksandr Koval; **S. 220:** oben Shutterstock/Monkey Business Images; vegetables Shutterstock/Olga Lyubkina; soup Shutterstock/Olinchuk; fruit salad Shutterstock/bonchan; scones Shutterstock/discpicture; sandwiches oben Shutterstock/Daniel Etzold; cakes links Shutterstock/Elena Larina; cakes rechts Shutterstock/Smit; sandwiches unten Shutterstock/Crepesoles; cream/jam Stefan Höhne, Berlin; **S. 221:** cheese Shutterstock/Evgeny Karandaev; tea Shutterstock/Victor1; milk Shutterstock/Texturis; bread Shutterstock/LandscaperY; cornflakes Shutterstock/Oliver Hoffmann; present Shutterstock/Vasilius; **S. 222:** turkey Shutterstock/veleknez; **S. 223:** oben links Shutterstock/Olga Lyubkina; oben rechts Shutterstock/viki2win; unten Shutterstock/Robert Spriggs; **S. 224:** oben Shutterstock/amasterphotographer; unten Shutterstock/nito; **S. 225:** unten Shutterstock/SergiyN; **S. 226:** Cornelsen/Trevor Burrows Photography; **S. 229:** oben Shutterstock/Gordon Ball LRPS; unten Shutterstock/Aleksey Patsyuk; **S. 230:** oben Shutterstock/AnnaIA; unten Shutterstock/Koshevnyk; **S. 231:** minibus Fotolia/ art_zzz; bus Shutterstock/Rob Wilson; car Shutterstock/risteski goce; **S. 236:** oben Shutterstock/montego; **S. 238:** links Shutterstock/rui vale sousa; rechts Shutterstock/Baloncici; **S. 241:** Shutterstock/fritz16; **S. 242:** Cornelsen/Trevor Burrows Photography.

Zu Beginn und am Ende des Unterrichts

Guten Morgen, Frau …	**Good morning, Mrs/Miss …** *(bis 12 Uhr)*
Guten Tag, Herr …	**Good afternoon, Mr …** *(ab 12 Uhr)*
Entschuldigung, dass ich zu spät komme.	**Sorry I'm late.**
Auf Wiedersehen. / Pfiati. / Bis morgen.	**Goodbye. / See you tomorrow.**

Du brauchst Hilfe

Können Sie/Kannst du mir bitte helfen?	**Can you help me, please?**
Auf welcher Seite sind wir, bitte?	**What page are we on, please?**
Was heißt … auf Englisch/Deutsch?	**What's … in English/German?**
Können Sie/Kannst du mir bitte … buchstabieren?	**Can you spell …, please?**
Können Sie es bitte an die Tafel schreiben?	**Can you write it on the board, please?**

Hausaufgaben und Übungen

Tut mir leid, ich habe mein Schulheft nicht dabei.	**Sorry, I don't have my exercise book.**
Kann ich bitte vorlesen?	**Can I read, please?**
Ich verstehe diese Übung nicht.	**I don't understand this exercise.**
Ich kann Nummer 3 nicht lösen.	**I can't do number 3.**
Entschuldigung, ich bin noch nicht fertig.	**Sorry, I haven't finished.**
Ich habe … Ist das auch richtig?	**I have … Is that right too?**
Tut mir leid, das weiß ich nicht.	**Sorry, I don't know.**
Was haben wir (als Hausaufgabe) auf?	**What's for homework?**

Wenn es Probleme gibt

Kann ich es auf Deutsch sagen?	**Can I say it in German?**
Können Sie/Kannst du bitte lauter sprechen?	**Can you speak louder, please?**
Können Sie/Kannst du das bitte noch mal sagen?	**Can you say that again, please?**
Kann ich bitte das Fenster öffnen/zumachen?	**Can I open/close the window, please?**
Kann ich bitte zur Toilette gehen?	**Can I go to the toilet, please?**

Partnerarbeit

Kann ich mit Julian arbeiten?	**Can I work with Julian?**
Kann ich bitte dein Lineal/deinen Filzstift/… haben?	**Can I have your ruler/felt tip/…, please?**
Danke. / Vielen Dank.	**Thank you. / Thanks a lot.**
Du bist dran.	**It's your turn.**

Classroom English

All together, please.	Alle zusammen, bitte.
Are you ready?	Bist du/Seid ihr bereit?
Be quiet, please.	Sei/Seid bitte ruhig.
Can I help you?	Kann ich dir/euch helfen?
Choose a partner.	Wähle/Wählt eine/n Partner/in.
Clean the blackboard, please.	Bitte wische die Tafel.
Collect the ..., please.	Sammle bitte den/die ... ein.
Come to the front, please.	Komme/Kommt bitte nach vorne.
Cut out/fold/glue the pieces.	Schneide/Falte/Klebe die Teile.
Don't shout out.	Rufe/Schreie nicht.
Everybody join hands.	Fasst euch alle an den Händen.
Go back to your chairs/tables, please.	Geht bitte zurück zu euren Stühlen/Tischen.
Good job. / Well done.	Gut gemacht.
Have you finished?	Bist du/Seid ihr fertig?
I'm in class.	Ich bin im Unterricht.
I've got a worksheet/some pictures for you.	Ich habe ein Arbeitsblatt/einige Bilder für dich/euch.
Let's play a game/sing a song.	Lasst uns ein Spiel spielen/ein Lied singen.
Listen carefully/again.	Hört genau/noch einmal zu.
Look at me/the blackboard, please.	Schaut bitte zu mir/zur Tafel.
Match the pictures and the words.	Ordne die Bilder und Wörter einander zu.
Open your (exercise)book, please.	Bitte öffne/öffnet dein/euer Buch/Arbeitsheft.
Open/Shut the door/window, please.	Bitte öffne/schließe die Tür/das Fenster.
Please, take out your ...	Bitte holt eure ... heraus.
Put the pictures in the right order.	Ordnet die Bilder in der richtigen Reihenfolge.
Raise your hand(s), please.	Bitte hebe/hebt deine/eure Hand/Hände.
Ready, steady, go.	Auf die Plätze, fertig, los.
Roll the dice (again).	Würfele (nochmal).
Speak after me, please.	Sprecht mir bitte nach.
Speak up, please.	Sprich bitte lauter.
Stand in twos.	Stellt euch zu zweit nebeneinander auf.
Stand/sit in a (semi-)circle, please.	Bitte stellt euch in einem (Halb-)Kreis auf.
Stop talking, please.	Bitte hört auf zu reden.
That's it.	Das war's. / Das ist es.
Try again.	Versuch/Versucht es nochmal.
Very good/nice.	Sehr gut/schön.
We need two teams/groups.	Wir brauchen zwei Teams/Gruppen.
What can you see in the picture?	Was kannst du auf dem Bild sehen.
What's this?	Was ist das?